The Rise and Fall of the
New Deal Order, 1930–1980

THE RISE AND FALL
OF THE
NEW DEAL ORDER,
1930–1980

EDITED BY

Steve Fraser and
Gary Gerstle

PRINCETON UNIVERSITY PRESS

Princeton, New Jersey

CONTENTS

Introduction   ix
GARY GERSTLE AND STEVE FRASER

PART I: *THE NEW DEAL POLITICAL ORDER:*
             EMERGENCE AND CRYSTALLIZATION,
             1929–1960

      1   Industrial Conflict and the Coming of the New
             Deal: The Triumph of Multinational Liberalism
             in America   3
             THOMAS FERGUSON

      2   Why the Great Depression Was Great: Toward
             a New Understanding of the Interwar
             Economic Crisis in the United States   32
             MICHAEL A. BERNSTEIN

      3   The 'Labor Question'   55
             STEVE FRASER

      4   The New Deal and the Idea of the State   85
             ALAN BRINKLEY

      5   From Corporatism to Collective Bargaining:
             Organized Labor and the Eclipse of Social
             Democracy in the Postwar Era   122
             NELSON LICHTENSTEIN

      6   Cold War—Warm Hearth: Politics and the
             Family in Postwar America   153
             ELAINE TYLER MAY

PART II: *THE NEW DEAL POLITICAL ORDER:*
           DECLINE AND FALL, 1960–1980

    7   Was the Great Society a Lost Opportunity?   *185*
         IRA KATZNELSON

    8   The Failure and Success of the New Radicalism   *212*
         MAURICE ISSERMAN AND MICHAEL KAZIN

    9   The Rise of the "Silent Majority"   *243*
         JONATHAN RIEDER

   10   The Changing Shape of Power: A Realignment
         in Public Policy   *269*
         THOMAS BYRNE EDSALL

         Epilogue   *294*
         STEVE FRASER AND GARY GERSTLE

         List of Contributors   *299*

         Index   *301*

INTRODUCTION

WHEN Ronald Reagan assumed office in January of 1981, an epoch in the nation's political history came to an end. The New Deal, as a dominant order of ideas, public policies, and political alliances, died, however much its ghost still hovers over a troubled polity. *The Rise and Fall of the New Deal Order, 1930–1980* is thus intended as a historical autopsy. All of its contributors probe the mystery of how something so grandly complex as the New Deal order was born, then mastered a notoriously fractious country, and finally disintegrated. The question is a compelling one: the passions, bitterness, recriminations, and anxieties of our contemporary political life are all unthinkable except in reference to the politics, ideology, and morality that have come to be associated with the New Deal order.

The ten essays assembled here offer some startlingly new interpretations of the anomalies, ironies, and paradoxes that have long contributed to the mystery of the New Deal order: why the Great Depression lasted so long; how the Democratic party could simultaneously accommodate poor workers and wealthy capitalists in its coalition; why the 'labor question' lost its central importance in American politics almost from the day the labor movement finally achieved some enduring political power; how a liberalism so focused on issues of class inequality in the 1930s came to focus entirely on the issue of racial inequality in the 1960s; why economic abundance generated political and cultural conservatism in the 1950s and radicalism in the 1960s; and how the Democratic party managed to alienate, in the late 1960s and early 1970s, those constituents who had been its most diehard supporters.

In addition to their commitment to illuminating such basic questions in political history, the authors also share a particular generational experience. By and large they matured intellectually during the years when the Democratic party and its liberal agenda lost power and appeal. The witnessing of a political era's eclipse has imparted to many of these essays a sober and ironic tone, appropriate to political analyses that stress missed opportunities, unintended consequences, and dangerous but inescapable compromises. Such a tone is a far cry from the celebration of the New Deal characteristic of those scholars, like Arthur Schlesinger, Jr., and Eric Goldman, who witnessed first-hand that remarkable and seductive burst of political energy in the mid-1930s.[1] It is equally distant from the condemnatory terms in which young, angry 1960s radicals like those who wrote for *Studies on the Left* cast the New Deal and modern liberalism.[2] The intellectual passions of the 1930s and 1960s took shape in a climate that assumed the political era ushered in by the New Deal would go on forever. Our sobriety reflects the fact that the era no longer lives; that it belongs, as it were, to history.

ELECTORAL SYSTEMS AND POLITICAL ORDERS

The essays in this volume are arranged chronologically to follow the emergence, crystallization, and decomposition of a political order. Our notion of "political order" draws its conceptual inspiration from the notion of "electoral system" and "party system" developed by political scientists and the "new political historians" in recent years. These scholars have depicted American political history since 1800 in terms of relatively long periods of electoral stability punctuated by brief but intense political upheavals and electoral realignments. In each of the five periods of electoral stability (1800–1820s, 1820s–1850s, 1850s–1890s, 1890s–1930s, 1930s–1970s), the major parties had a fixed relationship to an electoral coalition; the size of the parties' respective coalitions, in turn, determined the relationship that prevailed between the two parties—in particular, whether one dominated or whether the two struggled on a relatively equal footing. Thus the fourth electoral system, ushered in by the crisis of the 1890s, made the Republican party the dominant one in national affairs for thirty-five years; and the fifth electoral system, ushered in by the Great Depression, brought the Democrats and their New Deal agenda to power for a period of about forty years.[3]

This approach diminishes the importance of particular political actors—presidents, senators, and others—as well as of the normal two-, four-, and six-year electoral cycles. It elevates, by contrast, the importance of economic events and social trends. Fundamental changes in political life—those which produce a change in party systems—are seen as issuing from crises in the nation's economy, social structure, and political culture. Thus the dissolution of the second party system of Whigs and Democrats in the 1850s was tied to irresolvable conflicts over slavery; the dissolution of the third-party system in the 1890s occurred amid a devastating economic depression and fundamental challenges to capitalism embodied in the Populist and labor revolts of those years; and the collapse of the fourth-party system in the 1930s likewise reflected economic distress and political revolt.

In probing why such fundamental historical events are required to change party systems, the new political historians have generally offered "ethnocultural" explanations. American voters, at least from the mid-nineteenth to the mid-twentieth century, they have argued, viewed political parties as the protectors of their most treasured beliefs and vital interests: their religions, their ethnic traditions, their families and their neighborhoods. Voters thus developed profound emotional loyalties to parties; these loyalties, in turn, influenced individual electoral behavior far more than rational reflections on a party's platform or short-term, instrumental calculations of the likely return on casting a ballot for one party or another. Such loyalties were not easily forsaken. Only major economic and social crises triggered broad shifts in loyalty from one party to another.[4]

The dominance of the Democratic party and its liberal agenda in the period from the 1930s to the 1970s is inconceivable apart from the emotional bond tying millions of voters—especially Catholic and Jewish voters climbing out of their big-city ghettos in the North—to Franklin Delano Roosevelt and the New Deal. The nature of that emotional bond is an issue that a number of essays in this volume investigate. But other essays explore the economic elites, policy-making networks, and political ideologies and programs that shaped the distribution of power and influenced the era's political character. It is precisely these elites, programs, and ideologies—factors in the nation's political life that students of electoral systems have tended to neglect—that our term "political order" is meant to encompass.[5] The New Deal order never operated with the kind of precision and effortlessness implied by a word like "system"; but it did possess an ideological character, a moral perspective, and a set of political relationships among policy elites, interest groups, and electoral constituencies that decidedly shaped American political life for forty years.

The New Deal Political Order: Emergence and Crystallization, 1929–1960

Thomas Ferguson's opening essay focuses on the economic elite whose power, money, and ambition were crucial to the reelection of Roosevelt in 1936 and to the long-term dominance of the New Deal political order. Members of this elite shared two characteristics: first, they were located in capital-intensive sectors of American industry where labor costs formed a relatively small part of overall expenditures; and, second, they dominated their industries in international trade. These economic circumstances allowed these capitalists to tolerate prolabor legislation on the one hand and to demand an international policy of free trade on the other. They were the ones who occupied the "backrooms" of Roosevelt's administration of 1935–36, supplying policymakers to draft the National Labor Relations Act and Social Security Act and to engineer the New Deal's sudden turn from economic nationalism to free trade.

Ferguson explains why this "industrial bloc" first broke off from the united business community that had coalesced behind McKinley in 1896 and then "realigned" itself with the Democratic party. He reconstructs the private world of money, policy, and partisanship that is so central a part of modern American politics. In the process of this reconstruction, he dispels the persistent and popular myth that the business community was monolithic in its attitude toward the New Deal. He shows how labor and a portion of capital can coexist—and simultaneously pursue their interests—in the same political party. And, finally, he renders comprehensible why the second New Deal was so politically different from the first, and why the political solutions embodied in those 1935 reforms—unlike those of 1933—endured.

Michael A. Bernstein's essay examines another persistent riddle about the Great Depression, namely, why it lasted far longer than any other cyclic downturn in American history. His explanation hinges on the unique coincidence of a cyclic downturn with a fundamental secular transition. The 1929 crash occurred at a time when investment dynamism had already shifted to such new consumer-driven industrial and commercial sectors as food processing, mass retailing, household appliances, medical care, and recreation; but the cumulative size of these new sectors, in terms of investment activity and employment, was simply too small in the 1930s to lead an overall economic recovery. Thus, even as firms in these sectors quickly recovered their sales, investors, and profitability, they could not overcome the drag imposed on the economy by those old sectors, like primary metals, textiles, and lumber, that still accounted for such large shares of national output and employment. Had the panic of 1929 occurred at a later point in this secular transition, when the new sectors had added some heft to their lean, energetic frames and the old sectors had shrunk to a size more befitting their advanced age, the trauma of a decade-long depression might well have been averted.

Bernstein deepens Ferguson's argument that divisions within the business community are crucial to an adequate understanding of the politics of the depression years. One would expect entrepreneurs of the newer consumption-oriented industries to have been drawn to specific sorts of political strategies reflecting their firms' economic resiliency and their buoyant faith in a bountiful future. And, as Steve Fraser points out in his essay on the 'labor question,' this was indeed the case. Mass merchandisers, urban real-estate developers, clothing, appliance, and office goods manufacturers—and their banking, trade union, and intellectual allies—formed, as early as the 1920s, a proto-Keynesian elite eager to use the state to stimulate consumption, to redistribute income, and even to intervene in financial and labor markets. Such state policies, they believed, would trigger a revival of production and thus the return of prosperity. This vision had already attracted (by the mid-1920s) such political reformers as Louis Brandeis and Felix Frankfurter, labor leaders like Sidney Hillman, and industrial relations experts like William Leiserson and Morris Cooke. And when the Great Depression convulsed the world of politics, discrediting the policies of reigning elites and quickening the movement of "new immigrants"—especially its working-class component—for full political and social enfranchisement, this new political elite saw its opportunity and seized a portion of state power. Members of this elite were both the architects and the administrators of that famed New Deal welfare state that had taken shape by 1937: a rambling collection of state agencies, including the Departments of Labor and Interior, the Works Projects Administration, the National Labor Relations Board, the National Resources Planning Board, the Rural Electrification Agency, and the Federal Reserve.

This momentous political development was laced with irony and ambiguity. The more this new elite and its labor movement allies succeeded in their goals, the more workers would find themselves integrated into a mass consumer society and stripped of a specific class identity. On the other hand, this "mass consumption" coalition encountered opposition, even in the 1930s, on all sides: from conservative sectors of the labor movement; from the South; from old sectors of capital and their banking allies; from small businessmen. And then the severe recession of 1937 challenged the very legitimacy of the New Deal itself, provoking a far-reaching reevaluation of the political project that New Deal policymakers had so confidently undertaken.

That reevaluation—and its consequences for American politics—are the subjects of Alan Brinkley's essay "The New Deal and the Idea of the State." Focusing on the ideological and political disarray in Roosevelt's administration in 1937, he does not discern the kind of programmatic coherence that Fraser and Ferguson argue characterized the New Deal political elite by 1936. In Brinkley's eyes, ideological eclecticism rather than coherence characterized the New Deal from 1932 through 1936. The political and economic pressures of 1937, however, forced New Dealers—such men as Alvin Hansen, Marriner Eccles, Harry Hopkins, Harold Ickes, Thurman Arnold, and Henry Wallace—to articulate and defend their ideological vision. Such pressure yielded two quite different visions, one calling on the state to regulate capitalist institutions and the other calling on the state merely to stimulate economic growth through the use of fiscal and monetary powers. Brinkley labels the first vision "regulatory" and the second "Keynesian"; and he shows how the Keynesian vision gradually, but firmly, in the years 1937 to 1945, pushed the regulatory vision from the corridors of power. Above all, the experience of war—and especially a revived faith in capitalism which that experience engendered—secured, in Brinkley's view, the ascendancy of the Keynesian over the regulatory approach.

Brinkley's argument that Keynesianism triumphed only in the 1940s seems to contradict Fraser's claim that it already reigned in 1936. But the contradiction is more semantic than real, reflecting the significantly different meanings that the two authors impute to Keynesianism. Keynesianism, in Brinkley's eyes, signified the use of the state's fiscal and monetary powers to maintain a healthy macroeconomic environment. Keynesianism, in Fraser's eyes, involved extensive intervention by the state in capital, labor, and consumer markets—to the point of regulating corporate business practices and of assigning the state the role of employer, builder, and (on rare occasions) manufacturer. What made both these approaches Keynesian was their shared goal of using the state to stimulate consumption and to distribute the fruits of capitalism on an ever greater scale. But the markedly different means each espoused for achieving those goals necessarily tied Keynesianism to two very different kinds of political programs. Following the useful lead of Theda Skocpol and Margaret Weir, we might label the New Dealers' more radical, regulatory program "social Keynesianism," and their more conservative, fiscal-oriented program "commercial Keynesianism."[6] We could then suggest that the regulatory approach favored by many New Dealers in 1936 and 1937 was a form of social Keynesianism that fell into eclipse during the war years as advocates of a commercial Keynesianism won the key battles within the policy and party elites for control of the American state. Such a perspective would underscore the importance of Keynesian thinking from the late 1930s on, while allowing for the dramatic 1940s change in state policies emphasized by Brinkley.

Nelson Lichtenstein demonstrates in his essay "From Corporatism to Collective Bargaining" that proponents of social Keynesianism, though confined by the early 1940s to the progressive wing of the labor movement and the "left-liberal" wing of the Democratic party, doggedly carried on their battle for political power (and the control of the state that such power bestowed). Labor movement progressives like Walter Reuther and Philip Murray and their left-liberal allies in the Democratic party discerned in the structure and operation of such wartime agencies as the War Labor Board and Office of Price Administration a model of democratic, national planning—what Lichtenstein calls corporatism—that could be applied to a reconverted peacetime economy. Almost all the planning ideas involved securing for American workers full employment, high wages, and adequate welfare provisions. They drew their ultimate justification from the stimulus that such a welfare state would give capitalism through the dramatic expansion in levels of personal consumption. When their efforts to introduce such social democratic notions were rebuffed first by corporate titans like General Motors and then by an increasingly conservative Democratic party, the labor progressives sought to build their economic and political strength. They launched "Operation Dixie," a campaign to organize Southern workers, and they mobilized support for the formation of a truly "progressive" political party. "Operation Dixie" foundered on racism, while their third-party efforts—though yielding Henry Wallace's Progressive party—succumbed to cold war passions. Only in 1948 and 1949 did labor progressives relinquish their corporatist dreams and accept the political solution forced on them: the pursuit of economic security through a private, depoliticized system of collective bargaining. Only then did social Keynesianism drop entirely out of American politics.

Brinkley's and Lichtenstein's essays both force us to treat the 1940s, rather than the 1930s, as the politically formative years of the New Deal order. Only in the mid-to-late 1940s did the fate of modern liberalism come to depend on the successful operation of a high-consumption capitalist economy; only in those years did commercial Keynesians, those policymakers who wanted to exercise only the fiscal and monetary powers of the state, gain dominance in the Democratic party and over the state's administrative structure. The creation of this political economy was a wrenching political experience, lasting more than fifteen years and involving mammoth conflicts, not simply between workers and capitalists but between different blocs of capitalists and between contending groups of policymakers. And even in 1950, this political economy had not overcome all sources of resistance. The South still stood outside these new economic arrangements, as did many poor who had to survive in a haphazard welfare system. The incomplete integration of the South and the poor meant, of course, the incomplete integration of American blacks; it meant that race would necessarily loom larger and larger in American politics.

Those Americans who were fully integrated into this political economy—the unionized sectors of the working class and the rapidly expanding ranks of securely employed, well-paid, white-collar workers—found themselves surrounded by lush advertising images of the private satisfactions to be gained from spending and consuming. The definition of the good life that was thus implied—stressing the superiority of leisure to work, of individual expressiveness to social solidarity, and of private, family life to public, civic life—long antedated the 1950s. As Steve Fraser notes in his 'labor question' essay, the extension of mass production and scientific management techniques to ever greater sectors of American industry in the decade of World War I had thoroughly transformed the world of work and play. The skilled craftsman who found justification in work for his very essence had become, by 1930, an endangered species; so too had the unskilled laborers whose abysmal working conditions had aroused such political anxiety about the capacity of capitalist society to deliver a decent life to wage earners. In their places arose a new kind of worker, the semiskilled operative, whose modicum of skill commanded some respect and whom employers strenuously tried to acclimate to the hierarchical, bureaucratic character of the modern workplace. These workers, who formed the natural constituency for the CIO, found their political voice during the New Deal years. They demanded that their workplaces be governed by an enlightened rule of law and that employers respect the workplace rights that their unions had established; but, lacking the autonomy and skill that had made work the central element of the nineteenth-century craftsman's identity, they increasingly sought personal satisfaction not in "workers control" but in the glittering array of goods and entertainments made available by the marketplace. By 1950, millions of these unionized workers had won the job security and wage levels necessary to participate fully in the consumer marketplace; so too had the growing masses of white-collar, corporate workers.

Elaine Tyler May's essay "Cold War—Warm Hearth" explores this unprecedented mass focus on consumption as well as the "peculiar," family-centered form it took in the 1950s. The consumption mania of the 1950s—homes, cars, TVs, hi-fis, nylon stockings, and "bar-b-q" grills—has long been regarded as a central feature of post–World War II culture. What has remained somewhat obscure is why this wave of consumption should have focused so much on home and family. May argues that Americans seized on home and family life for two interrelated sets of reasons. First, the highly organized and bureaucratized character of work life—true for both blue- and white-collar workers—made home life seem correspondingly individualized and free. Second, the cumulative shock of depression, world war, cold war, and the threat of nuclear annihilation inclined individual Americans to forsake the frightening public world of politics for the comforting and secure private world of family. Suburbanization—and the breakup of familiar communities and extended kin networks that it implied—ensured that the *nuclear* family would become the focus for this private life; so did the new "scientific" gospel on the expressive and liberating possibilities inherent in family life. Middle-class Americans relied heavily on professional expertise, especially on the psychiatrists, social workers, and counselors who promised to help them become more expressive, in sexual and other ways, with their marriage partners.

For all these reasons, the 1950s apotheosis of home and family cannot be considered a triumph for traditional values. To the contrary, the emphases on consumption, scientific expertise, and personal and individual expressiveness all underscore the essentially modernist and secularist character of 1950s private life—at least for those participating in the economy of abundance and consumerism. This modernist version of private life may be viewed as an intrinsic part of the New Deal order. Its emphasis on consumption made it an integral part of the nation's mass production economy; its glorification of individual expressiveness in the family compensated for the impersonality of public life; and its infatuation with professionals and scientific expertise partook of the same rationalist, hierarchical principles driving state social and economic policy.

This "fit" between 1950s public and private life was hardly perfect. The espousal of modernist values in private life would generate enormous anxieties among husbands and wives, parents and children, as they strove to fulfill, often unsuccessfully, their hopes for individual expressiveness within a traditionalist, patriarchal form of family organization. Substantial numbers of families, moreover, located especially in the rural and small-town South and Midwest and in urban, ethnic districts of the Northeast, resisted the modernist code of May's middle-class suburban families, and cleaved instead to a traditionalism rooted in Protestant or Catholic spiritual codes. Some briefly found a political voice in Joseph McCarthy's attacks on the Eastern Establishment, liberalism, and cosmopolitanism. Still, those who found their search for individual expressiveness blocked or who clung to traditionalist codes discovered few political outlets for their dissatisfactions. They were marginal players in the political arena defined by the New Deal order.

The New Deal Political Order: Decline and Fall, 1960–1980

No single event undermined the New Deal order; no particular individual, or even group of individuals, dug its grave. Decay began to set in as a result of growing gaps between what the New Deal order promised its constituents—in terms of citizenship rights, affluence, individual expressiveness, and a stable international order under American auspices—and what it actually delivered. A gap emerged first in the early 1960s in regard to the disenfranchised and poverty-stricken status of American blacks; another appeared in the moral turbulence and growing drain of international military commitments on domestic prosperity occasioned by the Vietnam War; and a third and related gap appeared in middle-class youth's alienation from the highly organized, bureaucratized character of the New Deal order that, they felt, stifled their quest for authenticity and individuality. Political tensions began to accumulate as result. These tensions were aggravated by the often vacillating and halfhearted efforts of Democratic party elites to make good on the promises of equality and opportunity so essential to the legitimacy of their political order. At some point in the 1960s and early 1970s, each smoldering tension would trigger a political explosion. The cumulative effects of such explosions would shatter the Democratic party as a majority party and discredit its liberal doctrines. By the mid-1970s, as a result, the New Deal political order had ceased to exist.

The mobilization of American blacks in the greatest movement for racial equality since Reconstruction is a well-told and -analyzed story that we do not recount in this volume.[7] But that story forms the essential backdrop to Ira Katznelson's essay "Was the Great Society a Lost Opportunity?" Katznelson subjects to careful examination Daniel Patrick Moynihan's 1969 contention that the Johnson Administration squandered an "immense [political] opportunity" offered it by the civil rights movement: namely, to pass a full employment and incomes maintenance program that would have permanently solved the problem of American poverty. In Katznelson's eyes, such a program would have required the Democratic party to adopt European-style social democratic policies calling for extensive state interventions in labor and income markets. Such a social democratic turn was simply not possible in the 1960s. The reason, Katznelson argues, lies not in some fundamental, timeless antithesis between American political culture and social democratic ideas; it lies instead in the closing off in the 1940s of a social democratic initiative that the left wing of the New Deal and progressive elements of the labor movement had nurtured since the mid-1930s.

Katznelson furthers Brinkley's and Lichtenstein's argument that the 1940s were watershed years in modern American political life. Not only did those years encompass the triumph of commercial Keynesianism and the transformation of the labor movement from a social democratic insurgency into a mere interest group; they encompassed as well the substitution of race for class as the great, unsolved problem in American life. These 1940s transformations decisively shaped and limited the social programs of the 1960s. Policymakers of the 1960s, influenced by an economics profession committed to commercial Keynesian doctrines, would not contemplate extensive state interferences in capital and labor markets. The labor movement showed little inclination to use the War on Poverty to raise fundamental questions about the distribution of income and power in American society. As a result of the labor movement's timidity on the one hand and the growing force of the civil rights movement on the other, the War on Poverty became entirely associated with the problems of black Americans. Katznelson admires the inventiveness and boldness of Great Society policymakers in pushing the limits of the ideological framework in which they operated. But he also stresses the futility of their task. They could not possibly have solved the problem of poverty—black or white—without more extensive state controls of capitalist institutions and markets. And their inability to challenge the increasingly popular view that the Great Society was meant to aid only black Americans would soon stir up resentment against the Democratic party among poor and working-class whites.

Tensions within the Democratic party over the issues of poverty and race had already become apparent during the halcyon days of 1960s prosperity. They became much more serious as the costs of defending the "free world" and, in particular, of fighting the Vietnam War began to force cutbacks in domestic social spending. The growing European and Japanese challenge to American economic superiority further strained the nation's resources and began generating a string of economic woes, many of which to this day remain unsolved: inflation, declining investment and productivity, unmanageable budget deficits, and negative trade balances. In political terms, these pressures called into question two economic principles central to the New Deal order: first, that consumer capitalism's benefits were to be extended to ever greater numbers of Americans; and, second, that the state, through its fiscal and monetary powers, was to stimulate the production and distribution of economic abundance.

This brewing racial-economic crisis, on its own, would probably have been sufficient to undermine the New Deal order. But an assault on this order and its majority party came from a cultural source as well—middle-class youth who began rejecting the materialism, consumerism, and familial-based personal life that were so central to the New Deal order's definition of the "good life." This cultural revolt and the ways in which it fueled, in the 1960s, a radical student movement intent on eliminating racism, poverty, technocracy, and imperialism from American life form the subjects of Maurice Isserman and Michael Kazin's essay "The Failure and Success of the New Radicalism."

Isserman and Kazin root the student revolt in the stultifying character of 1950s private life. Told by the purveyors of mass culture and mass consumption that "a time of unending affluence and total freedom of choice was at hand," the young sought to experience a wide range of activities and to explore all aspects of their individuality. Above all, they sought "authenticity." Though the young cast this revolt in generational terms—as a revolt against their parents—their search for authenticity bears a striking resemblance to the search for personal expressiveness that Elaine Tyler May argues was so central to the family lives of the parents themselves. Seen from this perspective, the children may have been espousing an expanded, radicalized version of their own parents' values; 1950s domesticity, with its rhetorical emphasis on personal freedom, may have been the nursery of 1960s rebellion.

The younger generation's inclination to cast themselves in opposition to their parents was therefore deeply ironic. It also triggered momentous upheavals in both private and public life. The young rejected a host of values associated with 1950s adult, married life: the dogged pursuit of economic security, sexual monogamy, and, ultimately, patriarchy. Carrying the search for authenticity into all areas of public life—universities, corporations, government—the young produced a radical attack on the bureaucratic, hierarchical, and rationalist principles that underlay production and politics in the New Deal order.

In a cynical age, this radical disaffection might have developed along nihilist or narcissistic lines. But the moral awakening spawned by the cold war made many young people eager to join a crusade to save their society from the hypocritical practices—especially the tolerance of racism and poverty at home and the support of right-wing dictators abroad—that so compromised American democratic ideals. Isserman and Kazin analyze the emergence and collapse of this radical movement from the hopeful days of the civil rights protests, through the massive protests against the Vietnam War, to the self-destructive violence that set in once students began despairing, in the late 1960s, of ever changing the "system." While the authors duly note the failure of the New Left to achieve its stated political agenda, they argue that this movement altered, in enduring ways, popular attitudes toward race, gender, and authority. It also delivered the final blow to the New Deal order by opening up a gaping hole between two vital Democratic party constituencies: on one side stood a coalition of blacks and middle-class whites committed to an agenda of racial and sexual equality, social welfare, and moral modernism; on the other side gathered working-class and lower-middle-class whites, largely Catholic in the North and Protestant in the South, calling for a reassertion of such traditional values as patriarchy, patriotism, law and order, hard work, and self-help. By the late 1970s Democratic politicians found it impossible to design a politics to please both constituencies. As a result the Democratic party lost its majority status as well as the ability to define the nation's political agenda. In its place appeared a revived Republican party brandishing the political agenda of the New Right.

Jonathan Rieder's essay "The Rise of the 'Silent Majority' " traces the process by which working-class and lower-middle-class whites, South and North, abandoned the Democratic party first for George Wallace in 1968 and then for the Republican party of Ronald Reagan. From the earliest days of the New Deal order, these groups had embraced the Democratic party's economic liberalism for its frank recognition of the inequalities in wealth and power prevalent throughout American society. By contrast, they tolerated but were discomfited by the national party's racial and international liberalism. Both these constituencies were also traditionalist in moral outlook, suspicious of the secularism, rationalism, and emphasis on individual expressiveness that was so intrinsic a part of the New Deal order. Their class experience and moral traditionalism, in combination, made them suspicious of distant (and rootless) technocratic and bureaucratic elites and gave their political outlook a distinctly proto-populist air. A populist opposition seemed to cohere around McCarthy in the early 1950s, but the timing was premature. The Republican right needed another decade or two in the political wilderness to shed its own elitist roots and fashion a language and agenda appropriate for a conservative populist movement. Opportunities abounded in the 1960s as the dismantling of the Southern caste system triggered mass defections among white southerners. The implementation of antipoverty and affirmative action legislation, meanwhile, generated a sense of class injustice—"reverse discrimination"—

among large numbers of ethnic whites in the North. These grievances quickly became part of a moral critique of "limousine liberalism." White traditionalists, North and South, saw black and student
rioting, flag burning and contempt for the police, drug use and street
crime, sexual promiscuity, and the blurring of gender distinctions as
multiple signs of a single moral crisis of extraordinary proportions.
George Wallace was the first to articulate this moral crisis in national
political affairs; Ronald Reagan made it a leitmotif of his triumphant
rise to the pinnacle of American politics. By 1980 the whole of the
liberal vision that had taken shape during the New Deal years—not
just its moral modernism but its belief in the state as an agent of economic prosperity and income redistribution—stood discredited
among large parts of the American population.

    These essays point to the complexity of the New Deal order's de-
cline and collapse: economics, race, and morality each played a central role in this political drama. They also suggest an overarching
logic to the system's fall. The state's rhetorical commitment to distrib-
uting civil rights and economic abundance to all its citizens inevitably
pushed race to the very center of national politics; the nation's growing military obligations diminished the economic resources necessary
to solve or at least mitigate the brewing racial crisis; and the importance attached (by purveyors of mass culture and ideologues of a
modernist domesticity) to achieving a full and expressive personal life
predictably resulted in an insatiable hunger for "authenticity" and
autonomy in all social spheres. Did these particular dynamics, in combination, necessitate the explosion of unruly, ugly, and often violent
passions over issues of race and morals that so dominated and disfig-
ured 1960s politics? Several essays suggest an affirmative answer.
Tension between moral traditionalists and moral modernists in the
Democratic party, Rieder reminds us, was present from the New Deal
order's earliest days. The New Deal order's unabashedly modernist
character intensified these tensions and was bound, sooner or later,
to provoke the moral outrage of traditionalists. A second source of
tension resulted from the failure of the Democratic party and organized labor, in the 1930s and 1940s, to transform, through wage legislation and unionization, the South's social structure. Such failures,
analyzed by Fraser and Lichtenstein in their essays, meant that an
extraordinary kind of judicial fiat—itself, though cloaked in constitutional language, a kind of violence—would be necessary to integrate southerners (and especially blacks) into the New Deal order.
Such coercion provoked widespread, often violent, resistance. Given
the deep roots of 1960s conflict, it would have taken an unusually
prescient set of Democratic party policymakers to defuse social ten-

sions and remedy social problems. But, as Katznelson reminds us, Great Society policymakers, imprisoned by the 1940s ideological framework they inherited, lacked the necessary intellectual autonomy and clarity. And even if they had somehow managed to step outside their own history and devise a set of wise social policies, they might have found their policies thwarted by the nation's strained economic base.

Thomas Byrne Edsall, in this volume's concluding essay "The Changing Shape of Power," asks whether the Republican renaissance of the 1970s and early 1980s marks the birth of a new, Republican-dominated political order. He quickly concludes that this is not the case, largely because American political parties, as a result of electoral reform and the intrusion of mass media on electoral campaigns, are rapidly losing their dominance over the American political process. He does suggest, however, that a different kind of political order has taken shape, one in which a new elite—"a small, often interlocking, network of campaign specialists, fund-raisers, and lobbyists"—has usurped the political party's role of defining government policy and electoral strategy. This new elite, expert at raising money and at identifying and molding "public" opinion, has concentrated political power in the hands of the wealthy to a degree unimaginable in a party-dominated system. The result has been a fundamental "policy realignment" in which government policy, regardless of whether Republicans or Democrats control Washington, favors the well-to-do and penalizes the poor. The most telling evidence of this development can be found in the growing inequality in income distribution these last ten years. While some of this inequality reflects the nation's loss of high-paying manufacturing jobs and their replacement by low-paying service-sector jobs, another portion reflects deliberate government policy: namely, a regressive tax policy and a campaign to weaken organized labor. These policies are most clearly associated with Reagan and his refurbished Republican party; and Edsall argues that this party's core of affluent and religious voters will give Republicans an important edge in fund-raising and thus in presidential campaigning. But even if the Democrats manage to win a national election, they too would champion distributional policies that favored the affluent over the poor. Such continuity, at bottom, reflects the declining influence in Democratic party circles of workers and the poor—and of their institutional representatives, labor unions and political clubhouses. It reflects as well striking increases in the party power of affluent, middle-class Democrats. Politics in late-twentieth-century America, Edsall provocatively concludes, is a game increasingly played by and for the wealthy. The poor have lost both the ability to influence policy and the will to participate in electoral politics.

The New Deal order is dead. Yet the problems bedeviling that order from the early 1960s live on: class and racial antagonisms, the resentments of status and power, the corruptions and frustrations of engorged federal bureaucracies, the antipodes of authority and resistance, still occupy a central place in our nation's political life. Whether we are witnessing the birth of a new political order, and whether such a new order will address these troubling and divisive issues more successfully than the New Deal order, remain unclear.

NOTES

1. See Arthur Schlesinger, Jr., *The Age of Roosevelt*, 3 vols. (Boston: Houghton Mifflin, 1957–1960), and Eric Goldman, *Rendezvous with Destiny: A History of Modern American Reform* (New York: Knopf, 1952).

2. For examples of writing in this vein, see Barton Bernstein, "The New Deal: The Conservative Achievements of Liberal Reform," in Bernstein, ed., *Toward a New Past: Dissenting Essays in American History* (New York: Pantheon, 1968), 263–88; and Ronald Radosh, "The Myth of the New Deal," in Radosh and Murray N. Rothbard, eds., *A New History of Leviathan* (New York: E. P. Dutton, 1972), 146–86.

3. The seminal works in this approach include V. O. Key, Jr., "A Theory of Critical Elections," *Journal of Politics* 17 (February 1955): 3–18; Key, "Secular Realignment and the Party System," *Journal of Politics* 21 (May 1959); William Nisbet Chambers and Walter Dean Burnham, eds., *The American Party Systems: Stages of Political Development*, 2d ed. (New York: Oxford University Press, 1975); Burnham, *Critical Elections and the Mainsprings of American Politics* (New York: Norton, 1970); James L. Sundquist, *Dynamics of the Party System: Alignment and Realignment of Political Parties in the United States* (Washington, D.C.: The Brookings Institution, 1973); Paul Kleppner, *The Cross of Culture: A Social Analysis of Midwestern Politics, 1850–1900* (New York: Free Press, 1970); Kleppner, *The Third Electoral System, 1853–1892: Parties, Voters, and Political Cultures* (Chapel Hill, N.C.: University of North Carolina Press, 1979); Kleppner, ed., *The Evolution of American Electoral Systems* (Westport, Conn.: Greenwood Press, 1981); Richard J. Jensen, *The Winning of the Midwest: Social and Political Conflict, 1888–96* (Chicago: University of Chicago Press, 1971).

4. See Kleppner, *The Third Electoral System*, for a fully developed example of ethnocultural explanations; see also Richard Oestreicher, "Urban Working-Class Political Behavior and Theories of American Electoral Politics, 1870–1940," *Journal of American History* 74 (March 1988): 1257–86.

5. For recent works within the "electoral system" paradigm that remedy

this neglect, see Jerome M. Clubb, William H. Flanigan, and Nancy H. Zingale, *Partisan Realignment: Voters, Parties, and Government in American History* (Beverly Hills, Calif.: Sage Publications, 1980); and William E. Gienapp, *The Origins of the Republican Party, 1852–1856* (New York: Oxford University Press, 1987). See also Richard L. McCormick, "The Realignment Synthesis in American History," *Journal of Interdisciplinary History* 13 (Summer 1982): 85–105.

6. "Margaret Weir and Theda Skocpol, "State Structures and the Possibilities for 'Keynesian' Responses to the Great Depression in Sweden, Britain, and the United States," in Peter B. Evans, Dietrich Rueschemeyer, and Skocpol, eds., *Bringing the State Back In* (Cambridge: Cambridge University Press, 1985), 108, 151n. "Social Keynesianism" is the invention of Weir and Skocpol; "commercial Keynesianism," the invention of Robert Lekachman (*The Age of Keynes* [New York: Random House, 1966], 287).

7. Important analyses of this movement include David J. Garrow, *Bearing the Cross: Martin Luther King, Jr., and the Southern Christian Leadership Conference* (New York: William Morrow, 1986); Adam Fairclough, *To Redeem the Soul of America: The Southern Christian Leadership Conference and Martin Luther King, Jr.* (Athens, Ga.: University of Georgia Press, 1987); Clayborne Carson, *In Struggle: SNCC and the Black Awakening of the 1960s* (Cambridge, Mass.: Harvard University Press, 1981); Aldon D. Morris, *Origins of the Civil Rights Movement: Black Communities Organizing for Change* (New York: Free Press, 1984); August Meier and Elliot Rudwick, *CORE: A Study in the Civil Rights Movement, 1942–1968* (New York: Oxford University Press, 1973); Frances Fox Piven and Richard A. Cloward, "The Civil Rights Movement," in *Poor People's Movements: Why They Succeed, How They Fail* (New York: Pantheon, 1979), 181–263; Allen J. Matusow, *The Unraveling of America: A History of Liberalism in the 1960s* (New York: Harper and Row, 1984), chaps. 3, 4, 7; William H. Chafe, *Civilities and Civil Rights: Greensboro, North Carolina and the Black Struggle for Equality* (New York: Oxford University Press, 1980); Sara Evans, *Personal Politics: The Roots of Women's Liberation in the Civil Rights Movement and the New Left* (New York: Knopf, 1979); Harvard Sitkoff, *The Struggle for Black Equality, 1954–1980* (New York: Hill and Wang, 1981).

PART I

*The New Deal Political Order:
Emergence and Crystallization,
1929–1960*

1

Industrial Conflict and the Coming of the New Deal: The Triumph of Multinational Liberalism in America

THOMAS FERGUSON

*I*N OCTOBER 1929, the stock market crashed. Over the next few months the market continued dropping, and a general economic decline took hold. As sales plummeted, industry after industry laid off workers and cut wages. Farm and commodity prices tumbled, outpacing price declines in other parts of the economy. A tidal wave of bankruptcies engulfed businessmen, farmers, and a middle class that had only recently awakened to the joys of installment buying.

While the major media, leading politicians, and important businessmen resonantly reaffirmed capitalism's inherently self-correcting tendency, havoc spread around the world. By 1932, the situation had become critical. Many currencies were floating and international finance had virtually collapsed. World trade had shrunk to a fraction of its previous level. In many countries one-fifth or more of the work force was idle. Homeless, often starving, people camped out in parks and fields, while only the virtual collapse of real-estate markets in many districts checked a mammoth liquidation of homes and farms by banks and insurance companies.

In this desperate situation, with regimes changing and governments falling, a miracle seemed to occur in the United States, the country that, among all the major powers in the capitalist world economy, had perhaps been hit hardest. Taking office at the moment of the greatest financial collapse in the nation's history, President Franklin D. Roosevelt initiated a dazzling burst of government actions designed to square the circle that was baffling governments elsewhere: how to enact major social reforms while preserving both democracy and capitalism. In a hundred days his administration implemented a series of emergency relief bills for the unemployed; an Agricultural Adjustment Act for farmers; a bill (the Glass-Steagall Act, also sometimes referred to as the "Banking Act of 1933") to "reform" the banking structure; a Securities Act to reform the Stock Exchange; and the National Industrial Recovery Act, which in effect legalized cartels in American industry. Roosevelt suspended the convertibility of the dollar into gold, abandoned the gold standard, and enacted legislation to promote American exports. He also presided over a noisy public investigation of the most famous banking house in the world: J. P. Morgan & Co.

For a while this "first New Deal" package of policies brought some relief, but sustained recovery failed to arrive and class conflict intensified. Two years later, Roosevelt scored an even more dramatic series of triumphs that consolidated his position as the guardian of all the millions, both people and fortunes. A second period of whirlwind legislative activity produced the most important social legislation in American history—the Social Security and Wagner acts—as well as measures to break up public utility holding companies and to fix the price of oil. The president also turned dramatically away from his earlier economic nationalism. He entered into agreements with Britain and France informally to stabilize the dollar against their currencies and began vigorously to implement earlier legislation that empowered Secretary of State Cordell Hull to negotiate a series of treaties reducing U.S. tariff rates.[1]

After winning one of the most bitterly contested elections in American history by a landslide (and giving the coup de grace to the old Republican-dominated "System of '96"), Roosevelt consolidated the position of the Democrats as the new majority party of the United States.[2] He passed additional social welfare legislation and pressured the Supreme Court to accept his reforms. Faced with another steep downturn in 1937, the Roosevelt team confirmed its new economic course. Rejecting proposals to revive the National Recovery Administration (NRA) and again devalue the dollar, it adopted an experimental program of conscious "pump priming," which used government spending to prop up the economy in a way that foreshadowed the "Keynesian" policies of demand management widely adopted by Western economies after 1945. This was the first time this had ever been attempted—unless one accepts the Swedish example, which was virtually contemporaneous.[3]

Roosevelt and his successive New Deals have exercised a magnetic attraction on subsequent political analysts. Reams of commentary have sought to elucidate what the New Deal was and why it evolved as it did. But while the debate has raged for over forty years, little consensus exists about how best to explain what happened.

Many analysts, including most of those whose major works shaped the historiography of the last generation, have always been convinced that the decisive factor in the shaping of the New Deal was Franklin D. Roosevelt himself.[4] They hail his sagacity in fashioning his epoch-making domestic reforms. They honor his statecraft in leading the United States away from isolationism and toward Atlantic Alliance. And they celebrate the charisma he displayed in recruiting millions of previously marginal workers, blacks, and intellectuals into his great crusade to limit permanently the power of business in American life.

Several rival accounts now compete with this interpretation. As some radical historians pose the problem, only Roosevelt and a handful of advisers were farsighted enough to grasp what was required to save capitalism from itself.[5] Accordingly, Roosevelt engineered sweeping attacks on big business for the sake of big business's own long-run interest. (A variation on this theme credits the administration's aspirations toward reform but points to the structural constraints capitalism imposes on any government as the explanation for the New Deal's conservative outcome.)

Another recent point of view explains the New Deal by pointing to the consolidation and expansion of bureaucratic institutions. It deemphasizes Roosevelt as a personality, along with the period's exciting mass politics. Instead, historians like Ellis Hawley (in his latest essays) single out as the hallmarks of the New Deal the role of professionally certified experts, and the advance of organization and hierarchical control.[6]

Some of these arguments occasionally come close to the final current of contemporary New Deal interpretation. This focuses sharply on concrete interactions between polity and economy (rather than bureaucracy per se) in defining the outcome of the New Deal. Notable here are the (mostly West German) theorists of "organized capitalism," several different versions of Marxist analysis, right-wing libertarian analysts who treat the New Deal as an attempt by big business to institutionalize the corporate state, and Gabriel Kolko's theory of "political capitalism."[7]

These newer approaches provide telling criticisms of traditional analyses of the New Deal. At the same time, however, they often create fresh difficulties. "Organized capitalism," "political capitalism," or the libertarian "corporate state" analyses, for example, are illuminating with respect to the universal price-fixing schemes of the NRA. But the half-life of the NRA was short even by the admittedly unstable standards of American politics. The historic turn toward free trade that was so spectacularly a part of the later New Deal is scarcely compatible with claims that the New Deal institutionalized the collective power of big business as a whole, and it is perhaps unsurprising that most of this literature hurries over foreign economic policy. Nor are more than token efforts usually made to explain in detail why the New Deal arrived in its classic post-1935 form only after moving through stages that often seemed to caricature the celebrated observation that history proceeds not along straight lines but in spirals. It was, after all, a period in which the future patron saint of American Internationalism not only raised more tariffs than he lowered but also openly mocked exchange-rate stability and the gold standard, promoted cartelization, and endorsed inflation.[8] Similarly, theorists who treat the New Deal chiefly as the bureaucratic design of credentialed administrators and professionals not only ignore the significance of this belated opening to international trade in the world economy, but they also do less than full justice to the dramatic business mobilization and epic class conflicts of the period.

Nor do any of these accounts provide a credible analysis of the Democratic party of the era. Then, as now, the Democratic party fits badly into the boxes provided by conventional political science. On the one hand, it is perfectly obvious that a tie to at least part of organized labor provides an important element of the party's identity. But on the other, it is equally manifest that no amount of co-optation accounts for the party's continuing collateral affiliation with such prominent businessmen as, for example, Averell Harriman. Why, if the Democrats truly constituted a mass labor party, was the outcome of the New Deal not more congruent with the traditional labor party politics of Great Britain and Germany? And, if the Democratic party was not a labor party, then what force inside it was powerful enough to contain the CIO and simultaneously launch a sweeping attack on major industrial interests? These analyses also slip past the biggest puzzle that the New Deal poses. They offer few clues as to why some countries with militant labor movements and charismatic political leaders in the depression needed a New Order instead of a New Deal to control their work force.

In this essay I contend that a clear view of the New Deal's world historical uniqueness and significance comes only when one breaks with most of the commentaries of the last thirty years, goes back to primary sources, and attempts to analyze the New Deal as a whole in the light of industrial structure, party competition, and public policy. Then what stands out is the novel type of political coalition that Roosevelt built.[9] At the center of this coalition, however, are not the workers, blacks, and poor who have preoccupied liberal commentators, but something else: a new "historical bloc" (in Gramsci's phrase) of capital-intensive industries, investment banks, and internationally oriented commercial banks.

This new kind of power bloc constitutes the basis of the New Deal's great and, in world history, utterly unique achievement: its ability to accommodate millions of mobilized workers amid world depression. Because capital-intensive firms use relatively less direct human labor (and that often professionalized and elaborately trained), they were less threatened by labor turbulence. They had the space and the resources to envelop, rather than confront, their work force. In addition, with the momentous exception of the chemical industry, these capital-intensive firms were both world and domestic leaders in their industries. Consequently, they stood to gain from global free trade. They could, and did, ally with important international financiers, whose own minuscule work forces presented few sources of tension and who had for over a decade supported a more broadly international foreign policy and the lowering of traditionally high American tariffs.

THE RISE OF THE MULTINATIONAL BLOC, 1918–1929

At the center of the Republican party during the System of '96 was a massive bloc of major industries, including steel, textiles, coal, and, less monolithically, shoes, whose labor-intensive production processes automatically made them deadly enemies of labor and paladins of laissez-faire social policy.[10] While a few firms whose products dominated world markets, such as machinery, agitated for modest trade liberalization (aided occasionally by other industries seeking specific export advantages through trade treaties with particular countries), insistent pressures from foreign competitors led most to the ardent promotion of high tariffs.[11]

Integral to this "National Capitalist" bloc for most of the period were investment and commercial bankers. They had abandoned the Democrats in the 1890s when "Free Silver" and Populist advocates briefly captured the party. The financiers' massive investments in the mid-1890s and after, in huge trusts that combined many smaller firms, gave them a large, often controlling, stake in American industry, and brought them much closer to the industrialists (especially on tariffs, which Gold Democrats had abominated), and laid the foundation for a far more durable attachment to the GOP.[12]

World War I disrupted these close relations between American industry and finance. Overnight the United States went from a net debtor to a net creditor in the world economy, while the tremendous economic expansion induced by the war destabilized both the United States and the world economy. Briefly advantaged by the burgeoning demand for labor, American workers struck in record numbers and for a short interval appeared likely to unionize extensively.[13] Not surprisingly, as soon as the war ended a deep crisis gripped American society. In the face of mounting strikes, the question of U.S. adherence to the League of Nations, and a wave of racial, religious, and ethnic conflicts, the American business community sharply divided.

On the central questions of labor and foreign economic policy, most firms in the Republican bloc were driven by the logic of the postwar economy to intensify their commitment to the formula of 1896. The worldwide expansion of industrial capacity the war had induced left them face to face with vigorous foreign competitors. Consequently, they became even more ardent economic nationalists. Meeting British, French, and, later, German and other foreign competitors everywhere, even in the U.S. home market, they wanted ever higher tariffs and further indirect government assistance for their export drives. Their relatively labor intensive production processes also required the violent suppression of the great strike wave that capped the boom of 1919–20 and encouraged them to press the "Open Shop" drive that left organized labor reeling for the rest of the decade.

This response was not universal in the business community, however. The new political economy of the postwar world pressured a relative handful of the largest and most powerful firms in the opposite direction. The capital-intensive firms that had grown disproportionately during the war were under far less pressure from their labor force. By the end of the war the biggest of them had also developed into not only American but world leaders in their product lines. Accordingly, while none of them were pro-union, they preferred to conciliate rather than to repress their work force. Those which were world leaders favored lower tariffs, both to stimulate world commerce and to open up other countries to them. They also supported American assistance to rebuild Europe, which for many of them, such as Standard Oil of New Jersey and General Electric, represented an important market.

Joining these latter industrial interests were the international banks. Probably nothing that occurred in the United States between 1896 and the depression was so fundamentally destructive to the System of '96 as the World War I–induced transformation of the United States from a net debtor to a net creditor in the world economy. The overhang of both public and private debts that the war left in its wake struck directly at the accommodation of industry and finance that defined the Republican party. To revive economically and to pay off the debts, European countries had to run export surpluses. They needed to sell around the world, and they, or at least someone they traded with in a multilateral trading system, urgently needed to earn dollars by selling in the United States. Accordingly, along with private or governmental assistance from the United States to help make up war losses, the Europeans required a portal through the tariff walls that shielded Republican manufacturers from international competition.

The conflict between these two groups runs through all the major foreign policy disputes of the 1920s: the League of Nations, the World Court, and the great battles over tariffs, among others. Initially, the older, protectionist forces won far more than they lost. They defeated the League, kept the United States out of the World Court, and raised the tariff to ionospheric levels. But most trends in the world economy were against them. Throughout the 1920s the ranks of the largely Eastern internationalist bloc swelled.

Parallel to the multinational bloc's increasing numbers was its growing unity of interest, as problems with the British over oil and cables were resolved. As the bloc closed ranks, it discovered it could achieve its immediate foreign-policy objectives by working unofficially around the Congress with key executive-branch functionaries and New York Federal Reserve Bank officials.

Along with its increasing internal homogeneity, the multinational bloc enjoyed several other long-run advantages, which helped enormously in overcoming the new bloc's relative numerical insignificance vis-à-vis its older rival. The newer bloc included many of the largest, most rapidly growing corporations in the economy. Recognized industry leaders with the most sophisticated managements, these concerns embodied the norms of professionalism and scientific advance that in this period fired the imagination of large parts of American society. The largest of them also dominated major American foundations, which were coming to exercise major influence not only on the climate of opinion but on the specific content of American public policy. And, what might be termed the "multinational liberalism" of the internationalists was also aided significantly by the spread of liberal Protestantism; by a newspaper stratification process that brought the free trade organ of international finance, the *New York Times*, to the top; by the growth of capital-intensive network radio in the dominant Eastern, internationally oriented environment; and by the rise of major news magazines. These last promised, as Raymond Moley himself intoned while taking over at what became *Newsweek*, to provide "Averell [Harriman] and Vincent [Astor] . . . with means for influencing public opinion generally outside of both parties."[14]

Closely paralleling the business community's differences over foreign policy was its split over labor policy. Analysts have correctly stressed that the 1920s were a period of violent hostility toward labor unions. But they have largely failed to notice the significant, sectorally specific modulation in the tactics and strategy employed by American business to deal with the labor movement.

The war-induced boom of 1918–19 cleared labor markets and led to a brief but sharp rise in strikes and the power of labor. A White House conference called by Wilson to discuss the situation ended in stalemate. John D. Rockefeller, Jr., and representatives of General Electric urged conciliatory programs of "employee representation" (company-dominated, plant-specific works councils). Steel and other relatively labor intensive industries, however, rejected the approach. Led by Elbert Gary, head of U.S. Steel, they joined forces, crushed the great steel strike of 1919, and organized the American Plan drives of the 1920s.

Rockefeller and Gary broke personal relations. Rockefeller supported an attack on the steel companies by the Inter-Church World Movement, an organization of liberal Protestants for which he raised funds and served as a director. Later he organized a consulting firm, Industrial Relations Counsellors, to promote nonconfrontational "scientific" approaches to labor conflict. Industrial Relations Counsellors assisted an unheralded group of capital-intensive firms and banks throughout the 1920s—a group whose key members included top management figures of General Electric and Standard Oil of New Jersey, and partners of the House of Morgan. Calling themselves the "Special Conference Committee," this group promoted various programs of advanced industrial relations.[15]

Industrial Relations Counsellors worked with the leading figures of at least one group of medium-sized firms. Perhaps ironically, they were organized in the Taylor Society, once the home of Frederick Taylor's well-known project for reorganizing the labor process. Two types of firms comprised this group: technically advanced enterprises in highly cyclical (hence, in the 1930s, highly depressed) industries like machine tools, and medium-sized "best practice" firms in declining sectors. Mostly located in the Northeast, these latter firms hoped that the introduction of the latest management and labor relations techniques would afford them cost advantages over burgeoning low-wage competitors in the American South. Forming a sort of flying buttress to the core of the multinational bloc, most of these firms strongly favored freer trade, while several future New Dealers, including Rexford Tugwell and Felix Frankfurter, worked with them.[16]

The leading figures in Industrial Relations Counsellors and their

associates (who included, notably, Beardsley Ruml, head of the Spelman Fund, a part of the Rockefeller complex that began funding the
first university-based industrial relations research centers) played important roles in virtually all major developments in labor policy across
the 1920s. These included the campaign that forced the steel industry to accept the eight-hour day; the milestone Railway Labor Act;
and the increasing criticism of the use of injunctions in labor disputes
(a legal weapon that was an essential element of the System of '96's
labor policy) that eventually led to the Norris-LaGuardia Act.

Under all these accumulating tensions the elite core of the Republican party began to disintegrate. The great boom of the 1920s exacerbated all the tensions over labor and international relations just described, while it greatly enhanced the position of the major oil
companies and other capital-intensive firms in the economy as a
whole (see table 1.1). Though their greatest effects came after the
downturn in 1929, other "secondary"—that is, idiosyncratic or transitory—tensions also multiplied during the boom. One, which affected partisan competition even in the 1920s, concerned investment
banking. A flock of new (or suddenly growing) houses sprang up and
began to compete for dominance with the established leaders: the
House of Morgan and Kuhn, Loeb. In time these firms would produce a generation of famous Democrats: James Forrestal of Dillon,
Read; Averell Harriman of Brown Brothers Harriman; Sidney Weinberg of Goldman, Sachs; John Milton Hancock and Herbert Lehman
of Lehman Brothers.[17]

In commercial banking, rivals also began to contest Morgan's position. The Bank of America rose rapidly to become one of the largest
commercial banks in the world. Though the competition did not yet
take partisan form, the bank bitterly opposed Morgan interests,
which attempted to use the New York Federal Reserve Bank against
it. Morgan also was hostile to Joseph Kennedy and other rising financial powers.

The cumulative impact of all these pressures became evident in
the election of 1928. Some of the investment bankers, notably Averell
Harriman, turned to the Democrats. Enraged by the House of Morgan's use of the New York Fed to control American interest rates for
the sake of its international objectives, Chicago bankers, led by First
National's Melvin Traylor, organized and went to the Democratic
convention as a massed body. These were portentous developments
indeed. At the time, however, they were overshadowed by the dramatic, but brief, effort of major elements of the strongly protectionist
chemical industry, notably several members of the DuPont family, to
try to take over the Democratic party. Repelled by Al Smith's shock-

TABLE 1.1
LARGEST AMERICAN INDUSTRIALS, 1909–1948
(RANKED BY ASSETS)

Company	1909	1919	1929	1935	1948
U.S. Steel	1	1	1	2	3
Standard Oil of N.J.	2	2	2	1	1
American Tobacco	3	19			17
Int'l Mercantile Marine	4	12			
Anaconda	5	14	8	8	19
Int'l Harvester	6	13	17	14	18
Central Leather	7				
Pullman	8				
Armour	9	3	14	20	
American Sugar	10				
U.S. Rubber	11	8			
American Smelting & Refining	12	17			
Singer	13				
Swift	14	4	19	19	
Consolidation Coal	15				
General Electric	16	11	11	13	9
ACF Industries	17				
Colorado Fuel & Iron	18				
Corn Products Refining	19				
New England Navigation	20				
General Motors		5	3	3	2
Bethlehem Steel		6	5	7	12
Ford		7	6	6	10
Socony Mobil		9	7	4	5
Midvale Steel		10			
Sinclair Oil		15	16	16	15
Texaco		16	9	11	6
DuPont		18	12	9	7
Union Carbide		20			14
Standard Oil of Ind.			4	5	4
Standard Oil of Calif.			10	10	11
Shell			13	15	
Gulf			15	12	8
General Theater Equip.			18		
Kennecott			20	18	
Koppers				17	
Sears Roebuck					13
Westinghouse					16
Western Electric					20

Source: A.D.H. Kaplan, *Big Enterprise in a Competitive Setting* (Washington, D.C.: Brookings Institution, 1962), 140ff.

ing embrace of tariffs, most of the multinational bloc stayed with Republican presidential hopeful Herbert Hoover who, though still ostensibly committed to the traditional GOP position on tariffs, signaled his willingness to countenance several multinational-supported policies: German (and other) foreign investment in the United States, American investment abroad, and "unofficial" American intervention in European affairs.[18]

ECONOMIC CATASTROPHE AND "NATIONAL RECOVERY," 1929–1935

The onset of the Great Depression opened a new phase in the decay of the now creaking System of '96. As the depression grew worse, demands for government action proliferated. But Hoover opposed deficit-financed expenditures and easy monetary policies.[19] After the British abandoned the gold standard in September 1931 and moved to establish a preferential trading bloc, the intransigence of Hoover and the financiers locked the international economy onto a collision course with American domestic politics. Increasingly squeezed industrialists and farmers began clamoring for government help in the form of tariffs even higher than those in the recently passed Smoot-Hawley bill; they also called for legalized cartels and, ever more loudly, for a devaluation of the dollar through a large increase in the money supply.

Concerned, as Federal Reserve minutes show, at the prospect that the business groups and farmers might coalesce with angry, bonus-marching veterans, and worried by French gold withdrawals and fears that not only farmers and workers, but leading bankers, might go bankrupt, the Fed briefly attempted to relieve the pressure by expansionary open-market operations. But after a few months, the policy was abandoned as foreigners withdrew more gold and bankers in Chicago and elsewhere complained that the drop in short-term interest rates was driving down interest rates on short-term government debt (and thus bank profits, which, given the scarcity of long-term debt and the disappearance of industrial loans in Federal Reserve districts outside of New York, now depended directly on these rates).[20]

Hoover's commitment to gold, however, began driving inflationist, usually protectionist, businessmen out of the GOP to the Democrats. Their swarming ranks triggered a virtual identity crisis among Republican party regulars. As familiar rules of thumb about the growth of the world economy grew increasingly anachronistic, the mushrooming sentiment for monetary expansion and economic nationalism scrambled the calculations of the contenders for the Democratic nomination.

The developing situation called for the highest kind of political judgment from aspiring presidential candidates. At this point a legendary political operative came out of retirement to advise Franklin D. Roosevelt. Colonel Edward House had been a longtime adviser to Woodrow Wilson and was normally an ardent champion of low tariffs and the League of Nations; but, perhaps most important for the first New Deal, he was now closely associated with Rockefeller interests.[21] Along with the more famous Brains Trust, which functioned largely as a transmission belt for the ideas of others, including, notably, investment bankers from Lehman Brothers, House helped chart Roosevelt's early path. It was calculated to blur his image and make him acceptable to all factions of the party. Making overtures to William Randolph Hearst and other like-minded businessmen, Roosevelt repudiated his earlier strong support for the League of Nations, talked rather vaguely of raising tariffs, and began showing an interest in major revision of the antitrust laws.[22]

The tactics were successful. Coming into office at the very darkest moment of the depression, with all the banks closed, Roosevelt moved immediately to restore business confidence and reform the wrecked banking structure. The real significance of this bank reform, however, has been misperceived. With the world economy reeling, the shared interest in a liberal world economy that normally (i.e., when the economy was growing) bound powerful rivals together in one political coalition was disappearing. In this once-in-a-lifetime context, what had previously been secondary tensions between rival financial groups now suddenly came briefly, but centrally, to define the national political agenda. With workers, farmers, and many industrialists up in arms against finance in general and its most famous symbol, the House of Morgan, in particular, virtually all the major non-Morgan investment banks in America lined up behind Roosevelt. And, in perhaps the least appreciated aspect of the New Deal, so did the now Rockefeller-controlled Chase National Bank.

In the eighteen months previous to the election, relations between the Rockefeller and Morgan interests had deteriorated drastically. After the crash of 1929 Equitable Trust, which Rockefeller had purchased and in the late 1920s had sought to build up, had been forced to merge with the Morgan-oriented Chase National Bank. The merger caused trouble virtually from the beginning. Thomas W. Lamont and several other banking executives allied with Morgan attempted to block the ascent of Winthrop Aldrich, the brother-in-law of John D. Rockefeller, Jr., to the presidency of the Chase. Their efforts, however, proved unsuccessful, and Aldrich quickly, if apparently rather tensely, assumed an important role in Chase's management. But when Rockefeller attempted to secure a loan for the construction of Rockefeller Center (which threatened [Pierre] DuPont and Raskob's Empire State Building, already under construction and unable to rent all its space with the collapse of real-estate values), the bank seems not to have gone along. The chief financing had to come instead from Metropolitan Life. An old dispute between two transit companies, one controlled by the Morgans and the other by the Rockefellers, also created problems.[23]

Though sniping from holdover employees continued for several years, operating control of Chase passed definitely out of Morgan hands in late 1932. With longtime Chase head Albert Wiggin retiring, Aldrich was announced as the next chairman of the bank's governing board, and plans were made to reorganize the board of directors.

In the meantime, the East Texas oil discoveries dropped the price of oil to ten cents a barrel. This quickly brought the entire oil industry to the brink of disaster. Becoming more interested in oil and domestic recovery, and less in banking, the Rockefeller interests urged a substantial relief program on Hoover, who brusquely rejected it. Almost simultaneously top Rockefeller adviser Beardsley Ruml, then still at the helm of the Spelman Fund and a prominent Democrat, began promoting a complicated plan for agricultural adjustment. At Chicago the Roosevelt forces accepted some of its basic concepts just ahead of the convention.[24]

Only a few days before the 1932 presidential election, Morgan discovered that high Chase officials were supporting Roosevelt.[25] Colonel House's daughter was married to Gordon Auchincloss, Aldrich's best friend and a member of the Chase board. During the campaign and transition period, House and Vincent Astor, Roosevelt's cousin and also a member of the reorganized Chase board, passed messages between Roosevelt and Chase.[26]

A few days after Roosevelt was inaugurated, Chase and the investment bankers started their campaign, both in public and in private, for a new banking law. Aldrich made a dramatic public plea for the complete separation of investment and commercial banking. Then he began personally to lobby Roosevelt and high administration officials. As Secretary of Commerce Daniel Roper reported to Roosevelt in March 1932:

> I have had a very interesting and refreshing conversation with Mr. W. W. Aldrich. . . . I also suggest that you consider calling in, when convenient to you, Senators Glass and Bulkley and Mr. Aldrich to discuss the advisa-

bility and necessity for dealing not only with the divorcement of affiliates from commercial banks but the complete divorcement of functions between the issuance of securities by private banks over whom there is no supervision and the business of commercial banks. We feel that this suggestion should be incorporated in the Glass Banking Bill.[27]

Aldrich also joined the ancestral enemies of the banks—William Randolph Hearst, Samuel Untermeyer, South Dakota senator Peter Norbeck, and others promoting Ferdinand Pecora's investigation of J. P. Morgan & Co. He cooperated fully with the investigation, promoted "reforms," and aided investigators examining the Wiggin era at Chase. "I found Aldrich sympathetic to the last degree of what the president is trying to do," noted Colonel House to Roper in October 1933. House continued:

I advised him to tell the Banking Committee the whole story. He is prepared to do this, and has gone to the country today to write his proposed testimony in the form of a memorandum, a copy of which he is to send me tomorrow morning. He intimated that if there was any part of it that I thought should be changed he would consider doing so. . . . He tells me that his Board is back of him and some few of the leading bankers. However, most of them are critical and many are bitter because of what they term his not standing with his colleagues.[28]

These efforts came to fruition in the Glass-Steagall Act. By separating investment from commercial banking, this measure destroyed the unity of the two functions whose combination had been the basis of Morgan hegemony in American finance. It also opened the way to a financial structure crowned by a giant bank with special ties to capital-intensive industry—oil.

With most of the (Morgan-dominated) banking community opposed to him, Roosevelt looked toward industry for allies. By now an uncountably large number of firms, for reasons discussed earlier, were actively seeking inflation and, usually, an abandonment of the gold standard. For more than a year, for example, Royal Dutch Shell, led by Sir Henri Deterding, had been campaigning to get Britain, the United States, and other major countries to remonetize silver. At some point—it is impossible to say exactly when—Deterding and his American financial adviser Rene Leon began coordinating efforts to secure some kind of reflation with James A. Moffett, a longtime director and high official of the Standard Oil Company of New Jersey, and a friend and early supporter of Roosevelt.[29]

While they campaigned to expand the money supply, a powerful group of industrialists, large farm organizations, and retailers organized separately for the same general end. Led by Bendix, Remington

Rand, and Sears Roebuck, they called themselves "The Committee for the Nation." As Roosevelt took over in the spring of 1933, contributions from Standard Oil of New Jersey and many other industrial firms were swelling this committee's war chest.[30] The committee was vigorously pushing the president to go off the gold standard.

Working closely with sympathizers in the Treasury Department, the banks fought back. Federal Reserve minutes show the Executive Committee of the System Open Market Committee distinguishing between "technical" and "political" adjustments of the money supply, with the political adjustments designed to head off demands for reflation.[31] But the industrialists could not be denied. Moffett and Leon found legal authority for Roosevelt to go off gold during the banking crisis, when even the banks conceded the step to be briefly necessary. Later the same pair teamed up to reach Roosevelt at the crucial moment of the London Economic Conference and persuaded him to send the famous telegram destroying the hope for informal agreements on currency stabilization devoutly wished for and almost achieved by James P. Warburg and other international financiers.[32] Still pressured by the Committee for the Nation and the oil companies, Roosevelt embarked on his famous gold-buying experiments in the autumn, driving most of the banks to distraction. Roosevelt also continued with the National Recovery Administration, whose name wonderfully symbolized the truly national character of the political coalition forged by the extreme economic circumstances of the early 1930s: protectionist industrialists (whose ranks had been swelled by the collapse of world trade), oilmen desperate for price controls, anti-Morgan and pro-oil-industry bankers, and farmers.

PHOENIX RISES: ECONOMIC UPTURN AND THE RETURN OF THE MULTINATIONAL BLOC

This first New Deal was desperately unstable. Once the worst phase of deflation ended and the economy began slowly to revive, industries with good long-term prospects in the world economy would start exploring ways to resume profitable overseas business. In time, this search would necessarily bring them back in the direction of the international banks, which (with the obvious exceptions noted above) generally opposed the NRA, and away from the economic nationalists, for most of whom the NRA initially represented the promised land. In addition, the NRA's halfhearted and incoherently designed attempt to supplement price mechanisms with administrative processes for the allocation of resources bitterly divided its natural constituency of protectionist businessmen.

Not surprisingly, therefore, the NRA began to self-destruct almost from the moment it began operations. Free traders fought with protectionists; big firms battled with smaller competitors; buyers collided with suppliers. The result was chaos. The situation was especially grave in the oil industry. There the majors and the smaller independent oil companies stalemated in the face of massive overproduction from the new East Texas fields.[33]

As the industries fought, labor stirred. A bitter series of strikes erupted as the ambiguous wording of the National Recovery Act's 7a clause, guaranteeing employee representation, came to be interpreted as securing "company" rather than independent trade unions.[34]

With the pressure beginning to tell on Roosevelt, he looked around for new allies. He sponsored an inquiry into foreign economic policy conducted by Beardsley Ruml, which recommended freer trade. Simultaneously he allowed Secretary of State Cordell Hull to promote reciprocal trade treaties in a series of speeches. The prospect of a change in U.S. tariff policy drew applause from segments of the business community that had mostly been hostile to Roosevelt. The Council on Foreign Relations sponsored a symposium at which journalist Walter Lippmann declared that freedom itself could probably not be maintained without free trade.[35]

As the first New Deal coalition disintegrated under the impact of interindustrial and class conflicts, Roosevelt turned more definitely toward free trade. He pushed through Congress a new bill (bitterly opposed by steel, chemicals, and other industries) giving Hull the authority to negotiate lower tariffs and then let him build support for the trade treaties.

The rest of the New Deal's program stalled. With their public support already eroded, the NRA and other measures were declared unconstitutional by the Supreme Court. Largely out of ideas, anxiously eyeing the activity of the Left, the prospect of strikes, especially in the steel industry, and sporadic urban disorders, Adoph A. Berle conveyed his deep pessimism to fellow administrators as they toured New York and New England:

> Mr. Berle stressed the need for prompt action in any program of economic security. He dreads the coming winter. While the City of New York has gotten along better in the past months than was to be expected, the City's finances are near the exhaustion point. Mr. Berle also states that the "market" was "jittery" about the credit of the federal government. Another complete financial collapse is distinctly possible if "Wall Street" should decide to "dump" U.S. bonds, which Mr. Berle thinks it might be foolish enough to do. The Communists are making rapid gains in New

trol scheme. With its implementation, the greatest of major American industries achieved near-complete price control for a generation.[43]

The powerful appeal of the unorthodox combination of free trade, the Wagner Act, and social welfare was evident in the 1936 election. A massive bloc of protectionist and labor-intensive industries formed to fight the New Deal. Together with the House of Morgan (which had reasons of its own to oppose Roosevelt), the DuPonts recruited many of these firms into the Liberty League. They were joined by some firms hoping to find a Republican candidate to run a milder New Deal.[44]

But Standard Oil could not abide Alfred Landon, who had once been in the oil business as an independent in Kansas. On the eve of the Republican convention, Standard dramatically came out against him.[45] In addition, a furious battle raged in the Republican camp over Hull's reciprocal trade treaties. Landon, who was at the moment surrounded by advisers from major banks, including James Warburg and figures from both Chase and Morgan, originally favored them. But the Chemical Foundation and many industrialists were bitterly opposed. At the Republican convention the latter group prevailed during the writing of the platform. For a few weeks thereafter, however, it appeared that the free traders would nevertheless win out. Landon repudiated that part of the platform and ran as a free trader.[46]

But the protectionists did not give up. Organizing many businesses into the "Made in America Club," and backed by Orlando Weber of Allied Chemical and other top executives, Chemical Foundation president Francis Garvan and journalist Samuel Crowther, author of a book called *America Self-Contained* who enjoyed close ties with many businessmen, began kamikaze attacks to break through the cordon of free-trading advisers who were attempting to wall off Landon. Eventually they succeeded in getting their message through. Crowther optimistically noted, in a letter to Garvan in 1936, that George Peek, Chemical Foundation adviser and staunch protectionist, had succeeded in getting Landon's ear:

> On the foreign trade and gold, Landon was extremely interested and he gave no evidence of ever before having heard of either subject. . . .
> George Peek went back and forth over this subject, in terms of Landon's own business, and Landon seemed thus to get a grasp of what it was all about. . . . Peek hammered the subject of the tariff and of our whole foreign trade program and, although he could not say positively that Landon accepted it as his paramount issue, he did believe that by the time he left, Landon had begun to realize something and that he would go further.[47]

Though Warburg and the other bankers repeatedly warned him against it in the strongest possible terms, Landon began to waver. In mid and late September his campaign began to criticize Hull's treaties.

His attacks alienated many multinationalists, who had watched with great interest Roosevelt's effort to stabilize the dollar. When, after speeches by First National's Leon Fraser and others, Roosevelt opened negotiations with Britain and France, the New Deal began to look like a good deal to them. It became still more attractive when the Tripartite Money Agreement was announced in September and after the Roosevelt administration raised reserve requirements on bank deposits, as many bankers had been demanding. As Landon's attacks on the trade treaties increased (but, be it noted, while many of his polls were holding up, including the *Literary Digest*'s, which had never been wrong), a generation of legendary American business figures began backing out of the Republican campaign. On active service in war and peace, Henry Stimson, who had already backed the treaties, refused to support Landon and withdrew from the campaign. On October 18, as spokesmen for the Rockefeller interests debated issuing a veiled criticism of the Liberty League, came the sensational announcement that James Warburg, who since his noisy public break with FDR two years before had waged unremitting war on the New Deal and frequently advised Landon, was switching to Roosevelt out of disgust with Landon's stand on the trade treaties. Only a couple of days after Warburg released his rapturous public encomium to Hull, Dean Acheson, Warburg's friend and former associate at the Treasury Department, did exactly the same thing. So did cotton broker William Clayton, who also resigned from the Liberty League. On October 29 at

> a mass meeting in the heart of the Wall Street District, about 200 business leaders, most of whom described themselves as Republicans, enthusiastically endorsed yesterday the foreign trade policy of the Roosevelt Administration and pledged themselves to work for the President's reelection.
>
> After addresses by five speakers, four of whom described themselves as Republicans, the Meeting unanimously adopted a resolution praising the reciprocal trade policy established by the Roosevelt Administration under the direction of Secretary of State Cordell Hull. . . . Governor Landon's attitude on the reciprocal tariff issue was criticized by every speaker. They contended that if Landon were elected and Secretary Hull's treaties were revoked, there would be a revolution among conservative businessmen.[48]

While the Republicans switched, the Democrats fought. The Bank of America and New Orleans banker Rudolph Hecht, who was just coming off a term as president of the American Bankers Association, bulwarked the "Good Neighbor League," a Roosevelt campaign vehicle. Lincoln and Edward Filene supported the president to the hilt, as did sugar refiner Ellsworth Bunker, a major importer from the Caribbean. Sidney Weinberg of Goldman, Sachs came back into the campaign and raised more money for Roosevelt than any other single person. Behind him trailed a virtual Milky Way of non-Morgan banking stars, including Averell Harriman of Brown Brothers Harriman; James Forrestal of Dillon, Read; and probably John Milton Hancock of Lehman Brothers.

From the oil industry came a host of independents, including Sid Richardson, Clint Murchison, and Charlie Roesser, as well as Sir Henri Deterding, James A. Moffett of Standard Oil of California, W. Alton Jones of Cities Services, Standard Oil of New Jersey's Boris Said (who helped run Democratic Youth groups), and M. L. Benedum of Benedum-Trees. Top executives of Reynolds Tobacco, American Tobacco, Coca-Cola, International Harvester, Johnson & Johnson, General Electric, Zenith, IBM, Sears Roebuck, ITT, United Fruit, Pan Am, and Manufacturers Trust all lent support. Prodded by banker George Foster Peabody, the *New York Times* came out for Roosevelt, as did the Scripps-Howard papers.[49]

In the final days of the campaign, as Landon furiously attacked social security, Teagle of Standard Oil of New Jersey, Swope of GE, the Pennsylvania Retailers Association, the American Retail Federation, and the Lorillard tobacco company (Old Gold), among others, spoke out in defense of the program. Last, if scarcely least, the firm that would incarnate the next thirty years of multinational oil and banking, the Chase National Bank, loaned the Democratic National Committee $100,000.

The curtain fell on the New Deal's creation of the modern Democratic political formula in early 1938. When the United States plunged steeply into recession, the clamor for relief began again as it had in 1933. Pressures for a revival of the NRA also mounted. But this time Roosevelt did not devalue the dollar. With billions of dollars in gold now squirreled away in the Fed, thanks to administration financial policies and spreading European anxieties, early 1930s fears of hoarding and runs on gold had vanished. As a consequence, reflation without formal devaluation or a revival of the NRA became a live option. Rockefeller adviser Beardsley Ruml proposed a plan for deficit spending, which Roosevelt implemented after versions won approval from Teagle and nearly all the important bankers, including Morgan. Aldrich then went on NBC radio to defend compensatory spending from attacks as long as it was coupled with measures for free trade (to the great annoyance of the DuPonts). Slightly later, the State Department, acting in secret with the Chase National Bank, and in public with the Catholic cardinal of Chicago and high business figures, set up a committee to promote renewal of the Reciprocal Trade Act in the wavering Corn Belt.[50] They were successful. National income snapped back and the multinational bloc held together. The fatal circle closed: for all the drama of the next half century, the national Democratic party was permanently committed: it was now a party of the comparatively advantaged, unified around the principle of comparative advantage, and simultaneously the party of the "people" (or "labor") opposed to the Republicans, the party of "big business."

While scarcely profound or "magical,"[51] this process created illusions that ran very deep. Cultivated by the press, nourished by increasingly affluent business groups, and fiercely protected by two generations of (often handsomely rewarded) scholars, this view of the Democrats and the New Deal left ordinary Americans alternately confused, perplexed, alarmed, or disgusted, as they tried to puzzle out why the party did so little to help unionize the South, protect the victims of McCarthyism, promote civil rights for blacks, women, or Hispanics, or, in the late 1970s, combat America's great "right turn" against the New Deal itself.[52] To such people, it always remained a mystery why the Democrats so often betrayed the ideals of the New Deal. Little did they realize that, in fact, the party was only living up to them.

NOTES

This essay is a greatly abbreviated version of my "From Normalcy to New Deal: Industrial Structure, Party Competition, and American Public Policy in the Great Depression," *International Organization* 38, no. 1 (Winter 1984), reprinted by permission of MIT Press. See also my *Critical Realignment: The Fall of the House of Morgan and the Origins of the New Deal* (New York: Oxford University Press, forthcoming).

1. The first of several New Deal reciprocal trade measures passed rather early in Roosevelt's first term, but, as explained below, it had virtually no immediate effect on the administration's essentially protectionist trade policy.

2. The "System of '96" is a reference to the discussion of "party systems" and American electoral behavior by analysts such as V. O. Key and Walter Dean Burnham.

3. The role of "Keynesian" public finance versus a bulging export surplus in leading the Swedish revival of the mid and latter 1930s has been extensively debated: the weight of the evidence suggests that the Swedish gov-

ernment did not vigorously implement the advanced monetary and fiscal proposals that were undeniably in the air. I should also note that this paragraph's clear distinctions and exact datings of the New Deal's "Keynesian Turn" are taken over unchanged from my "Normalcy to New Deal" essay. I therefore find inexplicable the recent claim by M. Weir and T. Skocpol that my essay "mistakenly conflates the labor regulation and social insurance reforms of 1935–36 with Keynesianism." See their "State Structures and the Possibilities for 'Keynesian' Responses to the Great Depression in Sweden, Britain, and the United States," in P. Evans, D. Rueschemeyer, and T. Skocpol, eds., *Bringing the State Back In* (New York: Cambridge University Press, 1985), 154.

4. See, for example, Arthur Schlesinger, Jr., *The Age of Roosevelt*, 3 vols. (Boston: Houghton Mifflin, 1957–60); William Leuchtenburg, *Franklin D. Roosevelt and the New Deal* (New York: Harper & Row, 1963); and Frank Freidel, *Franklin D. Roosevelt*, 4 vols. (Boston: Little, Brown, 1952–).

5. See, for example, Barton Bernstein, "The New Deal: The Conservative Achievements of Liberal Reform," in Bernstein, ed., *Toward a New Past: Dissenting Essays in American History* (New York: Pantheon, 1968), and Ronald Radosh, "The Myth of the New Deal," in Radosh and Murray N. Rothbard, eds., *A New History of Leviathan* (New York: E. P. Dutton, 1972), 146–86.

6. See, for example, Ellis Hawley's "The Discovery and Study of a Corporate Liberalism," *Business History Review* 52, no. 3 (1978): 309–20. In contrast, his classic *The New Deal and the Problem of Monopoly* (Princeton: Princeton University Press, 1962) does not emphasize these themes. See also Alfred Chandler and Louis Galambos, "The Development of Large Scale Economic Organizations in Modern America," in E. J. Perkins, ed., *Men and Organizations* (New York: Putnam, 1977). It appears that Weir and Skocpol's "Keynesian Responses," and other recent essays in the "state managers" vein, represent something of a synthesis of this view and the older "pluralist" approach—with the conspicuous difference that the state manager theorists rely almost entirely on secondary sources.

7. For a review of the West German work see H. A. Winkler, ed., *Die Grosse Krise in America* (Göttingen: Vandenhoech & Ruprecht, 1973). Perhaps the finest of the libertarian writings are those by Murray Rothbard—see his "War Collectivism in World War I" and "Herbert Hoover and the Myth of Laissez-Faire," both in Radosh and Rothbard, *New History of Leviathan*; for Kolko's views see his *Main Currents in Modern American History* (New York: Harper & Row, 1976). See also Kim McQuaid, *Big Business and Presidential Power* (New York: William Morrow, 1983) and Robert Collins, *Business Response to Keynes* (New York: Columbia University Press, 1980).

8. Some commentators, such as Elliot Rosen in his very stimulating *Hoover, Roosevelt, and the Brains Trust* (New York: Columbia University Press, 1977), have questioned the existence of "two New Deals." These doubts, however, are difficult to sustain if one systematically compares the policies pursued during each period, as, for example, in the incomplete inventory that opened this essay.

9. On the notions of coalitions and investor blocs, see my "Elites and Elections, or What Have They Done to You Lately: Toward an Investment Theory of Political Parties and Critical Realignment," in Benjamin Ginsberg and Alan Stone, eds., *Do Elections Matter?* (Armonk, N.Y.: M. E. Sharpe, 1986), 164–88, and "Party Realignment and American Industrial Structure: The Investment Theory of Political Parties in Historical Perspective," in Paul Zarembka, ed., *Research in Political Economy*, (Greenwich, Conn.: JAI Press, 1983), 6:1–82.

10. See my "Party Realignment," sec. 4. The shoe industry was singular because in contrast with most other charter members of the Republican bloc, its firms directly confronted a giant trust, United Shoe Machinery. As a consequence, they were far more likely to harbor doubts about the wisdom of "big business" and often went over to conservative Democrats.

11. This discussion neglects a modest movement for very limited trade liberalization promoted by several sectors in the pre-1914 period.

12. For the merger movement of the 1890s, see my discussion in "Party Realignment." Railroad mergers, organized by leading financiers, were also a part of the consolidation of this bloc.

13. For reasons of space, notes for most secondary sources have had to be eliminated in this section. See "Normalcy to New Deal." Also eliminated are that essay's lengthy theoretical sections and a detailed specification of which firms and sectors belonged to the various blocs discussed below.

14. For the *New York Times*, see below; the Moley quotation is from a June 13, 1936, entry in his "Journal," now in the Moley Papers, Hoover Institution, Stanford, Calif. Astor and Harriman were the most important of the magazine's owners. Moley later moved much further to the right. (Most archives used in this project are adequately indexed; box numbers are provided for the reader's convenience only where confusion seems likely.)

15. The sources for this and the following paragraphs are mostly papers scattered through several archives, including the Rockefeller Archive Center at Tarrytown, N.Y. For the dominance of Standard Oil and General Electric within the group, see J. J. Raskob to Lammot DuPont, November 26, 1929, Raskob Papers, Eleutherian Mills–Hagley Foundation, Wilmington, Del. Industrial Relations Counsellors seems to have coordinated the meetings of the group for most of the 1920s.

16. Several (Northeastern) textile executives played leading roles within this group, which produced the otherwise inexplicable sight of a handful of textile men supporting Franklin D. Roosevelt during the second New Deal, and which for a brief period generated some interesting, if ultimately unimportant, wrinkles in the Hull-Roosevelt trade offensive in the mid-1930s. Boston merchant E. A. Filene, who established (and controlled) the Twentieth Century Fund, and who ardently championed what might be labeled the "retailers' dream" of an economy built on high wages and cheap imports, was deeply involved with this group. The small businessmen of the Taylor Society differed very slightly with their big-business allies on entirely predictable issues: antitrust and financial reform. Supreme Court justice Louis D.

Brandeis, who is usually credited as a major inspiration for many New Deal measures, had once served as Filene's attorney and remained closely associated with him and his brother A. Lincoln Filene.

17. Because many of these bankers were Jewish, the competition with Morgan almost immediately assumed an ugly tone. J. P. Morgan, Jr., quietly encouraged Henry Ford's circulation of the notorious *Protocols of the Elders of Zion* in the early 1920s, and later his bank forbade Morgan Harjes, the firm's Paris partner, to honor letters of credit from Manufacturers Trust, a commercial bank with strong ties to Goldman, Sachs and Lehman Brothers. See Thomas Lamont to V. H. Smith at Morgan Grenfell, January 10, 1927, Box 111, Lamont Papers, Baker Library, Harvard University. For more on the astonishing Morgan-Ford interaction, see Henry Ford to J. P. Morgan, Jr., May 7, 1921, and Morgan to Ford, May 11, 1921, Ford Archives, Henry Ford Museum, Dearborn, Mich.

18. See "Normalcy to New Deal," 72–79. Historians of this period have typically made rather too much of Hoover's criticism of foreign loans, since in its later stages it was encouraged by the Morgan bank.

19. In her *American Business and Foreign Policy* (Boston: Beacon Press, 1971), 137–38, Joan Hoff Wilson cites a Hoover "diary" in the Hoover Presidential Library as the authority for an account in which Hoover worked against the bankers. Box 98 of the Lamont Papers contains transcriptions of the telephone conversations to which the "diary" refers. The transcriptions not only refute every detail of Hoover's account but actually record Lamont's specific instructions to the president to conceal the origins of the moratorium. (As Lamont signed off from the first conversation: "One last thing, Mr. President . . . if anything, by any chance, ever comes out of this suggestion, we should wish to be forgotten in this matter. This is your plan and nobody else's.") A mass of supporting correspondence in the file confirms the authenticity of these transcripts while raising many more questions about the "diary." (Hoover often harbored private misgivings about both his policies and his advisers—but he never consistently acted upon these doubts.)

20. See Gerald Epstein and Thomas Ferguson, "Loan Liquidation and Industrial Conflict: The Federal Reserve and the Open Market Operations of 1932," *Journal of Economic History* 44, no. 4 (1984) for details.

21. Rosen, *Brains Trust*, 113, argues that House's influence on Roosevelt ebbed after March 1932. But the aging House could scarcely be expected to provide the daily memoranda and speeches that Roosevelt then needed. There is a sense in which House and all of Roosevelt's early advisers were supplemented, and in part supplanted, by many other forces then coming to life in the Democratic party; however, House always remained a major actor in the New Deal.

22. The Newton Baker Papers now at the Library of Congress, Washington, D.C., and the Franklin D. Roosevelt papers at the Roosevelt Library in Hyde Park, N.Y., contain a mass of material on the primary and convention battles (e.g., the letters between Baker and Ralph Hayes in the Baker Papers). Rosen, *Brains Trust*, chaps. 9 and 10, presents considerable detail on the busi-

ness opposition to FDR's nomination, and is very good on the stop-Roosevelt forces' manipulation of the press.

23. For Lamont's dramatic bid to block Aldrich, see Aldrich interviews, Chase Manhattan Bank Oral History project, November 29, 1961, now in the Winthrop W. Aldrich Papers, Baker Library, Harvard University; for apprising me of the Rockefeller Center financing controversy I am grateful to Robert Fitch, whose own work on urban development and American political structures involved a lengthy period of work in the Rockefeller Archives. For the subway battle see the *New York Times*, July 31, and August 27 and 31, 1932; and Cynthia Horan, "Agreeing with the Bankers: New York City's Depression Financial Crisis," in P. Zarembka, ed., *Research in Political Economy* (Greenwich, Conn.: JAI Press, 1986), vol. 8.

24. Agricultural economist M. L. Wilson is normally identified as the author of the adjustment plan. For Rockefeller's role in financing Wilson's early work see Rosen, *Brains Trust*, 180; see p. 178 for Ruml's role in the famous Wilson-Rexford Tugwell meeting on the eve of the convention.

25. See the crucial letters of Thomas W. Lamont to various business associates and attached memoranda in Box 123 of the Lamont Papers and my discussion of them in "Elites and Elections."

26. Some of these are in the House Papers, Yale University Library; others, in the Aldrich Papers. See, for example, the House-Auchincloss correspondence in the former.

27. Secretary of Commerce Daniel Roper to Franklin D. Roosevelt, March 28, 1932, Roosevelt Library. This is one of many documents relating to Aldrich's vast lobbying efforts; other aspects of this legislation involved fairly heated exchanges between the Bank of America and the National City Bank of New York. While not as enduringly significant as the separation of investment from commercial banking, these conflicts persisted for some years and complicated the position of the National City Bank during much of the New Deal.

28. House to Roper, October 21, 1933, House Papers.

29. The chief source for most of what follows are the personal papers of Rene Leon, copies of which are now in my possession. See also the correspondence between Walter Lippmann and Leon, now in the Lippmann Correspondence at Yale, and between Moley, Leon, and Deterding in the Moley Papers. Moffett later joined Standard of California.

30. The Frank Vandertip Papers at Columbia University, New York City, contain the financial records of the Committee for the Nation during this period. The Standard Oil contributions are plainly listed there.

31. See, for example, the Minutes of the Executive Committee of the Open Market Committee, September 21, 1933; these are in the George Harrison Papers, Columbia University and available at the Federal Reserve Bank of New York. Copies also appear in the Minutes of the Directors Meetings of the Federal Reserve Bank of Boston for October 4, 1933, and other dates.

32. When Mrs. Rene Leon originally told me of her husband's efforts to block the efforts of Warburg and the other financiers at the London Confer-

ence, she could not remember the name of the businessman who had assisted him. The Leon Papers make it obvious that Moffett was the man, as, independently, Mrs. Leon subsequently wrote me. A copy of what is perhaps the urgent telegram sent to warn FDR against Warburg's efforts, which Mrs. Leon remembers her husband dispatching, can be found in Raymond Moley's papers relating to the London Conference. When the telegram came into Moley's hands is not clear; but this and other files in the Moley Papers contain numerous messages from Leon and even Deterding himself.

33. See, among others, Norman Nordhauser, *The Quest for Stability* (New York: Garland, 1979), chap. 8. I have profited greatly from the material in the J. R. Parten Papers (in Parten's possession).

34. See, among many sources, Sidney Lens, *The Labor Wars* (Garden City, N.Y.: Doubleday, 1973), 288ff.

35. See Walter Lippman, "Self-Sufficiency: Some Random Reflections," *Foreign Affairs*, January 1934.

36. "Memorandum on the Views Relating to the Work of the Committee on Economic Security Expressed by Various Individuals Consulted," National Archives Record Group 47, Public Record Office, Washington, D.C. The interviews reported in the memo occurred "on a trip to New England and New York on August 11–21, 1934." I am grateful to Janet Corpus for bringing this memo to my attention.

37. It is impossible to inventory all of the relevant citations here, but see the material in Record Group 47 of the National Archives and, especially, the material in Box 31 of the Ralph Flanders Papers, Syracuse University Library, Syracuse, N.Y.

38. Some authors suggest that because strike rates went from ionospheric in 1934 to merely stratospheric in 1935, the Wagner Act cannot have been adopted in response to pressure from labor. In fact, the expiration of the NRA determined when the soaring overall rate of class conflict would affect the statutes. The Supreme Court decision declaring the NRA unconstitutional came only days ahead of the law's lapse. Obviously, what follows on the origins of the Wagner Act hardly suffices as a treatment of the rise of labor during the New Deal. I largely discuss elite responses to mass protest; I do not pretend to be offering a theory of the labor movement.

39. See, for example, Charlton Ogburn to William Green, January 7, 1935, Box 282, W. Jett Lauck Papers, University of Virginia.

40. See Sloan's remarkable letter to J. J. Raskob. October 23, 1934, Raskob Papers.

41. In the Twentieth Century Fund deliberations, some railroad leaders, noting the Wagner bill's similarity to the Railway Labor Act, supported its passage; Industrial Relations Counsellors opposed some of its key provisions; and nearly all the businessmen sought an equivalent "unfair labor practice" provision applying to unions. The AFL attorney Charlton Ogburn, however, won out. Some aspects of New Deal tax policy (which was certainly not radical) should probably also be viewed as evidence of labor's rising power.

42. Morgan had sought to repeal Glass-Steagall. Aldrich blocked this, but

had to accept a shift of power within the Fed from the New York Bank to the Board of Governors in Washington, which the Bank of America and other non–New York bankers championed. The almost simultaneous legislation aimed at breaking up public utility holding companies drove another nail into the coffin of the House of Morgan, for that bank totally dominated the industry, especially after Insull's bankruptcy.

43. The Parten Papers, along with those of Interior Secretary Ickes at the Library of Congress and those of Texas governor James Allred, now in the University of Houston Library, Houston, Texas, contain large amounts of material on oil issues. See, as one example, Franklin D. Roosevelt to Governor E. W. Marland of Oklahoma, May 17, 1935 (copy in the Allred Papers).

44. Despite the co-presence of the DuPont and most Morgan interests in the GOP in this period, I would caution against the interpretation, popular in the 1930s and now showing signs of revival, of the existence of a unified "Morgan-DuPont" group. A reading of much correspondence on both sides has persuaded me that this simply did not exist during this time period.

45. See Bernard Baruch to Eugene Meyer, May 20, 1936, Baruch Papers, Seeley Mudd Library, Princeton University. Meyer was at that time helping to run the Landon campaign. Note that in autumn 1935 Standard had helped turn aside Hoover's bid for the 1936 nomination (see Herbert Hoover to Lewis Strauss, September 23, 1935, Lewis Strauss Papers, Hoover Presidential Library).

46. The Chemical Foundation Papers at the University of Wyoming in Laramie contain much material on Francis P. Garvan's efforts to promote protectionism around the time of the convention. See especially Garvan's correspondence with F. X. Eble and Samuel Crowther, in Box 11-2.

47. Samuel Crowther to Francis P. Garvan, July 18, 1936, Box 11-2, Chemical Foundation Papers.

48. *New York Times*, October 29, 1936, 10.

49. The details of all the high-level switches around the trade issues and the complex positions of some large interests (such as the Rockefellers) cannot be discussed here for reasons of space. Note, however, George Foster Peabody to A. H. Sulzberger of the *New York Times*, December 5, 1935, on the importance of good coverage for FDR and Sulzberger's accommodating reply of December 12, both in the George Foster Peabody Papers, Box 50, Library of Congress. Peabody held a large demand note on Roosevelt's Warm Springs, GA., Foundation.

50. For some documentation on the trade committee, see Aldrich Papers, Box 67. For Ruml's role in the deficit spending plan, see Robert Collins, *Business Response to Keynes* (New York: Columbia University Press, 1981), 69ff.

51. "Ferguson," write Weir and Skocpol in "Keynesian Responses," p. 114, "[is] unmistakably a writer in the peculiarly American 'Beardsian' tradition" who attributes "magical powers" to business. Who could complain about a comparison with the greatest of all American political analysts (who, we now learn, was basically right about the founding fathers; see Robert Maguire and Robert Ohsfeldt, "Economic Interests and the Constitution: A

Quantitative Rehabilitation of Charles A. Beard," *Journal of Economic History* 44 [June 1984]: 509–19)? Serious readers of this essay, however, will recognize that the only "magical" power possessed by the New Deal's business supporters is their ability to remain invisible to historians.

52. Thomas Ferguson and Joel Rogers, *Right Turn: The Decline of the Democrats and the Future of American Politics* (New York: Hill & Wang, 1986), analyze at length the movement of various industrial groups in and out of the party during the decline of the New Deal. The explanation put forward there can usefully be contrasted with, for example, Thomas Byrne Edsall, *The New Politics of Inequality* (New York: W. W. Norton, 1984), which continues to portray the GOP as the party of big business, while analyzing the Democrats mainly in demographic terms.

2

Why the Great Depression Was Great: Toward a New Understanding of the Interwar Economic Crisis in the United States

Michael A. Bernstein

> The essential point to grasp is that in dealing with capitalism
> we are dealing with an evolutionary process. It may seem
> strange that anyone can fail to see so obvious a fact. . . . Yet
> that fragmentary analysis which yields the bulk of our propo-
> sitions about the functioning of modern capitalism persis-
> tently neglects it.
>
> —Joseph A. Schumpeter

To THIS day there exists no general agreement about the causes of the unprecedented duration of the depression of the 1930s in the United States. Several contemporary observers attempted to account for the Great Depression in terms of the collapse of a "mature capitalism." But after the war, their views appeared hysterical and exaggerated as the industrialized nations sustained dramatic rates of growth, and as the economics profession became increasingly preoccupied with the development of Keynesian theory and the management of the mixed economy. Nevertheless, the refusal of the depression economy to react well to the numerous and powerful potions devised for its recovery was then and remains now a puzzle for anyone involved in or concerned with the New Deal.

The protracted character of the Great Depression was the basis of a dramatic and profound change in American institutions and politics. Indeed, except for Lincoln and the Civil War, it is hard to think of another presidential administration so singularly and exclusively defined by a single great problem. At no time, from the moment FDR assumed office until, at the earliest, the outbreak of war in Europe, did the depression recede from the forefront of national politics. It began and ended all presidential and party calculations. Like some chronic disease that, despite occasional remissions, would not go away, it mortally threatened not only the economy but the body politic. Every major piece of legislation that endures on the statute books and in popular memory—the NRA, the Wagner Act, TVA, Social Security, the Securities and Exchange Commission, mandated budget deficits—was addressed to its remedy. For eight years, the political fortunes of the Roosevelt regime crested and fell with each oscillation in the stock market or lengthening of the bread lines. The persistence of the depression scrambled political alliances and compelled New Dealers to abandon one recovery policy after another. Corporatism, state planning, trust-busting, and Keynesianism came and went and came again and still the Great Depression proved incurable. Its very intractability suggests that something more fundamental, immune to all the experimental innovations of public policy, was awry at the very core of the country's economy. This essay attempts to probe that underlying malady.

Although the American economy has suffered several financial panics in its history, none has had the legacy of the panic of 1929. It was not until the outbreak of war in Europe that industrial production reached its precrash peak levels and the unemployment rate fell below a decennial average of 18 percent. There is no greater puzzle in American economic history than the persistent failure of investment activity during the depression of the 1930s to generate a full recovery. Most economic theorists have tried to solve this puzzle by focusing on what they conceive to be a variety of mechanisms that interfered with the establishment of equilibrium in product, labor, and capital markets after the trough was reached in 1932–33. In particular, it has been argued that obstacles to the appropriate adjustment of prices and wages upset the nation's marketplace, causing unprecedented levels of idle capacity and unemployment. These obstacles have been identified as ranging from "sticky prices" administered by highly concentrated and powerful firms, to excessively high wages maintained by union pressure, political rhetoric, and the provisions of section 7a of the National Industrial Recovery Act. In short, the prevailing view is that the persistence of the slump was the direct outgrowth of distortions in price mechanisms imposed by large firms, government, and labor unions.[1]

A price-theoretic approach to understanding the interwar slump in general, and interwar unemployment in particular, has a great many adherents and a not inconsiderable amount of intellectual appeal. But it is not beyond empirical criticism and refutation. Prices fell by almost one-third in the early thirties. The extent of so-called administered pricing in producers' and consumers' markets in interwar America has never been shown to be very large. The proportion of the American labor force that was organized in the interwar period, while high by historical standards, was not as high as in other industrialized nations where recovery obtained sooner. These facts leave one unpersuaded that price (and wage) inflexibility explains the longest depression in American economic history.

An older tradition in the literature, first formulated during the depression itself, argued that modern capitalist economies inevitably reached a stage of slow growth and ultimate stagnation. In particular, some economic theorists and historians looked on the interwar period of American economic development as the final stage of internally generated accumulation. They argued that the American economy was moribund by the 1930s, and was revived only by the impact of wars, state expenditures, and the penetration of foreign markets.[2] What the stagnation theorists focused on were those characteristics of the early-twentieth-century economy which seemed to presage an end to the endogenous growth of the system. By the interwar period the geographic expansion of the United States had ceased, and so had the dramatic rates of increase in infrastructural and heavy investment. Population growth had also slowed, along with the rate of immigration. The opportunities offered by foreign markets were reduced by increasingly protectionist policies, and an unequal distribution of income in the nation generated tendencies toward underconsumption.

The stagnation theorists were right to root the Great Depression in secular (that is, long-term) changes in the American economy.[3] But the crucial secular change was not the permanent exhaustion of capitalism's capacity for investment and accumulation—a theory obviously belied by the performance of world capitalism since 1945—but rather a new structure of consumer demand that had triggered profound shifts in the composition of investment and industrial output. By the 1920s, the structure of demand in the interwar American economy reflected a long-term transition to what might be called high-income spending behavior: from 1923 to 1929, for example, consumer spending on clothing, housing, and utilities all fell while spending on food, tobacco, household appliances, medical care, and recreation rose.[4] As a consequence, patterns of investment changed, encouraging a shift in both the composition of national output and in the distribution of employment opportunities from the old to the new sectors. But the financial crash "caught" the secular transition at a very early and vulnerable point. In 1929 and 1930, those firms located in the dynamic sectors of the economy were simply not present in sufficient numbers to lead a general economic recovery. It was this interaction of business cycle and secular trend that accounted for the length of the Great Depression, not the cycle or the trend alone.[5] Had there been no financial disruption in 1929, the secular transition to a consumer economy would have proceeded relatively smoothly. Had the crash occurred at a later point in the long-term trend of development, when the newer industries were more fully established, the length of the disruption would have been significantly shortened. Profitable new enterprises would have been more resilient to cyclic setbacks. Their surplus funds would have been ample, and eventually they would have been able to finance their own recovery. Most important, perhaps, business expectations would have been less depressed, and net investment commitments would have increased at an earlier date.

As a direct result of a secular rise in national income, new, more affluent consumer markets emerged during the interwar period—markets that showed greater potential and faster rates of growth than others that had figured prominently in the past in total consumption expenditures. In a certain sense, this changing pattern of consumer demand was the result of the kind of behavior originally described by Ernst Engel in his now classic studies of demand. Engel found that as people grew richer, they spent proportionately less on basic foods, clothing, and housing and more on manufactures and, as they grew still more affluent, on services.[6] These shifts in consumer demand in the interwar period had important macroeconomic consequences. The new pattern of consumer demand differentially affected industries—benefiting some, harming others. The result was that an uneven growth of industrial sectors became apparent even before 1929. Certain major industries such as textiles, iron and steel, and lumber saw their markets weaken; others, notably appliances, chemicals, and processed foods, faced a new set of opportunities, but were not yet sufficiently strong to sustain a high rate of macroeconomic growth.

Compounding the difficulty posed by the emergence of new consumption patterns, interwar changes in the distribution of income and the impact on the distribution of buying power occasioned by the rapid deflation after the crash in 1929 played an important role in hampering the recovery process. The lower 93 percent of the nonfarm population saw their per capita disposable income fall during the boom of the later twenties. The evidence suggests that the interwar years offered relatively limited opportunities for the rapid development of new mass markets.[7] Not until the 1940s and after was the distribution of income sufficiently broad to allow for the full emergence of the markets and firms that were beginning to grow during the interwar era. Although the high-income environment of the 1920s spawned a new composition of aggregate demand—due to changes in middle-class spending behavior—it also created a demand constraint on the growth of new markets in the form of a highly skewed distribution of income. The severe cyclic reduction in disposable income after 1929 only magnified this obstacle to the transformation of the structures of economic growth.

The distribution of buying power, distorted as it was by the postcrash fall in the price level, also played a role in hampering the timely growth of the dynamic sectors. By 1932 the purchasing power of those still employed had risen greatly because of rapid deflation. Insofar as these income recipients tended to be businessmen and professionals, the demand for luxury items, high-priced durables such as large cars, and nonessential services such as entertainment and tourism, rose. Deflation did not, of course, bolster the purchasing power of those who had lost their jobs, except to the extent that they owned assets, borrowed funds, or received relief payments. Thus, a falling price level did not strengthen consumption as a whole; rather, it redirected consumer expenditures toward product markets geared mainly to high-income recipients. This shift in demand patterns intensified the difficulties of the industries most damaged by the depression. Their markets shrank as the number of inactive workers rose. In more dynamic sectors, the demand emanating from those still employed was not large enough, nor was it sufficiently dispersed among a broad spectrum of commodities, to generate a large advance in revenues and thereby a robust recovery.

The divergent growth potentials of American industries during the interwar period can be broadly discerned from the changing pattern of demand for capital goods by major manufacturing sectors. Movements in the demand for capital goods indicate which industries were expanding and which were contracting during the interwar years. As the composition of final consumer demand changed during the period, so the derived demand for investment inputs was altered. The consumption patterns of the twenties favored the emergence and expansion of certain industries and generated a slower rate of growth, if not actual contraction, for others.[8]

For example, an average of 2.1 percent of the total real expenditures on productive facilities in the American economy during the twenties was made in the processed foods sector. That average rose to 2.5 percent during the decade of depression, paralleling the change in the share of consumer spending going to processed foods.

By contrast, in the textile industry the mean was 1.54 percent during the twenties and 1.2 percent during the thirties. The same shrinkage occurred in the lumber industry, where the relevant figures are 0.8 percent in the 1920s and 0.4 percent in the 1930s. In the petroleum sector there was expansion as the average share rose from 0.6 percent in the twenties to 1 percent during the thirties. Certain relatively new industries expanded quickly during the interwar years. Aircraft production and chemicals manufacturing were two sectors where the rate of investment in new productive facilities was high. There was also a rise in investment in the manufacture of office machinery and related equipment, absorbing an average of 3.3 percent of real total domestic investment during the twenties and 3.9 percent in the thirties. In iron and steel production there was also a moderate increase in the investment share, but this expansion was limited to firms producing for appliance, food container, and other new markets. The automobile sector experienced a slight rise in its investment share, but again such expansion was limited to firms producing newer styles of cars equipped with what had previously been regarded as luxury items.

Changes in investment activity offer a broad overview of the varied experience of American industries during the 1929 downturn. A closer examination of the source of these variations requires explicit attention to the changing strength of particular markets during the interwar period. Such an investigation helps to show the actual shifts in patterns of consumer expenditure and sectoral investment. These alterations in the composition of economic activity had profound implications for the direction and speed of economic recovery in the wake of the crash. Following are brief descriptions of how certain industries could benefit from and respond positively to the secular and cyclic forces at work in the interwar economy.

Iron and Steel.

In the case of iron and steel firms, those least affected by the Great Depression produced for newer markets in lighter steels and in tin plate. The shift in markets experienced by iron and steel producers in the interwar period may be seen in table 2.1. The downward trend in railway and construction demand was due to the secular decline in population growth and the slower rate of territorial expansion. Whatever strength in markets existed was found in such sectors as food containers and miscellaneous manufacturing. Indeed, once the depression occurred, steel plate and rails fell in importance as a percentage of total industry shipments, while the rank of shipments of black plate (for tinning) rose from seventh to third, and the

TABLE 2.1
PERCENTAGE OF TOTAL STEEL OUTPUT
CONSUMED BY MAJOR INDUSTRIES, 1922–1939

Industry	1922	1926	1929	1939
Railways	22	23.5	17	9.3
Construction	15	19.5	16.5	13.1
Automobiles	10	14.5	18	18.1
Oil, gas, mining	10	9.5	10.5	5.5
Export trade	7	5	5.5	6.5
Food containers	4	4	5	9.4
Machinery	NA[a]	4	3	3.8
Agriculture	4	4	5.5	1.9
Miscellaneous	28	16	19	32.4[b]

Sources: Homer B. Vanderblue and William L. Crum, *The Iron Industry in Prosperity and Depression*, 146; E. D. McCallum, *The Iron and Steel Industry in the United States*, 186; *Iron Age*, 117 (January 7, 1926), 7; Standard and Poor's, *Industry Surveys* (June 27, 1947), section 2, pp. s3–s6.

[a] Data not available.
[b] Includes pressing and stamping, and jobbers.

rank of strip steel rose from sixth to fourth. From 1925 to 1934, as plate and rail manufacturing capacity fell, sheet mill capacity rose by 44.6 percent.[9] Thus, profitable avenues of steel production shifted from heavy structural markets to fabricators' markets, consumer and producer hardware, and new alloys.

The investment behavior of firms serving these markets demonstrates their relative well-being in a time of severe economic distress. For example, rolling mills continued investment during the 1930s aimed at standardizing shapes and improving the ductility of the product. The American Steel and Wire Company spent $4.7 million in 1935 on new rod mills and wire machines; National Steel, the only firm in the industry not to run a deficit in 1932, maintained an aggressive investment policy with respect to its continuous hot-strip rolling operations and was one of the few firms to maintain a flexible pricing policy throughout the depression decade. Inland Steel Company, having served heavy-product markets throughout the 1920s, altered the focus of its investment in the 1930s in order to shift "the emphasis in production from heavy steel (rails, plates, structurals) for the capital goods industries to lighter steel (sheets, strip, tin plate) for the consumer industries." It is not surprising, therefore, that of the twelve largest steel companies, Inland and National secured the highest operating profits (13.1 percent and 9.2 percent, respectively, of gross fixed assets) for the period 1936–40.[10]

With the onset of the crash, several major markets in iron and steel contracted. Automobile output fell by almost four million vehicles in the first three years of the downturn. Oil pipeline mileage built in the 1930s was 60 percent less than the 1920s total. Construction came to a halt. It was in the markets for light, flat-rolled steels (sheets, strip, and tin plate) where earnings continued to grow. These steels were used in the newer markets such as household appliances and food containers (especially cans); their percentage of total industry shipments rose from 25.8 percent to 40 percent later in the decade. By 1938 the railroads consumed only 6.1 percent of the nation's hot-rolled steel, while abandoning eleven thousand miles of track by 1939. The automobile producers were similarly affected, their consumption of steel falling by close to four million net tons from 1930 to 1932.[11] It would take the advent of World War II to reverse this decline in the heavy-products division of the industry.

Automobiles.

The automobile industry had two outstanding problems in the interwar period: the slowing in the absolute rate of growth of its market, due to a decrease in the growth rate of the population and a general decline in the income held by most of the nonfarm population, and the difficulty of stimulating demand for its product during a depression. In the first three years of the Great Depression the number of cars in use declined only 10 percent, but with the relatively large number of new vehicles on the road because of the boom of the 1920s, the amount of unused mileage per car (that is, service life) rose 37 percent. Scrap rates of used cars consequently fell. There was accordingly a dramatic shift in the age composition of the stock of cars owned. An idea of the magnitude of the problem may be gained from data on replacement sales. In 1913, three out of every four cars sold in the United States were net additions to the national total; by 1924 the ratio fell to one in every three; and by 1927 replacement sales accounted for three-fourths of total production. The inevitable result occurred in 1931, when 755,000 fewer new cars were made than the total number scrapped, replaced, or stored by owners. Some firms were so concerned about the used car problem that they attempted to ship used vehicles to foreign markets (where there was no competition) and undertook payment schemes to reward dealers for each used car scrapped. During the 1930s the industry "took greater punishment than most others because a new car was not an essential in a home where the breadwinner was out of work."[12]

It is difficult to distinguish between secular and short-run mechanisms contributing to the poor auto sales performance of the 1930s. The immediate cause, namely, the depressed purchasing power of the population, is obvious enough. But superimposed on this were long-term developments in automobile and tire manufacture and in road building that made cars last longer. Operating costs were also falling because of improvements in fuels, lubricants, and repair techniques. All these developments lengthened the service life of cars and increased the impact of a fall in national income on the sales of new vehicles. The "increased durability of automobiles [rendered] the industry more subject to large cyclical swings and [increased] its resemblance as regards economic position to residential building."[13]

Many automobile producers responded to the depression in classic fashion, by cutting prices. This created intense problems for independent companies producing luxury cars, such as Auburn, Duesenberg, and Packard. Yet the price-cutting strategy was not overly successful. The Maxwell Company (later to become Chrysler) had already experienced such a problem when in 1923 it cut prices on all models by a hundred dollars and experienced no increase in sales. As a result, by 1932 many firms in the industry hesitated to make substantial price cuts when their impact on revenues was uncertain and, with lower volume obtaining, their effect could be catastrophic. Car manufacturers found that sales could be stimulated more by changes in the operating characteristics of their product than by lowering retail prices—prices that represented only one-third of the cost of using a car throughout its life.[14]

Many car manufacturers turned to style changes and technical innovation to increase sales volume. There were systematic attempts to provide "more car for less money." Vehicle weights increased, as did wheelbases and horsepower ratings. Many of the changes provided auxiliary instrumentation or minor additions. No real effort was made to develop a simple, cheap "depression car." Indeed, one such experiment was a market failure. The number of engine models and body types per make did not change. "The fact remains that instead of tending toward offering 'raw' transportation [during the 1930s], the cheaper cars of the period presented many features hitherto associated exclusively with the more expensive makes." As part of this nonprice response to poor sales performance, most automakers continued annual model design changes throughout the 1930s.[15] Special trade-in allowances on used cars and installment buying plans were also introduced.

In the absence of a constant or rising rate of durable goods purchases in the 1930s, automobile firms suffered relatively more than nondurable goods manufacturers.[16] The lessons of the depression were well learned. After the artificial stimulus of wartime production had played out, the industry moved into a new era of style development and technical change in the 1950s and 1960s. Moreover, until the fuel embargo of the seventies, design and technical developments focused on appearance, advertising convenience, and luxury rather than on durability or efficiency.

Food Products.

Several factors were responsible for the dynamic behavior of food producers during the thirties. Low consumer income generated by the downturn appears to have encouraged the purchase of relatively cheap and nutritious processed foods. Government expenditures for unemployment relief may have further enhanced the demand for such foods. The depression-inspired increase in the number of homemakers holding jobs also qualitatively altered the demand for food products. And there were long-term trends, involving the increase in the spread of household appliances and automotive transportation, that increased the derived demand for and access to processed food products.[17]

Short-run developments fit well with secular changes in technology (in both the plant and the home) and the rising labor force participation rate of women. It was only with improved methods of home storage and preparation that cheaper food products could be successfully marketed. In addition, the demand for appliances was directly linked with the alteration in the sexual division of labor. The increasing entrance of women into the labor force dated from the end of World War I. It was not limited to young women. While the participation rate of women twenty to twenty-four years old rose from 37.5 percent in 1920 to 45.6 percent in 1940, that of women of prime marriage age (twenty-five to forty-four years) rose even faster, from 21.7 percent to 30.5 percent. The hardship of the depression obviously encouraged greater labor force participation by women from households where the primary income earner was idle or on short time. Full-time domestic labor by women was virtually impossible in a period of massive unemployment. Consequently, demand increased for cheaper foods that could be stored and prepared more easily.[18] Food producers responded to the long-term and cyclic opportunities that the 1930s provided. These opportunities were realized by technical change, product innovation, and the development of new methods of distribution.

Important developments in the techniques of food processing dated from the end of World War I. Most involved the preparation of canned and frozen foods. By the thirties, these innovations had reached the operational stage and attenuated the impact of the 1929 downturn. Although canning output fell off from 1929 to 1931, there was a swift recovery by 1935. In 1931, output stood at 160 million cans of foodstuffs; by the end of the decade, this figure had more than doubled. At the other end of the pipeline, retailers saw the merit of canned foods in terms of their ease of storage, reliability of supply, opportunities for advertising, and potential for customer self-service. As can shipments increased and won an ever-increasing share in the revenue of shippers, there were competitive reductions in transportation costs that further improved the canners' market. The reduction in domestic working time, which increased as the depression worsened, was compensated for by a greater reliance on canned items. This was paralleled by investment in nutrition and agricultural research (especially hybridization) and in machinery for the washing, peeling, trimming, grinding, and cutting of raw produce.[19]

Developments in frozen food processing were not as impressive as those in canning. Nevertheless, they did play a role in stimulating investment in the industry during the depression decade. Clarence Birdseye sold his patents and trademarks to the General Food Corporation in 1929 after many years of research. By 1930 the company marketed a full line of frozen poultry, meat, fish, and sixteen varieties of fruits and vegetables. Even so, the frozen foods market was initially limited by the lack of refrigeration in homes and stores, which in turn was due to technical bottlenecks and high costs.[20] Immaturity in storage technology also brought into question the quality and reliability of the product. This was especially the case with meats. The low rate of consumer acceptance also had roots in the competition of retail butchers, who provided personalized attention to customers. But there was substantial progress in expanding the frozen foods market during the thirties. In 1933, for example, only 516 stores in the country had refrigeration capacity. That number grew to approximately 15,000 by the end of the decade. As early as 1934, easily accessible freezers for use in stores were commercially developed.[21]

Associated with the dynamic impact of process and product innovation in food manufacture was the articulation of more efficient and sophisticated mechanisms of distribution. Improvements in packaging materials, cans, and glassware, called forth by the dynamism of firms in the food industry, allowed for the wider and more appealing distribution of the industry's products. Concentrated food retailing in the form of supermarkets increased enormously with the pressures of reduced demand in the thirties. The scale economies of supermarket retailing allowed for effective competition with the small grocery store; they were due, in part, to the greater reliability and variety of supplies that the large stores and chains developed.[22]

From 1935, when there were 300 supermarkets in the nation, to 1939, when there were 4,982, the average annual increase in supermarket retailing was almost 1,200 stores. Linked with this marketing development was the increased use of advertising in various media. By 1932, the food industry ranked second among all manufacturing sectors in annual expenditures on national magazine advertisements.[23]

Petroleum and Chemicals.

The petroleum industry's relative success in the 1930s was largely due to long-run developments in related markets that stimulated the demand for petroleum products and spurred technical progress and product innovation. In addition, expansion in their markets encouraged aggressive marketing by oil companies, resulting in better distribution and sometimes lower prices.

The growth of automotive transportation in the thirties, a major stimulus to the industry's depression performance, continued a trend dating back to the end of World War I. Coupled with this expansion was a steady development in the surfaced road system that served to enhance the demand for cars. In the ten years prior to the depression, highway mileage had already doubled. In the thirties, the increase was slightly more than double. In the same period, exemplifying the increasing reliance of the population on automotive transportation, the average annual consumption of gasoline per car rose from 525 to 648 gallons. One in every 5.2 people regularly traveled by car in 1929; that ratio rose to one in every 4.5 by 1941.[24]

Throughout the 1920s the automobile industry had improved its product by increasing engine compression ratios and by moving up to six-cylinder design. These developments, carrying over into the depression decade, expanded the demand for gasoline both extensively and with respect to quality. Larger engines required more fuel; enhanced compression ratios required fuel with better octane ratings. Refineries both expanded output during the thirties and continually revamped their cracking technologies to improve the quality of gasoline. Linked with this derived demand from automobile users was an increase in the need for lubricants that further improved refinery revenues.[25]

The markets in home heating, aviation, and railroading also supported the petroleum industry during the depression. The advent of the oil burner in the twenties, both in homes and in commercial establishments, generated an increased demand for refinery output. From 1929 to 1941 this trend continued as the introduction of oil heat steadily increased. The diesel locomotive created and expanded the demand for yet another distillate product. Just over 1.7 million barrels of diesel fuel were consumed in the last four years of the depression. And by the end of the decade, an entirely new sector—aviation—made its presence felt, demanding still newer refinery products for its equipment.[26]

As in the petroleum sector, firms in the chemical industry profited from new market linkages and techniques of production during the depression. Of major importance was the drive to innovate, both to cut costs and to meet the needs of downstream industries for new and better products. As a result, the focus of investment activity in this industry during the thirties was on technical innovation and product development rather than on simply seeking a rebound in standard output and sales. The bulk of the derived demand for chemical products came from the rayon and petroleum producers and, to a lesser extent, rubber, metals, and paper corporations. Radio and motion-picture production generated an increased need for chemicals. Tanners, soap boilers, paint mixers, and glassmakers also populated the chemical producers' market more heavily than ever before. Automobile firms increased their purchase of such inputs as rubber compounds and synthetic lacquers and also stimulated more metallurgical research in order to improve chassis and engines. And the depressed conditions prevailing gave added incentive to investment to improve on output recovery rates and the utilization of the wastes and by-products of reactions.[27]

In petroleum and chemical production, improvements in technology and innovation in products were intimately linked. During the thirties, efforts dating to the previous decade to achieve continuous processing came to fruition and provided a cheaper alternative to the earlier batch production of chemicals and petroleum distillates. The downturn of 1929 stimulated further efforts to reduce costs. For petroleum producers, major emphasis was placed on the development of new refining methods; in chemicals, the concern was to automate the control of reaction temperature, pressure, volume, duration, and other attributes such as pH level.[28]

Stone, Clay, and Glass Products.

Building materials and glass typically exhibit a high degree of sensitivity to movements in the business cycle because the sales of the sector depend on the (also cyclically volatile) volume of construction activity. But from the mid-1930s on, this industry performed remarkably well. Long-term developments in market opportunities, along with the impact of government policies in the short run, made this possible.

For the glass division, secular developments were particularly important. High import tariffs, along with the inflated wages that they encouraged, aided the early development of modern glassmaking from 1880 to 1920. By 1915, the nation met its own glass needs and created a surplus for export for the first time. The rise of the automobile industry after 1900 bolstered the market for plate glass that had previously been limited to construction needs. And although Prohibition and the demise of gas lighting lowered the demand for bottles, globes, and chimneys, other markets were developed that provided further opportunities for growth.[29]

From the turn of the century, the industry embarked on an era of development based on new processes and products. Perhaps most important for this growth between 1890 and 1920 was the tenfold rise in the demand for glass in food packaging. Glass became the favored choice of food processors because of its relatively low price, its superiority in holding vacuum seals, its sanitary properties, and its virtues as a display device to aid sales. Further, its unique flexibility with respect to coloring, size, and shape allowed for distinctive trademark designs. The Pure Food and Drug Act of 1906 enhanced the public's confidence in the quality of prepackaged foods, and the act's insistence on specified weight tolerances (to avoid fraud) increased the demand for uniform glass containers.[30]

During the depression, the glass industry benefited from the continued growth of new markets for its output. The spread of electrification stimulated the demand for refrigerated foods, many of which were packaged in glass, and for electric bulbs—a wholly new product. During the thirties, increases in the demand for lighting and packaging glassware were mostly uninterrupted. From mid-decade on, electrification (both private and New Deal inspired) was a crucial aspect of this development, because of both its direct effect on the demand for light bulbs and its indirect effect (given the spread of refrigeration) on the demand for glass food containers.

The surprisingly strong performance of the building materials division in the latter half of the thirties reflected government expenditures on residential and public-facility construction. The Works Progress Administration alone built or renovated 2,500 hospitals, 5,900 school buildings, 1,000 airfields, and 13,000 recreation sites.[31]

It appears, therefore, that the relative success of this industry was due to a combination of factors. The development of new consumer markets provided a secular stimulus to the glass division. Government stabilization and relief policies during the depression aided the building materials producers. Both secular mechanisms and the intervention of government lent this industry a dynamism that served it well during the crisis of the thirties.

The changing composition of consumer and investment demand, combined with the cyclic problems of the early thirties, generated a severe structural unemployment problem. The limited size of the dynamic sectors made the absorption of the unemployed exceedingly difficult. The net result was a continuation of the unpropitious demand conditions facing the economy as a whole. Any large increase in employment had to come from a general revival of all sectors.

A comparison of net investment data for the 1930s with the interwar ranking of industries with respect to their share of national employment and value of output provides further demonstration of the uneven development of major industries that interfered with recovery. In table 2.2, the evidence shows that sectors where net investment recovered relatively quickly after the trough of 1932 had low shares of national employment and national value-product. Conversely, those industries that in the interwar period accounted for large shares of employment and output engaged in little if any net expansion in the immediate wake of the crash. Notable examples of the former are food products, tobacco products, chemicals, and petroleum products—precisely those sectors most stimulated by the new patterns of consumer spending at the time. Of the latter, the best demonstrations are afforded by textile mill products, lumber products, primary metal industries, and transportation equipment.

Thus, a massive structural unemployment problem emerged during the thirties that in the absence of an exogenous shock like war would have taken some time to solve. But this problem, which began to emerge prior to 1929, was not derived from interferences with the price mechanism of labor markets. Rather, it was one of mobilizing the necessary capital, information, and confidence to retrain and reallocate the labor force in conformity with prevailing employment trends and opportunities. Indeed, there had been a steady decline since the early twenties in the percentage of national employment accounted for by the manufacturing and construction sectors. The same decline took place in agriculture and mining. In the service industries, such as transportation, trade, finance, selected services, and government operations, there was a rise.[32] Even if there had been no financial crash in 1929, these trends show that structural unemployment would have been a recurrent problem in the interwar period.

The Great Depression must be viewed as an event triggered by random historical and institutional circumstances, but prolonged by the timing of the process of long-term industrial development in the

TABLE 2.2
DATA ON INDUSTRIAL RECOVERY IN THE 1930s

Industry	Net investment in equipment as percentage of 1929 level			Share of national employment by rank			Share of national value-product by rank		
	1937	1938	1939	1931	1933	1935	1931	1933	1935
Chemicals and allied products	369.9	256.6	401	32	27	25	20	18	14
Stone, clay and glass products	850.3	422.9	306.3	29[a]	30[a]	24[a]	46[a]	40[a]	41[a]
Petroleum and coal products	131.9	50.1	21.2	23	22	21	8	2	4
Tobacco products	130.2	85.6	159.6	19	54[b]	67[b]	10	11	10
Food and kindred products	178.2	61.2	115.7	18[c]	13[c]	14[c]	1[c]	1[c]	2[c]
Nonelectrical machinery	96.9	58.5	148.9	NA[d]	NA	NA	NA	NA	NA
Apparel and other textile products	32.6	Neg.[e]	114.4	15[f]	12[f]	18[f]	19[f]	20[f]	19[f]
Rubber and plastic products	22.2	14.8	74	30	28	32	27	27	22
Transportation equipment	34.7	8	53.2	12	18	8	2	4	1
Paper and allied products	27.4	8.6	29.5	20	19	17	14	13	12
Primary metal industries	38.6	Neg.	Neg.	4	2	1	5	3	3
Fabricated metal products	18.7	25.3	100.2	NA	NA	NA	NA	NA	NA
Printing and publishing	Neg.	Neg.	Neg.	16	15	13	4	5	7
Leather and leather products	19	Neg.	3.6	36	35	38	36	34	35
Lumber and wood products	Neg.	Neg.	Neg.	5	7	3	25	23	18
Textile mill products	Neg.	Neg.	Neg.	3	3	3	3	3	3

Sources: U.S. Bureau of the Census, Census of Manufactures, relevant years; U.S. Bureau of Labor Statistics, Capital Stock Estimates for Input-Output Industries: Methods and Data, Bulletin 2034, 1979; U.S. Internal Revenue Service, Statistics of Income, relevant years; L. Chawner, "Capital Expenditures for Manufacturing Plant and Equipment—1915 to 1940," Survey of Current Business (March, 1941); L. Chawner, "Capital Expenditures in Selected Manufacturing Industries," Survey of Current Business (May, 1941); L. Chawner, "Capital Expenditures in Selected Manufacturing Industries—Part II," Survey of Current Business (December, 1941). I am indebted to Charles Bowman of the U.S. Department of Labor and John Musgrave of the U.S. Department of Commerce for providing me with some unpublished data used in this table.

[a] Glass products only.
[b] Cigarettes only.
[c] Meat packing only.
[d] Data not available.
[e] Neg. indicates net disinvestment in relevant year.
[f] Men's clothing only.

United States—in particular, by a transition in the structure of consumer and investment demand in the interwar period. The financial machinery of the American economy, caught in heavy deflation, was not equal to the task of pushing open the doors to the patterns of growth characteristic of the postwar era.

The problem of delayed recovery and the peculiar difficulties created by the incipient reordering of America's industrial structure in the 1930s were quickly overcome by World War II. The war provided a twofold stimulus. The more mature industries of the interwar period were brought out of their doldrums by the particular demands of making war. The new industries were pulled along by government orders, both through their contribution to a general increase in economic activity and through their particular demands on sectors such as petroleum, chemicals, electronics, and aviation. Indeed, the war itself spawned the development of other new industries, products, and processes. Thus, the 1940s helped to lay the foundation of prosperity in the 1950s and 1960s. Indeed, it has been suggested that wartime production and military procurement during the Korean conflict, cold war, and Vietnam War have been responsible for the prosperity of the American economy in the entire postwar era.[33]

By the 1970s, however, the postwar prosperity of the American economy was in jeopardy. Much like the crisis of the interwar period, the persistent instability of the seventies raised fears about the long-term viability of capitalism and made a mockery of the optimism of the "New Frontier" and the "Great Society." Indeed, in the 1970s, the performance of the American economy was somewhat similar to that of the 1930s. In both decades, the growth rate of the gross domestic product (that is, the gross national product net of output produced abroad to which residents have title) fell after several years of robust expansion. Unemployment rates reached disquieting levels, and the attendant downturns were persistent rather than transitory. At the beginning of each of these decades, profound exogenous shocks—in one case, the stock market crash; in the other, skyrocketing oil prices—triggered the difficulties that followed. And in both cases formidable political and intellectual obstacles prevented the adoption of appropriate countercyclic policies.

If in fact the 1970s seem, in economic historical terms, to be similar to the 1930s, is this the result of a simple isomorphism or is there a deeper connection? It may be that the technical requirements of making war (in the 1940s, 1950s, and 1960s) and confronting the perceived Soviet challenge in the cold war, while providing a fiscal stimulus, interfered with the kinds of innovation and economic dynamism necessary for continued growth. For example, during the

1930s the Ford Motor Company began experimenting with the development of plastic car bodies. Such research was abandoned with the inflow of war orders in 1939. The American steel industry by 1950 was ready to engage in the full-scale development of new mechanized processes and the scaling-down of capacity in anticipation of the shrinkage of wartime orders. The Korean conflict reversed this trend. It is now well documented that the strategic weapons buildup of the early sixties, along with the escalation of the space program to undertake a manned mission to the moon, slowed the rate of technological innovations in those markets in which the American economy has been challenged in recent years. And some experts say today that the Strategic Defense Initiative of the Reagan administration inappropriately distorted an entire generation of research in applied physics, engineering, and aeronautics. The "spillover" effects of military research may not be as profound or useful as proponents have suggested.[34]

Innovative effort was the key in the thirties and remains essential today to the sustained development of the capitalist economy. Although certain *industries* in a given stage of development may prosper or wane, individual *firms* may transcend the exigencies of the secular process. Some of course do not; they constitute the failures of business life. But for those enterprises willing and able to develop new products, revamp existing production technologies, and engage in newer and more aggressive forms of distribution, continued accumulation is the prize. The more firms there are in an economy that can adapt and change in these ways, the better off the aggregate economy will be at a given point in time and the faster it will grow. Wartime mobilization and procurement jeopardize the possibility of renewed productive lives for specific firms insofar as they divert attention from invention and focus it upon uniformity, regularity, and volume. To be sure, some military contracts require for their execution the fabrication of entirely new plant, equipment, and tools (the building of sophisticated aircraft and naval vessels is an obvious example). But even here, it may be that for the economy as a whole there are few resources and little energy left for innovative drive in the production of consumption goods or of capital goods used in the production of consumption goods.

Wartime stimuli and defense spending, although providing a general expansion of the national product that can aid the emergence of new industries and techniques and protect the sales of more mature sectors, may also encourage a technological conservatism that has negative long-run consequences. Had the American automobile industry developed plastic car bodies in the 1930s, had the steel industry developed more mechanized processes as early as the mid-1950s, would the hardships afforded by foreign competition obtain in the U.S. economy to the same extent today? This speculation implies that America's contemporary foreign competitors, whose industries were rebuilt after war in the relative absence of military demands, may be enjoying the consequences of the "Arsenal of Democracy" of the 1940s, 1950s, and more recent decades.

How ironic it was that World War II laid the basis for a new era of government intervention in economic affairs. The fiscal experience of the war years gave confidence for the postwar use of government tax and spending policies to "tame" the business cycle. But the war had another legacy: the emergence of a military-industrial complex. Military-industrial procurement during and since the forties, while it afforded temporary support for the growth of the national economy, interfered with the more qualitative development of the economy with respect to technology, labor training, and managerial skill. A decline in productivity growth-rates and international competitiveness has been the inevitable and unfortunate outcome. The business cycles of the last two decades have as a consequence been quite difficult to subdue. What the war gave us by way of an education in policy-making has perhaps now proved less useful. For it also interrupted and deformed the continuing evolution and growth of the American economy. The Great Depression of the 1930s places this present-day misfortune in sharp relief.

Notes

1. It is beyond the scope of this essay to give a full survey of the literature to which I allude here. Some good examples of the arguments I have summarized may be found in Michael M. Weinstein, *Recovery and Redistribution under the NIRA* (New York: North-Holland, 1980); Gardiner C. Means and Adolf A. Berle, *The Modern Corporation and Private Property* (New York: Harcourt, Brace & World, 1968); and S. H. Slichter, "Corporate Price Policies as a Factor in the Recent Business Recession," *Proceedings of the Academy of Political Science* 18 (January 1939): 20–33.

2. Some very good examples of the stagnation literature are G. E. McLaughlin and R. J. Watkins, "The Problem of Industrial Growth in a Mature Economy," *American Economic Review* 29 (March 1939): supp., 1–14; A. H. Hansen, "Economic Progress and Declining Population Growth," *American Economic Review* 29 (March 1939): 1–15; J. M. Keynes, "Some Economic Consequences of a Declining Population," *Eugenics Review* 29 (April 1937): 13–17; and D. Weintraub, "Effects of Current and Prospective Technological Developments upon Capital Formation," *American Economic Review* 29 (March

1939): supp., 32. Also see M. Kalecki, "The Problem of Effective Demand with Tugan-Baranovski and Rosa Luxemburg," in his *Selected Essays on the Dynamics of the Capitalist Economy, 1933–1970* (New York: Cambridge University Press, 1971); Paul A. Baran and Paul M. Sweezy, *Monopoly Capital: An Essay on the American Economic and Social Order* (New York: Monthly Review Press, 1966), chaps. 5–7; and P. Patnaik, "A Note on External Markets and Capitalist Development," *Economic Journal* 82 (December 1972): 1316–23.

3. Examinations have been made of the instability of the interwar years in terms of long-term development factors, but they have been concerned with economies other than that of the United States. Ingvar Svennilson undertook such an investigation of the Western European nations in his *Growth and Stagnation in the European Economy* (Geneva: United Nations Economic Commission for Europe, 1954). The experience of the Canadian economy during the Great Depression was studied in these terms by A. E. Safarian, *The Canadian Economy in the Great Depression* (Toronto: University of Toronto Press, 1959). Erik Dahmen did the same in his classic study of Swedish industry between the world wars, *Entrepreneurial Activity and the Development of Swedish Industry: 1919–1939*, trans. A. Leijonhufvud (Homewood, Ill.: Richard D. Irwin, 1970). With the possible exception of Joseph A. Schumpeter's *Business Cycles: A Theoretical, Historical, and Statistical Analysis of the Capitalist Process* (New York: McGraw-Hill, 1939), only one study by an American economist has explicitly called for the analysis of economic fluctuations in the United States in a long-term historical perspective that emphasizes qualitative as well as quantitative evidence, and that is R. A. Gordon's "Business Cycles in the Interwar Period: The 'Quantitative-Historical' Approach," *American Economic Review* 39 (May 1949): 47–63. Also see the intriguing article by R. R. Keller, "Factor Income Distribution in the United States during the 1920s: A Reexamination of Fact and Theory," *Journal of Economic History* 33 (March 1973): 252–73.

4. See J. Frederic Dewhurst and Associates, *America's Needs and Resources* (New York: Twentieth Century Fund, 1947), 80–82; and William H. Lough, *High-Level Consumption* (New York: McGraw-Hill, 1935), app. A. Also see U.S. Department of Commerce, Bureau of the Census, *Historical Statistics of the United States: Colonial Times to 1970*, pt. 1, series G470–494 (Washington, D.C.: U.S. Government Printing Office, 1975), p. 320.

5. See Lewis Kimmel, *The Availability of Bank Credit: 1933–1938* (New York: National Industrial Conference Board, 1939); and B. S. Bernanke, "Nonmonetary Effects of the Financial Crisis in the Propagation of the Great Depression," *American Economic Review* 73 (June 1983): 257–76.

6. See G. J. Stigler, "The Early History of Empirical Studies of Consumer Behavior," *Journal of Political Economy* 62 (April 1954): 95–113. Engel first published his findings in 1857 in his "Die Productions und Consumtionsverhaltnisse des Konigreichs Sachsen," reprinted in *International Statistical Institute Bulletin* 9, no. 1, supp. 1.

7. On the fate of the 93 percent of the nonfarm population, see C. F. Holt, "Who Benefited from the Prosperity of the Twenties?" *Explorations in*

Economic History 14 (July 1977): 277–89; see also F. Stricker, "Affluence for Whom?—Another Look at Prosperity and the Working Class in the 1920s," *Labor History* 24 (Winter 1983): 5–33. Simon Kuznets estimated that the share of income received by the top 5 percent of recipients rose from 25.76 percent to 32.12 percent in 1932. Thereafter, the share hovered at around 28 percent, until the 1940s, when it fell below 20 percent. Raymond Goldsmith estimates the same share to be 30 percent throughout the first half of the thirties and argues that it fell to 20.9 percent in 1947 and to just below 20 percent by 1962. See Jeffrey G. Williamson and Peter H. Lindert, *American Inequality: A Macroeconomic History* (New York: Academic Press, 1980), 315–16; and Simon Kuznets, *Shares of Upper Income Groups in Income and Savings* (New York: National Bureau of Economic Research, 1953), 637. Robert J. Lampman, in his *Changes in the Share of Wealth Held by Top Wealth-Holders, 1922–56*, NBER Occasional Paper no. 71 (New York: National Bureau of Economic Research, 1960), discusses increasing income inequality in the United States prior to 1929. In a sample of thirty-three large and middle-sized American cities for the years 1929–33, Horst Mendershausen shows that the absolute dispersion of incomes fell, while the relative dispersion (i.e., inequality) of incomes rose. See his *Changes in Income Distribution during the Great Depression*, vol. 7 of *Studies in Income and Wealth* (New York: National Bureau of Economic Research, 1946).

8. The evidence for the following discussion is compiled and reported in J. Frederic Dewhurst and Associates, *America's Needs and Resources*, app. 21.

9. See Carroll R. Daugherty et al., *The Economics of the Iron and Steel Industry* (New York: McGraw-Hill, 1937), 1: 53–54, 320, 364–65, 447; and C. H. Hession, "The Metal Container Industry," in W. Adams, ed., *The Structure of American Industry* (New York: Macmillan, 1961), 430–67. Nonintegrated steel producers, according to Daugherty and his associates, tended to improve their economic position in the 1930s owing to the fact that the markets in which they excelled (finished, rolled products) were far better off than those in which the large integrated producers were dominant (rails and structural shapes).

10. William T. Hogan, *Economic History of the Iron and Steel Industry in the United States* (Lexington, Mass.: D. C. Heath, 1971), vol. 3, pts. 4–5, 1148, 1201, 1244, 1246, 1267; and Gertrude C. Schroeder, *The Growth of Major Steel Companies, 1900–1950* (Baltimore: Johns Hopkins University Press, 1953), 175.

11. Hogan, *Economic History of the Iron and Steel Industry*, vol. 3, pts. 4–5, 1119–20, 1297–99, 1306–67.

12. John W. Scoville, *Behavior of the Automobile Industry in Depression* (n.p. 1935), 3 (quotation), 19–27; Arthur Pound, *The Turning Wheel: The Story of General Motors through Twenty-Five Years, 1908–1933* (Garden City, N.Y.: Doubleday, Doran, 1934), 373–74; Philip H. Smith, *Wheels within Wheels: A Short History of American Motor Car Manufacturing* (New York: Funk & Wagnalls, 1968), 96, 115; Harold A. Baker, *Marketing and Consumption Trends in the Automobile Industry, 1929–1933* (Chicago, 1938), 196–97; and General Motors

Corporation, *The Dynamics of Automobile Demand* (New York: General Motors Corporation, 1939), 8.

13. See Scoville, *Behavior of the Automobile Industry*, 13–14; and General Motors Corporation, *The Dynamics of Automobile Demand*, 69–70, 88. From just over $1 billion in 1926, the national expenditure for car parts, tires, and the like fell almost 41 percent to $592 million in 1933. This decline was not entirely cyclic.

14. See Baker, *Marketing and Consumption Trends*, 200; E. D. Kennedy, *The Automobile Industry: The Coming of Age of Capitalism's Favorite Child* (New York: Reynal and Hitchcock, 1941), 229; John W. Scoville, *Reasons for the Fluctuations in Automobile Production* (Ohio State University Publications, 1938), 54; General Motors Corporation, *The Dynamics of Automobile Demand*, 31, 89, 94; and Scoville, *Behavior of the Automobile Industry*, 16.

15. See Scoville, *Behavior of the Automobile Industry*, 9; Baker, *Marketing and Consumption Trends*, 195–96, 198; and H. B. Vanderblue, "Pricing Policies in the Automobile Industry," *Harvard Business Review* 17 (Summer 1939): 392. Also see Robert Paul Thomas, "An Analysis of the Pattern of Growth of the Automobile Industry: 1895–1929" (Ph.D. diss., Northwestern University, 1965).

16. See Kennedy, *The Automobile Industry*, 321–22; and General Motors Corporation, *The Dynamics of Automobile Demand*, 95.

17. As noted in U.S. Department of Agriculture, *Technology in Food Marketing* (Washington, D.C.: U.S. Government Printing Office, 1952), 9. Public recognition of the nutritional value of canned foods was enhanced by the 1930 McNary-Mapes Amendment to the Food and Drug Act of 1906 which set standards for food labeling and the listing of ingredients and additives.

18. See U.S. Department of Commerce, *Historical Statistics of the United States: Colonial Times to 1970*, pt. 1, series D26-62, pp. 131–33.

19. See E. C. Hampe and M. Wittenberg, *The Lifeline of America: Development of the Food Industry* (New York: McGraw-Hill, 1964), 118, 130–31.

20. This is not to say that innovation in refrigeration equipment was lacking. In 1930, tunnel air-blast freezers were developed in Canada, as were freezers using movable refrigerated plates. The fog freezer was developed in 1933, the immersion freezer in 1939. Thus, "despite the depression, the rise of the frozen-food industry began in the 1930s" (U.S. Department of Agriculture, *Technology in Food Marketing*, 11–13).

21. The full acceptance of frozen meat packing also had to await the development of effective wrapping materials—the most important (with respect to its technical superiority and inherent display characteristics) being cellophane by the DuPont Corporation. See Hampe and Wittenberg, *The Lifeline of America*, 154–55 and chap. 7. Also see U.S. Department of Agriculture, *Technology in Food Marketing*, 20.

22. See Alfred D. Chandler, Jr., *The Visible Hand: The Managerial Revolution in American Business* (Cambridge: Harvard University Press, 1977), 233–39.

23. As reported in *The National Advertising Records* (New York: Denney,

1929–34). Also see Hampe and Wittenberg, *The Lifeline of America*, 273, 316, 322–24.

24. See H. F. Williamson et al., *The American Petroleum Industry: The Age of Energy, 1899–1959* (Evanston, Ill.: Northwestern University Press, 1963), 446, 604–5, 651–55, 694. Yet another factor in the improved market conditions facing the industry was the demand from farms. The number of tractors in use increased by about 750,000 in the 1930s.

25. See ibid., 457, 605, 667–68.

26. See ibid., 448, 455, 642–43, 660, 663, 666.

27. See Williams Haynes, *American Chemical Industry* (New York: Van Nostrand, 1948–54), 4:5–6, 5:6–7, 31, 38, 297. The soil conservation and crop restriction programs of the New Deal, created by the Agricultural Adjustment Act, also increased the demand for fertilizers and other agronomic chemicals.

28. See ibid., 5:37, 226; and Williamson et al., *The American Petroleum Industry*, 374–75, 624–25. Also see John McLean and Robert Haigh, *The Growth of Integrated Oil Companies* (Norwood, Mass.: Plimpton Press, 1954), chap. 19.

29. See Warren C. Scoville, *Revolution in Glass-Making: Entrepreneurship and Technological Change in the American Industry, 1880–1920* (Cambridge: Harvard University Press, 1948), 82, 248–49, 253–55, 257–59, 261–62; Pearce Davis, *The Development of the American Glass Industry* (Cambridge: Harvard University Press, 1949), chaps. 9–10; and J. M. Hammer, "The Glass Industry," and P. A. Hughes, "The Plate Glass Industry," both in J. G. Glover and W. B. Cornell, eds., *The Development of American Industries: Their Economic Significance* (Englewood Cliffs, N.J.: Prentice-Hall, 1932).

30. See Scoville, *Revolution in Glass-Making*, 252–56; and Davis, *The Development of the American Glass Industry*, pp. viii, 220–21.

31. See William E. Leuchtenberg, *Franklin D. Roosevelt and the New Deal, 1932–1940* (New York: Harper & Row, 1963), 125–26.

32. See U.S. Department of Labor, Bureau of Labor Statistics, *Employment and Earnings* (June 1968), (Washington, D.C.: U.S. Government Printing Office, 1968), vol. 7, no. 1, p. 11, as cited in John P. Henderson, *Changes in the Industrial Distribution of Employment: 1919–1959*, Bulletin no. 87 (University of Illinois, Bureau of Economic and Business Research, 1959), 10.

33. See, for example, Baran and Sweezy, *Monopoly Capital*.

34. See J. C. Furnas, "Ford's Leftover Idea," *New York Times*, February 16, 1983, p. A-30; Henry W. Broude, *Steel Decisions and the National Economy* (New Haven: Yale University Press, 1963), chap. 5; and J. E. Ullmann, "The Arms Race and the Decline of U.S. Technology," *Journal of Economic Issues* 17 (June 1983): 565–74. Also see Robert W. Degrasse, Jr., *Military Expansion, Economic Decline: The Impact of Military Spending on U.S. Economic Performance* (New York: Council on Economic Priorities, 1983).

3   *The 'Labor Question'*

STEVE FRASER

I

W HEN Franklin Roosevelt first appeared on the na-
tional stage of American public life, as a youthful assistant secretary
of the navy, many of his contemporaries considered the 'labor question' the primal problem confronting the Western world. Even in the
United States, where socialist and labor politics had barely scratched
out a beachhead, the 'labor question' nonetheless assumed this onto-
logical status. Thus, on the eve of World War I, Louis Brandeis
noted, "The labor question is and for a long time must be the paramount economic question in this country."[1] But even that was an un-
derstatement. Everyone from Woodrow Wilson to Big Bill Haywood
acknowledged that the 'labor question' was not merely the supreme
economic question but the constitutive moral, political, and social dilemma of the new industrial order.

From Versailles, President Wilson cabled Congress:

> The question which stands at the front of all others amidst the present
> great awakening is the question of labor . . . how are the men and women
> who do the daily labor of the world to obtain progressive improvement in
> the conditions of their labor, to be made happier, and to be served better
> by the communities and the industries which their labor sustains and ad-
> vances?[2]

For a president facing a world undone by war and revolution, the
'labor question' was fraught with danger. For others, like progressive
ideologue Frederick Howe, it contained an exalting revelation:

> My own class did not want such a world [a world of equality—SF]. And
> there was but one other class—the workers . . . Labor would not serve
> privilege . . . By necessity labor would serve freedom, democracy, equal
> opportunity for all . . . The place for the liberal was in labor's ranks . . .
> My political enthusiasm was now for a party of primary producers.[3]

Momentarily, the editors of the *New Republic* were swept away:

> We have already passed to a new era, the transition to a state in which labor will be the predominating element. The character of the future democracy is largely at the mercy of the recognized leaders of organized labor.[4]

For some, answering the 'labor question' thus promised not only to permanently alter the relationship between Labor and Capital, but in so doing to eliminate the immorality of exploitation, the social inequality and antagonism fostered by great aggregations of wealth, the threat to democratic politics represented by overbearing corporate power and pelf, and even the causes of global and imperialist war.

Along with FDR, a whole political generation matured during this "golden age" of the 'labor question'—men and women later principally responsible for the great reforms and realignments of the second New Deal: Felix Frankfurter and his band of political lawyers, including Ben Cohen, James Landis, Tom Corcoran, Alger Hiss, and future CIO chief counsel Lee Pressman; future cabinet members Frances Perkins, Harold Ickes, and Henry Wallace; senatorial New Dealers Robert Wagner and Robert LaFollette, Jr.; CIO founders John L. Lewis, Sidney Hillman, Clinton Golden, and Len DeCaux; social engineering reformers Harlow Person, Jett Lauck, and Morris Cooke; and future NLRB chairmen Edwin Smith, William Leiserson, and Harry Millis. Yet within the new political and industrial order they helped create, the 'labor question' no longer resonated with its accustomed power. By the time of Roosevelt's death in 1945, it had been eclipsed not only as the animating problem of national politics, not only as the unsolved central dilemma of the social order, but even as the "paramount economic question in this country."

Paradoxically, however, just as the 'labor question' receded like some faint echo from the distant political past, the new labor movement rose in a crescendo of industrial and political power. Indeed, if the new Democratic party crystallizing around the reform agenda of the second New Deal was not a mass labor party, it was nonetheless a party very much resting on the labor movement, on the insurgent CIO particularly. Somehow the political chemistry of the New Deal worked a double transformation: the ascendancy of labor and the eclipse of the 'labor question'.

This metamorphosis was clearly marked by (1) the dying away of the antimonopoly movement and its venerated ideology of productive labor as the core of oppositional politics; (2) the gradual repudiation of all third- or labor-party pretensions by the CIO leadership; (3) the legalization and federalization of industrial unionism and its subordination to the rule of administrative law under the Wagner Act; (4) metaphors of social integration, such as "security," "consumption," "interest," that supplanted metaphors of pariahdom like "rights" and "power"; (5) the replacement of the "workers control" of 1919 by "full employment" in 1946 as the animating issue of the postwar period; and (6) a global New Deal, not socialism, that circumscribed the far horizon of labor's vision.

By the end of World War II, the overriding issue in domestic affairs (arguably even in the realm of international politics) had become the American Standard of Living. The ASL was, in a sense, the favored answer to the 'labor question', draining it of its moral preeminence, its political threat, and its elemental social significance. The struggle over power and property, which had supplied the friction and frisson of politics since at least the Gilded Age, was superseded by the universal quest for more—goulash capitalism. Mass politics replaced class politics. Labor ceased to be a great question or even a mass movement containing within it the seeds of a wholly new future. As an institutionalized interest group it had become part of the answer, contributing to and drawing its just deserts from the cornucopia of American mass production and consumption.

Yet a question yawns. How was it that "Labor" came to be both fundamentally more important yet fundamentally less threatening to the American polity, to its newly created administrative state and its new ruling coalition?

An answer converges from two directions: (1) transformations in the macrodynamics of national politics culminating in the crystallization of a new political elite whose prescriptions for economic reform and recovery mated well with the social psychology and organizational imperatives of the new labor movement; (2) profound, if largely invisible, revolutions in the micropolitics of production and consumption, in the very anthropological framework of working-class life out of which the 'labor question' originally arose.

*　*　*

When, in the era of World War I, workers all over the world raised the cry for workers' control, they did so from the standpoint of a skilled elite (both industrial and pre-industrial) whose whole way of life was threatened with extinction, or at least marginalization, by the new forces of Fordism and Taylorism. But artisanal and industrial craftsmen were not the only ones to challenge the prevailing system of authority at work. 'Industrial democracy', a rubric as evocative and imprecise as "workers' control" but considerably more respectable, commanded equally widespread attention. The war and postwar period turned out to be the occasion for a plethora of experiments in redesigning the architecture of power at the workplace and even beyond the workplace. Works councils, shop delegates, profit sharing, corporate parliaments, all inspired visions, some would say delusions, of social partnership, of a new democratic dispensation where once the martial imperatives of coercive hierarchy commanded obedience.

The *New Republic*, aware that democracy was being subjected to "tests of unprecedented severity throughout the world," concluded that democracy's future "depends . . . upon the capacity of employers and workers to harmonize democratic ideals of freedom with the voluntary self-discipline essential to efficient production."[5] Industrial democrats like Felix Frankfurter were at pains to point out the need for independent vehicles of working-class representation. A community of progressive jurists and liberal-minded industrial engineers, along with circles of politically active businessmen, sought ways of restoring some sense of democratic participation to the otherwise stultifying regime of mass production, a regime that could no longer take for granted the submissiveness of its subjects. Ludlow and Lawrence before the war, Seattle and Pittsburgh after it, marked the longitude and latitude of a new geopolitics of class where armed confrontations, immigrant risings, municipal general strikes, and mass industrial unionism menaced the terrain. Equally unsettling, if less visible, was the disintegration of the traditional system of patrimonial authority of departmental foremen in mass production industries like auto where the costs of instability were becoming exorbitant, especially among the growing class of semiskilled workers. Somewhere, it was hoped, amid all the contending blueprints for industrial democracy, was a well-designed escape from "the bitterness of class war and the horrors that have paralyzed Russia."[6]

Notwithstanding the thousand and one subtle nuances of meaning, 'industrial democracy' was an idea whose time had come—or so it seemed. Yet so much was expected by so many from this proposed marriage of industry and democracy that no one could with confidence predict the health or longevity of the offspring, or, for that matter, whether a marriage subject to so many crosscutting desires might not fall apart without issue. Thus, industrial democracy might conceivably evolve as a new system of domination, that snare and delusion warned of by the Wobblies and cynically plotted by more hard-boiled industrialists. For those radical and skilled denizens of the modern factory, however, carriers of a democratic and egalitarian tradition already generations old, industrial democracy plausibly promised an end to hierarchy, centralized authority, and the degrading fragmentation of skills; it seemed, in a phrase, a new vehicle of liberation. For a heterogeneous milieu of personnel managers, social workers, efficiency experts, labor relations professionals, and social science academics; for socialists whose watchword was progress and progressives whose shibboleth was social partnership; for reformers loyal to the hoary tenets of antimonopoly politics and reformers like Frankfurter and Brandeis who deployed the populist rhetoric of antimonopoly to express an entirely new industrial dispensation; and for a small circle of socially conscious trade unionists, industrial democracy suggested a social compromise, the 'British way', a new system of integration for a society so explosively fractious it sometimes seemed, in the superheated atmosphere of war and revolution, on the verge of disintegration.

II

The Taylor Society, the institutional home of scientific management, had drifted steadily to the left during and after the war. Until Taylor's death in 1915, the American "science of management" was very much management's science. It was elitist and totalitarian in spirit, evincing a kind of nineteenth-century Stakhanovism whose Benthamite utilitarian psychology lacked any sense of the need for cultural transformation arising out of the destruction of craft and peasant cultures.

After Taylor's death the Society's formal conception of the industrial polity became increasingly syndicalist, envisioning the democratic integration of functional groups in a rationalized production system. Industrial relations mediators like William Leiserson, personnel managers like Meyer Jacobstein, scientific management consultants like Harlow Person, all of whom would play conspicuous roles in the labor politics of the New Deal, knew that the era of the "Prussian method" needed to end. Industrial authority should rest on the consent of the governed, so to speak, not merely because that was only fitting in a society so saturated in the maxims of liberalism, but because those precious psychic and social energies unleashed by the process of autonomous, self-imposed discipline were simply not reachable through the imperious command of others.

Their outlook tended to converge with that of certain progressive trade unionists—Sidney Hillman particularly, who was lionized by progressives everywhere as the architect of a 'new unionism'. Within the men's clothing industry Hillman helped fashion a new system of labor relations that embraced scientific management on condition that it be accompanied and accomplished by mechanisms of democratic—that is, union—control. Hillman, in collaboration with leading members of the Taylor Society, especially Cooke, Otto Beyer, and Harlow Person, as well as Frankfurter and economist Leo Wolman, sought both to introduce the rule of law on the shop floor—a constitutional order for labor-management relations—and install scientifically determined standards of production, formulated and agreed to by all parties. What really made the 'new unionism' new, and so appealing, however, was Hillman's distinctive genius for translating the axioms of industrial democracy into the lingua franca of dozens of shop-floor ethno-cultures.[7]

Up until this time, the new science of personnel management was deployed almost exclusively among the English-speaking skilled craftsmen. The immigrant unskilled were left to the less subtle ministrations of the "Prussian method." People like Leiserson and Cooke were convinced that the 'new unionism' of the ACW opened up an incomparably more felicitous avenue of acculturation and socialization by inviting the participation of the new immigrant working class in a controlled system of trade union and industrial decision making. They rejected both the facile belief in some natural harmony between Labor and Capital as well as the fatalism that conflict between them was inevitable and irreconcilable. This new techno-managerial and social science milieu saw in the formal procedures of industrial democracy a way "to obtain the consent of employees to their continued participation in the further development of the capitalist mode." What was required, then, was not only a major reform in the organizational mechanics and jurisprudence of industrial labor relations, but a root-and-branch transformation in the social and psychological dynamics of the workplace.[8]

Cooke not only encouraged the growth of particular trade unions, but proposed the creation of national unions to facilitate planning in the economy at large. Moreover, Cooke's version of economic planning—in contradistinction to the artificial scarcities achieved or at least hoped for by trade associations and oligopolies in older industrial sectors—assumed that "in itself any increase in the production of essential commodities is a desirable social end." Consequently, in the twenties the Taylor Society became the crossroads for a set of newer, mass-consumption-oriented industries—mass merchandisers like Filenes and Macy's; urban real estate developers like the Greenfield interests in Philadelphia; newer investment banks that underwrote the mass consumer sector like Lehman Brothers and Goldman, Sachs; mass-consumer-oriented banks with diversified investments in real estate, fire insurance, furniture, lumber, the movies, agricultural finance, and various consumer services like Bank of America and the Bowery Savings Bank; industries like clothing, housing construction and supplies, dry goods, office equipment and supplies, appliances; capital goods suppliers to mass market producers; a wide variety of producer service organizations including management consultants and foundations—all associated with the exponential growth in the size and depth of the urban mass market.[9]

Cooke's 1928 presidential address to the Taylor Society anticipated the next decade's agenda of industrial reform: "The interests of society—including those of the workers—suggest some measure of collective bargaining. . . . Effective collective bargaining implies the organization of the workers on a basis extensive enough—say nation-wide—as to make this bargaining power effective." Inevitably, he argued, in an economic world of complex interdependence, one populated with "national trade organizations; national and even international standards and sales syndicates; the vertical and horizontal integration of widely different industries, inter-industry research organizations; and in 'combinations' of one sort and another," adversarial industrial relations must "gradually give way" and labor organizations would be given "that functional status in the industrial process which is now denied." It was essential, from the standpoint of effective management, Cooke maintained, "to look upon some organization of the workers, such as labor unions, as a deep social need."

In this "new day of scientific management, high wages and standards of living, mass production, quick changes, cooperation, mechanical improvement," it was necessary to have strong labor organizations "ready to grapple with any group of employers guilty either of cupidity or industrial illiteracy." A mass-consumption economy and culture, Cooke noted, was recasting the immemorial struggle between the haves and the have-nots. It was no longer a matter of "the full dinner pail," but "the full garage"; now gasoline rather than bread and perhaps later a "share in the world's highest culture" were at stake. Cooke was equally alert to the dangers of "craft sectarianism and job separatism" that plagued the AFL, making it averse to any kind of organizational experimentation. The organized labor movement was compelled to adjust or perish.[10]

As a premonition of the main organizational, economic, and political objectives of the new labor movement one could scarcely ask for more—or from someone better positioned to simultaneously assess the internal dynamics of labor and industry. One can say more. A decade before Flint and the Memorial Day Massacre, a Great Depression away from the general strikes of Minneapolis and San Francisco, several AFL conventions prior to John L. Lewis's celebrated assault on William Hutcheson, the CIO already existed. It existed, that is, strictly as a managerial-political formation. On the eve of the depression it had a strategy—national industrial unionism; a social perspective—functional integration within a finely reticulated, interdependent economy of complex, large-scale bureaucratic organizations; a political economy—planned, expanded production and state-sanctioned redistribution of income in the interests of security and consumption; a general staff—not only Hillman and Lewis but their key economic and social engineering advisers including Cooke, Jett Lauck, Harlow Person, and Leiserson; a cadre school—Brookwood—where such key future CIO operatives as Kathryn Pollack Ellickson, John Brophy, Eli Oliver, David Saposs, and dozens of anonymous trade union militants, who would go on to become the organizers of the Steel Workers Organizing Committee, the Packinghouse Workers Organizing Committee, the Textile Workers Organizing Committee, and the like either taught or studied; and an ideology—industrial democracy, the Marxism of the professional middle class, wise to the class antinomies of industrial society but sanguine enough to believe in their pacific supersession by science and abundance.[11]

Most fundamentally, the CIO already existed as an embryonic strategic alliance, its incipient leadership already integrated, via the left wing of the scientific management movement, into the political circles around Frankfurter and Brandeis. These circles included such potentially potent influentials as Senators Norris, Wagner, and La-Follette; lawyer activists outside the labor movement including Tom Corcoran and Ben Cohen, and those already or soon to be invited inside the family of labor, including Lee Pressman, Max Lowenthal, Nathan Witt; and progressive social and political activists such as Frances Perkins and Harold Ickes. Those political relationships also entailed ties to institutional networks of businessmen, labor-minded social scientists, and unorthodox economists gathered around the Twentieth Century Fund and Russell Sage Foundation, or, like Waddill Catchings and William T. Foster, associated with consumer-oriented investment houses. While something far less coherent than a shadow government, it was nonetheless a new political elite whose legislative and administrative innovations during the second New Deal would decisively shape the political and economic ecology within which the CIO would discover its niche.

III

Yet what made all the political scheming and social dreaming so agonizingly imprecise was that no one had any really firm idea of just what the message of industrial democracy meant—at ground level—first of all to those politically alert circles of industrial artisans; second, to the newest and fastest growing species of industrial labor, the semiskilled machine tender; last, to the massed, silent armies of the new immigrant working class. Indeed, especially in the last case, no one could even be sure the message had penetrated their ranks at all.

From the standpoint of the craft militant, the advent of bureaucratic-hierarchical management atop a system of mass, semiskilled production represented a root-and-branch expropriation of his social existence and identity. Partisans of workers' control movements, certainly the most uncompromising of industrial democrats, resisted both before and after the war the inexorable processes of de-skilling and the evisceration of what has been called the "culture of control." Ushered in by scientific management, with its chronometry, its impersonally determined and externally imposed piece rates, bonus systems, and job ladders, its ingenious designs for serial production to be undertaken by a whole new class of semiskilled operatives, this new industrial order promised the social extermination of a whole social species. In this beleaguered world, the 'labor question' remained what it had always been since the heyday of the social gospel in the Gilded Age and earlier—not only or even primarily a class question, but a moral one, a matter of autonomous manhood, of redemptive brotherhood and communal rebirth.[12]

All of this had very little to do with the toils and troubles of those old-world peasants suffering the irremediable process of marginalization. For Italian, Polish, and southeast European casual laborers and unskilled factory operatives, who poured in and out of the country in extraordinary numbers until the war ended transatlantic travel, the ideology of productive labor and the program of workers' control exerted little appeal. In the heart of Pennsylvania steel country, eastern European immigrants remained old-country "worker-farmers," tending and in part subsisting on their small garden plots. Arriving from decomposing peasant societies, they were already familiar with mobile, migratory agricultural and urban wage labor and the cash economy. But the experience was so recent and unsettling that the desire for survival, security, and above all for landholding remained potent. Wages in the New World were hoarded in the hope of reproducing the valued landed social structure of the Old. Socially, these cultures in transit remained profoundly deferential.[13]

Indeed, for the most recently arrived unskilled, who lacked political perspective or experience with voluntary, non-kinship-based organizational life—without a vision of the industrial world put together differently—resistance to industrial society was only outwardly similar to that of their more skilled and assimilated co-workers. Their strikes—Lawrence before the war, the steel strike immediately after it—more closely resembled episodic communal rebellions—peasant jacqueries or the rising of the fascio in Sicily—than they did acts rooted in the immediate experience of work itself. These prospective "citizens of industry," even as they became naturalized citizens in the 1920s, were concerned less with the procedural formalities of industrial due process, and more with securing the ancient attachments of kin and community corroded by the factory and the market. For them the moral codes of industrial democracy—the spiritual hygiene of disciplined work, economic group and individual self-interest, the iniquity of ascribed values—were at first less than compelling.[14]

In the end, however, the power of industrial rationalization proved ineluctable. The worlds of the impassive peasant and craft militant were undermined utterly, especially during and after the war as the regime of mass production extended its reach across the industrial landscape. The gap between them closed, or rather was filled by a new generation of workers, bound neither to the communal republicanism of the skilled elite nor to the patriarchal traditionalism of the Old World.

During the two decades preceding the depression the very category of common labor and its ganglike structure became far less common. Attention was reoriented to the individual's performance. A new species of semiskilled machine tender emerged, whose work demanded a new repertoire of talents—judgment, observation, control, and measurement, as opposed to the undifferentiated routines of the unskilled. The electrification of production, observed Cooke and Philip Murray, created a new emphasis on "sustained attention; correct perception, quick reaction"; on nervous poise and intelligent coordination. By its very nature such work was subject to more systematic and finely tuned external control and monitoring, at which scientific management excelled; it also elicited new habits at and away from work. Together with the alchemic powers of the mass market and mass culture, whose impact on the desires and behavior of the second-generation immigrant was already conspicuous by the 1920s, it helped fashion the new labor force. And it was precisely this new species, the heterogeneous and more individuated precipitate of various traditional ethno-occupational milieux—often the urbanized sons of immigrants and urbanized blacks as well as "native" Protestant workers—who, precisely because they had lost their anchorages in the closed cultural world of kin, craft, community, and culture, became the natural constituency of industrial democracy and the CIO.[15]

The rise of the semiskilled worker, organically connected to the processes of mass production, did not of course entail the instantaneous obliteration of the industrial and urban crafts. Tool and die makers, die setters, and factory maintenance mechanics, for example, persisted and resisted the ravages of the depressed economy. In the auto and electrical industries, tool and die makers and machinists especially comprised the indispensable cadre of the new industrial unions, the UAW and the UE. If semiskilled operators comprised the CIO's mass constituency, it was a certain kind of skilled worker, experienced politically as well as in trade union matters, who supplied the movement's élan and organizational genius.[16]

But skilled workers comprised a milieu heterogeneous in background. They included both production and nonproduction workers. Some were quite secular and even anticlerical; others were attracted by liberal currents of Catholic social thought then deeply dividing the church.

Often in the United States for several generations, or immigrants from the British isles, skilled workers frequently were experienced trade unionists, and not infrequently acquainted with some version of radical labor or nationalist politics—the Pan-Slavic revolutionary nationalism of the Serbs and Croats, for example, or the syndicalism of Italian artisans or the belligerent atheism of Lithuanian or Bohemian "free thinkers." And yet their motivations were often at the same time deeply conservative. The depression, and the accompanying downgrading of skilled jobs (both with respect to pay and job content), presented a mortal threat to their social status, about which they were acutely conscious: "We were just part of the common mass, you might say. And that's what got us really thinking a lot about unionism," remembered an early UE activist. The locus of UAW support was often in body plants where de-skilling was intense among metal finishers and welders who were often responsible for the waves of quickie strikes and shop-floor struggles for control that followed the Flint sit-down. For such people the CIO, at least in part and particularly in its emphasis on meticulously defined seniority provisions, was a protective device with which to defend hard-won social position.[17]

While the machinists and tool and die makers of the UAW and UE invariably comprised the militant and radical democratic cadre of the CIO, other industrial craftsmen, especially among urban tradesmen and non-production-line workers, were more tradition-bound, less deracinated. Their status-consciousness was embedded in patterns of neighborhood, ethnic, and familial solidarity. For them, shop-floor politics were an extension of the politics of civil society. In even the most cosmopolitan and industrialized urban centers—the "Back of the Yards" neighborhood of Chicago, for example, or in the more isolated, self-absorbed ethnic worlds of Pennsylvania steel towns with their own saloons, groceries, butchers, bankers, newspapers, and clothing stores—small-scale, self-contained ethnic social economies reproduced in relative isolation social hierarchies in which craftsmen enjoyed an honored position even if employed by the corporate world outside the ethnic community. Members of the Steelworkers Independent Union, for instance, men of skill and self-conscious dignity, were also opposed to the centralizing tendencies of industrial unionism and were bound up in the exclusionary fraternal world of the Knights of Pythias. In Flint, a self-conscious labor aristocracy dating from the carriage- and wagon-making era maintained close relations with the local business elite and was separated by a wide gulf of material possessions, social status, and security from the emerging migratory milieu of southeastern Europeans and Appalachians.[18]

The influence of these skilled traditionalists on shop-floor politics extended far beyond their own circle, precisely because of their social and cultural hegemony within the circumscribed universe of working-class neighborhood and ethnic life. Within the factory, first-generation unskilled immigrants—for whom work was an unadulterated curse from which they withdrew into the worlds of the tavern and fraternal lodge and the family's religious and secular rituals—were tied by customary relations of deference to their skilled, more worldly brethren. The very sociotechnical structure of industrial work gangs reinforced traditional deferential relations because of the nearly absolute power exercised by skilled gang leaders over the nature, duration, and pace of work, which imparted an intimidating vulnerability to the work experience of these immigrants. A network of authority thus linked the top and the bottom of the occupational hierarchy and generated in certain respects a deeply conservative community with an abiding respect for the institutions of private property, if not capitalism. After all, most Slavic and Italian peasant immigrants hailed from areas of marginal, small-scale, not latifundist agriculture, where the sense of property rights remained strong. For many, the fatalism, restricted mobility, patriarchy, and moral and educational parochialism of the old-world village were reinforced by the exigencies of industrial and urban life.[19]

For a long time, these hierarchical and organic relationships had defined the internal political dynamics of many AFL unions. The CIO insurgency immediately threatened the customary power and prestige of these shop-floor elites. New occupational groupings of semi-skilled machine tenders were themselves often ambitious, eager to perform a variety of jobs and advance up the job ladder. Ambitiousness about work—they "wanted better jobs, cleaner, mechanized, with some skills"—extended into the realm of consumption. Such ambitions were threatened by the depression. Especially as the wage differential between skilled, often German and Irish, tradesmen and the semiskilled narrowed, the former sensed a threat to established patterns of power and status, a mortal threat to the prerogatives of a craft-based and ethnically homogeneous elite self-conscious about its purported racial and cultural superiority.[20]

Meanwhile, the newer, historically more fluid sector of the shop floor—the semiskilled—was more ethnically dissociated, less enmeshed within networks of kin and community. For second-generation Italians, for example, the structures of patriarchal authority were already decomposing through exposure to schools and work outside the family and community. And, if anything, southern Italians tended to be more village oriented and less mobile than many Slovaks, Rumanians for example, among whom nationalism had some time ago supplanted more parochial attachments. Among various Slavic populations the courtship and marriage patterns of the second generation became noticeably less rigid and endogamous. Neighborhood ethnic parishes were gradually "Americanized" as old-country feasts, distinct village liturgies, local patron saints, and processionals were replaced by a more austere and devotional sacramental orthodoxy. The workplace became a site of resentment as the universalist criteria of merit and individual performance clashed with the real structures of racial-ethnic authority: "We didn't want to live like Hunkies anymore . . . treated like trash." Quintessentially urban, with a functional and instrumental but not existential relationship to their work, far more integrated as consumers into the mass market and more influenced by the media of mass culture than their parents, this new species of worker came closer to resembling Marx's "proletariat"—rootless, dispossessed, functionally interchangeable—than anything yet seen in America.[21]

Precisely because they were often alienated from the extended family, excluded from the charmed circle of craft, and instead integrated into the public worlds of work and citizenship more by bureaucratic than by primordial ties, they were receptive to the message of industrial unionism. However, the CIO might have remained little more than a general staff and officers corps without the electrifying electoral victory of 1936, which unleashed a mass movement of unprecedented militance and tactical boldness.

IV

The mass political mobilization of the thirties, enlisting legions of new voters from among the new immigrant working class (both in its first and second generations) and shaking the Democratic party to its foundations, should be considered ontologically prior to the mass labor struggles of the period. Even the great strikes of 1933–34—Minneapolis, San Francisco, Toledo, the textile general strike—and the near general strikes in auto and steel, even the waves of union organization that crested and receded under the frail wings of the Blue Eagle, were themselves politically inspired—inspired particularly by the NRA's clause 7a, which Lewis compared with the Emancipation Proclamation. Strikes and union organizing were in effect attempts to implement purported presidential policy.[22]

Labor—its leadership as well as its rank and file—looked to Washington, sensing that its fate hinged on the outcome of great struggles between contending elites for control of the new government and its administrative machinery. By mid-1935, when the Supreme Court's *Schecter* decision outlawed the NRA, the outlook was grim. The AFL's timidity demoralized thousands initially excited by 7a, while the political paralysis that plagued the anodyne recovery administration crippled whatever real potential it may have once possessed to improve labor standards and encourage unionization. But if *Schecter* seemed a declaration of war from the Right, it also served to mobilize the "keynesian" left, those mass-consumption-oriented political and business circles on the left wing of the New Deal. Simultaneously, populist and third-party movements proliferated, pressuring a temporizing president to abandon efforts at mollifying the hysterical business and political old guard. Between mid-1935, beginning with Roosevelt's reluctant endorsement of the Wagner Act, through the great landslide of 1936—that is, before the emergence of the CIO as a mass organization—all the legislative essentials of the "second New Deal"—the Wagner Act, the Social Security Act, the second banking act, the public utility holding company act, the wealth tax act—were installed. It was that triumph, one that penetrated key administrative agencies and executive departments as well as vital congressional committees, which helped transform the CIO from a strategic blueprint into a mass movement.

The relationship between the "second New Deal" and the 'new unionism' was organic. Above all, the "welfare state" was expressly designed by its chief architects to encourage and stimulate mass consumption: state intervention in the labor market, along with the state's credit policy, urban renewal, and so on, were tactical devices for achieving that larger strategic purpose.

Frances Perkins put it well as early as 1933: "As a Nation, we are recognizing that programs long thought of as merely labor welfare, such as shorter hours, higher wages, and a voice in the terms and conditions of work, are really essential economic factors for recovery, and for the technique of industrial management in a mass production age."[23] Similarly, the Wagner Act was expressly designed, by the senator, his chief economic adviser Leon Keyserling, and Isador Lubin, a close associate of Hillman's, as a device with which to both civilize and stabilize the politics of production and as part of a more general economic recovery program premised on expanded mass consumption.[24]

Alexander Sachs, an economist once associated with Lehman Brothers, not only shared this sympathy with industrial unionism, but expressed well the broader struggle over the structure of the political economy of which it was a part. In a memorandum to General Johnson, critical of some of the corporatist-inspired thinking that would culminate in the NRA, he cited as causes of the depression "policies which had the effect of sterilizing wealth and credit resources" as well as a lack of flexibility and initiative on the part of large corporations "sicklied o'er by the pale case of laissez-faire and liquidity complexes." The federal government, he argued, ought to sponsor public works and credit for housing and consumer durables. He feared instead that what was to become the NRA would, like the German cartel system, have the effect of "congealing the inflated capital values of the speculative era."[25]

The "speculative era" had long been the bête noire of the circle of lawyer-politicians gathered around Frankfurter and Brandeis. People like Benjamin Cohen, Thomas Corcoran, James Landis, and others, had never been wide-eyed worshipers of the free market. Beginning with Brandeis, they had all represented large corporations and investment houses—although invariably ones outside the orbit of the Morgan and Kuhn Loeb interests. Brandeis and Frankfurter, as architects of industrial democracy, maintained working relations with the Taylor Society and mounted their critique of overbearing corporate power in part from the standpoint of its strangulating inefficiencies. They shared a much more sophisticated view about the relationship between technology and economic concentration, while retaining a wise skepticism about the morals and motives of old-style corporate managements. For them, federal coercion was an unavoidable part of an assault, expressed ultimately in securities and banking and utilities legislation, on an older, entrenched bloc of infrastructural and primary goods industries and their financial allies in the investment banking community—circles committed to the open shop and opposed to the redistributive implications of a mass-consumption economy. This "securities bloc" was responsible in their eyes for the economic arteriosclerosis referred to by Sachs.[26]

The CIO strategists, including not only Hillman but Jett Lauck, Lewis's principal adviser on broad matters of political economy, shared this view about the relationships between industrial unionism and the restructuring of the political economy. Having played a significant role in the drafting of the NRA's labor provisions, Lauck's advice to Lewis during the fateful years of the middle thirties emphasized the need for government intervention and regulation to expand production, redistribute income, and expand mass purchasing power and government credit. And in 1934 he broached the idea of the UMW leaving the AFL to start a new labor federation.[27]

From Lauck's point of view, the politics of production were but one element in a social and political chemistry of greater complexity: the emergence of modern centralized industrial unions rooted in mass production, informed by modern managerial strategy, developing within the context of mass culture and consumption, and linked to a reform government in the national arena, was the framework within which the more intimate battles of the factory floor and union hall would take place. If the CIO helped fabricate a "new man"—existentially mobile, more oriented to consumption than production, familiar with the impersonal rights and responsibilities of industrial due process—then this new social identity was inconceivable apart from a political elite in command of the state, committed to a program of enlarged government spending, financial reform, and redistributive taxation, presiding over a reconstituted coalition in the realm of mass politics.

The CIO's debt to Roosevelt was thus from the very beginning greater than the president's obligations to the CIO—and the new labor leadership knew it. The CIO of course staunchly supported all the administration's labor and welfare initiatives, and often from a distinctly keynesian point of view. Its loyalty to Roosevelt was practically unconditional. It even included the administration's most bitterly contested attempts at court-packing and executive reorganization designed to strengthen the youthful agencies of the administrative state against enemies in Congress and the judiciary. When Lewis and Hillman created Labor's Non-Partisan League to politically mobilize industrial workers on behalf of Roosevelt's reelection in 1936, they did so in full consultation with, if not at the behest of, the administration's chief political operatives, including Farley, Berle, and Frankfurter. There was a real spiritual compatibility as well. At this, the zenith of the New Deal's reform zeal, the language of labor and the language of executive power were indistinguishable; the Non-Partisan League excoriated the "manipulators of other people's money and the exploiters of other people's labor" and proclaimed a "battle of the masses against the classes, of the people against the economic royalists."[28]

This concordance of views and interests permeated the proliferating agencies of the new administrative state. The Labor Department under Perkins was of course sympathetic. She was largely responsible for Hillman's initial elevation to a position of national political prominence under the NRA. Senator LaFollette, a longtime proponent of collective bargaining and keynesian reform of the political economy, used his subcommittee on civil liberties to actively aid CIO organizing drives. The subcommittee's chief counsel, John Abt, was close to the CP and would subsequently become Hillman's personal legal counsel. Subcommittee personnel conferred regularly with CIO cadre on the timing and content of testimony designed to expose the tyrannical and violent practices of the country's leading industrial corporations, especially in the steel industry. Job-hopping between the civil liberties committee, the NLRB, and the SWOC was common.[29]

Above all, the NLRB embodied this marriage of New Deal and new labor movement. It was conceived and administered to promote industrial unionism and at the national level was populated by sympathizers like Edwin Smith, Saposs, Nathan Witt, and others. The board's jurisdictional rulings openly favored the CIO and infuriated the AFL. Most galling and threatening to the preeminence of the AFL's skilled elite was the board's definition of the ideal bargaining unit as the largest practicable one. No wonder that AFL sachem Frey bitterly remarked to board chairman Madden early in 1937 that "there is an impression growing every day that your agents are definitely CIO."[30]

From the fall of 1936 through the summer of 1937 the industrial insurgency from below—beginning with the Flint sit-down and spreading irresistibly from sector to sector and city to city—moved in synchrony with the reform impulse from above. By mid-1937 the state agencies responsible for human capital and infrastructural development, for planning and for regulating the flow of public and private credit, were run by this newly empowered keynesian elite: the Labor Department under Perkins and the Interior Department under Ickes; the NLRB, and the agencies of relief and public works under Hopkins; the National Resources Planning Board run by Beardsley Ruml and Frederick Delano; the REA under Cooke and John Carmody; the various housing and mortgage finance agencies; and of course the Federal Reserve under the keynesian tutelage of Marriner Eccles. Together they comprised the "welfare state." And it was this "state" that the CIO-LNPL leadership exalted.

V

But other regions of the executive branch, not to mention substantial portions of the Congress, state legislatures, and municipal governments remained hostile to this new public policy perspective and program. Moreover, the mass-consumption–industrial-unionism strategy had yet to win a following among a great mass of entrepreneurs and wide sections of the middle class. Thus, the state itself became a locus of activity for contending elites, for the suddenly articulate armies of the shop floor, for the organizational dynamics of electoral politics and the brute force of the marketplace. It was a dangerously centerless system, tending toward dispersion. Any shift in the fortunes of the new regime would immediately reverberate within the CIO.

As the reaction against the Roosevelt administration set in, more or less coincident with the deep recession of 1937–38, it was apparent that the rise of the New Deal and the CIO were generating powerful countercurrents within the working class. The fratricidal civil war that erupted within the infant UAW between the Homer Martin faction and those tenuously allied groups led by cadre from the Socialist and Communist parties was symptomatic. The Martin group was diverse. There were Appalachian migrants raised on fundamentalist religion and racism who, once in Detroit, were sometimes recruited into the ranks of the Black Legion and Ku Klux Klan and evinced a deep, almost racial-religious, antipathy to the Polish Catholics of the city's industry. There was as well a heavy admixture of Coughlinite urban, Irish and German Catholics, largely mechanics, carpenters, electricians, and plumbers, first organized in 1934 with Father Coughlin's help through the Automotive Industrial Workers Association, centered in Chrysler's Dodge Division. They were elitist and attracted by the corporate authoritarianism of the Little Flower's priest.[31]

Martin's following evinced a deep antipathy toward the more secular, cosmopolitan, racially mixed, and often anticlerical if not irreligious, milieu under the radical leaderships of the socialist Reuther brothers and Adolph Germer or the Communist caucus led by George Addes and Wyndam Mortimer. Martin played on such anxieties in speeches and radio addresses that accused the CIO leadership of being tied "directly to Moscow."[32]

As the case of Homer Martin also suggests, the anthropological fault line not only divided the CIO from the AFL but ran straight through the CIO itself. In the eyes of old-stock German, Irish, and other skilled workers—tradesmen as well as nonproduction factory craftsmen—often tied to traditional urban Democratic party machines, the threatening rise of the semiskilled workers within the political hierarchy of production was closely associated with the ascendancy of the new immigrant within the New Deal Democratic party. At the same time, other more cosmopolitan circles of skilled production workers—secular and sometimes politically radical—tended to push the mass movement of the semiskilled to the left. These social anxieties created fissures within all the main CIO unions and erected definite boundaries beyond which the CIO leadership dared not venture politically. The congressional uproar over the wave of sit-down strikes helped focus a pervasive atmosphere of anti-Communist, anti-CIO sentiment that was most pronounced in, but not confined to, the traditional old-stock Catholic skilled milieu. It infected as well the younger, second-generation Catholic semiskilled production workers. Frequently, CIO organizers appealed to liberal Catholics like Father Francis Haas to use their influence among local priests in St. Louis, in the auto centers of Michigan, and elsewhere to counteract anti-Communist–CIO propaganda.[33]

Susceptibility to the politics of anticommunism was, then, a function of a deeper estrangement from the rational-materialist posture of the CIO leadership and its allies in the left wing of the Democratic party. The CIO effort to integrate blacks into its industrial and political coalition—its active campaigns for equal rights on and off the job—further exacerbated these tensions. The child labor provisions of the CIO-supported Fair Labor Standards Act incited the opposition of the Catholic Church, always sensitive to state intrusions into family life and parochial school education, and further estranged sections of the Catholic working class.[34]

The CP and its most conspicuous CIO cadre and sympathizers thus became the lightning rod for animosities that had little to do with the party's loyalties to the Soviet Union. Ironically, then, anticommunism as a mass movement was profoundly anticapitalist insofar as it rebelled against the corporate, bureaucratic, centralizing, and statist tendencies of the modern industrial order. With equal irony "communism" in America only counted in the arithmetic of national and local politics to the degree it articulated the central assumptions and aspirations of the CIO and the New Deal.

This rainbow of social and cultural anxieties severely limited the political influence and perspective of the CIO. Noteworthy is the fact that a labor movement with a reputation for radicalism took no sides in the Spanish civil war. Practically, if not rhetorically, the leadership

retreated quickly from the tactical and political riskiness of the sit-
down strike. Differences between Lewis and Hillman emerged over
whether to sue for peace with the AFL. Meanwhile, that bitter rivalry
continued. While immediately a matter of organizational turf, it was
aggravated by deeper historical divisions. The tendency of old-stock,
Catholic, craft-based groups to vote against the New Deal–CIO alliance became pronounced in the 1938 congressional elections. By
mid-1938 the AFL launched an industrial counteroffensive, sponsor-
ing splits from the CIO in textile and in auto (where Homer Martin
rejoined the AFL) as well as a breakaway from the National Maritime
Union and even a "Progressive Miners" group to aggravate Lewis.
Simultaneously, an alliance of the AFL and the NAM (in particular, the
lawyers for the adamantly anti-union little steel companies) worked
assiduously to undermine the NLRB and the Wagner Act itself.[35]

Lewis's mounting exasperation with Roosevelt, first surfacing in
his angry denunciation of the president's disingenuous neutrality in
the Little Steel strike, dramatized the CIO's predicament. How quickly
the balance of forces had shifted. The SWOC, which had boomed after
the Roosevelt landslide, was deeply demoralized and withering away
by late 1937. Similarly, when the LNPL was first formed, the ground
swell of reform sentiment emboldened Hillman and Lewis to keep
alive, if only rhetorically, the possibility of an independent labor
party. To be sure, the first priority was Roosevelt's reelection, without
which fascism might triumph in America. Hillman made it clear that
labor only stood a chance politically if it talked "not Marxism, but
economic power" to the masses of the people. Still, he boldly announced himself "satisfied . . . we are laying the foundations for a
labor party."[36]

Just months later Gardner Jackson, New Deal functionary and adviser to Lewis, was worrying about how to offset the bad publicity
about violence and irresponsibility that was clearly hurting the CIO,
not only among middle-class people but within the ranks of the CIO
itself. By 1939, Murray was telling the CIO executive board, "We are
living in a wave and an age and an era of reaction." By the middle of
1940, Lee Pressman was reporting to that same board that "within
the past few weeks we have had to shift our emphasis from attempting to obtain new legislation to bending all efforts to defend the legislative protection which we now enjoy."[37]

It was the effort to crack the Solid South, politically and industri-
ally, that most tellingly revealed the inherent limitations of the New
Deal–CIO alliance. The Textile Workers Organizing Committee was
created when the second New Deal and the CIO were riding high, in

the spring of 1937. In the South, moreover, they depended utterly upon each other. Hillman's strategy as TWOC chairman (about which Lewis was dubious) was in part predicated on the political assistance of the administration through the NLRB as well as LaFollette's civil liberties subcommittee and those congressional Democrats promoting fair labor standards legislation aimed principally at the Southern textile industry. Meanwhile, the Roosevelt administration took steps to purge the Southern wing of the party of its conservative opponents, who, together with a revived Republican party, were managing to stalemate New Deal initiatives in Congress. The LNPL devoted itself to the defeat of these Southern reactionaries in the '38 primaries. The purge, the Fair Labor Standards Act, and TWOC's mass organizing campaign would together, it was hoped, recast the Democratic party, making of it an unequivocal instrument of economic and social reform.

This was political strategy at its grandest, since its success was predicated on the deliberate transformation of the South's political and social structure. Unionizing the South's key industry, textiles, together with the passage of minimum wages and hours legislation (the FLSA was drafted by Cohen, Corcoran, and Frankfurter in consultation with Hillman) would transform the closed Southern labor market and help break the political stranglehold of the planter and merchant-manufacturer oligarchy. Corcoran in particular thought the bill would shatter the monopoly of Southern Democratic politics by older corporate interests—the railroads and public utilities especially.[38]

The results proved far less grand than the strategy. The traditional patriarchal structures of Southern authority—the communal, small-town alliance of press, pulpit, property, and racial populism—survived. Although TWOC got off to a promising start, by the middle of 1938 it was collapsing all over the South as the recession made textile workers desperate and afraid. Roosevelt's purge was at best a partial success. The Fair Labor Standards Act did finally, although barely, manage to overcome a tenacious congressional opposition, an opposition that included the AFL, which refused to support the administration's bill even though Roosevelt designated it priority legislation. But the bill created a real wedge between the CIO-LNPL and the farmers lobby, which feared its impact on agricultural wages. The emasculated result was an act that exempted millions of workers from its coverage—only one-fifth of the work force fell under its provisions—while establishing the most minimal standards for those it did include; only 325,000 workers stood to benefit immediately from the act's initial twenty-five-cent minimum wage.[39]

VI

The FLSA was the last "act" of the New Deal. Soon the war in Europe would put a period to an era of reform, but not all at once. There were wartime battles in Congress and within the labyrinthine bureaucracy of home-front mobilization over who was to control the vastly expanded domestic economy. Meanwhile, all throughout the war the shop floor remained a contested arena where resentments about the inequalities of sacrifice demanded of industrial workers exploded in outlaw strikes in defiance of the CIO leadership. In retrospect, however, the drift of events seems unmistakable. The war demanded the suppression of unresolved social conflict and opened up all the state agencies of economic mobilization to the dominating influence of large-scale corporate interests. Lewis resisted and finally broke with Roosevelt officially in 1940. Hillman was convinced, however, that there were no other options for labor outside the precincts of the Democratic party. He was willing to trust the fate of the CIO to Roosevelt even though, or perhaps because, both the CIO and the New Deal had lost a good deal of their forward momentum. He sought a permanent place for the industrial union movement as an institutional component of the New Deal state, a state no longer able to innovate in the area of social and economic reform. To achieve that recognized position, moreover, entailed a similar accommodation in the industrial arena.

The industrial relations compact worked out by the industrial union leadership and the scientific management–keynesian milieu provided for job security, formal democratic grievance and representation procedures, and high wages and benefits, all in return for shop-floor stability self-consciously achieved at the expense of the less formal practices of shop-floor democracy. Growing segments of the business community accepted that basic arrangement. By 1939 most of the legal and extralegal challenges to the essentials of the Wagner Act were over. Hillman testified at congressional hearings on amending the Wagner Act that core companies, including USS, GE, American Woolen, and RCA, had long ago recognized the wisdom of the act and its procedures for collective bargaining. Carle Conway, chairman of the board of Continental Can, delivered a reprise on the way corporate thinking had changed:

Certainly anyone who has been in business during [the past 30 years] would have to be naive to think that management by and large desired collective bargaining or certain of the other reforms which labor has finally won . . . But isn't it also likely that better understanding of the basic fundamentals involved in the struggle over the last thirty years between labor and management can work toward harmonizing the two viewpoints into a common objective and so make collective bargaining and many of the other reforms operate in the interests of both labor and management?[40]

Nor was it merely the giants of American industry that began to accept industrial unionism as a feature of modern management. In the late thirties many steel mills on the verge of bankruptcy began to cooperate with SWOC, particularly with Clinton Golden, a former organizer for the ACW's 'new unionism' in the twenties and a close associate of Philip Murray and Morris Cooke. In return for stabilized and secure employment, Golden showed how SWOC could improve productivity by sharing in the determination and enforcement of production standards, more or less exactly in the manner that the Amalgamated had first done after the war.[41]

Thus the common ground for a close collaboration between modern management and centralized industrial unionism emerged clearly by the end of the decade. The history of UAW–GM relations after the heroic battle at Flint is illustrative. Immediately after Flint there was considerable truth in the romantic image of the UAW as a union of shop-floor solidarity, militancy, and democratic participation. Because stewards were prepared to act boldly, to lead strikes if necessary, grievances were settled rapidly and workers' powers expanded without regard to contractual formalities. Neither the central leadership of the UAW nor, more important, the national leadership of the CIO—Lewis and his appointed deputies, Hillman and Philip Murray, who effectively ran UAW affairs in the late thirties—nor GM management found this tolerable. The union sought institutional stability and normalizing of the collective bargaining relationship. The corporation expected maintenance of order and discipline and recognition of its prerogatives. And so a second conflict that pitted the International Union and GM management against rank-and-file shop-floor organizers supplanted the more celebrated battle between union and corporation. The emerging bureaucracy of the UAW took steps to dismantle the shop steward system, reduced the authority of local unions while augmenting the power of the International, appended a no-strike and management rights clause to the contract, and perfected the modern grievance procedure and committee system.[42]

None of this constituted the betrayal of some sacred trust. If the more radical promises of the New Deal—to seriously redistribute income, to systematically socialize the care of the needy and unfit, to democratize the councils of industry and government, to uproot the iniquities of racial and social caste—fell short, they did so for reasons more deeply implanted within the dynamics of the national political economy and within the social chemistry of the CIO itself. Even in the early years of the New Deal, when mass and general strikes and rank-and-file self-organization made independent labor politics and radical versions of industrial democracy seem less than utopian, countercurrents within and outside of the labor movement pressed toward a more conservative resolution. The presumptive momentum of complex, bureaucratic organization, the imperatives of corporate-led economic stability and growth, and the increasing power of the mass market and mass production to dissolve the ties of social solidarity, were enough, even by themselves, to overwhelm whatever contrary impulses were given life by the trauma of economic collapse and social chaos.

Finally, to the extent that this capitalist trauma gave rise to a culture of resistance, that culture was itself often profoundly conservative even while ushering in a new age. Over and over again the CIO insisted that what it sought above all else, whether in negotiating contracts with employers or in pressing its demands for social welfare legislation, was security. As early as 1934 in a BBC address, Hillman characterized the "quest for security" as the "central issue in this life of modern man." Ten years later, as the CIO's Political Action Committee mobilized to defend the New Deal, it proclaimed: "As a result of this war and the victory that will be achieved at the conclusion of it we must move forward to a broader program of social and economic security for the men and women of this nation." The CIO turned out to be engaged in a great project to protect the individual and the nuclear family from the vicissitudes of modern industrial society. For that, the moral and millenarian enthusiasms once invoked by the 'labor question' were no longer appropriate.[43]

NOTES

1. Quoted in Philippa Strum, *Louis D. Brandeis: Justice for the People* (Cambridge: Harvard University Press, 1984), 103.
2. Quoted in John Milton Cooper, *The Warrior and the Priest: Woodrow*

Wilson and Theodore Roosevelt (Cambridge: Harvard University Press, 1983), 264.

3. Frederick Howe, *Confessions of a Reformer* (New York, 1925), cited in Stanley Shapiro, "The Great War and Reform: Liberals and Labor, 1917–19," *Labor History*.

4. *New Republic*, June 29, 1918.

5. *New Republic*, February 1, 1919.

6. Strum, *Louis D. Brandeis*, esp. chap. 10; *Public*, May 4, 1918, 556–57, cited in Shapiro, "The Great War." Personal forms of authority and control persisted among skilled production and nonproduction workers, as inherent in the exercise of these skills was an element of discretion and autonomy.

7. Steven Fraser, "Dress Rehearsal for the New Deal: Shop-Floor Insurgents, Political Elites, and Industrial Democracy in the Amalgamated Clothing Workers Union," in Michael Frisch and Daniel Walkowitz, eds., *Working-Class America* (Champaign: University of Illinois Press, 1983).

8. Christopher L. Tomlins, *The State and the Unions: Labor Relations, Law, and the Organized Labor Movement in America, 1880–1960* (New York: Cambridge University Press, 1985), 81.

9. Morris Cooke to Sidney Hillman, April 15, 1920, Sidney Hillman Papers, Labor Management Documentation Center, New York State School of Industrial and Labor Relations, Cornell University. Peter Friedlander, in his unpublished manuscript "The Origins of the Welfare State: The Keynesian Elite and the Second New Deal," presents pathbreaking research on this network of business and political associations. It informs a good deal of the analysis of this essay.

10. "Some Observations on Workers Organizations," Presidential Address to the Fifteenth Annual Meeting of the Taylor Society in New York City, box 62, folder A, Morris Cooke Papers, FDR Library, Hyde Park. Cooke had no patience with welfare capitalism or company unions, which he largely considered "fakes, pure and simple" (Cooke to Robert Bruere, July 10, 1928, box 2, file 14, Cooke Papers). Anyone failing to see the utility and necessity of independent collective bargaining was not a worthy associate: "I make collective bargaining as essential to the proper conduct of industrial organization as modern tools" (Cooke to Boyd Fisher, April 13, 1922, box 8, file 65, Cooke Papers).

11. Fraser, "Dress Rehearsal"; Jonathan D. Bloom, "Brookwood Labor College, 1921–33: Training Ground for Union Organizers" (M.A. thesis, New York University, 1978). Lewis's taste for scientific management cooperation schemes originated in the UMW's arrangements with the Rocky Mountain Fuel Company in Colorado under Josephine Roche, an associate of Frankfurter's.

12. David Montgomery, "The 'New Unionism' and the Transformation of Workers' Consciousness in America," *Journal of Social History* (Summer 1974); Carmen Sirianni, "Workers' Control in Europe: A Comparative Sociological Analysis," in James E. Cronin and Carmen Sirianni, eds., *Work, Community, and Power* (Philadelphia, Pa.: Temple University Press, 1983); Henry

Eilbert, "The Development of Personnel Management in the United States," *Business History Review* (Autumn 1959). Both John L. Thomas, *Alternative America: Henry George, Edward Bellamy, Henry Demarest Lloyd, and the Adversary Tradition* (Cambridge: Harvard University Press, 1983), and Nick Salvatore, *Eugene V. Debs: Citizen and Socialist* (Champaign: University of Illinois Press, 1982), reveal the threads connecting the language and political culture of labor radicalism in the Gilded Age to its subsequent socialist and syndicalist mutations in the twentieth century.

13. Ewa Morawska, *For Bread with Butter: Life-Worlds of East Central Europeans in Johnstown, Pennsylvania, 1890–1940* (New York: Cambridge University Press, 1985), is particularly good on this persistence amidst great change of old-world cultures.

14. Morawska, *For Bread with Butter*; Edwin Fenton, *Immigrants and Unions, A Case Study: Italians and American Labor, 1870–1920* (reprint, New York, 1957). For some eastern European immigrants, however, the war aroused a latent nationalism and a powerful identification with struggles for democracy and national liberation in their homelands.

15. Morris Cooke and Philip Murray, *Organized Labor and Production: Next Steps in Industrial Democracy* (New York: Harper and Brothers, 1940); David Gartman, *Auto Slavery: The Labor Process in the American Automobile Industry, 1897–1950* (New Brunswick, N.J.: Rutgers University Press, 1986), 173, notes that within the auto industry both craftsmen and laborers lost ground to the new class of semiskilled assemblers, machine tool and press operators, and "machine-minders."

16. Nelson Lichtenstein, *Labor's War At Home: The CIO in World War II* (New York: Cambridge University Press, 1982); Ronald Schatz, *The Electrical Workers: A History of Labor at GE and Westinghouse, 1923–60* (Champaign: University of Illinois Press, 1983); Peter Friedlander, *The Emergence of a UAW Local, 1936–39: A Study of Class and Culture* (Pittsburgh: University of Pittsburgh Press, 1975); and Gartman, *Auto Slavery*, are all illuminating on this set of issues. The UAW's carefully orchestrated tool and die makers' strike of 1939, deliberately limited to only these skilled militants, was arguably responsible for arresting the union's life-threatening decline after the heroic days of Flint.

17. Mel Piehl, *Breaking Bread: The Catholic Worker and the Origins of Catholic Radicalism in America* (Philadelphia, Pa.: Temple University Press, 1982), notes that the liberal Association of Catholic Trade Unionists led by Father Charles Owen Rice, adviser to Philip Murray, exerted significant influence among steel, auto, electrical, and transport workers (p. 61); Schatz, *The Electrical Workers*, 89; Friedlander, *The Emergence*; Ronald Edsforth, *Class Conflict and Cultural Consensus: The Making of a Mass Consumer Society in Flint, Michigan* (New Brunswick, N.J.: Rutgers University Press, 1987); Gartman, *Auto Slavery*, 173. The National Recovery Administration further exacerbated this threat as employers tried using wage codes particularly to turn minimum wages into maximums (see Charles R. Roos, *NRA: Economic Planning* [New York: Da Capo Press, 1971]).

18. Robert A. Slayton, *Back of the Yards: The Making of a Local Democracy* (Chicago: University of Chicago Press, 1986); Barbara Newell, *Chicago and the Labor Movement* (Champaign: University of Illinois Press, 1961); Edsforth, *Class Conflict.* It is noteworthy that Chicago remained an essentially AFL town with few sit-downs through the thirties and that the CIO was not publicly sanctioned by the city's Roman Catholic officialdom until 1939, and that the UE remained insignificant while the UAW was restricted to the city's parts plants (see Newell, *Chicago and the Labor Movement*, 115, 130, 150–51, 167–68, 180–81).

19. David Brody, "Labor and the Great Depression—Interpretive Prospects," *Labor History* (Spring 1972); Josef J. Barton, *Peasants and Strangers: Italians, Rumanians, and Slovaks in an American City, 1890–1950* (Cambridge: Harvard University Press, 1975); Morawska, *For Bread with Butter.* There was a hard practicality to these deferential relations, as through their observance the immigrant often managed to first secure and then hold onto a job; his skilled betters frequently functioned as work-gang leaders with real, if informal, authority over such matters.

20. Schatz, *The Electrical Workers*, Morawska, *For Bread with Butter*, 276. Skilled positions in the steel industry, including rollers, blacksmiths, carpenters, etc., were monopolized by Americans and western Europeans whose racism helped block access to these jobs by eastern European immigrants as well as their offspring.

21. Silvano Tomasi, *Piety and Power: The Role of Italian Parishes in the New York Metropolitan Area, 1880–1930* (New York: Center for Migration Studies, 1975); Nicholas J. Russo, "Three Generations of Italians in New York City: Their Religious Acculturation," in Silvano M. Tomasi and Madeline H. Engel, eds., *The Italian Experience in the United States* (New York: Center for Migration Studies, 1970); Slayton, *Back of the Yards*, 62; quotation from Morawska, *For Bread with Butter*, 274; Lizabeth Cohen, "Learning to Live in the Welfare State" (Ph.D. diss., University of California, 1986); Humbert S. Nelli, *From Immigrants to Ethnics: The Italian-American* (New York: Oxford University Press, 1983); Barton, *Peasants and Strangers*; Edsforth, *Class Conflict.*

22. Kristi Andersen, *The Creation of a Democratic Majority, 1928–36* (Chicago: University of Chicago Press, 1979).

23. Cited in "He Fights for Labor," Labor Non-Partisan League pamphlet, p. 4, Hillman Papers.

24. James A. Gross, *The Making of the NLRB: A Study in Economics, Politics, and Law* (Albany: State University of New York Press, 1974), vol. 1. The Twentieth Century Fund, an assembly point for mass-consumer-oriented businessmen, social scientists, and economists, not only supported the essentials of the Wagner Act (with some qualifications), but supplied the NLRB with its most radical, original member, Edwin Smith, and its research director, David Saposs, one-time educational director for the Amalgamated. With respect to the Social Security Act, Marion Folsom of Kodak lobbied vigorously on its behalf (see Kim McQuaid, "Corporate Liberalism in the American Business Community, 1920–40," *Business History Review* [Autumn 1978]);

Marion Folsom to John B. Andrews, May 11, 1934, American Association of Labor Legislation papers, Tamiment Library, New York University; Social Security Project, Marion B. Folsom, Oral History Collection of Columbia University (hereafter cited as OHCCU), 1970; Tomlins, *The State and the Unions*, 119.

25. Frances Perkins, Oral History Memoir, OHCCU, p. 214; Roos, *NRA: Economic Planning*.

26. Friedlander, "Origins of the Welfare State"; Strum, *Louis D. Brandeis*; Max Lowenthal to Tom Corcoran, April 4, 1934, and July 12, 1935, and Lowenthal to "Tom and Ben," July 12, 1937, box 204, Thomas Corcoran Papers, Library of Congress; Donald A. Ritchie, *James M. Landis: Dean of the Regulators* (Cambridge: Harvard University Press, 1980); Felix Frankfurter to Bruce Bliven, December 4, 1930, Felix Frankfurter Papers, Library of Congress.

27. *Fortune*, October 1933; "Wagner Committee—1933," memo, box 285, William Jett Lauck Papers, University of Virginia; "Suggested Program for 1934–35, memo to Mr. Lewis," box 40, Lauck Papers.

28. Frances Perkins Memoir, OHCCU; Jacob Potofsky Memoir, OHCCU; James A. Farley Memoir, OHCCU; Kenneth Waltzer, "The American Labor Party" (Ph.D. diss., Harvard University, 1977); New York State Labor Non-Partisan League, "Declaration of Principles," July 16, 1936, Labor Non-Partisan League file, Hillman Papers.

29. Perkins used her influence with varying success to persuade industrialists like Swope, Chrysler, and Sloan of General Motors to come to terms with the new labor movement (see Perkins correspondence, Record Group 174, Department of Labor, Office of the Secretary, boxes 79 and 91; Jerrold Auerbach, *Labor and Liberty: The LaFollette Committee and the New Deal* [Bobbs-Merrill, 1966]). Lee Pressman's influence extended directly into the White House via his relationship with Tom Corcoran and through Corcoran to James Roosevelt (see "Memorandum on conference with Secretary Perkins," October 11, 1937, box 63, "Secretary of Labor" folder, Father Francis Haas Papers, Catholic University, Washington, D.C.).

30. Gross, *The Making of the NLRB*, 247–48.

31. Edsforth, *Class Conflict*; Irving Howe and B. J. Widick, *The UAW and Walter Reuther* (New York: Random House, 1949); Alan Brinkley, *Voices of Protest: Huey Long, Father Coughlin, and the Great Depression* (New York: Alfred A. Knopf, 1982), 140, 200–202; David O'Brien, "American Catholics and Organized Labor in the 1930s," *Catholic Historical Review* (October 1966).

32. Transcript of Homer Martin radio broadcast, wJR in Detroit and wGAR in Cleveland, n.d., box 20, Adolph Germer Papers, Wisconsin Historical Society, Madison.

33. Jacob Potofsky to Father Haas, July 8, 1937, and Haas to Monseigneur Tourenhart, August 10, 1937, box 63, Haas Papers.

34. Robert P. Ingalls, *Herbert Lehman and New York State's Little New Deal* (New York: New York University Press, 1975), 117–19. Even as staunch a CIO supporter as Father Rice opposed a federal housing project in Pittsburgh,

sensing a threat to the integrity of the local Catholic community (see Bruce
Stave, "Pittsburgh and the New Deal," in Braeman, Bremner, and Brody,
eds., *State and Local Levels*, vol. 2 of *The New Deal* [Ohio State University Press,
1975]). The far more conservative Catholic hierarchy in New York State opposed all federal and state child labor regulations for similar reasons.

35. Gross, *The Making of the NLRB*.

36. Newell, *Chicago and the Labor Movement*; Hugh T. Lovin, "The Fall of
the Farmer-Labor Parties," *Pacific Northwest Quarterly* (January 1971); Sidney
Hillman, speech to the General Executive Board of the Amalgamated Clothing Workers of America, April 19, 1936, Hillman Papers; *St. Louis Post-Dis-
patch*, April 26, 1937.

37. Gardner Jackson to Jett Lauck and "Memo for Mr. John L. Lewis on
Public Relations Suggestions," August 12, 1937, box 37, "Gardner Jackson"
folder, Lauck Papers; Executive Board Minutes of the CIO, June 13, 1939,
and June 3, 4, 5, 1940, AFL-CIO Headquarters, Washington, D.C.

38. Mordecai Ezekiel to Sidney Hillman, October 22, 1935, and February
10, 1938, Hillman Papers; Eziekel to Jett Lauck, May 3, 1938, box 35, Lauck
Papers; "Rendevous with Democracy: The Memoirs of 'Tommy the Cork,' "
with Philip Kooper, box 586a, Corcoran Papers. Arguably, this strategy pursued the objectives of the Rural Electrification Administration, the Tennessee
Valley Authority, the Resettlement Administration, and other related agencies as well as the more radical leanings of the purged group around Tugwell
within the Agriculture Department, which included Eziekel, Alger Hiss, Lee
Pressman, Jerome Frank, Beanie Baldwin, and Gardner Jackson, who viewed
agricultural reform as a way of recasting the political economy of the South
and thereby realigning the Democratic party.

39. James T. Patterson, *Congressional Conservatism and the New Deal: The
Growth of the Conservative Coalition in Congress, 1933–1939* (Lexington: University of Kentucky Press, 1967); CIO Executive Board Minutes, 1938–1941,
AFL-CIO Headquarters; James A. Gross, *The Reshaping of the NLRB: National
Policy in Transition, 1937–47* (Albany: State University of New York Press,
1981). While it is true that a combination of work relief projects and the FLSA
did eventually undermine the regional isolation of the Southern labor market and, most important, the New Deal's agricultural programs encouraging
the mechanization of cotton cultivation produced an out-migration of farm
labor, the full impact of these developments would not be registered for decades (see Gavin Wright, *Old South, New South: Revolutions in the Southern Economy since the Civil War* [New York: Basic Books, 1986]).

40. *New York Times*, July 27, 1939; "Correspondence, 1935–37," box 63,
Haas Papers; Carle Conway's address to the Annual Meeting of the Taylor
Society, 1939. Many personnel managers, reflecting the functional dispersion
of the firm, were quite sympathetic to the Wagner Act: "After so long a struggle . . . the principle of representation in employer-employee relations is definitely established. It has become increasingly clear that modern, complex,
large-scale corporations no longer admit of satisfactory individualized control and management" ("Employer-Employee Relations," September 1, 1935,

quoted in Robert E. Lane, *The Regulation of Businessmen: Social Conditions of Government Economic Control* [Hamden, Conn.: Archon Books, 1966], 129).

41. Clinton S. Golden and Harold J. Ruttenberg, *The Dynamics of Industrial Democracy* (1942; reprint, New York: Da Capo Press, 1975); Cooke and Murray, *Organized Labor and Production*; Morris Cooke to Beulah Amidon, July 14, 1938, Paul U. Kellogg Papers, New York School of Social Work.

42. Box 24 of the Adolph Germer Papers is most useful in documenting this control; R. J. Thomas Memoir, OHCCU; Lee Pressman Memoir, OHCCU; Lichtenstein, *Labor's War at Home*; Gartman, *Auto Slavery*.

43. "The Quest for Security," transcript of Sidney Hillman address on the BBC, November 18, 1934, Hillman Papers; Joseph Gaer, *The First Round: The Story of the CIO-PAC* (New York: Duell, Sloan, and Pearce, 1944); *A Turning Point in History*, National Citizens Political Action Committee pamphlet, August 5, 1944, Hillman Papers; "PAC Political Program 1944," Hillman Papers; Hillman speech at CIO Full Employment Conference, January 1944, Hillman Papers.

4 The New Deal and the Idea of the State

ALAN BRINKLEY

ALVIN HANSEN had been one of the principal economic advisers to the New Deal for nearly three years when he traveled to Cincinnati in March 1940 to speak to a group of businessmen. After his address, someone in the audience asked him what must have seemed a perfectly reasonable question: "In your opinion is the basic principle of the New Deal economically sound?" Hansen could not answer it. "I really do not know what the basic principle of the New Deal is," he replied. "I know from my experience in the government that there are as many conflicting opinions among the people in Washington under this administration as we have in the country at large."[1]

Hansen's confusion was not uncommon in the cluttered, at times incoherent, political atmosphere of the late New Deal. The Roosevelt administration had moved in so many directions at once that no one could make sense of it all. Everyone was aware, of course, of what the New Deal had done—of the laws it had helped pass, of the programs it had created, of the institutions it had launched or reshaped. But as Hansen suggested, few could discern in all this any "basic principle," any clear prescription for the future.

Only a few years later, however, most American liberals had come to view the New Deal as something more than an eclectic group of policies and programs. By the end of World War II, it had emerged as an idea: a reasonably coherent creed around which liberals could coalesce, a concept of the state that would dominate their thought and action for at least a generation. To some extent, battered and reviled as it has become, it remains at the center of American political life still.

This essay attempts to explain how and why liberal ideas of what the federal government should do evolved in response first to the recession of the late 1930s and then to the experience of World War II. The liberal concept of the state was not, of course, the only, or even the most important, factor in determining the form American government would assume. Nor was liberal ideology ever a uniform or static creed. But the broad outlines of what came to be known as "New Deal liberalism" remained fairly consistent for several decades after World War II; and those ideas played a major role at times in shaping the major expansions of federal responsibility that have transformed American government and, in more recent years, American politics.

I

The United States was one of the slowest of the advanced industrial nations to define an important social and economic role for its national government. The American state did not remain static, certainly, in the last decades of the nineteenth century and the first decades of the twentieth; but it grew slowly, haltingly, incompletely.[2] The Great Depression, which would have been a difficult challenge for any state, was doubly intimidating in the United States because Americans had as yet made few decisions about what their government should do and how it should do it. As a result, the New Deal was not only an effort to deal with the particular problems of the 1930s; it was also a process of building government institutions where none existed, of choosing among various prescriptions for an expanded American state.

Through the first four years of the Roosevelt administration, however, making choices seemed to be nearly the last thing New Dealers were interested in doing. Instead, they moved unashamedly, even boastfully, in innumerable directions, proud of their experimentalism, generally unconcerned about the eclecticism of their efforts. Richard Hofstadter may have exaggerated when he described it as a program bereft of ideologies, "a chaos of experimentation." The New Deal was, in fact, awash in ideologies. What it lacked, however, was any single principle to bind its many diverse initiatives together.[3] There were occasional cries, both in and out of the administration, for greater ideological coherence; predictions that without it, the New Deal would ultimately collapse in terminal confusion. But as long as the administration seemed politically unassailable and as long as the economy seemed on the road to recovery, it was easy to ignore such warnings.

In 1937, however, both the political and economic landscape

changed. The president's ill-advised plan for "packing" the Supreme Court, first proposed a few weeks after his second inauguration, sparked a long-festering revolt among conservatives within his own party and caused an erosion of both his congressional and popular strength from which he was never fully to recover. An even greater blow to the administration's fortunes, and to its confidence, was the dismaying and almost wholly unanticipated recession that began in October 1937—an economic collapse more rapid and in some ways more severe than the crash of 1929. The new recession quickly destroyed the illusion that the Great Depression was over. And it forced a serious reevaluation among American liberals of the policies and philosophy of the New Deal. Out of the tangle of ideas and achievements of the early New Deal, many came now to believe, had to come a coherent vision that could guide future efforts. It was necessary, in short, to define the concept of New Deal liberalism.

II

There were in the late 1930s a number of potential definitions available to those engaged in this effort, and there seemed little reason at the time to assume that any one of them would soon prevail. Two broad patterns of governance, in particular, competed for favor. Each had roots in the first years of the New Deal and in earlier periods of reform; each had important defenders.

For a time, at least, it seemed that the principal impact of the 1937 recession on American liberalism would be an enhanced belief in the value of an "administrative" or "regulatory" state, a government that would exercise some level of authority over the structure and behavior of private capitalist institutions. Efforts to reshape or "tame" capitalism had been central to American reform ideology since the late nineteenth century and had been particularly prominent in the first years of the New Deal. Indeed, believing that something was wrong with capitalism and that it was the responsibility of government to fix it was one of the most important ways in which progressives and liberals had defined themselves through the first decades of the twentieth century.

In the immediate aftermath of the 1937 collapse, a powerful group of younger New Dealers embraced this tradition again and, without fully realizing it, began to transform it. They were something of a fresh force within the New Deal, a new generation of liberals moving into the places vacated by the original "brain trusters," most of whom had by then departed from public life. Some occupied important positions of influence in the administration itself: Thomas

Corcoran (often considered their unofficial leader), Benjamin Cohen, Thurman Arnold, Leon Henderson, James Landis, and Robert Jackson, among others. Some made their influence felt as writers for the *New Republic*, the *Nation*, and other magazines and journals. Felix Frankfurter (who had once taught some of them at Harvard Law School and who had served as a one-man employment agency for New Deal agencies) maintained his links from Cambridge. Henry Wallace and Harold Ickes served at times as their allies in the cabinet. They were known as the "New Dealers," a term that had once referred to the administration and its supporters as a whole but that now usually described a particular group within that larger orbit.

Several things distinguished them from other members of the administration and other advocates of reform. One was their hostility to an idea that had entranced progressives for decades and had played a major role in the early years of the New Deal—the idea of an associational economy, in which government would promote and regulate the cartelization of private industries so as to reduce destructive competition and maintain prices. The associational vision had shaped the first and most celebrated of the New Deal's reform experiments, the National Recovery Administration of 1933–1935.[4] And the concept continued to evoke a vague, romantic affection in some corners of the administration. Donald Richberg and others continued to lobby in the late 1930s for a revival of NRA-like policies, and the president showed an occasional inclination to agree with them.[5] But to the younger liberals of the late 1930s, the failure of the NRA was proof of the bankruptcy of the associational vision. They referred repeatedly to the "NRA of unhappy memory," the "NRA disaster," the "ill-conceived NRA experiment." The attempt to create a cartelistic "business commonwealth" capable of ordering its own affairs had, they claimed, produced only increased concentrations of power and artificially inflated prices. "The NRA idea is merely the trust sugar-coated," the *Nation* argued, "and the sugar coating soon wears off."[6]

A second, related characteristic of these younger liberals was their rhetoric. Most rejected the conciliatory tone of the early New Deal, which had sought to draw the corporate world into a productive partnership with government. They favored, instead, the combative language of Franklin Roosevelt's 1936 campaign, with its sharp denunciation of "economic royalists." To much of the press and the public, what typified the "New Dealers" was a strong antipathy toward the corporate world and a fervent commitment to using government to punish and tame it.[7]

In fact, attitudes toward businessmen varied greatly among the "New Dealers," and almost none were as hostile to corporate capital-

ism as their rhetoric at times suggested. Some did indeed believe that
the new recession was a result of a corporate conspiracy: a deliberate
"strike" by capital, designed to frustrate and weaken the administration.[8] But even many of those who articulated this theory were careful to draw distinctions between "tyrannical" capitalists and those
more "enlightened" business leaders who were already embracing
some elements of the New Deal.

Whatever their opinions of corporate capitalism, however, virtually all the New Dealers agreed that a solution of the nation's greatest problems required the federal government to step into the marketplace to protect the interests of the public. The events of 1937 and
1938 had proved, they believed, that the corporate world, when left
to its own devices, naturally frustrated the spontaneous workings of
the market; that business leaders often conspired with one another
to impose high "administered prices" on their customers; that the result was an artificial constriction of purchasing power and hence an
unnecessarily low level of production. Only through a vigorous campaign against monopoly, therefore, could the economy be made to
operate at full capacity.

Thus, on the surface at least, the most powerful impulse within
the New Deal beginning early in 1938 was the revival of the old crusade against "monopoly." Rhetorical assaults on economic concentration echoed throughout the administration as New Dealers tried to
forge an explanation for the setbacks of the year before. The president made the issue the centerpiece of an important 1938 message to
Congress, in which he called for the creation of what became the
Temporary National Economic Committee to examine "the concentration of economic power in American industry and the effect of
that concentration upon the decline of competition." At about the
same time, Roosevelt appointed Thurman Arnold, a professor at
Yale Law School and a prolific political theorist, to succeed Robert
Jackson as head of the Antitrust Division of the Justice Department.
Arnold quickly made his office one of the most active and conspicuous in the federal government.[9]

In fact, however, it was not the "atomizers," the believers in the
Brandeisian concept of a decentralized, small-scale economy, who
were moving to the fore. While the antitrust activists of the late New
Deal used familiar antimonopoly rhetoric, their efforts had very little
to do with actually decentralizing the economy. They were committed, instead, to defending the consumer and to promoting full production by expanding the regulatory functions of the state.

The record of Thurman Arnold was one indication of the form
the "antimonopoly" impulse was now assuming. Arnold well de-

served his reputation as the most active and effective director in the history of the Antitrust Division. By the time he left the Justice Department in 1943, he had radically expanded both the budget and the staff of his division; and he had filed (and won) more antitrust cases than the Justice Department had initiated in its entire previous history.[10]

But Arnold was not using the antitrust laws to promote anything remotely resembling the Brandeisian concept of decentralization. On the contrary, he had been arguing for years, in his books, articles, and speeches, that the idea of "atomizing" the economy was nostalgic folly; that large-scale institutions were an inevitable, perhaps even desirable, consequence of industrialism; and that any effort to dismantle them would be not only futile but dangerous.[11] In *The Folklore of Capitalism*, his celebrated 1937 book chronicling the meaningless ideological "rituals" Americans used to disguise political and economic realities, he gave special attention to what he considered one of the most vacuous of such rituals—the antitrust laws. They were, he wrote, "the answer of a society which unconsciously felt the need of great organizations, and at the same time had to deny them a place in the moral and logical ideology of the social structure. They were part of the struggle of a creed of rugged individualism to adapt itself to what was becoming a highly organized society."[12]

The role of the Antitrust Division, Arnold believed, was not to defend "smallness" or to break up combinations, but to supervise the behavior of corporations. Size by itself was irrelevant. "I recognize the necessity of large organizations in order to attain efficient mass production," he wrote in 1939, shortly after assuming office. "I recognize that trust-busting for the mere sake of breaking up large units is futile." Three years later, as he neared the end of his tenure, he was saying the same thing, even more emphatically: "Big Business is not an economic danger so long as it devotes itself to efficiency in production and distribution. . . . There can be no greater nonsense than the idea that a mechanized age can get along without big business."

How was government to measure "efficiency in production and distribution"? Arnold's answer was simple: by the price to the consumer. Whatever artificially inflated consumer prices (and thus reduced economic activity)—whether it was the anti-competitive practices of a giant monopoly, the collusive activities of smaller producers acting to stabilize their markets, or (and here he raised the ire of some of his fellow liberals) the excessive demands of such powerful labor organizations as the building trades unions—was a proper target of antitrust prosecution. Any organization that did not harm the consumer, regardless of its size, had nothing to fear. Hence the anti-trust laws became in Arnold's hands vehicles for expanding the reg-ulatory scope of the state, not tools for altering the scale of economic organizations. Enforcement, he claimed, "is the problem of continu-ous direction of economic traffic. . . . The competitive struggle with-out effective antitrust enforcement is like a fight without a referee."[13]

In this, of course, Arnold was saying little that was inconsistent with the actual history of antitrust law enforcement, and certainly nothing that was inconsistent with the previous record of the New Deal in confronting economic concentration. It was, however, a state-ment sharply at odds with the long-standing ideology of antimonop-oly. Arnold's views were more reminiscent of Theodore Roosevelt's nationalistic view of the economy (or Thorstein Veblen's concern with efficiency) than of the more truly antimonopolist views of the popu-lists or Brandeis or the Wilson of 1912.[14] No one recognized that more clearly than the old Midwestern progressives to whom antitrust still meant (as William Borah put it in a hostile exchange during Ar-nold's confirmation hearings) "breaking up monopolies." Suspicious of Arnold from the start, they viewed his tenure in the Justice De-partment as a disaster—which, by their standards, it turned out to be. His success in using the antitrust laws to police rather than forestall "bigness" was a serious, perhaps final, blow to the old concept of those laws as the route to genuine decentralization. That was pre-cisely Arnold's intention.[15]

The TNEC, similarly, was an antimonopoly inquiry more in name than in substance. It included among its members such inveterate congressional antimonopolists as Borah, Rep. Hatton Sumners of Texas, and Sen. Joseph O'Mahoney of Wyoming (the chairman). But most of the congressional members soon lost both interest and faith in the committee as the real work of the investigation fell increasingly under the control of the young New Dealers appointed to represent the administration: Arnold, Jerome Frank, William O. Douglas, Isa-dor Lubin, and (directing the investigative staff) Leon Henderson, men far less concerned about the size of the institutions of the econ-omy than about their effect on consumers and their accountability to the state. At times subtly, at times explicitly, the TNEC inquiry de-bunked old antimonopolist assumptions that small enterprises were inherently preferable to large ones; it cited time and again the value of efficiencies of scale; and it sought to find new ways for the govern-ment to intervene in the economy to protect the public from the ad-verse effects of a concentration of power that it seemed to concede was now inevitable.[16]

The work of the TNEC dragged on for nearly three years. The

committee examined 655 witnesses, generated eighty volumes and over twenty thousand pages of testimony, published forty-four monographs, and, as time passed and the inconclusiveness of the enterprise became clear, gradually lost the attention of both the public and the president. Its final report, issued in April 1941, attracted virtually no serious attention in a nation already preoccupied with war; and the entire episode was soon largely dismissed as a "colossal dud" or, more charitably, a "magnificent failure." "With all the ammunition the committee had stored up," *Time* magazine commented at the end, "a terrific broadside might have been expected. Instead, the committee rolled a rusty BB gun into place [and] pinged at the nation's economic problems."[17]

The feeble conclusion of the TNEC inquiry illustrated the degree to which the antimonopoly enthusiasms of 1938 had faded by 1941. But the character of the inquiry during its three years of striving illustrated how the rhetoric of antimonopoly, even at its most intense, had ceased to reflect any real commitment to decentralization. If economic concentration was a problem, and most liberals continued to believe it was, the solution was not to destroy it, but to submit it to increased control by the state.

The New Dealers of the late 1930s used many different labels to describe their political ideas: "antimonopoly," "regulation," "planning." But while once those words had seemed to represent quite distinct concepts of reform, they described now a common vision of government—a vision of capable, committed administrators who would seize command of state institutions, invigorate them, expand their powers when necessary, and make them permanent forces in the workings of the marketplace. The task of liberals, William Douglas wrote in 1938, was "to battle for control of the present government so its various parts may be kept alive as vital forces of democracy." What Americans needed above all, Thurman Arnold argued, was a "religion of government which permits us to face frankly the psychological factors inherent in the development of organizations with public responsibility."[18]

James Landis, chairman of the Securities and Exchange Commission from 1935 to 1937 and later dean of Harvard Law School, published in 1938 a meditation on his own experiences in government in which he expressed something of this new faith. "It is not without reason," he wrote in *The Administrative Process*, "that a nation which believes profoundly in the efficacy of the profit motive is at the same time doubtful as to the eugenic possibilities of breeding supermen to direct the inordinately complex affairs of the larger branches of private industry." But the impossibility of finding "supermen" to manage the economy (as some progressives had once dreamed) was, Landis believed, not a reason to retreat from state activism. It was a reason to enlarge the federal bureaucracy, to substitute for the unattainable "super manager" the massed expertise of hundreds of individual administrators. "A consequence of an expanding interest of government in various phases of the industrial scene," he insisted, "must be the creation of more administrative agencies. . . . Efficiency in the processes of governmental regulation is best served by the creation of more rather than less agencies."[19]

Increasing the regulatory functions of the federal government was not, of course, an idea new to the 1930s. Curbing corporate power, attacking monopoly, imposing order on a disordered economic world—those had been the dreams of generations of reformers since the advent of large-scale industrialization. But the concept of an administrative state that was gaining favor in the late New Deal, while rhetorically familiar, was substantively different from the visions that had attracted reformers even five years earlier. Younger liberals continued to use the language of earlier reform impulses; but without ever quite saying so, they were rejecting one of the central features of those impulses.

For decades, American reformers had dreamed of creating a harmonious industrial economy, a system that could flourish without extensive state interference and produce enough wealth to solve the nation's most serious social problems. There had been widely varying ideas about how to create such an economy, from the associational visions of creating a smoothly functioning, organic whole out of the clashing parts of modern capitalism to the antimonopolist yearning for a small-scale decentralized economy freed of the nefarious influence of large combinations. But the larger dream—the dream of somehow actually "solving" the problems of modern capitalism—had been one of the most evocative of all reform hopes and the goal of most progressives and liberals who advocated an expanded state role in the economy.

By the end of the 1930s, faith in such broad solutions was in retreat. Liberal prescriptions for federal economic policy were becoming detached from the vision of a harmonious capitalist world. The state could not, liberals were coming to believe, in any fundamental way "solve" the problems of the economy. The industrial economy was too large, too complex, too diverse; no single economic plan could encompass it all. Americans would have to accept the inevitability of conflict and instability in their economic lives. And they would have to learn to rely on the state to regulate that conflict and instability.

This new vision of the state was in some ways more aggressive and assertive than the prescriptions it replaced. And it was the very limits of its ultimate ambitions that made it so. The new breed of administrators would operate from no "master plan." Nor would they ever reach a point where economic reforms obviated the need for their own services. They would, rather, be constantly active, ever vigilant referees (or, as Arnold liked to put it, "traffic managers"), always ready to step into the market to remove "bottlenecks," to protect efficiency and competition, and to defend the interests of consumers, who were replacing producers as the ultimate focus of liberal concern.[20] The regulators would not, could not, create lasting harmony and order. They would simply commit the state to the difficult task of making the best of an imperfect economic world.

The aggressively statist ideas of the new liberals aroused intense and constant controversy—controversy that revealed how untenable their position really was. The idea of perpetual intrusive government involvement in the workings of the economy, with no hope of ever setting things right in a way that would permit the government to withdraw, was a rebuke both to the anti-statist impulses deeply embedded in American political culture and to the natural yearning for simple, complete solutions to important problems. Even most liberals were never fully comfortable with the idea that there was no real "answer" to the economic question. So it is perhaps unsurprising that when an alternative "solution," with an appealing, almost dazzling simplicity, began to emerge, it found a ready, even eager, following.

III

While some New Dealers were expressing enthusiasm for an expanded regulatory state, others within the administration were promoting a different course of action that would ultimately become more important in shaping the future of liberalism. They proposed that the government make more energetic use of its fiscal powers—its capacity to tax and spend—to stimulate economic growth and solve social problems. Advocates of the fiscal approach, like advocates of regulation, were principally interested in aiding consumers and increasing mass purchasing power. But they seized on different tools. Theirs was a vision of an essentially compensatory government, which would redress weaknesses and imbalances in the private economy without directly confronting the internal workings of capitalism. Such a state could manage the economy without managing the institutions of the economy.

There were few signs early in 1937 that new, more ambitious fiscal policies were on the horizon. Instead, the administration began the year in a confident mood and seemed prepared to return to the still appealing orthodoxies of balanced budgets and reduced spending. The depression, it appeared, was finally over. Unemployment remained disturbingly high, to be sure, but other signs—factory production, capital investment, stock prices—were encouraging. Inspired by these apparent successes, fiscal conservatives pressed their case with an almost gleeful vigor.

Leading the campaign for "fiscal responsibility" was Secretary of the Treasury Henry Morgenthau, Jr., whose relentless private efforts to win Roosevelt's support for a balanced budget belied his public image as a passive sycophant with no strong ideas of his own. Morgenthau and his allies admitted that deficit spending had been necessary during the economic emergency, but they had never credited the concept with any real legitimacy. And now that the New Deal had "licked the Great Depression," as a treasury official wrote in 1937, it was time to put the nation's finances back in order. The president, who had never been fully reconciled to the budget deficits he had so consistently accumulated, was receptive to such arguments. In the spring of 1937 he agreed to a series of substantial cuts in federal spending that would, he believed, balance the budget in 1938.[21]

The idea of a balanced budget was appealing for reasons beyond inherited dogma. Morgenthau managed to persuade the president that only by eliminating deficits could the New Deal truly prove its success; federal spending, he argued, had become a crutch, propping up an economy that—because of the administration's achievements—could now stand on its own. Roosevelt, moreover, recalled the charges of fiscal irresponsibility he had leveled against Hoover in 1932 and saw a balanced budget as a way to vindicate his earlier attacks. Economists in the Treasury Department argued further that there was a danger now of inflation and that trimming the federal deficit would contribute to price stability.[22]

There were dissenters. Chief among them was Marriner Eccles, chairman of the Federal Reserve Board, who called efforts to balance the budget "dangerously premature" and defended deficits as "a necessary, compensatory form of investment which gave life to an economy operating below capacity."[23] But nothing could prevail against the sunny optimism and strenuous bureaucratic infighting of Morgenthau and his allies. "The President gave me . . . everything that I asked for," Morgenthau gloated in the spring of 1937. "It was a long hard trying fight but certainly at some time during the weeks that I argued with him he must have come to the conclusion that if he wants his Administration to go forward with his reform program he must have a sound financial foundation."[24]

The economic collapse of the fall of 1937 destroyed hopes for a balanced budget in 1938. More significantly, it discredited many of the arguments supporting those hopes. "No one can doubt," the *New Republic* wrote, "that the sudden withdrawal of hundreds of millions of dollars of federal relief funds, the smashing of thousands of projects all over the country, did contribute materially to the creation of our present misery."[25] Within a few months, even many erstwhile defenders of fiscal orthodoxy had come to believe that the spending cuts of the previous spring had been an important, perhaps even a decisive, cause of the recession. The center of power in the debate over fiscal policy suddenly shifted.

Morgenthau and his allies in the Treasury Department continued to argue strenuously for fiscal conservatism even in the face of the new disasters. But they were now arguing almost alone. Throughout the early months of 1938, Eccles arranged meetings with sympathetic administration officials to press the case for spending and quickly mobilized influential supporters—Henry Wallace, Harold Ickes, Harry Hopkins, Aubrey Williams, Leon Henderson, Lauchlin Currie, Mordecai Ezekiel, Beardsley Ruml, Isidor Lubin—committed to a vigorous new anti-recession program. In March, a group of spending advocates assembled in Warm Springs, where the president was vacationing. And while Williams, Ruml, and Henderson huddled at a nearby inn preparing ammunition, Hopkins sat with the president in the "Little White House," spread the evidence out on the rickety card table Roosevelt liked to use as a desk, and persuaded him to shift his course.[26] A few weeks later, the president sent a message to Congress proposing a substantial new spending program: an additional $1.5 billion for work relief, another $1.5 billion for public works, and an expansion of credit of approximately $2 billion. It was not enough, some critics maintained. But at a time when the nation's peacetime budget had never exceeded $10 billion, most considered $5 billion substantial indeed.[27]

What was particularly significant was the way Roosevelt explained the new proposals. In his first term, he had generally justified spending programs as ways to deal with particular targeted problems: helping the unemployed, subsidizing farmers or homeowners or troubled industries, redeveloping the Tennessee Valley. Now he justified spending as a way to bring the economy as a whole back to health.[28] "We suffer primarily from a lack of buying power," he explained in a fireside chat early in 1938 (its text drawn in part from a Beardsley Ruml memo). It was time for the government "to make definite additions to the purchasing power of the nation." He accompanied his announcement (as he was fond of doing) with references to the historical precedents for his decision:

> In the first century of our republic we were short of capital, short of workers and short of industrial production; but we were rich in free land, free timber and free mineral wealth. The Federal Government rightly assumed the duty of promoting business and relieving depression by giving subsidies of land and other resources.

> Thus, from our earliest days we have had a tradition of substantial government help to our system of private enterprise. But today the government no longer has vast tracts of rich land to give away. . . . [N]ow we have plenty of capital, banks and insurance companies loaded with idle money; plenty of industrial productive capacity and several millions of workers looking for jobs. It is following tradition as well as necessity, if Government strives to put idle money and idle men to work, to increase our public wealth and to build up the health and strength of the people—to help our system of private enterprise to function.[29]

Roosevelt's comfortable references to the past failed to mask the genuinely unprecedented nature of his statement. Government spending, the president now implied, was no longer a necessary evil, to be used sparingly to solve specific problems. It was a positive good, to be used lavishly at times to stimulate economic growth and social progress. Without fully realizing it, he was embracing the essence of what would soon be known as Keynesian economics. He was ushering in a new era of government fiscal policy.

In many respects, fiscal activism was no newer to the 1930s than the regulatory innovations with which it coexisted. Federal subsidization of private interests was as old as the federal government itself. But the kind of spending New Dealers supported throughout the 1930s, and the rationale they were gradually developing to justify it, suggested an important departure. In the past, government subsidies had almost always promoted the productive capacities of the nation. They had been designed to assist the builders of roads, bridges, dams, railroads, and other essential elements of the economic infrastructure. They had encouraged settlement of the West and the development of new agricultural frontiers. More recently, they had assisted banks and other financial institutions to weather the storms of the depression.

But ideas about government spending changed significantly in the late New Deal. Instead of advocating federal fiscal policies that would contribute directly to production and economic development, liberals pressed for policies that would promote mass consumption.

Alvin Hansen, one of the first important American economists to grasp and promote the teachings of Keynes, took note of this important shift in outlook. The best way to ensure a prosperous future, he was arguing in the late 1930s, was "to work toward a higher consumption economy," to make consumer demand the force driving production and investment instead of the other way around. And the most efficient way to create such demand was for the government to pump more spending power into the economy—through public works, social security, federal credit mechanisms, and other methods. "Consumption," he argued, "is the frontier of the future."[30]

IV

These two broad approaches to the problems of the economy—increased state regulation and increased use of fiscal policy—coexisted relatively easily in the late 1930s. Indeed, most New Dealers considered them two halves of a single strategy and seldom thought very much about the differences between them.[31]

What bound these two strategies together most closely was an assumption about the American economy that suffused liberal thought in the late 1930s and helped drive efforts to discover a new role for the state. Even before the 1937 recession, doubts had been growing within the New Deal about the nation's capacity ever again to enjoy the kind of economic growth it had experienced in the half-century before the Great Depression. The setbacks of 1937 only reinforced those concerns. The economy had been dragging for nearly a decade; sluggish growth and high unemployment were beginning to seem part of the natural order of things. Out of those fears emerged the concept of the "mature economy."[32]

The idea that economic expansion was not (and could not become) limitless drew from a long tradition of such predictions in America, stretching back at least to the nineteenth century. (It also anticipated some of the no-growth ideologies of the 1970s.) It had particularly close ties to Frederick Jackson Turner's "frontier thesis," which remained in the 1930s a staple of American historical interpretation. Sen. Lewis Schwellenbach of Washington, an ardent New Dealer (and later secretary of labor under Truman) suggested the connection in a 1938 speech: "So long as we had an undeveloped West—new lands—new resources—new opportunities—we had no cause to worry. We could permit concentration of wealth. We could permit speculation of our heritage. We could permit waste and erosion by wind and water, but we caught up with ourselves. We reached our Last Frontier."[33]

It was not simply the exhaustion of land and other natural resources that presented problems. Nor was it the slackening population growth of the 1930s, which had led many analysts to predict very slow future increases and a leveling off at 175 million around the year 2000.[34] The most important source of "economic maturity," defenders of the concept claimed, was the end of "capital accumulation." The great age of industrial growth was finally over. The basic industries were now built. No new sectors capable of matching railroads, steel, and automobiles as engines of expansion were likely to emerge. And since economic growth alone would no longer be sufficient to meet the needs of society, new forms of management were now essential if the nation's limited resources were to be sensibly and fairly allocated. "Hereafter," wrote the popular economist Stuart Chase, "unless I have completely misjudged the trend of the times and the temper of the people, economic systems are going to be run deliberately and directly for those ends which everybody knows they should be run for. . . . The welfare of the community will be paramount."[35]

The mature-economy idea provided powerful support to arguments for increasing the regulatory functions of the state. An economy in which dynamic growth was no longer possible placed nearly unbearable pressures on those in the marketplace to avoid risks and thus to collude to raise (or "administer") prices. Only a strong administrative state could combat this dangerous trend. But the same concept added strength to arguments for greater government spending as well. In the absence of large-scale private investment, only the government had the resources (and the broad "national" view of the economic problem) necessary to keep even modest economic growth alive.

The writings of Alvin Hansen illustrate how the belief in economic maturation was helping to fuse regulatory and spending ideas. Hansen agreed that "the age of capital investment is past"; and he explained the result with the idea of what he called "secular stagnation"—a concept that became one of his principal contributions to Keynesian theory (and one that Keynes himself never fully accepted). Private institutions, Hansen argued, had lost the ability to create large-scale economic growth; indeed, they were now likely actually to retard such growth through anti-competitive practices as they struggled to survive in a more difficult world. One solution, therefore, was vigorous antitrust efforts to restore fluidity to the marketplace. Like Keynes, however, Hansen believed that fluidity alone would not be enough. Government also had a responsibility to sustain and, when necessary, increase purchasing power to keep alive the higher levels of consumption upon which the mature economy would now have to rely. Regulatory and fiscal mechanisms would work together to produce economic growth.

But the partnership of the regulatory and compensatory visions, which for a time had seemed so natural and untroubled, did not last, at least not on equal terms. By 1945, the idea of the administrative state, which had seemed so powerful in the late 1930s, was in decline; and the faith in fiscal policy, so tentatively embraced in 1938, had moved to the center of liberal hopes. The reason for that change was not simply that the spending initiatives of the late 1930s seemed to work; even when they did, many liberals continued to consider spending little more than a temporary stopgap and continued to believe that more lasting statist solutions were necessary. The change was also a result of the American experience in World War II.

V

World War I spawned two decades of bitter recriminations among Americans who believed the nation had intervened in the conflict for no useful purpose. But it also helped shape bright dreams among progressives of a more harmonious economic world at home, dreams of a vaguely corporatist economy in which private institutions would learn to cooperate on behalf of the public interest and in which the state would preside benignly over a new era of growth and progress. Those dreams, however untrue to the realities of the wartime experience, fueled a generation of reform efforts and helped shape the early New Deal.[36]

In the 1940s, by contrast, the war itself—the reasons for it, the necessity of it—produced little controversy and few recriminations. But neither did it evoke among liberals anything comparable to the World War I enthusiasm for a reformed and reordered economy. On the contrary, the war helped reduce enthusiasm for a powerful regulatory state and helped legitimize the idea of a primarily compensatory government.

Many factors contributed to this wartime evolution of opinion. The political climate was changing rapidly: the Republicans had rebounded in the 1938 and 1940 elections; conservatives had gained strength in Congress; the public was displaying a growing antipathy toward the more aggressive features of the New Deal and a declining animus toward big business. Liberals responded by lowering their sights and modifying their goals.[37] The labor movement, similarly, encountered during the war intense popular hostility, along with strong pressure from the government to abandon its more ambitious political goals. Its accommodation with the state, and its alliance with the Democratic party, limited its capacity to act as an independent political force and to press for structural economic reforms.[38] Liberals who had once admired the collective character of some European governments looked with horror at the totalitarian states America was now fighting and saw in them a warning about what an excessively powerful state could become. And the emergence of an important American role in the world, which virtually all liberals came to believe must extend indefinitely beyond the end of the war, directed attention and energy away from domestic reform ideas.[39]

But the war had two more direct effects on liberal hopes for the state. It forced American government actually to attempt many of the aggressive managerial tasks that reformers had long advocated. The results of those efforts not only failed to increase faith in the ability of the state to administer a rationalized economy but actually diminished it. At the same time, the war spurred a revival of the economy that dispelled some of the doubts liberals had once harbored about the capacity of capitalism to expand and the ability of private institutions to govern themselves.

In the beginning, at least, many liberals expected otherwise. The war, they hoped, would strengthen the case for a government role in administering the economy and would enhance the influence and prestige of state bureaucracies and administrators. "We have learned already," wrote Clifford Durr in 1943,

> that we cannot obtain the production we need for waging the war as an undirected by-product of what we commonly refer to as "sound business principles." Neither can we expect such by-product to furnish us after the war with the standard of living which we shall be warranted in expecting. . . . There must be some over-all source of direction more concerned with [these] objectives than with the profits or losses of individual business concerns.[40]

Or as Herbert Emmerich, another New Deal official, wrote in 1941, "With a farewell to normalcy and an appreciation of the greater opportunities that the war crisis presents, public administrators today have an opportunity to enhance and permanently to establish the prestige of their calling in the United States."[41]

By 1945, however, the wartime experience had led most to conclude otherwise: that neither a new economic order nor active state management of the present one were necessary, possible, or desirable; that the existing structure of capitalism (including its relative independence from state control) represented the best hope for social progress; and that the government's most important task was less to regulate the private economy than to help it expand and to compensate for its occasional failures.

Even at the start, the government approached the task of organizing the economy for war in a way that suggested a degree of anti-statism. For two years before Pearl Harbor, the president and most of his principal advisers resisted the idea of creating a single, centralized locus of authority for mobilization and preferred instead to disperse power widely among an array of ad hoc committees, boards, and agencies. A series of production crises ultimately forced Roosevelt early in 1942 to create a single agency with a single director charged with supervising the war economy. But the shift was more apparent than real. Genuine authority remained divided, and the only ultimate arbiter of the chaos—Roosevelt himself—was always too preoccupied with other issues (or too incapacitated by his declining health) to resolve the confusion. World War II never produced a bureaucratic mechanism comparable to the War Industries Board of 1918; nor did it produce a production manager comparable to Bernard Baruch. There was, therefore, no comparable model of economic planning to fuel liberal hopes.[42]

The administration similarly resisted the idea of placing control of the wartime economy in the hands of professional civil servants or others from the permanent state bureaucracy. This was not, of course, entirely a matter of choice. The federal government, despite its considerable expansion during the 1930s, still lacked anything approaching sufficient bureaucratic capacity for managing a mobilization effort. The civil service and the professional political community had little experience or expertise in supervising the institutions of the industrial economy. The one major effort to "modernize" the federal bureaucracy and equip it to perform more advanced administrative tasks—Roosevelt's executive reorganization plan of 1938—had encountered substantial political opposition and had ultimately produced only modest reforms.[43] And so it was inevitable, perhaps, that the state would turn to the private sector for its administrative talent. But there was also an element of conscious preference to that choice. In the more conservative climate of the 1940s, Roosevelt preferred a conciliatory approach to war mobilization, an approach that liberal critics sometimes charged was an abdication of power to corporate figures but that the president believed was simply prudent politics.

The central agency of mobilization was the War Production Board, whose four-year existence was an almost endless bureaucratic ordeal. Roosevelt created the WPB in January 1942, only weeks after America's formal entry into the war, as the successor to a long string of failed organizational efforts. It was, he promised, to be the single production agency with a single manager for which many critics had been clamoring all along.[44] But the WPB failed on several levels to fulfill hopes for effective government supervision of the economy. It was, in the first place, not in any real sense a state institution at all. It was, rather, a collection of corporate executives and corporate lawyers, most of them still drawing salaries from their peacetime employers and working temporarily for the government for token payments (hence the label "dollar-a-year men," by which, like their World War I counterparts, they were generally known). Many of the leading WPB officials were implacably hostile to anything that smacked of centralized planning and considered it their mission not only to expedite war mobilization but to resist any attempt to make the war an occasion for the permanent expansion of the state.[45] "The arsenal of democracy . . . is still being operated with one eye on the war and the other on the convenience of big business," the always skeptical I. F. Stone wrote only months after the WPB began operations. "The progress made on production so far is the fruit of necessity and improvisation rather than of foresight and planning, and the men running the program are not willing to fight business interests on behalf of good will and good intentions."[46] The three years that followed strengthened such complaints, as Bruce Catton (who had served on the WPB) noted in a memoir published in 1948: "One consideration should guide all reconversion planning as the dollar-a-year men saw it; the old competitive patterns of the war economy must be preserved intact. When the last traces of the prewar economy evaporated, each industrialist must be able to pick up exactly where he had left off."[47]

For many liberals, then, the WPB served not as an inspiration but as an alarming indication of what government management of the economy could become: a mechanism by which members of the corporate world could take over the regulatory process and turn it to their own advantage. What made the WPB experience particularly disturbing, moreover, was that it was not an aberration. Corporate "capture" of state institutions had been a lament of many liberals for years; that the war not only failed to reverse that tendency, but seemed to advance it, raised questions about whether traditional forms of regulation were workable at all.

The actual performance of the WPB did little more to encourage hopes for state planning than its structure. Although it managed to avoid any genuine catastrophes, the agency was in continual administrative disarray. It was crippled from the start by its lack of adequate authority to resist other centers of power (most notably the military) in the battle for control of production decisions. It failed miserably to protect the interests of small business, despite strenuous efforts from both within the agency and without to force it to do so.[48] It suffered continually from the unwillingness of the president to support its decisions unreservedly; Franklin Roosevelt preferred to keep all potential power centers (and thus all possible rivals) in his administration relatively weak.

The WPB's inherent problems were magnified by the ineffectuality of its chairman, former Sears Roebuck executive Donald Nelson. Nelson was an earnest, intelligent, hardworking man, but he lacked the stature and, apparently, the will to stand up successfully to his competitors. By the beginning of 1943, his leadership of the WPB was in wide disrepute, nowhere more than within his own agency. "I am not at all certain that the views of Mr. Nelson prevail at WPB," one of Nelson's subordinates told a reporter in March 1943. "It seems to function as a sort of board of directors, with a lack of clear-cut direction as to where we are to go."[49] Harold Ickes was more blunt. "I think the WPB has fallen down badly on its job," he wrote late in 1942. "Nelson is the failure that many were afraid that he would be but hoped that he wouldn't be. He likes to please everybody which means that he has to make compromises. He frequently reverses himself or divides on a 50-50 basis when one claimant ought to be denied anything. He can't fire people."[50]

Nelson managed to hang on to his job for another year after some uncharacteristically decisive bureaucratic infighting. But he gradually lost the bulk of his authority to several new administrative structures.[51] In August 1944, he accepted a face-saving assignment to visit China on a presidential mission; when he returned a few months later, he resigned from the WPB. A man lionized in 1942 for his "inhuman" capacities as he took over "the biggest single job in the world" faded quietly into obscurity.[52]

Even some of the strongest supporters of federal regulatory efforts in the late 1930s found the experience of the war years discouraging. In 1937, Thurman Arnold had called on Americans to develop a "religion of government." By 1943, he was disillusioned and impatient with what he had seen of state control of the economy. "The economic planners are always too complicated for me," he wrote his friend William Allen White. "They were bound to get in power during a period of frustration"; but their time, he implied, had passed.[53] The dreams of an extensive regulatory state were coming to seem unrealistic, perhaps even dangerous. And that realization encouraged a search for other, less intrusive, vehicles of economic management.

VI

Declining faith in the managerial capacities of the state coincided with another development that had profound effects on liberal assumptions about the future: the revival of American capitalism. After a decade of depression, a decade of declining confidence in the economy and despair about the prospects for future growth, the industrial economy restored itself and, perhaps more important for the future of national politics, redeemed itself in a single stroke.[54]

In the process, it helped erode one of the mainstays of late-depression liberalism. The wartime economic experience—the booming expansion, the virtual end of unemployment, the creation of new industries, new "frontiers"—served as a rebuke to the "mature economy" idea and placed the concept of growth at the center of liberal hopes. The capitalist economy, liberals suddenly discovered, was not irretrievably stagnant. Economic expansion could achieve, in fact had achieved, dimensions beyond the wildest dreams of the 1930s. Social and economic advancement could proceed, therefore, without structural changes in capitalism and without continuing, intrusive state management of the economy. It could proceed by virtue of growth.

Assaults on the concept of "economic maturity" began to emerge as early as 1940 and gathered force throughout the war. Alvin Hansen himself partially repudiated the theory in 1941 ("All of us had our sights too low," he admitted).[55] The *New Republic* and the *Nation*, both of which had embraced the idea in 1938 and 1939, openly rejected it in the 1940s—not only rejected it, but celebrated its demise. The country had achieved a "break," the *Nation* insisted, "from the defeatist thinking that held us in economic thraldom through the thirties, when it was assumed that we could not afford full employment or full production in this country."[56]

But to believe that growth was feasible was not necessarily to believe that it was inevitable. "Enough for all is now possible for the first time in history," a 1943 administration study reported. "But the mere existence of plenty of labor, raw materials, capital, and organizing skill is no guarantee that all reasonable wants will be supplied—or that wealth will actually be produced." Except perhaps for the prospect of military defeat (a prospect seldom contemplated by most Americans), nothing inspired more fear during the war years than the specter of a peacetime economic collapse and a return to the high levels of unemployment that had been the most troubling and intractable problem of the 1930s. How to prevent that collapse now became the central element on the national political agenda; and for liberals, as for others, that meant a basic change in outlook. Instead of debating how best to distribute limited output and how most efficiently to manage a stagnant economy, reformers began to discuss how to keep the wartime economic boom—and the high levels of income and employment it had produced—alive in the postwar years. "Full employment" was the new rallying cry of liberal economists; all other goals gradually came to seem secondary. And the route to full employment, the war seemed to demonstrate, was not state management of capitalist institutions, but fiscal policies that would promote consumption and thus stimulate economic growth.[57]

The new approach was particularly clear in the deliberations of those committed to the idea of "planning," and above all, perhaps, in the work of the National Resources Planning Board. In the first years of the war (before its demise in 1943 at the hands of hostile congressional conservatives), the NRPB produced a series of reports outlining an ambitious program for postwar economic growth and security. It showed in the process how the "planning" ideal was shifting away from the vision of a rationally ordered economy (prominent in the early 1930s) and away from the idea of the activist, regulatory state (a central feature of late 1930s reform) and toward the concept of compensatory action. Planning would enable government to stimulate economic growth through fiscal policies. It would allow the state to make up for the omissions and failings of capitalism through the expansion of welfare programs. It need not involve increased state management of capitalist institutions.[58]

The NRPB had begun its life in 1933 under Harold Ickes in the Interior Department. And during its first half-dozen years of existence (under four different names and several different structures), it had generally reflected a view of planning derived from the city planning backgrounds of many of its members and from the regional planning experience of the Tennessee Valley Authority and other, smaller, New Deal projects. City planning and regional planning—the coordination of government programs in particular localities to reshape the social, physical, and economic environment—served for a time as microcosmic models for a larger concept of a planned society. The federal government, through a combination of public investment, public welfare, and extensive regulation, could become a major actor in the workings of the national economy, could direct its course, shape its future.[59]

The concept of planning to which the NRPB became principally committed in the first years of the war was subtly yet significantly different. The board continued to outline public works projects and to insist on their importance; but it usually portrayed such projects now less as vehicles for remaking the environment than as opportunities for countercyclic government spending. Its mission was to create a "shelf" of potential public undertakings, from which the government could draw projects "as insurance against industrial collapse and unemployment"; the intrinsic value of the projects as vehicles for urban or regional planning had become secondary. Welfare programs (and, above all, an expansion of the Social Security system) had, in the meantime, moved to the center of the NRPB prescription for federal social activism—both because such programs now appeared affordable (given the new abundance apparently within the nation's grasp) and because they could themselves serve the cause of growth by increasing and redistributing purchasing power.[60]

The board's 1942 report, *Security, Work, and Relief Policies* (released by the president early in 1943), outlined a program of "social security" of such breadth and ambition that it was widely dubbed the "American Beveridge Report," after the nearly simultaneous study that led to the creation of a new British welfare state. But the NRPB proposals were, in fact, significantly different from, and in some ways more extensive than, their British counterparts. The Beveridge Report restricted itself largely to a discussion of social welfare and insurance mechanisms; the NRPB proposed such mechanisms in the context of what it considered a larger goal: the maintenance of full employment.[61] The board's 1943 "National Resources Development Report" called explicitly for government programs to maintain a "dynamic expanding economy on the order of 100 to 125 billions of national income." Only a few years before, such a figure would have seemed preposterously high. "We must plan for full employment," members of the board wrote in a 1942 article explaining their proposals. "We shall plan to balance our national production-consumption budget at a high level with full employment, not at a low level with mass unemployment."[62]

The board did not altogether abandon its concern about state management of economic institutions. Even very late in its existence, it continued to include in its reports recommendations for expanded antitrust efforts, for new regulatory mechanisms, and for other extensions of the government's administrative role. One of its 1943 documents, in fact, spoke so explicitly about a drastic expansion of state control of the economy that it evoked rare applause from I. F. Stone, who generally decried the administration's "timidity," but who saw in the NRPB proposals "large and historic aims."[63]

But this lingering interest in what Franklin Roosevelt once dismissed as "grandiose schemes" was by now secondary—both to the members of the board themselves and, to an even greater extent, to other liberals interpreting its work—to the larger, simpler task of maintaining economic growth. "We know," the authors of the 1943 "Resources Development Report" wrote,

> that the road to the new democracy runs along the highway of a dynamic economy, to the full use of our national resources, to full employment, and increasingly higher standards of living. . . . We stand on the threshold of an economy of abundance. This generation has it within its power not only to produce in plenty but to distribute that plenty.

As columnist Ernest K. Lindley noted, "The most striking characteristic of the two [1943 NRPB] reports is their essential conservatism. The postwar is keyed to the restoration of the free enterprise system and its encouragement and stimulation."[64]

Central to this new emphasis on growth was the increasing influence of the ideas of John Maynard Keynes and of the growing number of American economists who were becoming committed to his theories. By the late 1930s, Keynes himself was already personally friendly with some of the leading figures of the New Deal. At the same time, leading American economists were becoming proponents of Keynesian ideas. Alvin Hansen, Mordecai Ezekiel, and Gardiner Means, for example, all of whom were active on the NRPB and all of whom reached broader audiences through their essays in economic journals and liberal magazines, had by the early years of the war become converted to at least a portion of Keynes's general theory.[65]

Hansen in particular—one of the principal authors of the 1943 NRPB reports—was in the early 1940s frequently described as "Keynes's American counterpart," "one of the most influential men in Washington," "the leader of a whole new economic school." He served as an illustration not only of the increasing impact of Keynes on American economists but of the way in which the American Keynesians were embracing only the most moderate aspects of an economic philosophy that, in Keynes's own hands, at times envisioned far more fundamental change. Hansen's earlier, celebrated concerns about "secular stagnation" were now muted. In their place was a faith in the ability of fiscal policy to ensure continued economic growth. "Clearly fiscal policy is now and will continue to be a powerful factor in the functioning of the modern economy," Hansen wrote in 1942. Such policies should be used, he continued, "to develop a high-consumption economy so that we can achieve full employment. . . . A higher propensity to consume can in part be achieved by a progressive tax structure combined with social security, social welfare, and community consumption expenditures."[66]

The wartime expansion had proved to liberals that given sufficient stimuli, the economy could grow at an impressive rate. Keynes's economic doctrines (and the larger constellation of ideas derived from them) suggested ways to introduce in peacetime the kinds of stimuli that had created the impressive wartime expansion. They offered, in fact, an escape from one of liberalism's most troubling dilemmas and a mechanism for which reformers had long been groping. They provided a way to manage the economy without directly challenging the prerogatives of capitalists. Growth did not necessarily require constant involvement in the affairs of private institutions, which (as the experience of wartime mobilization helped demonstrate) was both endlessly complex and politically difficult; it did not require a drastic expansion of the regulatory functions of the state. "To produce in plenty" required only the indirect manipulation of the economy through the use of fiscal and monetary "levers"; and to "distribute that plenty" required the creation of an efficient welfare system. Such measures were not (as some liberals had once believed) simply temporary stopgaps, keeping things going until some more basic solution could be found; they were themselves the solution.[67]

The renewed wartime faith in economic growth led, in short, to several ideological conclusions of considerable importance to the future of liberalism. It helped relegitimize American capitalism among a circle of men and women who had developed serious doubts about its viability in an advanced economy. It robbed the "regulatory" reform ideas of the late 1930s of their urgency and gave credence instead to Keynesian ideas of indirect management of the economy. And it fused the idea of the welfare state to the larger vision of sustained economic growth by defining social security mechanisms as ways to distribute income and enhance purchasing power. No other single factor was as central to the redefinition of liberal goals as the simple reality of abundance and the rebirth of faith in capitalism abundance helped to inspire.

VII

By the end of World War II, the concept of New Deal liberalism had assumed a new form; and in its assumptions could be seen the outlines of a transformed political world. Those who were taking the lead in defining a liberal agenda in the aftermath of the war still called themselves New Dealers, but they showed relatively little interest in the corporatist and regulatory ideas that had once played so large a role in shaping the New Deal. They largely ignored the New Deal's abortive experiments in economic planning, its failed efforts to create harmonious associational arrangements, its vigorous if short-lived antimonopoly and regulatory crusades, its open skepticism toward capitalism and its captains, its overt celebration of the state. Instead, they emphasized those New Deal accomplishments that could be reconciled more easily with the vision of an essentially compensatory government. They lauded the New Deal's innovations in social welfare and social insurance; a decade earlier many had considered such initiatives of secondary importance. They credited the New Deal with legitimizing government fiscal policy as a way of dealing with fluctuations in the business cycle and guaranteeing full employment; few liberals in the 1930s had understood, let alone supported, such policies. Above all, perhaps, postwar liberals celebrated the New Deal for having discovered solutions to the problems of capitalism that required no alteration in the structure of capitalism; for having defined a role for the state that did not intrude it too far into the economy. In earlier years, many liberals had considered the absence of significant institutional reform one of the New Deal's failures.

This transformation had proceeded slowly, at times almost imperceptibly, so much so that for a time many liberals were unaware that it had even occurred. But for those who cared to look, signs of the change were abundant. It was visible, for example, in the character of the postwar liberal community. The "planners," "regulators," and "antimonopolists" who had dominated liberal circles eight years earlier were now largely in eclipse, without much influence on public discourse. Thurman Arnold, Robert Jackson, and William Douglas were sitting on federal courts. Thomas Corcoran was practicing law. Benjamin Cohen was accepting occasional assignments as a delegate to international conferences. Leon Henderson, one of the last of the true "New Dealers" to hold a major administrative post during the war, had resigned as head of the Office of Price Administration in December 1942 and had become an embittered critic of the government's failures, convinced that without more assertive state planning and regulation the nation faced an economic disaster after the war.[68]

No comparably powerful network could be said to have emerged by 1945 to take their place; indeed, many liberals were now so preoccupied with international questions and with the emerging schism within their ranks over the Soviet Union that they paid less attention to domestic issues. But those who did attempt to define a domestic agenda were largely people fired with enthusiasm for the vision of a full-employment economy, people who considered the New Deal's principal legacy the idea of effective use of fiscal policy and the expansion of social welfare and insurance programs. In place of the "statist" liberals who had helped define public discourse in the 1930s were such people as Alvin Hansen, one of the architects of the principal liberal initiative of 1945, the Full Employment bill;[69] or Chester Bowles, the last director of the Office of Price Administration, whose 1946 book *Tomorrow Without Fear* called not for an expansion, or even a continuation, of the regulatory experiments with which he had been involved during the war but for an increased reliance on fiscal policy.[70]

The Democratic platform in 1944 was another sign of the changing political landscape. Four years earlier, the party had filled its platform with calls for attacks on "unbridled concentration of economic power and the exploitation of the consumer and the investor." It had boasted of the New Deal's regulatory innovations, its aggressive antitrust policies, its war on "the extortionate methods of monopoly."[71] The 1944 platform also praised the administration's antimonopoly and regulatory efforts—in a perfunctory sentence near the end. But most of its limited discussion of domestic issues centered on how the New Deal had "found the road to prosperity" through aggressive compensatory measures: fiscal policies and social welfare innovations.[72]

The changing landscape of liberalism was visible as well in some of the first retrospective celebrations of the New Deal, in the way early defenders of its legacy attempted to define its accomplishments. In 1948, Arthur M. Schlesinger, Jr., published an essay entitled "The Broad Accomplishments of the New Deal." The New Deal, he admitted, "made no fundamental attempt to grapple with the problem of the economies of concentration or of the decline in outlets for real investment." But that, he claimed, was not really the point. The New Deal's most significant accomplishments were much simpler and more important: "The New Deal took a broken and despairing land and gave it new confidence in itself. . . . All [Roosevelt's] solutions were incomplete. But then all great problems are insoluble."[73]

VIII

The importance of the New Deal lies in large part, of course, in its actual legislative and institutional achievements. But it lies as well in its ideological impact on subsequent generations of liberals and in its effects on two decades of postwar government activism. And in that light, the New Deal appears not just as a bright moment in which reform energies briefly prevailed but as part of a long process of ideological adaptation.

For more than half a century, Americans concerned about the impact of industrialization on their society—about the economic instability, the social dislocations, the manifest injustices—had harbored deep and continuing doubts about the institutions of capitalism. Relatively few had wanted to destroy those institutions, but many had wanted to use the powers of government to reshape or at least to tame them. And that desire had been a central element of "progressive" and "liberal" hopes from the late nineteenth century through the late 1930s.

The ideological history of the late New Deal, from the troubled years after 1937 through the conclusion of the war, is the story of a slow repudiation of such commitments and the elevation of other hopes to replace them. By 1945, American liberals, as the result of countless small adaptations to a broad range of experiences, had reached an accommodation with capitalism that served, in effect, to settle many of the most divisive conflicts of the first decades of the century. They had done so by convincing themselves that the achievements of the New Deal had already eliminated the most dangerous features of the capitalist system; by committing themselves to the belief that economic growth was the surest route to social progress; and by defining a role for the state that would, they believed, permit it to compensate for capitalism's inevitable flaws and omissions without interfering with its internal workings. Thus reconciled to the structure of their economy, liberals of the postwar world could move forward into new crusades—fighting for civil rights, eliminating poverty, saving the environment, protecting consumers, opposing communism, reshaping the world—crusades that would produce their own achievements and their own frustrations, and that would one day lead to another, still unfinished, ideological transformation.

NOTES

1. Hansen, "Toward Full Employment," speech at the University of Cincinnati, March 15, 1940, Alvin Hansen Papers, 3.10, Harvard University Archives, Cambridge, Mass.

2. See, for example, Morton Keller, *Affairs of State: Public Life in Late Nineteenth Century America* (Cambridge: Harvard University Press, 1977); and Stephen Skowronek, *Building an American State: The Expansion of National Administrative Capacities, 1877–1920* (Cambridge: Cambridge University Press, 1982).

3. Richard Hofstadter, *The Age of Reform* (New York: Alfred A. Knopf, 1955), 307. William Leuchtenburg challenges the idea of the New Deal's "ideological innocence" in *Franklin D. Roosevelt and the New Deal* (New York: Harper & Row, 1963), 34.

4. The best account of the origins of the NRA and its performance is Ellis

Hawley, *The New Deal and the Problem of Monopoly* (Princeton: Princeton University Press, 1966), 19–146.

5. Donald Richberg to Marvin McIntyre, March 10, 1938, and FDR to Richberg, January 15, 1941, both in Richberg MSS 2, Manuscripts Division, Library of Congress (hereafter, LC); James Farley speech in Winston Salem, N.C., February 6, 1940, Joseph Tumulty MSS 60, LC; "What Do They Mean: Monopoly?" *Fortune*, April 1938, 126; Robert Jackson, draft of unpublished autobiography, 1944, 135, Jackson MSS 188, LC. William Leuchtenburg contends that "the President believed deeply in the NRA approach and never gave up trying to restore it" (*Franklin D. Roosevelt and the New Deal*, 146).

6. George Soule, "Toward a Planned Society," *New Republic*, November 8, 1939, 31; "A New NRA," *Nation*, March 25, 1939, 337; Thurman Arnold, *The Folklore of Capitalism* (New Haven: Yale University Press, 1937), 221, 268; Arnold, "Feathers and Prices," *Common Sense*, July 1939, 6; David Cushman Coyle, "The Twilight of National Planning," *Harper's*, October 1935, 557–59. See also Hawley, *The New Deal and the Problem of Monopoly*, 143–146.

7. The existence of an informal network of liberals in the late 1930s was the subject of frequent comment in the popular press. See, for example, Joseph Alsop and Robert Kintner, "We Shall Make America Over: The New Dealers Move In," *Saturday Evening Post*, November 12, 1938, 8–9; Beverly Smith, "Corcoran and Cohen," *American Magazine*, August 1937, 22; Alva Johnston, "White House Tommy," *Saturday Evening Post*, July 31, 1937, 5–7; "A New NRA," 337. Surviving correspondence among members of the group helps confirm such reports. See, for example, Archibald MacLeish to Thomas Corcoran, May 2, 1942, MacLeish MSS 5, LC; MacLeish to Felix Frankfurter, January 26, 1940, MacLeish MSS 8, LC; William Douglas to Thurman Arnold, February 8, 1938, and Arnold to Douglas, February 11, 1938, both in Douglas MSS 14, LC; Hugo Black to Harold Ickes, August 15, 1935, Black MSS 34, LC; Benjamin Cohen to Hugo Black, February 2, 1938, Black MSS 23, LC.

8. The idea of a "capital strike" was most prominently associated at the time with Assistant Attorney General Robert Jackson, known in 1937 as a favorite of the president. Jackson used the phrase and explained the concept in a controversial speech before the American Political Science Association on December 29, 1937 (Jackson MSS 30, LC). So eager was the administration to believe this explanation that late in 1937 the president ordered the FBI to launch an investigation into the possibility of a criminal conspiracy. His evidence for the charge was extraordinarily frail: an unsubstantiated letter from a hotel waiter in Chicago who reported overhearing a conversation among railroad executives. They were, the waiter reported, conspiring to lay off workers as part of an "unemployment boycott" that would force Roosevelt "and his gang" to "come to terms." The FBI found no evidence to support the charge (Vasilia N. Getz to Roosevelt, November 19, 1937, Roosevelt to Homer Cummings, November 26, 1937, and J. Edgar Hoover to Roosevelt, December 11, 1937, all in Corcoran MSS 203, LC). See also "The Administration Strikes Back," *New Republic*, January 5, 1938, 240; Arthur D. Gayer,

"What Is Ahead?" *New Republic*, February 2, 1938, 391; George Soule, "What Has Happened—And Whose Fault Is It?" *New Republic*, February 2, 1938, 381; Irving Brant to Thomas Corcoran, January 5, 1938, Brant MSS 5, LC.

9. FDR to Robert Jackson, August 19, 1937, and Isador Lubin to Marvin McIntyre, August 25, 1937, both in President's Secretary's File (hereafter, PSF) 77, Franklin D. Roosevelt Library, Hyde Park, New York (hereafter, FDRL). Wayne C. Taylor to FDR, March 26, 1938; draft of "Monopoly Message," n.d., 1938; Huston Thompson to McIntyre, April 25, 1938: all in Official File (hereafter, OF) 277, FDRL. Samuel Rosenman, ed., *The Public Papers and Addresses of Franklin D. Roosevelt*, 13 vols. (New York: Random House, 1938–1950), 8: 305–20; Alsop and Kintner, "We Shall Make America Over," 86; Public Resolution No. 113, 75th Congress, "To create a temporary national economic committee," OF 3322, FDRL; "Trustbuster's Goal," *Business Week*, February 22, 1941, 35; Homer Cummings to FDR, April 21, 1938 (and accompanying memorandum from Arnold), OF 277, FDRL; Gene M. Gressley, "Thurman Arnold, Antitrust, and the New Deal," *Business History Review* 38 (1964): 217; Walter Millis, "Cross Purposes in the New Deal," *Virginia Quarterly Review* 14 (1938): 359–61.

10. "Trust Buster Benched," *Time*, February 22, 1943, 32–34; Corwin Edwards, "Thurman Arnold and the Antitrust Laws," *Political Science Quarterly* 58 (1943): 353–55; J. David Stern to Robert S. Allen, December 9, 1939, Thurman Arnold MSS, University of Wyoming; Leuchtenburg, *Franklin D. Roosevelt and the New Deal*, 259–60.

11. "Do Monopolies Retard or Advance Business Recovery?" *Town Meeting*, January 30, 1939, 11–12, 16; "How Far Should Government Control Business?" *Consensus* 23 (March 1939): 17; Arnold R. Sweezy, "Mr. Arnold and the Trusts," *New Republic*, June 8, 1942, 803–4.

12. Arnold, *The Folklore of Capitalism*, 211.

13. Arnold, "Feathers and Prices," 5–6; Thurman Arnold, "Confidence Must Replace Fear," *Vital Speeches*, July 1, 1942, 561. See also Arnold, *The Bottlenecks of Business* (New York: Harcourt Brace Jovanovich, 1940), 124; Arnold, "The Abuse of Patents," *Atlantic Monthly*, July 1942, 16.

14. Even Brandeis, the patron saint of antimonopoly, viewed the antitrust laws more as regulatory mechanisms than as vehicles for overt "trust-busting." But Brandeis and his allies always believed that regulation could itself prevent economic concentration, that restriction of unfair trade practices would forestall the creation of large combinations. He wrote in 1933: "I am so firmly convinced that the large unit is not as efficient—I mean the very large unit—as the smaller unit, that I believe that if it were possible today to make the corporations act in accordance with what doubtless all of us would agree should be the rules of trade no huge corporation would be created, or if created, would be successful." Arnold embraced no such assumptions. For an important discussion of Brandeis's regulatory philosophy, see Thomas K. McCraw, *Prophets of Regulation* (Cambridge: Harvard University Press, 1984), 94–109, 135–42; and McCraw, "Rethinking the Trust Question," in McCraw,

ed., *Regulation in Perspective: Historical Essays* (Boston: Harvard Business School, 1981), 1–55.

15. Hearings before a subcommittee of the Committee on the Judiciary, United States Senate, 75th Cong., 3d sess., March 11, 1938, in Wendell Berge MSS 15, LC; Henry Hyde to William Borah, July 6, 1938, Walter Williams to Borah, February 23, 1939, both in Borah MSS 772, LC. Borah's hostility toward Arnold was undoubtedly in part a result of the condescending description of Borah's own career in *The Folklore of Capitalism*: "Men like Senator Borah founded political careers on the continuance of such antitrust crusades, which were entirely futile but enormously picturesque, and which paid big dividends in terms of personal prestige" (p. 217).

16. Max Lerner to Thurman Arnold, December 4, 1938, Arnold MSS. See, especially, Adolf A. Berle, Jr., "Memorandum of Suggestions," July 12, 1938, and Berle to Steve Early, July 15, 1938, both in OF 3322, FDRL. Berle's lengthy memorandum, written at the request of Jerome Frank and Thurman Arnold, was intended to provide a "foundation for one branch of the investigation"; and its suggestions were apparently of significant influence. Much of the report focused on what Berle called "unwarranted assumptions" that the TNEC should avoid—most notably the assumption that there was any inherent connection between the size of an enterprise and its efficiency, competitiveness, or humaneness.

17. "Final Statement of Senator Joseph C. O'Mahoney, Chairman of the TNEC, at the Closing Public Session," March 11, 1941, reprint in Raymond Clapper MSS 182, LC; O'Mahoney to FDR, April 2, 1941, OF 3322, FDRL; Raymond Moley, "Monopoly Mystery," *Saturday Evening Post*, March 30, 1940, 9–11, and "Business in the Woodshed," ibid., May 6, 1940, 62, 68; Emmet F. Connely, "Let Business Roll Its Own: The TNEC, Stuart Chase, and the New Financing," *Harper's*, May 1940, 644–51; Lawrence Dennis, "The Essential Factual Details about the TNEC," privately circulated business newsletter, October 17, 1938, OF 3322, FDRL; "Twilight of TNEC," *Time*, April 14, 1941, 86–87; "TNEC: Magnificent Failure," *Business Week*, March 22, 1941, 22–27; Robert Brady, "Reports and Conclusions of the TNEC," *Economic Journal* 53 (1943): 415; Richard N. Chapman, "Contours of Public Policy, 1939–1945" (Ph.D. diss., Yale University, 1976), 152–53.

18. William Douglas to Karl Llewelyn, December 20, 1938, Douglas MSS 18, LC; Arnold, *The Folklore of Capitalism*, 389.

19. James M. Landis, *The Administrative Process* (New Haven: Yale University Press, 1938), 24–25. McCraw, *Prophets of Regulation*, 212–16, analyzes Landis's argument.

20. Arnold, *Bottlenecks of Business*, 122–26.

21. Herbert Stein, *The Fiscal Revolution in America* (Chicago: University of Chicago Press, 1969), 114–18; Dean L. May, *From New Deal to New Economics: The American Liberal Response to the Recession of 1937* (New York: Garland Books, 1981), 95.

22. Stein, *Fiscal Revolution*, 91–100; May, *From New Deal to New Economics*, 17–37.

23. Stein, *Fiscal Revolution*, 93. The quoted phrases are from Morgenthau's description of Eccles's advice to the president.

24. May, *From New Deal to New Economics*, 89.

25. Bruce Bliven, "Confidential: To the President," *New Republic*, April 20, 1938, 328.

26. May, *From New Deal to New Economics*, 123–25, 132–33.

27. Stein, *Fiscal Revolution*, 109–15.

28. Theda Skocpol and Margaret Weir, "State Structures and the Possibilities for Keynesian Responses to the Great Depression in Sweden, Britain, and the United States," in Peter B. Evans, Dietrich Rueschemeyer, and Skocpol, eds., *Bringing the State Back In* (New York: Cambridge University Press, 1985), 132–36.

29. Franklin D. Roosevelt, *The Public Papers and Addresses of Franklin D. Roosevelt* (New York: Macmillan, 1941), 1938 volume:240–41, 243.

30. Hansen, "Toward Full Employment," March 15, 1940, Hansen MSS, 3.10. "Perhaps I am getting to Keynesian," Hansen joked to Sir Dennis H. Robertson. Hansen to Robertson, September 29, 1939, ibid. See also Hansen, "Economic Progress and Declining Population Growth," *American Economic Review* 29 (1939): 1–15, a published version of Hansen's presidential address the previous year before the *American Economic Association*.

31. Leon Henderson, for example, served simultaneously as one of the leading advocates of increased spending and one of the architects of such regulatory efforts as the TNEC. When Roosevelt traveled back to Washington after the meeting in Warm Springs at which he agreed to increase his budget requests, Robert Jackson and Benjamin Cohen joined him on the train. In the course of the trip, they persuaded him to launch a vigorous antitrust campaign as a natural complement to the spending efforts (see Robert H. Jackson, draft of unpublished autobiography, 1944, p. 131, Jackson MSS 188, LC).

32. For a thoughtful analysis of the "mature economy" idea, see Theodore Rosenof, *Patterns of Political Economy in America: The Failure to Develop a Democratic Left Synthesis, 1933–1950* (New York: Garland Publishing, 1983), 39–46.

33. Schwellenbach speech in Seattle, July 15, 1938, Schwellenbach MSS 3, LC.

34. The prediction came from a 1938 report—*The Problems of a Changing Population*—published by the National Resources Committee (which later became the National Resource Planning Board). In fact, the population exceeded 175 million before the 1960 census (Philip W. Warken, *A History of the National Resource Planning Board, 1933–1943* [New York: Garland Publishing, 1979], 85–86).

35. Stuart Chase, "Freedom from Want," *Harper's*, October 1942, 468.

36. The best description of the World War I economic mobilization and of the gap between the reality of its performance and its later image is Robert D. Cuff's, *The War Industries Board: Business-Government Relations during World War I* (Baltimore: Johns Hopkins University Press), 7, 147–55, 220, 268–69,

and passim. See also Robert D. Cuff, "American Mobilization for War 1917–1945: Political Culture vs. Bureaucratic Administration," in N. F. Dreisziger, ed., *Mobilization for Total War: The Canadian, American, and British Experience, 1914–1918, 1937–1945* (Waterloo, Ont.: Wilfred Laurier University Press, 1981), 80; David M. Kennedy, *Over Here: The First World War and American Society* (New York: Oxford University Press, 1980), 113–43. William E. Leuchtenburg, "The New Deal and the Analogue of War," in John Braeman et al., eds., *Change and Continuity in Twentieth-Century America* (Columbus: Ohio State University Press, 1964), 81–143, suggests the degree to which the legacy of World War I served as an inspiration to New Deal efforts.

37. On public attitudes toward big business in the 1930s, see Louis Galambos, *The Public Image of Big Business in America, 1880–1940* (Baltimore: Johns Hopkins University Press, 1975), 222–52. "In the Great Depression," Galambos argues, "middle-class Americans mounted only a brief and rather feeble attack on big business. . . . [N]ew bureaucratic norms muffled hostility toward corporate enterprise, and on the eve of the Second World War they helped to ease Americans into an acceptance of big business" (pp. 246–47).

38. See Nelson Lichtenstein, *Labor's War at Home: The CIO in World War II* (New York: Cambridge University Press, 1982), 9–25; Bruce Catton, *The War Lords of Washington* (New York: Harcourt, Brace and Company, 1948), 92–96; Mike Davis, "The Barren Marriage of American Labor and the Democratic Party," *New Left Review* 124 (1980): 43–50.

39. Barry D. Karl, *The Uneasy State: The United States from 1915 to 1945* (Chicago: University of Chicago Press, 1983), makes a case for the central importance of anti-statism in twentieth-century America; see esp. pp. 1–7, 155–81, 205–39. See also Theodore Rosenof, "Freedom, Planning, and Totalitarianism: The Reception of F. A. Hayek's *Road to Serfdom*," *Canadian Review of American Studies* 5 (Fall 1974): 149–65, which assesses the impact of von Hayek's anti-statist tract of 1940 on American liberal thought; and Robert D. Cuff, "Commentary," in James Titus, ed., *The Home Front and War in the Twentieth Century* (United States Air Force Academy, 1984), 114–16.

40. Clifford Durr, "The Postwar Relationship Between Government and Business," *American Economic Review* 33 (1943): 47. See also George Soule, "The War in Washington," *New Republic*, September 27, 1939, 205–6; "New Deal Plans Industry Council," *Business Week*, March 20, 1943, 15.

41. Cuff, "American Mobilization for War 1917–1945," 83.

42. James MacGregor Burns, *Roosevelt: The Soldier of Freedom* (New York: Harcourt Brace Jovanovich, 1970), 190–94; Otis L. Graham, Jr., *Toward a Planned Society: From Roosevelt to Nixon* (New York: Oxford University Press, 1976), 69–72; Richard Polenberg, *War and Society: The United States, 1919–1945* (Philadelphia, Pa.: J. B. Lippincott Company, 1972), 6–9; Eliot Janeway, *The Struggle for Survival: A Chronicle of Economic Mobilization in World War II* (New Haven: Yale University Press, 1951), 123–25. Hugh Gregory Gallagher, *FDR's Splendid Deception* (New York: Dodd, Mead, 1985), offers a controversial blunt appraisal of Roosevelt's physical and mental condition in his last years; see esp. pp. 178–206.

118   *Alan Brinkley*

43. See Barry Karl, *Executive Organization and Reform in the New Deal* (Chicago: University of Chicago Press, 1963), and Richard Polenberg, *Reorganizing Roosevelt's Government, 1936–1939: The Controversy over Executive Reorganization* (Cambridge: Harvard University Press, 1966). Discussions of the limits of state capacity and the influence of those limits on the New Deal include Theda Skocpol, "Political Response to Capitalist Crisis," *Politics and Society* 10 (1980): 155–201; Skocpol and Kenneth Finegold, "State Capacity and Economic Intervention in the New Deal," *Political Science Quarterly* 97 (1982): 255–78; James T. Patterson, *The New Deal and the States: Federalism in Transition* (Princeton: Princeton University Press, 1969), 201–7. The lack of "state capacity" to manage the economy had been most conspicuously visible during the NRA experiment of 1933–35.

44. Paul A. C. Koistinen, "The Hammer and the Sword: Labor, the Military, and Industrial Mobilization, 1920–1945" (Ph.D. diss., University of California, Berkeley, 1964), 60–77; Koistinen, "Mobilizing the World War II Economy: Labor and the Industrial-Military Alliance," *Pacific Historical Review* 42 (November 1973): 443–78; Chapman, "Contours of Public Policy," 91–93; Donald M. Nelson, *Arsenal of Democracy: The Story of American War Production* (New York: Harcourt, Brace and Company, 1946), 25–193; Michael Straight, "Victory on the Factory Front," *New Republic*, January 26, 1942, 105–6.

45. Nelson, *Arsenal of Democracy*, 329–48; Koistinen, "The Hammer and the Sword," 663; "Don Nelson's Men," *Business Week*, July 4, 1942, 46–58; Julius Krug to Manly Fleischmann, November 23, 1943, Krug MSS 1, LC; "The Pain and the Necessity," *Time*, June 29, 1942, 18; "The War Production Board: Is It?" *Fortune*, March 1943, 94–97; "Truman and Nelson," *New Republic*, June 29, 1942, 879–80; Marver Bernstein, "Political Ideas of Selected American Business Journals," *Public Opinion Quarterly* 17 (1953): 258–67; David Vogel, "Why Businessmen Distrust Their State: The Political Consciousness of American Corporate Executives," *British Journal of Political Science* 8 (1978): 45–78; Roland N. Stromberg, "American Business and the Approach of War, 1935–1941," *Journal of Economic History* 13 (1953): 58–78; Edwin M. Epstein, "The Social Role of Business Enterprise in Britain: An American Perspective: Part I," *The Journal of Management Studies* 13 (1976): 212–33.

46. I. F. Stone, "Nelson and Guthrie," *Nation*, June 27, 1942, 731.

47. Catton, *The War Lords of Washington*, 247.

48. Ibid., 310–11; John Morton Blum, *V Was for Victory: Politics and American Culture During World War II* (New York: Harcourt Brace Jovanovich, 1976), 124–31; Nelson, *Arsenal of Democracy*, 269–89; Jim F. Heath, "American War Mobilization and the Use of Small Manufacturers, 1939–1943," *Business History Review* 46 (1972): 317–19. Roosevelt wrote to James F. Byrnes late in 1942: "This Small Business problem has baffled me, as you know, for nearly two years. We have not met it—and I am not sure that it can be met." He raised the "wild idea" of appointing Joseph Kennedy to head the Smaller War Plants Corporation, an agency he had created within the WPB to protect

the interests of small business. Kennedy refused the offer, explaining (according to Byrnes) that he doubted "that anyone could accomplish anything of value to small business," and that certainly no accomplishments were possible given the limited authority of the swpc. (FDR to Byrnes, December 18, 1942, and Byrnes to FDR, January 14, 1943, OF 4735-F, FDRL).

49. "The War Production Board: Is It?" 94.

50. Harold Ickes to Lady Bird Johnson, August 13, 1942, Ickes MSS 161, LC. See also Julius Krug to Manly Fleischmann, November 23, 1943, Krug MSS 1, LC, in which Krug says sarcastically of Nelson: "Don is back from his interesting trip so that we now again have the cool, courageous, decisive leadership to which we have become accustomed."

51. Early in 1943, Nelson's critics in the administration (and in the War Department in particular) persuaded the president to fire him and appoint Bernard Baruch to head the wpb in his stead. But Nelson got wind of the decision before it was publicly announced and managed to preempt it by dismissing Ferdinand Eberstadt, one of his most powerful and controversial deputies, and in the process made a conspicuous public demonstration of decisiveness. Roosevelt quietly backed down and allowed Nelson to remain in office. See Catton, *The War Lords of Washington*, 205–7; Robert K. Murray, "Government and Labor During World War II," *Current History* 37 (1959): 146–49; Charles E. Wilson to FDR, August 23, 1944, and Harold Ickes to FDR, April 17, 1943, both in OF 4735, FDRL; Harry S. Truman to Lou E. Holland, June 20, 1942, Senatorial File 116, Harry S. Truman Library (hereafter, HSTL), Independence, Missouri; I. F. Stone, "Nelson vs. Wilson," *Nation*, September 22, 1944, 259–60; Nelson, *Arsenal of Democracy*, 381–90; Blum, *V Was for Victory*, 117–31.

52. " 'Dear Charlie,' " *Time*, September 4, 1944, 18–19; J. P. McEvoy, "The Nation's Busiest Businessman," *Reader's Digest*, June 1942, 41–43; "Nelson Gets World's Biggest Single Job," *Life*, January 26, 1942, 29.

53. Arnold to White, September 9, 1943, White MSS C413, LC.

54. Between 1939 and 1944, the American GNP (measured in constant dollars) grew by more than 50 percent. Although the bulk of the growth was a result of military production, the consumer economy expanded by 12 percent during the same years. Unemployment, the most persistent and troubling economic problem of the 1930s, all but vanished (Alan S. Milward, *War, Economy, and Society: 1939–1945* [Berkeley and Los Angeles: University of California Press, 1977], 63–65; Blum, *V Was for Victory*, 90–93).

55. Alvin Hansen, "Planning Full Employment," *Nation*, October 21, 1941, 492.

56. "Is There a New Frontier?" *New Republic*, November 27, 1944, 708–10; "A New Bill of Rights," *Nation*, March 20, 1943, 402; Stein, *The Fiscal Revolution in America*, 175–77.

57. National Resources Planning Board (hereafter, NRPB), "National Resources Development Report for 1943," p. 4, PSF 185, FDRL; Milward, *War, Economy, and Society*, 330. Wartime public opinion polls suggested that the majority of the public was coming to believe that postwar economic

growth offered the best route to meeting the nation's social needs and that interest in government job programs was waning (see Office of Public Opinion Research, "Presenting Post-War Planning to the Public," OF 4351, FDRL; Harlow S. Person to Morris L. Cooke, October 3, 1944, President's Personal File, 940, FDRL.

58. Chapman, "Contours of Public Policy," 30–31, 342–45, 358; Office of Facts and Figures, "War Aims and Postwar Policies," March 17, 1942, MacLeish MSS 5, LC; Milward, *War, Economy, and Society*, 330.

59. Philip J. Funigiello, *The Challenge to Urban Liberalism: Federal-City Relations during World War II* (Knoxville: University of Tennessee Press, 1978), 11, 180–85, 197; Graham, *Toward a Planned Society*, 52–58; Chapman, "Contours of Public Policy," 342–43.

60. Frederic Delano et al. to FDR, August 24, 1943, OF 1092, FDRL; NRPB, "Post-War Plan and Program," February 1943, Senatorial File 43, HSTL.

61. NRPB, *Security, Work, and Relief Policies* (Washington, D.C.: Government Printing Office, 1942). Beveridge claimed that full employment was a "basic assumption" of his own plan, and it is clear that he believed his social welfare and insurance proposals—proposals considerably more extensive than those of the NRPB—would contribute to that end. But the Beveridge Report contained no direct mechanisms for ensuring full employment, and indeed Beveridge himself warned against the accumulation of public debt in pursuit of social goals. The NRPB proposed, in addition to aggressive use of federal spending, making the government the employer of last resort; and its members had few inhibitions about deficit spending as a means to that end (see, e.g., Eveline M. Burns, "Comparison of the NRPB Report with the Beveridge Report," December 26, 1942, PIN.8, 167, Public Records Office [hereafter, PRO], London). T. J. Woofter, Jr., to Roger Evans, April 20, 1943, and Alvin Hansen to Beveridge, July 3, 1943, both in William Beveridge MSS, XI-31, British Library of Political and Economic Science, London School of Economics.

62. NRPB, "National Resources Development Report"; NRPB, "The NRPB in Wartime," *Frontiers of Democracy* 8 (February 1942): 143. See also memorandum to Stephen Early (telephone summaries), February 4, 1943, OF 1092 (5), FDRL; L. B. Parker to Rep. Harry Sheppard, March 11, 1943, OF 4351 (2), FDRL; Bruce Bliven, Max Lerner, and George Soule, "Charter for America," *New Republic*, April 19, 1943, 528; J. Raymond Walsh, "Action for Postwar Planning," *Antioch Review* 3 (1943): 153–61.

63. I. F. Stone, "Planning and Politics," *Nation*, March 20, 1943, 405. See also "Postwar Portent," *Newsweek*, March 22, 1943, 31–34, and L. G. Rockwell, "The National Resource Planning Board in the United States," *Public Affairs* 6 (1942): 9–13.

64. NRPB, "National Resources Development Report," p. 4; Ernest K. Lindley, "How the Postwar Reports Came to Be," *Newsweek*, March 22, 1943, 27. Bliven, "Charter for America," 539–42, is a good example of how some liberals gave more emphasis to the NRPB's proposals for structural reform

than did the NRPB itself. See also Chapman, "Contours of Public Policy," 363; Harold Smith to FDR, April 27, 1942, OF 788, FDRL.

65. William O. Douglas to Keynes, July 29, 1937, Douglas MSS 8, LC; Felix Frankfurter to Alfred Harcourt, February 2, 1939, MacLeish MSS 8, LC; Archibald MacLeish to Keynes, July 8, 1941 and October 10, 1944, both in MacLeish MSS 12, LC; Chapman, "Contours of Public Policy," 11–13. See Robert Lekachman, *The Age of Keynes* (New York: Random House, 1966), 124–43, for a discussion of the rise of an indigenous American "Keynesian school" of economists after 1937.

66. Richard Strout, "Hansen of Harvard," *New Republic* December 29, 1941, 888–89; Alvin Hansen and Guy Greer, "The Federal Debt and the Future," *Harper's*, April 1942, 500; Hansen, "Wanted: Ten Million Jobs," *Atlantic*, September 1943, 68–69.

67. Skidelsky, "Keynes and the Reconstruction of Liberalism," *Encounter*, 29–32; Stein, *Fiscal Revolution*, 169–96; Donald T. Critchlow, "The Political Control of the Economy: Deficit Spending as a Political Belief, 1932–1952," *Public Historian* 3 (1981): 5–22; Herbert Feis, "Keynes in Retrospect," *Foreign Affairs* 29 (1951): 576–77; Alfred H. Bornemann, "The Keynesian Paradigm and Economic Policy," *American Journal of Economics and Sociology* 35 (1976): 126–28.

68. One revealing glimpse of Henderson's bitterness after 1942 is in a report by Richard Miles of the British embassy in Washington of a dinner party in late 1943 at which Henderson was a guest and during which he spoke harshly (and apparently constantly) about the abysmal state of liberal government (Redvers Opie to Gladwyn Jebb, November 30, 1943, F0371-35368, PRO).

69. Alvin Hansen, "Suggested Revision of the Full Employment Bill," Hansen MSS, 3.10.

70. Chester Bowles, *Tomorrow Without Fear* (New York: Simon & Schuster, 1946).

71. "Democratic Platform of 1940," reprinted in Democratic National Committee, *Democratic Campaign Handbook* (1940), 84–90.

72. "The 1944 Democratic Platform," *Democratic Digest*, August 1944, 13, 27.

73. Arthur M. Schlesinger, Jr., "The Broad Accomplishments of the New Deal," in Seymour Harris, ed., *Saving American Capitalism* (New York: Alfred A. Knopf, 1948), 78, 80.

For their generosity in commenting on earlier drafts of this essay, the author is grateful to Daniel Aaron, Brian Balogh, Robert Cuff, Frank Freidel, Gary Gerstle, Hugh Heclo, Bradford Lee, Mark Leff, William Leuchtenburg, Nelson Lichtenstein, Richard L. McCormick, Michael McGerr, James T. Patterson, Roy Rosenzweig, Judith Shklar, and Theda Skocpol.

5   From Corporatism to Collective Bargaining: Organized Labor and the Eclipse of Social Democracy in the Postwar Era

NELSON LICHTENSTEIN

*I*N RECENT years the decline of the trade union movement and the eclipse of the liberal ideology it long sustained has thrown into question the political assumptions and organizational structures upon which the New Deal system of social regulation has rested. While the postwar generation of economists and social scientists once found the social and political "settlement" of the 1940s a bulwark of pluralist democracy and progressive economic advance, contemporary observers have been far more critical. Because of its very stability, the "labor-capital accord" that emerged after World War II may well have foreclosed the possibility of a more progressive approach to American capitalism's chronic difficulties, made manifest in the Great Depression itself, and then, more than a generation later, in the social tensions that accompanied the latter-day erosion of American industry's world hegemony. In this process the peculiarly American system of interclass accommodation that jelled in the 1940s—a decentralized system characterized by extremely detailed, firm-centered collective bargaining contracts, a relatively low level of social welfare spending, and a labor market segmented by race, gender, region, and industry—stood counterposed to the once hopeful effort to expand the welfare state and refashion American politics along more "European," explicitly social democratic lines.[1]

The turning point came between 1946 and 1948 when a still powerful trade union movement found its efforts to bargain over the shape of the postwar political economy decisively blocked by a powerful remobilization of business and conservative forces. Labor's ambitions were thereafter sharply curbed, and its economic program was reduced to a sort of militant interest group politics, in which a Keynesian emphasis on sustained growth and productivity gain-sharing replaced labor's earlier commitment to economic planning and social solidarity. This forced retreat narrowed the political appeal of labor-liberalism and contributed both to the demobilization and division of those social forces which had long sustained it.

UNION POWER

The dramatic growth of the organized working class put the American system of industrial relations at a crossroads in 1945. In the years since 1933 the number of unionized workers had increased more than fivefold to over fourteen million. About 30 percent of all American workers were organized, a density greater than at any time before and a level that for the first time equaled that of northern Europe. Unions seemed on the verge of recruiting millions of new workers in the service trades, in white collar occupations, across great stretches of the South and Southwest, and even among the lower ranks of management.[2] "Your success has been one of the most surprising products of American politics in several generations," Interior Secretary Harold Ickes told a cheering CIO convention just after Roosevelt's 1944 reelection. "You are on your way and you must let no one stop you or even slow up your march." Three years later, the sober-minded Harvard economist Sumner Slichter still counted U.S. trade unions "the most powerful economic organizations which the country has ever seen."[3]

It was not size alone that contributed to this assessment. The élan so noticeable in many sections of the labor movement rested upon a degree of union consciousness, in some cases amounting to working-class loyalty, that would today seem quite extraordinary. The mid-1940s were no period of social quiescence, for the war itself had had a complex and dichotomous impact on working Americans. On the one hand it had provided them with a taste of postwar affluence and had attuned them to the daily influence of large, bureaucratic institutions like the military and the government mobilization agencies. But the labor shortages of that era and the social patriotic ideology advanced by government and union alike engendered a self-confident mood that quickly translated itself into a remarkable burst of rank-and-file activity. Led by shop stewards and local union officers, hundreds of thousands of workers had taken part in a wildcat strike movement that had focused on a militant defense of union power in the workplace itself. And the now forgotten series of postwar general strikes called by central labor councils in Oakland, California; Lancaster, Pennsylvania; Stamford, Connecticut; and Akron, Ohio are indicative of the extent to which working-class activity still retained an occasionally explosive character even in the later half of the 1940s.[4]

The economic power wielded by American trade unions was by its very nature political power, for the New Deal had thoroughly politicized all relations between the union movement, the business community, and the state. The New Deal differed from previous eras of state activism not only because of the relatively more favorable political and legislative environment it created for organized labor but, perhaps even more important, because the New Deal provided a set of semipermanent political structures in which key issues of vital concern to the trade union movement might be accommodated. Although the industry codes negotiated under the National Recovery Administration were declared unconstitutional in 1935, the Fair Labor Standards Act established new wage and hour standards three years later. The National Labor Relations Board established the legal basis of union power and provided the arena in which jurisdictional disputes between the unions might be resolved, while the National War Labor Board had provided a tripartite institution that both set national wage policy and contributed to the rapid wartime growth of the new trade unions. The successive appearances of these agencies seemed to signal the fact that in the future as in the past, the fortunes of organized labor would be determined as much by a process of politicized bargaining in Washington as by the give and take of contract collective bargaining.[5]

As a result of the wartime mobilization the United States seemed to advance toward the kind of labor-backed corporatism that would later characterize social policy in northern Europe and Scandinavia. Corporatism of this sort called for government agencies, composed of capital, labor, and "public" representatives, to substitute rational, democratic planning for the chaos and inequities of the market. The premier examples of such corporatist institutions in 1940s America were the War Labor Board and its wartime companion, the Office of Price Administration—administrative regimes that began to reorder wage and price relations within and between industries. Although union officials often denounced both agencies for their accommodation of politically resourceful business and producer groups, the maintenance of institutions such as these were nevertheless seen by most liberal and labor spokesmen as the kernel of a postwar "incomes" policy. That policy would continue the rationalization of the labor market begun during the war, set profit and price guidelines, and redistribute income into worker and consumer hands. These agencies were usually staffed by individuals somewhat sympathetic to their consumer and trade union constituencies and headed by New Dealers like Chester Bowles and William H. Davis who recognized the legitimacy of labor's corporate interests.[6]

The War Labor Board, for example, socialized much of the trade union movement's prewar agenda, thus making seniority and grievance systems, vacation pay and night-shift supplements, sick leave and paid mealtimes, standard "entitlements" mandated for an increasingly large section of the working class. Likewise, the Little Steel wage formula, although bitterly resisted by the more highly paid and well organized sections of the working class, had enough loopholes and special dispensations to enable low-paid workers in labor-short industries to bring their wages closer to the national average. Thus black wages rose twice as rapidly as white, and weekly earnings in cotton textiles and in retail trade increased about 50 percent faster than in high-wage industries like steel and auto.[7] By the onset of postwar reconversion, WLB wage policy was explicitly egalitarian. "It is not desirable to increase hourly earnings in each industry in accordance with the rise of productivity in that industry," declared a July 1945 memorandum. "The proper goal of policy is to increase hourly earning generally in proportion to the average increase of productivity in the economy *as a whole*."[8]

LABOR'S VISION

Since contemporary trade unions have often been equated with "special interest politics," it is important to recognize that the American trade union movement of the immediate postwar era, and especially its industrial union wing, adopted a social agenda that was broad, ambitious, and not without prospects for success. The unions thought the welfare of the working class would be advanced not only, or even primarily, by periodic wage bargaining but through a political realignment of the major parties that would give them a powerful voice in the management of industry, planning the overall political economy and expansion of the welfare state. The union agenda was never an entirely consistent one, but its thrust meshed well with the corporatist strain that characterized late New Deal social policy.

This perspective was most graphically manifest in the demand for tripartite industry governance, embodied in the Industry Council Plan put forward by CIO president Philip Murray early in the war. The industry council idea represented an admixture of Catholic social reformism and New Deal era faith in business-labor-government cooperation. Under the general guidance of a friendly government, the Industry Council Plan contemplated the fusion of economic and political bargaining at the very highest levels of industry governance. Here was the essence of the CIO's corporatist vision: organized labor would have a voice in the production goals, investment decisions, and employment patterns of the nation's core industries. "The Industry Council Plan," wrote Philip Murray, "is a program for democratic economic planning and for participation by the people in the key decisions of the big corporations." Such important elements of the union movement's wartime agenda as the Guaranteed Annual Wage, industry-wide bargaining, and rationalization of the wage structure could be won only through this initiative.[9]

If the CIO plan had something of an abstract air about it, the proposals put forward by the young autoworker leader, Walter Reuther, had a good deal more political bite. Reuther rose to national prominence in 1940 and 1941 with a widely publicized "500 planes a day" plan to resolve the military aviation bottleneck through a state-sponsored rationalization of the entire auto/aircraft industry. Reuther proposed a tripartite Aircraft Production Board that would have the power to reorganize production facilities without regard for corporate boundaries, markets, or personnel. It would conscript labor and work space where and when needed and secure for the UAW at least a veto over a wide range of managerial functions. Winning wide support among those New Dealers who still retained a commitment to social planning, the Reuther plan was ultimately delayed and then defeated by an automobile industry both hostile to social experimentation and increasingly well represented within the government's wartime production agencies.[10]

The Reuther plan nevertheless cast a long shadow, for it contained hallmarks of the strategic approach so characteristic of labor-liberalism in the 1940s: an assault on management's traditional power made in the name of economic efficiency and the public interest, and an effort to shift power relations within the structure of industry and politics, usually by means of a tripartite governmental entity empowered to plan for whole sections of the economy. Thus did auto executive George Romney declare, "Walter Reuther is the most dangerous man in Detroit because no one is more skillful in bringing about the revolution without seeming to disturb the existing forms of society."[11]

Indeed, the union movement defined the left wing of what was possible in the political affairs of the day. Its vision and its power attracted a species of political animal hardly existant today, the "labor-liberal" who saw organized labor as absolutely central to the successful pursuit of his political agenda. After 1943 the CIO's new Political Action Committee put organizational backbone into the northern Democratic party, and the next year its "People's Program for 1944" codified many of the central themes that would define liberalism in the immediate postwar years: big-power cooperation, full employment, cultural pluralism, and economic planning.[12] "Labor's role in our national progress is unique and paramount," affirmed Supreme Court justice William O. Douglas as late as 1948. "It is labor, organized and independent labor, that can supply much of the leadership, energy and motive power which we need today."[13]

But labor-liberalism was never a coherent or static doctrine, and in the mid-decade years its opinion-molding, policy-oriented adherents had made a subtle shift in their thinking about how the political economy could be made both efficient and just. New Dealers who had once entertained "underconsumptionist" assumptions of U.S. economic maturity and stagnation had been startled by the remarkable success of the American mobilization effort. Structural changes in the distribution of economic power, such as those envisioned by the CIO's various schemes for tripartite governance of industry, now seemed less necessary to ensure economic growth and full employment. "Our phenomenal economic success in the forties is a tribute to the resiliency of the system," declared economist Seymour E. Harris in the introduction to a 1948 collection of essays by Leon Keyserling, Alvin Hansen, Chester Bowles, and other New Dealers. *Saving American Capitalism: A Liberal Economic Program* saw a Keynesian program of demand stimulation, social welfare expenditure, and economic planning for specific industry sectors and geographic regions as the "blueprint for a second new deal," designed to assure that "capitalism is not but a passing phase in the historical process from feudalism to socialism."[14] High on this liberal agenda was a long-overdue expansion of Social Security and unemployment insurance, elaboration of a system of national health insurance, and a commitment to full employment. Union wage demands were of particular social usefulness, for now the labor movement's traditional demand for higher income meshed easily with the emerging Keynesian view that aggregate demand must be sustained and income redistributed to avoid a new slump.

During World War II many liberals had seen the regulatory apparatus of the federal government as the key arena in which such plans for postwar reconstruction might be generated. But their failure to prevent corporate domination of the reconversion process, combined with their disappointment that the long-sought Employment Act of 1946 eschewed real economic planning, forced those economists and administrators who had championed a progressive reconversion program to look elsewhere, primarily to the union movement where the economic muscle and voting strength of labor's battalions might yet advance their agenda. Thus Donald Montgomery, the former Agriculture Department consumer counsel who resigned when that department undermined wartime price controls, took over the UAW's Washington office, and in 1945 emerged as the author of "Purchasing Power for Prosperity," the UAW's left-Keynesian manifesto in the 1945–46 GM strike. Likewise, Robert Nathan, who had played a central role in shaping the abortive reconversion schemes of the Office of War Mobilization and Reconversion, reemerged in 1947 as the author of the CIO's "Nathan Report," which advocated a classwide wage increase as a way of repairing the damage done by the collapse of price controls and fulfilling the redistributive economic program the Truman administration was unwilling to inaugurate.[15]

LABOR AND THE SEARCH FOR A RECONVERSION WAGE PROGRAM

The CIO hoped to take the tripartite, corporatist model of wage-price bargaining that had emerged during the war and use it to bridge the uncertain political currents of the reconversion era. The industrial union federation wanted a National Production Board that would preside over the reconversion of defense plants to civilian production, maintain a semblance of price control, and establish a set of wage guidelines designed to defend working-class incomes. As CIO president Philip Murray told a 1944 labor meeting, "Only chaos and destruction of our industrial life will result if employers look to the war's end as an opportunity for a union-breaking, wage cutting, open-shop drive, and if labor unions have to resort to widespread strikes to defend their very existence and the living standards of their members."[16] To forestall such a prospect, the CIO in March 1945 sponsored a "Labor-Management Charter" with William Green of the AFL and Eric Johnston, the corporate liberal president of the U.S. Chamber of Commerce. Consisting of a list of often irreconcilable platitudes hailing the virtues of unfettered free enterprise and the rights of labor, the charter nevertheless symbolized the CIO's hope for cooperation with the liberal wing of American capitalism in stabilizing postwar industrial relations along roughly the lines established during the war. "It's Industrial Peace for the Postwar Period," headlined the *CIO News*. In return for management support for the unamended Wagner Act and a high-wage, high-employment postwar strategy, the unions pledged to defend "a system of private competitive capitalism" including "the inherent right and responsibility of management to direct the operations of an enterprise."[17]

The businessmen with whom the CIO hoped to work were collective bargaining progressives and moderate Keynesians who favored a countercyclic fiscal policy and a degree of structural reform as the minimum program necessary to stabilize postwar capitalism. Often influenced by the Committee for Economic Development and the Twentieth Century Fund, they also supported the 1946 Full Employment Act in something like its original, liberal form. Among these progressive industrialists with whom the CIO sought an alliance, in addition to the Chamber of Commerce's Eric Johnston, who called for a "people's capitalism" in the postwar era, was Paul Hoffman of the Studebaker Corporation, who took pride in his company's harmonious relationship with organized labor. But the most famous of these progressives was undoubtedly Henry J. Kaiser, the maverick West Coast industrialist who had built his empire on New Deal construction projects and wartime contracts. Hardly an opponent of government planning or public works spending, Kaiser's good relations with the unions and the pioneering health-care facilities at his shipyards and mills added to his reputation as a social liberal. In 1945 he won strong UAW cooperation for a well-publicized effort to convert the giant Willow Run bomber plant to civilian car production.[18]

Implementation of a new wage-price policy was one of the key elements in such an accord with the liberal wing of the business community, so state action was essential. The CIO wanted a 20- or 30-percent increase in real wages to make up for the elimination of overtime pay at the end of the war, and many New Dealers like Commerce Secretary Henry Wallace and William Davis, now head of the Office of Economic Stabilization, considered such a wage boost essential to maintain living standards and avoid the long-feared postwar downturn.[19]

Such forecasts were music to CIO ears, but the political and social base for such a liberal postwar prospect had already been eroded. Since 1938 labor-liberalism had been on the defensive, stymied by the defection of Southern agriculture from the New Deal coalition, by the political rejuvenation of a conservative manufacturing interest during World War II, and by the reemergence of long-standing ethnic and social tensions within the urban Democratic party. Certainly emblematic of this stalemate was Harry Truman's selection as vice-president in 1944, replacing Henry Wallace, the labor-liberal favorite. FDR's successor was not a New Dealer, but a border-state Democrat, a party centrist whose political skill would lie in successfully presiding over an increasingly factionalized party coalition.[20]

Truman certainly recognized that in order to govern, the unions and their liberal allies had to be accommodated—this was the lesson that Clark Clifford would drill home in his famous strategy memorandum on the 1948 campaign—but even before the cold war came to dominate its outlook, the personnel of his administration took on a particularly parochial outlook. Within a year virtually all of FDR's cabinet resigned, to be replaced by men like John Snyder, a Missouri banker now at the Office of War Mobilization and Reconversion who would come to have an "ideological fear" of Walter Reuther. California oilman Edwin Pauley, now at the Navy Department, sought industry exploitation of the government's rich oil reserves.[21] Moreover, Truman had none of the patrician equanimity with which FDR faced the leaders of the labor movement. Although the President prided himself on his humble origins, he found emotionally jarring and somehow illegitimate the power and resources now commanded by trade union leaders. Thus Clark Clifford remembered a bitter 1946 showdown with the United Mine Workers' John L. Lewis as "the moment when Truman finally and irrevocably stepped out from the shadow of FDR to become President in his own right."[22]

Truman's inadequacies aside, the CIO had profoundly misjudged the tenor of the postwar business community. The progressive industrialists with whom the industrial union federation hoped to achieve an accord were in fact a relatively uninfluential minority. Key business spokesmen were those practical conservatives who presided over the core manufacturing firms in the unionized steel, electrical, auto, rubber, and transport industries. Led by men such as John A. Stephens of U.S. Steel, Ira Mosher of the National Association of Manufacturers, and Charles E. Wilson of General Motors, these industrialists had emerged from the war with enormous sophistication and self-confidence. Unlike their counterparts in continental Europe, or even in the British Isles, who had been tarred with the brush of collaboration or appeasement, American business leaders found the wartime experience one of both commercial success and political advance. They felt in little need of the kind of state-sponsored labor-management collaboration that helped legitimize a mixed capitalist economy in Germany, France, and Italy in the immediate postwar era.

These industrialists recognized the potential usefulness of the new industrial unions as stabilizers of the labor force and moderators of industrial conflict, but they also sought the restoration of managerial prerogatives that wartime conditions had eroded in the areas of product pricing, market allocation, and shop-floor work environment. They were intensely suspicious of the kind of New Deal social engineering favored by labor, and only with some reluctance did they accommodate themselves to the modest degree of economic stimulation that would later go by the name "commercial Keynesianism." Looking forward to a postwar boom, they wanted to be free of government or union interference in determining the wage-price relationship in each industry.[23] Thus the long-awaited Labor-Management conference that President Truman convened in November 1945 was doomed to failure. No accord proved possible on either the prerogatives of management or the scope of legitimate union demands, and on the crucial issue of a general wage policy, the CIO got nowhere. Philip Murray offered industry a de facto policy of labor peace in return for a pattern wage increase, which Truman had endorsed in a speech of October 30, but the opposition was so great that the issue never secured a place on the formal conference agenda.[24]

The CIO faced resistance not only from industry but from within the labor movement itself. The AFL unions had never been as committed as the CIO to the tripartite bargaining arrangements of the war era, and these unions demanded a return to free and unrestricted collective bargaining. In part this stemmed from the AFL's tradition of Gompersarian voluntarism, but it also reflected the contrasting organizational base of the two labor federations. The CIO industrial unions were overwhelmingly concentrated in the manufacturing sector of the economy where they faced oligopolistically organized employers who were themselves capable of imposing a new wage pattern. But only 35 percent of AFL membership lay in this heavy industrial sector, while construction, transportation, and service trades proved the federation's most important centers of strength. These decentralized, and now booming, sectors of the economy were less subject to the pattern-setting guidelines established by core firms like General Motors and U.S. Steel. With almost seven million members in 1945, the AFL was not only 30 percent larger than the CIO but actually growing more rapidly, in part because its flexible model of mixed craft and industrial unionism seemed to fit more closely the actual contours of the postwar economy than did the CIO brand of mass organization. This meant that although CIO unions like the Steelworkers and the UAW remained innovative and powerful institutions, their political and organizational weight was often less impressive than it seemed.[25]

Although he was an industrial unionist, John L. Lewis spoke most forthrightly for the AFL viewpoint. Repeated clashes between the UMW and the Roosevelt administration during the war had soured the mine leader on the kind of state-sponsored industrial planning arrangements he had once advocated as the CIO's first president. Lewis was now determined to exercise his union's power unfettered by a new set of federal regulations. "What Murray and the CIO are asking for," declared Lewis at the Labor-Management conference, "is a corporate state, wherein the activities of the people are regulated and constrained by a dictatorial government. We are opposed to the corporate state."[26]

THE GM STRIKE AND AMERICAN LIBERALISM

This stalemate led directly to the General Motors strike, actually begun while the conference remained in session, and then to the general strike wave that spread throughout basic industry in the winter of 1946. Like Walter Reuther's other wartime "plans," the GM strike program made a strong appeal to the "national" interest, this time not so much in terms of rationalized production and democratic control, but as part of the emerging Keynesian consensus that a substantial boost in mass purchasing power would be necessary to avoid a postwar depression. The UAW's demand that industry pacesetter GM raise wages by some 30 percent without increasing the price of its product seemed adventuresome in a collective bargaining negotiation; even more so was its demand that GM "open the books" to demonstrate its ability to pay. The company quickly denounced these UAW demands as European-style socialism, but they were in fact little more than standard OPA price-setting procedures now translated into the language of collective bargaining.[27]

While this program was formally directed against the giant automaker, it was in practice a union demand against the state as well, for its ultimate success rested upon the ability of an increasingly embattled OPA to resist industry pressure and enforce price guidelines well into the postwar era. This program won Reuther a wave of support, both within the UAW, where it prepared the way for his election as union president, and among influential liberals who identified with the union effort. A union-sponsored "National Citizens Committee on the GM-UAW Dispute" lauded the UAW's determination to lift "collective bargaining to a new high level by insisting that the advancement of Labor's interest shall not be made at the expense of the public." And a strike support committee, headquartered at NAACP offices in New York, quickly enrolled such luminaries as Eleanor Roosevelt, Wayne Morse, Reinhold Niebuhr, Walter White, and Leon Henderson.[28]

Reuther and the rest of the CIO won an 18.5-cent wage increase during the postwar round of strikes and negotiations that ended in the late winter of 1946. But the effort to turn this struggle into a downward redistribution of real income was decisively repulsed, first by the adamant opposition of industrial management, second by Truman administration vacillation (OWMR director John Snyder played the key role here), and finally by division and timidity within trade union ranks, especially after Philip Murray made it clear that the Steelworkers' union would not turn its mid-winter strike into a political conflict with the Truman administration over the maintenance of price controls.

The 1946 strike settlement ended left-liberal hopes that organized labor could play a direct role in reshaping class relations for the society as a whole. Thereafter Reutherite social unionism gradually tied its fate more closely to that of industry and moved away from a strategy that sought to use union power to demand structural changes in the political economy. Instead the UAW worked toward negotiation of an increasingly privatized welfare program that eventually succeeded in providing economic security for employed autoworkers. But just as postwar liberalism gradually reduced its commitment to national planning and eschewed issues of social and economic control, so too did the UAW abandon the quest for labor participation in running the automobile industry. And just as liberalism increasingly came to define itself as largely concerned with the maintenance of economic growth and an expansion of the welfare state, so too would the UAW and the rest of the labor movement define its mission in these terms.[29]

Taft-Hartley and American Politics

Although the immediate postwar strike wave had proven the largest since 1919, the pattern wage increases won by the UAW and other major unions soon evaporated under the galloping inflation let loose when government price controls were cut back during the summer. In the fall, therefore, all the major unions had to return to the bargaining table to demand another round of wage increases. Unions that sought to improve on postwar wage patterns, such as the Railway Brotherhoods and the UMW, now found that "free" collective bargaining of the sort advocated by John L. Lewis brought them into bitter confrontations with the government. The frequent strikes and annual pay boosts of this era, which industry used to raise prices, were at least partially responsible for creating the conservative, antilabor political climate that gave Republicans their large victory in the 1946 elections and then culminated in the passage of the Taft-Hartley Act in 1947.[30]

Passage of the Taft-Hartley Act over President Truman's veto proved a milestone, not only for the actual legal restrictions the new law imposed on the trade unions, but as a symbol of the shifting relationship between the unions and the state during the late 1940s. The law sought to curb the practice of interunion solidarity, eliminate the radical cadre who still held influence within trade union ranks, and contain the labor movement to roughly its existing geographic and demographic terrain. The anti-Communist affidavits, the prohibition against secondary boycotts, the enactment of section 14b allowing states to prohibit the union shop, the ban on foreman unionism—all these sections of the law had been on the agenda of the National Association of Manufacturers and other conservative groups since 1938. Of course, Taft-Hartley was not the fascist-like "slave labor law" denounced by the AFL and CIO alike. In later years, unions like the Teamsters prospered even in right-to-work states, while the bargaining relationship between employers and most big industrial unions was relatively unaffected by the new law.[31] But if Taft-Hartley did not destroy the union movement, it did impose upon it a legal/administrative straitjacket that encouraged contractual parochialism and penalized any serious attempt to project a classwide political-economic strategy.

This explains the union movement's enormous hostility to Taft-Hartley. As CIO counsel Lee Pressman put it in 1947, "When you think of it merely as a combination of individual provisions, you are losing entirely the full impact of the program, the sinister conspiracy that has been hatched." Union leaders correctly recognized that the act represented the definitive end of the brief era in which the state served as an arena in which the trade unions could bargain for the kind of tripartite accommodation with industry that had been so characteristic of the New Deal years. At the very highest levels a trust had been broken, which is why Philip Murray declared the law "conceived in sin."[32] Taft-Hartley had altered the whole texture of the sociopolitical environment, and the failure of the congressional Democrats to repeal the law in 1949 proved the final blow for many unionists. As Arthur Goldberg, who replaced Lee Pressman as CIO lawyer, sadly put it in late 1949, the law had "in its most fundamental aspect created great changes in our industrial *mores* with incalculable effects."[33]

The SEARCH FOR POLITICAL REALIGNMENT

If the tide of public sentiment, congressional votes, and administration policy all seemed to be shifting against the unions, these organizations were not without the resources to mount a counterattack.

There were two elements in this strategy: the first, Operation Dixie, the CIO campaign to organize the South, was carefully planned and well funded; the second, labor's search for a political alternative to Truman, and quite possibly to the Democratic party, represented more of an unfocused mood than a program of action. Nevertheless, both of these efforts were not without the prospect of some real impact on the body politic; but in both cases failure became almost inevitable when the Communist issue and the cold war became a central focus of domestic politics in postwar America.

In the mid-1940s the fate of the trade unions and of the movement for black freedom were more closely linked than at any other time in American history. American blacks were overwhelmingly proletarian, and after almost two million had been enrolled in labor's ranks, the fight for civil rights entered a much larger and more dynamic phase, putting it near the top of the national political agenda. In cities like Detroit and Pittsburgh, and even in Birmingham and Memphis, the trade unions played a vanguard role during the 1940s. This was hardly because of the racial egalitarianism of their rank and file (white working-class racism was probably on the rise after 1943); rather, unionists with any sort of strategic vision recognized the simple organizational necessity of forging a union movement with at least a minimal degree of interracial solidarity.[34] Thus the NAACP's Harold Preece concluded that the CIO had become a "lamp of democracy" after his multistate tour of the old Confederacy in mid-1941. "The South has not known such a force since the historic Union Leagues in the great days of the Reconstruction era."[35]

Of course, this link between CIO-style unionism and the mobilization of an increasingly self-confident black movement was instantly appreciated by the political leadership of the white South, whose militant opposition to even the most attenuated New Deal reforms can be dated from the birth of this interracial alliance in the late 1930s. The CIO therefore sought to break the political power of the Bourbon South, both at home and in Congress, by striking at its heart, the bastions of racial segregation and low-wage labor in the deep South. During the war both labor federations had made substantial inroads in that region, organizing more than 800,000 new workers.[36] In 1944 the CIO's new Political Action Committee had mobilized war workers in Alabama and Texas shipyards to defeat such well-known labor baiters as Martin Dies and Joe Starnes. And in Winston-Salem, wartime organization of the heavily black Reynolds Tobacco Company overnight transformed that city's NAACP chapter into the largest and most vital in the seaboard South, which in turn opened local politics to black participation for the first time since the Populist era.[37]

Beginning in mid-1946, Operation Dixie sought to replay these local breakthroughs on an even larger scale, in the process mobilizing an interracial electorate that could realign the very shape of Southern politics. "When Georgia is organized . . . ," predicted Van Bitter, CIO southern organizing director, "you will find our old friend Gene Talmadge trying to break into the doors of the CIO conventions and tell our people that he has always been misunderstood."[38]

But Operation Dixie was a thorough failure. The CIO put up a million dollars, recruited some two hundred organizers, and opened scores of offices throughout the South. Not to be outflanked, the AFL almost immediately opened its own rival campaign to bring authentic "American" unionism to the region. While some inroads were made in 1946 and 1947, the resistance from the political and industrial leadership of the white South proved overwhelming, and the proportion of union nonfarm labor in the South declined from just above 20 percent in 1945 to something under 18 percent ten years later. Meanwhile, white supremacists made the CIO-PAC a whipping boy in each election season, and with the rise of the Dixiecrats and the defeat of such pro-union racial moderates as Claude Pepper and Frank Graham later in the decade, the Southern congressional delegation was even more monolithically reactionary in 1950 than it had been five years before.[39]

Operation Dixie's failure was cause and consequence of the stalemate in domestic politics that characterized the early postwar years. To have organized the South in the late 1940s would have required a massive, socially disruptive interracial campaign reminiscent of the CIO at its most militant moment in the late 1930s—indeed, a campaign not dissimilar from that which the modern civil rights movement would wage in the 1960s. Moreover, it would have required the kind of federal backing, both legal and ideological, offered by the Wagner Act in the 1930s and the Supreme Court's *Brown* decision twenty years later.

Although many of the political ingredients for such a symbiosis were available, such a campaign never jelled in 1946 and 1947. First, the white South was economically and politically stronger in 1946 than it had been ten or twelve years earlier. The New Deal's massive intervention in the agricultural economy of that region had revived cotton and tobacco cultivation and begun a process of financial subsidy and farm mechanization that tilted the balance of power in the rural South still further to the political and social interests of large landowners. In the long run New Deal agricultural policies would proletarianize millions of rural blacks and set the stage for the transformation of the Democratic party and the civil rights movement of the 1960s, but in the late 1940s such displacement merely generated a labor surplus that depopulated the countryside and intensified racial competition at the bottom of the labor market.[40] Moreover, direct federal pressure upon the white South would remain quite timid in the postwar years, notwithstanding the celebrated bolt of the Dixiecrats at the 1948 Democratic convention. Reluctant to fragment the crumbling Democratic coalition, Truman tried long and hard to accommodate both civil rights liberals and Southern white supremacists. "The strategy," an assistant later explained, "was to start with a bold measure and then temporize to pick up the right-wing forces."[41]

The government's timidity was matched by that of organized labor and its liberal allies. Red-baiting and race-baiting had long been staples of Southern anti-unionism, but instead of directly confronting these attacks, CIO leaders sought to deflect Southern xenophobia by excluding Communists and other radicals from participation in Operation Dixie. Thus resources of the Communist-led trade unions and of Popular Front institutions like the Southern Conference for Human Welfare and the Highlander Folk School were shunted aside.[42] Of course, CIO anticommunism was not alone responsible for the defeat of Operation Dixie; the decisive battles in the key textile mill towns were over by the end of 1946, before this issue became all-consuming. But the labor movement's internal conflict may well have turned a tactical defeat into a disorganized rout. For example, two of the most dynamic unions in the postwar South, the Mine, Mill and Smelter Workers, and the Food and Tobacco Workers, were heavily black organizations hospitable to the Communists. By 1949 locals of these unions were being systematically raided by anti-Communist CIO unions. The crisis came to a head in Alabama when Murray's own Steelworkers broke the Mine, Mill local that represented militant black iron miners around Birmingham. Recruiting their cadre from elements close to the KKK, USW ¹ ,cals in northern Alabama blended anticommunism with overt racism to raid the Mine, Mill union and destroy one of the black community's most progressive institutions. The legacy of this fratricidal conflict extended well into the 1960s when Birmingham became synonymous with brutal white resistance to the civil rights movement.[43]

The cold war's chilling effect on domestic politics also sealed the fate of labor-liberal efforts to find an effective vehicle that could stem the rightward drift in national politics. Until the spring of 1948 labor-liberals almost uniformly repudiated Truman as their presidential candidate and proposed replacing him with men as different as Dwight D. Eisenhower and William O. Douglas. More significant, the structure of the Democratic party also came under scrutiny. The CIO, the new Americans for Democratic Action, and the AFL favored its "realignment," either by liberalization of the South or, if that failed, the explusion of the Dixiecrats. Moreover, there was still enough interest in the formation of a third party to create at least a serious debate within some of the major unions—notably the UAW—and within sections of the liberal community. Mainstream union leaders had always held a dichotomous view of this subject. In the short run (that is, before the next election), unionists rejected the third-party idea on the grounds that it would "divide progressive forces." But when unionists looked further down the line, the labor party idea seemed more attractive. In 1946 C. Wright Mills found that among CIO national officers, 65 percent favored such a new political initiative in ten years' time.[44]

Yet as the Democratic party declined in both its liberalism and its electability, the union determination to preserve the unity of "progressive" forces seemed increasingly tenuous. Thus in the spring of 1946, John Dewey, Norman Thomas, and Walter Reuther, all identified with the anti-Communist wing of American liberalism, issued a call for a National Educational Committee for a New Party. A year later, the UAW's secretary-treasurer, the socialist Emil Mazey, told local union presidents to take "concrete action in building an independent labor party of workers and farmers." So unsure was Reuther of Truman's reelection that he scheduled a unionwide third-party political education meeting for January 21, 1949, the day after Thomas Dewey's presidential inauguration.[45]

Ironically, it was the actual formation of a third party—the Progressive party, which ran Henry Wallace for president—that put a decisive end to such political experimentation and brought the industrial union wing of the labor movement even closer to the Democratic party. For nearly a decade Wallace had enjoyed remarkable support in labor-liberal circles; as late as 1947 his vision of a global New Deal and great-power collaboration coincided with that of many liberals and the entire CIO wing of the labor movement. But his candidacy brought into sharp relief two issues that would prove crucial to the political reformulation of postwar labor-liberalism. The first was the Marshall Plan, and more generally the effort to integrate into an American-dominated world order the shattered economies of the industrialized West and commodity-producing South. Although initially greeted with some skepticism even by anti-Communist union leaders like Walter Reuther, the Marshall Plan won strong endorsement from most liberals as their hopes for the construction of a purely domestic full-employment welfare state declined, and as the

Truman administration advanced the European Recovery Program as a key to international trade and North Atlantic prosperity.[46]

The second issue raised by the Wallace candidacy was the legitimacy of the Communists in American political life, and more broadly the possibility that Popular Front politics might have a continuing relevance in postwar America. Wallace refused to accept the postwar settlement that was emerging abroad and at home. He wanted détente with the Soviet Union (accepting its control of Eastern Europe) and saw the Marshall Plan as little more than an effort to drive Western Europe into the straitjacket constructed by a newly hegemonic American capitalism. At home he denounced Taft-Hartley, defended those unions that defied its sanctions, and tried to ally himself with the most advanced forms of civil rights militancy.[47]

By 1948 the Wallace candidacy was therefore anathema, for it represented a break with what was becoming fundamental in postwar America: alignment with the government in the battalions of the new cold war and exclusion of the Communists from the political arena. This was made explicit in a January 1948 CIO executive council resolution rejecting the Progressive party and endorsing the Marshall Plan. A powerful Wallace movement threatened to taint the CIO with the badge of disloyalty. "The real issue," asserted the ever cautious Philip Murray, "is the jeopardy in which you place your Unions."[48] Truman's well-crafted opening to the labor-liberals—his Taft-Hartley veto message in June 1947, his accommodation of the urban coalition's pressure for federal civil rights action in the summer of 1948, and his pseudopopulist "Give 'm Hell, Harry" presidential campaign in the fall—solidified labor-liberal ties with the Democratic party. Although the trade unions might still differ privately on bargaining goals or even their approach to Taft-Hartley, any divergence from the CIO election strategy was tantamount to organizational treason, which was in fact one of the charges leveled against several unions expelled from the CIO in 1949.[49]

Organized labor's failure to build its own political party may well have been overdetermined, even in an era when its organizational strength reached a twentieth-century apogee. The peculiarities of the American electoral system, the concentration of union strength in a relative handful of states, the ideological pressures generated by the cold war, and the continuing ethnic and racial divisions within the working class are but the most obvious factors that sealed labor's alliance with the Democratic party. But the costs of this political marriage still require calculation. Even in the urban North the Democratic party rarely offered the representatives of organized labor more than a subordinate role in the development of its political program. The CIO bargained with the Democratic party "much as it would with an employer," admitted PAC head Jack Kroll in the early 1950s.[50]

Two important consequences flowed from this dilemma. At the level of national policy formation, organized labor had no effective vehicle through which it could exert systematic pressure upon either the Democratic party or the state apparatus. The trade unions maintained an extensive lobbying operation in Washington and in most state capitals, but on any given issue of interest to their membership, they were forced to rebuild the labor-liberal coalition all over again. Thus labor took justifiable credit for the reelection of Truman in 1948, but it proved incapable of translating this vote into a coherent congressional majority after Congress convened three months later. In turn, this radical disjunction between the relative solidity of the working-class vote and the weakness of its political representation contributed to the demobilization and depoliticization of a large part of the American working class in these years. Denied access to a political leadership that could articulate their specific class-oriented interests, workers found their consciousness shaped either by the parochial interests of their union, or, more likely, by the vaguely populist rhetoric of mainsteam Democrats.[51]

PRIVATIZATION OF THE WELFARE STATE

After 1947 the defensive political posture adopted by even the most liberal of the CIO unions enhanced the apparent appeal of a narrowly focused brand of private-sector collective bargaining. For example, the conservative victory in the 1946 congressional elections had a dramatic impact on Walter Reuther's own thinking. In a radio debate of May 1946, well before the elections, Reuther told his audience that rhetoric about a "government controlled economy" was a big-business scare tactic. The real question, he said, is "how much government control and for whose benefit." But in the wake of the massive Republican victory of November 1946 Reuther made a rhetorical about-face, now urging "free labor" and "free management" to join in solving their problems, or a "superstate will arise to do it for us."[52] Or as Reuther put it in another context, "I'd rather bargain with General Motors than with the government . . . General Motors has no army."[53]

General Motors and other big companies also sought a long-range accommodation with their own unions. General Motors wanted to contain unionism within what it considered its "proper sphere"; otherwise, declared Charles Wilson, the "border area of collective bargaining will be a constant battleground between unions and management."[54] To executives like Wilson this fear was exacerbated by the realization that inflationary pressures generated by cold war military spending would be a permanent feature of the postwar scene. The UAW effort to link company pricing policy to a negotiated wage package in 1946 had been staved off by GM, but the company realized that disruptive strikes and contentious annual wage negotiations, especially if couched as part of a broader offensive against corporate power, merely served to embitter shop-floor labor relations and hamper the company's long-range planning.

Therefore in the spring of 1948—just after the Czech coup and during the months when Congress debated an administration request for a $3.3 billion military procurement package—GM offered the UAW a contract that seemed to promise social peace even in an era of continuous inflation. Two features were central to the new social order: first, an automatic cost-of-living adjustment keyed to the general price index; second, a 2-percent "annual improvement factor" wage increase designed to reflect, if only partially, the still larger annual rise in GM productivity. To GM, such permanently escalating labor costs would prove tolerable because this industrial giant faced little effective competition, either foreign or domestic, so it could easily "administer" any price increases made necessary by the new labor contract.[55]

The agreement was a dramatic, even a radical, departure from past union practice. Reuther himself had rejected wage escalation until early 1948, and a Twentieth Century Fund survey of union leaders taken later the same year revealed that more than 90 percent opposed COLA clauses in their contracts. With the general wage declines of 1921, 1930–32, and 1938 still a living memory, most union leaders instinctively rejected the premise upon which the GM-UAW contract was based: the emergence of a new era of inflationary prosperity and relative social peace. Labor leaders thought such schemes foreclosed the possibility of a large increase in the real standard of living, and they continued to fear that such a wage formula would become a downhill escalator when the inevitable postwar depression finally arrived. The UAW, for example, described the 1948 GM pact as only a "holding action" that protected GM workers until the labor-liberal coalition could replace it with more comprehensive sociopolitical guidelines.[56]

But when the 1949 recession turned out to be less than the depression many had expected, the gateway was open to the further elaboration of such an accommodation between the big unions and the major corporations. Again, the UAW pioneered the way, with a new agreement, a five-year "Treaty of Detroit" that provided an im-proved COLA and AIF and a $125-a-year pension. *Fortune* magazine hailed the 1950 UAW-GM contract as "the first that unmistakably ac-cepts the existing distribution of income between wages and profits as 'normal' if not as 'fair.' . . . It is the first major union contract that explicitly accepts objective economic facts—cost of living and produc-tivity—as determining wages, thus throwing overboard all theories of wages as determined by political power and of profits as 'surplus value.' " By the early 1960s the COLA principle had been incorporated in more than 50 percent of all major union contracts, and in the in-flationary 1960s and 1970s it spread even wider: to Social Security, to some welfare programs, and to wage determination in some units of the government and nonunion sector.[57]

Just as the negotiation of COLA agreements came in the wake of the union movement's forced retreat from the effort to reshape the Truman administration's early economic policy, so too did the new interest in pension and health and welfare plans represent a parallel privatization of the labor movement's commitment to an expanded welfare state. Initially, American trade unionists overwhelmingly fa-vored a public, federal system for financing social benefits like pen-sions, health care, and unemployment insurance. Both the CIO and AFL worked for the passage of the Wagner-Murray-Dingell bill, a 1945 proposal that would have liberalized and federalized the Amer-ican social welfare system in a fashion not dissimilar to that envi-sioned by the British government's pathbreaking Beveridge Report of 1942, which laid the basis for the welfare state constructed by the postwar Labour government.[58]

But the same forces that gutted the Full Employment Act of 1946 also destroyed labor-backed efforts to raise the social wage in these same postwar years. "Nothing more clearly distinguishes the post-war political climate of the USA from that of Great Britain than the al-most unqualified refusal of its legislature to respond to proposals for social reform," wrote the British political scientist Vivian Vale. The United States devoted about 4.4 percent of GNP to Social Security in 1949, a proportion less than half that of even the austere economies of war-torn Western Europe.[59]

Organized labor still found company-funded pension and health schemes distasteful—their coverage was incomplete, their financing was mistrusted, and they smacked of old-fashioned paternalism—but the political impasse faced by postwar unionists seemed to offer no alternatives.[60] The UMW made the first important postwar commit-ment in this area when John L. Lewis fought for an employer-funded health and welfare system in the spring of 1946. His several wartime years of conflict with the government had soured Lewis on the whole idea of the liberal administrative state. He found, for example, that when federal authorities seized actual control of the coal mines in 1943 and 1946, little changed in terms of the safety or health of UMW workers. Lewis would feel confident only if the UMW itself played the decisive role in providing safety, health, and retirement benefits in the mines. His struggle over this issue entailed a series of strikes and legal confrontations with the administration, but the UMW's ultimate success proved crucial in reducing labor's support of a federal effort in this area. Thus in 1948, after Lewis had finally established the UMW health and welfare program, he told the embattled advocates of Truman's national health insurance scheme that the UMW would no longer stand in support of this initiative.[61]

Unlike Lewis, mainstream union leaders never abandoned their formal commitment to an expanded welfare state, but at the same time they retreated, if more subtly, to a more parochial outlook. Immediately after the disastrous midterm elections of 1946, CIO leaders announced that they were not going to wait "for perhaps another ten years until the Social Security laws are amended adequately." Instead they would press for pensions and health benefits in their next collective bargaining round. Some unionists of a more explicitly social democratic outlook, like Walter Reuther and William Pollock of the Textile Workers, theorized that if employers were saddled with large pension and health insurance costs, they would join "shoulder to shoulder" with labor-liberal forces to demand higher federal payments to relieve them of this burden.[62] But such assumptions proved naive. The big unions themselves no longer saw an increase in federal welfare expenditures as an urgent task. And after the steel and auto unions established the heavy-industry pension and health benefit pattern in 1949, employers were more than ready to fold these additional costs into their product prices. Moreover, managers recognized that company-specific benefits built employee loyalty, and at some level they understood that a social wage of minimal proportions was advantageous to their class interest, even if their own firm had to bear additional costs as a consequence.[63]

Despite these limitations, it looked as if the "key" wage and benefit bargains negotiated by the big unions would generate the kind of classwide settlement in the United States that was characteristic of industry-labor relationships in northern Europe. Beginning in 1946 there were four distinct collective bargaining "rounds" in which the wage pattern hammered out in the steel or auto industry became the standard applied in rubber, meatpacking, electrical products, and other core industries. Similiarly, pensions, health benefits, and supplemental unemployment payments were also copied by many large employers, both union and nonunion, private and public.[64]

But this sort of pattern bargaining had a remarkably anemic life. It never spread much beyond the oligopolistically structured core industries, and even there it required a strong union that could take labor costs out of competition to make the pattern stick. Where unions were weak, as in electrical products and textiles, or where competition was fierce, as in automotive parts and food processing, wage and benefit guidelines established in Detroit or Pittsburgh were reproduced only imperfectly. For example, in the Detroit-area auto parts industry only about a quarter of all companies, employing 40 percent of the work force, followed the big-three pattern.[65] Similarly, cost-of-living adjustments were rarely extended to workers in those segments of the labor market outside the core industrial/governmental sector. As a result, wage disparities increased dramatically within the postwar working class. The relatively egalitarian wage patterns of the mid-1940s began to erode even in the high employment years of the Korean War, but they underwent a truly radical deterioration in the inflationary era after 1965 when workers outside of the primary labor market found themselves defenseless against renewed inflation and labor-cost competition (see table 5.1).[66]

THE POSTWAR LEGACY

The weakness of the postwar welfare state and the extreme fragmentation inherent in the American system of industrial relations did much to redivide the American working class into a unionized segment that until recently enjoyed an almost Western European level of social welfare protection, and a still larger stratum, predominantly young, minority, and female, that was left out in the cold. Because so much of the postwar social struggle has taken place at the level of the firm rather than within a broader political arena, this American system has reinforced the postwar economy's tendency to construct segmented and unequal labor markets. This multitiered system of industrial relations has served to erode solidarity within the working class and has made it difficult to counter claims that welfare spending and social equity are harmful to economic growth. The classic resentment felt by many blue-collar workers toward those on state-supported welfare has one of its roots in the system of double taxation the organized working class has borne in the postwar era. Union workers pay to support two welfare systems: their own, funded by a "tax" on their total pay periodically renegotiated in their contract,

TABLE 5.1
AVERAGE WEEKLY EARNINGS OF PRODUCTION OR NONSUPERVISORY WORKERS AS A
PERCENTAGE OF AUTOWORKERS' AVERAGE WEEKLY EARNINGS

Year	Auto ($)	Miscellaneous Manufacturing (%)	Apparel (%)	Retail Trade (%)
1947	56.51	76.3	71.2	—
1950	74.85	69.4	59.6	53.1
1955	99.84	64.9	49.8	48.8
1960	115.21	64.5	49.0	50.1
1965	147.63	57.8	45.1	45.1
1970	170.07	64.4	49.6	48.5
1975	259.53	56.5	43.0	41.9
1980	394.00	53.6	41.0	37.4
1983	524.80	50.6	38.2	32.6

Source: U.S. Department of Labor, *Handbook of Labor Statistics*, Bulletin 2217, Washington, D.C., 1984, pp. 201–3.

and that of the government, paid for by a tax system that grew increasingly regressive as the postwar years advanced. In turn, organized labor has come to be perceived (and all too often perceives itself) as a special-interest group, in which its advocacy of welfare state measures that would raise the social wage for all workers has taken on an increasingly mechanical quality.[67]

Among other consequences, these divisions within the working class and between labor and its erstwhile allies have progressively weakened political support for the structures of the welfare state erected in the New Deal era. American unions remain supporters of Social Security, national health insurance, and minority-targeted welfare programs, but their ability to mobilize either their own members or a broader constituency on these issues declined during most of the postwar era. A militant civil rights movement, not the unions, put these issues back on the national agenda for a time in the 1960s. Moreover, labor's postwar abdication from any sustained struggle over the structure of the political economy has had its own debilitating consequences. As older industries decline, it has both sapped the loyalty of the labor movement's original blue-collar constituency and at the same time deprived the unions of any effective voice in the contemporary debate over the reorganization of work technology or the reindustrialization of the economy.

NOTES

1. Although not uncritical of the New Deal labor relations system, the most comprehensive example of pluralist scholarship remains Derek C. Bok and John T. Dunlop, *Labor and the American Community* (New York: Simon and Schuster, 1970), 207–28. More critical assessments of the postwar "settlement" include Michael Piore, "Can the American Labor Movement Survive Re-Gomperization?" *Proceedings, Industrial Relations Research Association Thirty-Fifth Annual Meeting*, 1982, 30–39; Samuel Bowles, David M. Gordon, and Thomas E. Weisskopf, *Beyond the Waste Land: A Democratic Alternative to Economic Decline* (Garden City, N.Y.: Anchor Press/Doubleday, 1983), 70–75; Robert Kuttner, *The Economic Illusion: False Choices between Prosperity and Social Justice* (Boston: Houghton Mifflin, 1984), 26–49, 136–86; Mike Davis, *Prisoners of the American Dream* (London: Verso, 1986), 102–27; and David Brody's influential synthesis, *Workers in Industrial America: Essays on the Twentieth-Century Struggle* (New York: Oxford University Press, 1980), 173–257.

2. Leo Troy, "The Rise and Fall of American Trade Unions: The Labor Movement from FDR to RR," in Seymour Martin Lipset, ed., *Unions in Transition* (San Francisco, 1986), 75–89.

3. *Proceedings of the Seventh Constitutional Convention of the CIO*, Chicago, November 20–24, 1944, 313; Sumner Slichter, *The Challenge of Industrial Relations* (Ithaca, N.Y.: Cornell University Press, 1947), 4.

4. For a discussion of the war years see Nelson Lichtenstein, *Labor's War at Home: The CIO in World War II* (New York: Cambridge University Press, 1982); and George Lipsitz, *Class and Culture in Cold War America: "A Rainbow at Midnight"* (South Hadley, Mass.: J. F. Bergin Publishers, 1982), 37–86.

5. For contrasting discussions of the way in which state functions accommodated and influenced the new labor movement see Theda Skocpol, "Political Response to Capitalist Crisis: Neo-Marxist Theories of the State and the Case of the New Deal," *Politics and Society* 10 (1980): 155–201; and Christopher Tomlins, *The State and the Unions: Labor Relations, Law, and the Organized Labor Movement in America, 1880–1960* (New York: Cambridge University Press, 1985), 197–328 passim.

6. Of course, the term *corporatism* would not have been used in the 1940s to describe these structural arrangements because of corporatism's close identification with Fascist ideology. But in the last two decades scholars on both sides of the Atlantic have noted the presence of a corporatist strain within the body politic of liberal capitalist society, especially in northern Europe where once-stable capital-labor accords have begun to crumble. Such scholarship has largely focused on these countries. See especially the work of Philippe Schmitter, "Still the Century of Corporatism?" in *Trends toward Corporatist Intermediation*, ed. Philippe Schmitter and Gerhard Lehmbruch (Beverly Hills, Calif.: Sage Publications, 1982); Wyn Grant, ed., *The Political Economy of Corporatism* (New York: Cambridge University Press, 1983); Leo Panitch, *Working-Class Politics in Crisis: Essays on Labor and the State* (London:

Verso, 1986), 132–86; and Charles S. Maier, *Recasting Bourgeois Europe: Stabilization in France, Germany, and Italy in the Decade after World War I* (Princeton, N.J.: Princeton University Press, 1975). For the United States see the pioneering work of Ellis Hawley, *The New Deal and the Problem of Monopoly: A Study in Economic Ambivalence* (Princeton, N.J.: Princeton University Press, 1966) and his unpublished essay, "Techno-Corporatist Formulas in the Liberal State, 1920–1960: A Neglected Aspect of America's Search for a New Order," as well as the recent comparative work of Margaret Weir and Theda Skocpol, "State Structures and the Possibilities for a 'Keynesian' Response to the Great Depression in Sweden, Britain, and the United States," in Peter B. Evans et al., *Bringing the State Back In* (New York: Norton, 1984), 132–49. See also Ron Schatz, "From Commons to Dunlop and Kerr: Rethinking the Field and Theory of Industrial Relations" (Paper presented at the Woodrow Wilson International Center for Scholars, March 29, 1988).

7. U.S. Department of Labor, *Termination Report of the National War Labor Board* (Washington, D.C.: Government Printing Office, 1947), 150–55, 211–291; 338–402; Paul Sultan, *Labor Economics* (New York: Henry Holt and Company, 1957), 71.

8. As quoted in Craufurd Goodwin, *Exhortation and Controls: The Search for a Wage Price Policy, 1945–1971* (Washington, D.C.: Brookings Institution, 1975), 13.

9. Philip Murray, "Industry Councils: The CIO Prosperity Program," October 22, 1946, in box A4, Murray Papers, Catholic University of America. See also Merton W. Ertell, "The CIO Industry Council Plan: Its Background and Implications" (Ph.D. diss., University of Chicago, 1955).

10. David Brody, "The New Deal in World War II," in John Braeman et al., *The New Deal: The National Level* (Columbus: Ohio State University Press, 1975), 281–86.

11. George R. Clark, "Strange Story of the Reuther Plan," *Harper's*, 184 (1942): 649.

12. Alonzo Hamby, *Beyond the New Deal: Harry S. Truman and American Liberalism* (New York: Columbia University Press, 1973), 33–38; Norman D. Markowitz, *The Rise and Fall of the People's Century: Henry A. Wallace and American Liberalism, 1941–1948* (New York: Free Press, 1973), 124–54; Joseph Gaer, *The First Round: The Story of the CIO Political Action Committee* (New York: Duell, Sloan and Pearce, 1944), 187–221.

13. *Proceedings of the Tenth Constitutional Convention of the CIO*, Portland, Ore., November 22–26, 1948, 270.

14. Seymour E. Harris, ed., *Saving American Capitalism: A Liberal Economic Program* (New York: Alfred A. Knopf, 1948), 4; for an extended discussion of the shift in liberal thinking, see Alan Brinkley, "The New Deal and the Idea of the State," in this volume.

15. Byrd L. Jones, "The Role of Keynesians in Wartime Policy and Postwar Planning, 1940–1946," *American Economic Review* 62 (1972): 125–33; "Washington Bureau of UAW to Fight on National Front," *United Automobile Worker*, March 1, 1943; John Moutoux, "Reconversion and Pricing Policies

Assailed by CIO Groups as Unjust," *PM*, May 13, 1945; Joel Seidman, *American Labor from Defense to Reconversion* (Chicago: University of Chicago Press, 1953), 244–47.

16. Victor Reuther, *The Brothers Reuther and the Story of the UAW* (Boston: Houghton Mifflin, 1976), 247–48; Walter Reuther, "The Challenge of Peace," box 1, UAW Ford Department Collection, Archives of Labor History and Urban Affairs, Wayne State University (hereafter ALHUA); *Proceedings of the Seventh Constitutional Convention of the CIO*, Chicago, November 20–24, 1944, 39.

17. *New York Times*, March 29, 1945; *CIO News*, April 1, 1945.

18. Howell Harris, *The Right to Manage: Industrial Relations Policies of American Business in the 1940s* (Madison: University of Wisconsin Press, 1982), 110; on Henry Kaiser see Eliott Janeway, *The Struggle for Survival* (New Haven, Conn.: Yale University Press, 1950), 249–53; and Janeway, "Adventures of Henry and Joe in Autoland," *Fortune* 38 (1946): 96–103.

19. Barton Bernstein, "The Truman Administration and Its Reconversion Wage Policy," *Labor History* 4 (1965): 216–25.

20. Robert Garson, *The Democratic Party and the Politics of Sectionalism, 1941–1948* (Baton Rouge: Lousiana State University Press, 1974), 94–130.

21. Alan Wolfe, *America's Impasse: The Rise and Fall of the Politics of Growth* (Boston: South End Press, 1981), 18–21; Hamby, *Beyond the New Deal*, 53–85 passim.

22. Bert Cochran, *Harry S. Truman and the Crisis Presidency* (New York: Funk and Wagnalls, 1973), 208.

23. Harris, *The Right to Manage*, 111–18, 129–58; Robert M. C. Littler, "Managers Must Manage," *Harvard Business Review* 24 (1946): 366–76. See also David Brody, "The Uses of Power I: Industrial Battleground," in his *Workers in Industrial America*, 173–214 passim; and Ron Schatz, *The Electrical Workers: A History of Labor at General Electric and Westinghouse, 1923–60* (Urbana: University of Illinois Press, 1983), 167–71.

24. U.S. Department of Labor, *The President's National Labor-Management Conference*, Bulletin 77 (Washington, D.C.: Government Printing Office, 1945), 12–24; *New York Times*, November 9, 1945; *CIO News*, November 26, 1945. For a larger analysis of the postwar corporate offensive, see Robert Griffith, "Forging America's Postwar Order: Politics and Political Economy in the Age of Truman" (Paper presented at the Harry S. Truman Centennial, Woodrow Wilson International Center for Scholars, September 1984).

25. U.S. Department of Labor, *Labor-Management Conference*, 18–19; Christopher L. Tomlins, "AFL Unions in the 1930s: Their Performance in Historical Perspective," *Journal of American History* 65 (March 1979): 1021–42.

26. As quoted in Melvyn Dubofsky and Warren Van Tine, *John L. Lewis: A Biography* (New York: Quadrangle, 1978), 456–57.

27. Walter Reuther, "Our Fear of Abundance," in Henry Christman, ed., *Walter Reuther: Selected Papers* (New York: Macmillan Company, 1961), 13–21; Barton Bernstein, "Walter Reuther and the General Motors Strike of 1945–46," *Michigan History* 49 (September 1965): 260–77; Irving Howe and

B. J. Widick, *The UAW and Walter Reuther* (New York: Random House, 1949), 97–101; Donald Montgomery, "The Product Standard in OPA Price Ceilings," January 16, 1945, and Montgomery to Philip Murray, March 6, 1945, both in UAW-Montgomery Collection, box 10, ALHUA.

28. "Report of the National Citizens Committee, December 1945," in file UAW-CIO—1945, box 29, Paul Sifton Papers, Library of Congress; and "National Committee to Aid Families of General Motors Strikers," in file Labor Union Contributions, box A336, NAACP Papers, Library of Congress.

29. Barton Bernstein, "The Truman Administration and Its Reconversion Wage Policy," *Labor History* 6 (Fall 1965), 214–31. For a good discussion of the changing character of the liberal economic agenda, see Wolfe, *America's Impasse*, 13–79; and Brinkley, "The New Deal and the Idea of the State."

30. Seidman, *American Labor from Defense to Reconversion*, 233–44.

31. James A. Gross, *The Reshaping of the National Labor Relations Board: National Labor Policy in Transition, 1937–1947* (Albany: State University of New York Press, 1981). See also Harris, *Right to Manage*, 121–25; and R. Alton Lee, *Truman and Taft-Hartley: A Question of Mandate* (Lexington: University of Kentucky Press, 1966), 236.

32. CIO, *Proceedings of the Ninth Constitutional Convention*, Boston, October 13–17, 1947, 22, 186, 189.

33. CIO, *Proceedings of the Eleventh Constitutional Convention*, Cleveland, October 31–November 4, 1949, 124.

34. Jack Bloom, *Class, Race, and the Civil Rights Movement* (Bloomington: Indiana University Press, 1987), 59–70; August Meier and Elliott Rudwick, *Black Detroit and the Rise of the UAW* (New York: Oxford University Press, 1979); Herbert Garfinkel, *When Negroes March: The March on Washington Movement in the Organizational Politics of FEPC* (Glencoe, Ill.: Free Press, 1959); Michael Honey, "Labor, the Left, and Civil Rights in the South: Memphis, Tennessee during the CIO Era, 1937–1955," in Gerald Erickson and Judith Joel, eds., *Anti-Communism, the Politics of Manipulation* (Minneapolis: University of Minnesota Press, 1987); and Judith Stein, "Blacks and the Steel Workers Organizing Committee" (Paper delivered at the Seventh Annual North American Labor History Conference, Wayne State University, Detroit, October 1985). For a contrary view that emphasizes a continuing pattern of CIO racial discrimination, see Robert Norrell, "Caste in Steel: Jim Crow Careers in Birmingham, Alabama," *Journal of American History* 73 (December 1986): 669–701.

35. Harold Preece, "The South Stirs," *The Crisis* 48 (October 1941): 318.

36. "Murray Says Labor Should Be in Politics," *New York Times*, April 21, 1946; F. Ray Marshall, *Labor in the South* (Cambridge, Mass.: Harvard University Press, 1967), 225–27; Garson, *The Democratic Party*, 1–54 passim.

37. James Foster, *The Union Politic: The CIO Political Action Committee* (Columbia: University of Missouri Press, 1975), 28–29; Everett Carll Ladd, Jr., *Negro Political Leadership in the South* (Ithaca, N.Y.: Cornell University Press, 1966), 58–61; Winston-Salem Membership Report, July 31, 1946, box

C141, file North Carolina State Conference, in NAACP Papers, Library of Congress.

38. "CIO Will Seek End of Poll Tax," *New York Times*, April 11, 1946, 30; "Unionized South Will Oust Reaction, Murray Declares," *Wage Earner*, April 12, 1946, 3; *Proceedings of 1946 Convention of the CIO*, November 18–22, 1946, 194.

39. Marshall, *Labor in the South*, 229–66, 276; Michael Honey, "Labor and Civil Rights in the Postwar South: The CIO's Operation Dixie" (Paper delivered at the Southern Labor Studies Conference, Atlanta, September 1982); see also Barbara Griffith, *The Crisis of American Labor: Operation Dixie and the Defeat of the CIO* (Philadelphia: Temple University Press, 1988), 22–45, 161–76.

40. Gavin Wright, *Old South, New South: Revolutions in the Southern Economy since the Civil War* (New York: Basic Books, 1986), 226–69 passim; Weir and Skocpol, "State Structures," 143–45.

41. Quotation taken from Joseph Huthmacher, ed., *The Truman Years* (Hinsdale, Ill.: Franklin Watts, 1972), 111.

42. Griffith, *Crisis of American Labor*, 139–60; Anne Braden, "Red, White, and Black in Southern Labor," in Ann Fagan Ginger and David Christiano, eds., *The Cold War against Labor* (Berkeley, Calif.: Meiklejohn Civil Liberties Institute, 1987), 648–60.

43. Marshall, *Labor in the South*, 258–60; Neil Irvin Painter, *The Narrative of Hosea Hudson* (Cambridge, Mass.: Harvard University Press, 1979), 329–34). Hudson was a black Communist, purged by the CIO, whose graphic account of Southern labor illustrates both the potential and the tragedy of its history in the 1930s and 1940s.

44. Brody, "The Uses of Power II: Political Action," in *Workers in Industrial America*, 215–21.

45. Ibid., 222–25; *United Automobile Worker*, October 1, 1948. See also Mike Davis, "The Barren Marriage of American Labour and the Democratic Party," *New Left Review* 124 (1980): 72–74.

46. Hamby, *Beyond the New Deal*, 185–86; Michael Hogan, "American Marshall Planners and the Search for a European Neocapitalism," *American Historical Review* 86 (April 1981): 44–72; and Federico Romero, "Postwar Reconstruction Strategies of American and Western European Labor," Working Paper no. 85/193, European University Institute, Department of History and Civilization, San Domenico di Fiesole, Italy.

47. Markowitz, *Rise and Fall of the People's Century*, 242–60.

48. CIO Executive Board Minutes, January 22–23, 1948, 220, ALHUA. See also Mary Sperling McAuliffe, *Crisis on the Left: Cold War Politics and American Liberalism, 1947–1954* (Amherst: University of Massachusetts Press, 1978), 3–47.

49. McAuliffe, *Crisis on the Left*, 41–47; Harvey A. Levenstein, *Communism, AntiCommunism, and the CIO* (Westport, Conn.: Greenwood Press, 1981), 280–97, 330–40; Brody, "The Uses of Power," 226–28.

50. Foster, *The Union Politic*, 199.

51. Davis, *Prisoners of the American Dream*, 97–100; The decline in working class voting has been the most visible manifestation of this depoliticization process; see Thomas Edsall, *The New Politics of Inequality* (New York: W. W. Norton, 1984), 141–201; and Thomas Ferguson and Joel Rogers, *Right Turn: The Decline of the Democrats and the Future of American Politics* (New York: Hill and Wang, 1986), 61–67.

52. "Are We Moving toward a Government Controlled Economy?" May 30, 1946; and UAW Press Release, December 7, 1946, in box 542, Walter Reuther Collection, ALHUA.

53. Lester Velie, *Labor, U.S.A.* (New York: Random House, 1958), 64.

54. Frederick Harbison, "The UAW-General Motors Agreement of 1950," *Journal of Political Economy* 58 (October 1950): 402.

55. Stephen Amberg, "Liberal Dmocracy and Industrial Order: Autoworkers under the New Deal" (Ph.D. diss., Massachusetts Institute of Technology, 1987), 118; Kathyanne El-Messidi, "Sure Principles midst Uncertainties: The Story of the 1948 GM-UAW Contract" (Ph.D. diss., University of Oklahoma, 1976), 48–107 passim; Daniel Bell, "The Subversion of Collective Bargaining: Labor in the 1950s," *Commentary*, March 1960, 697–713.

56. W. S. Woytinsky, *Labor and Management Look at Collective Bargaining: A Canvas of Leaders' Views* (New York: Twentieth Century Fund, 1949), 105–9; El-Messidi, "Sure Principles," 60; "UAW Press Release on GM Contract," May 25, 1948, box 72, file 5, UAW-Montgomery Collection, ALHUA.

57. Russell Davenport, *U.S.A.: The Permanent Revolution* (New York: Fortune Magazine, 1951), 94; George Ruben, "Major Collective Bargaining Developments—A Quarter Century Review," reprinted from Bureau of Labor Statistics, *Current Wage Developments* (Washington, D.C.: Government Printing Office, 1974), 46–47.

58. Monte M. Poem, *Harry S. Truman versus the Medical Lobby* (Columbia: University of Missouri Press, 1979), 29–43; Woytinsky, *Labor and Management Look at Collective Bargaining*, 128–40.

59. Vivian Vale, *Labour in American Politics* (London: Barnes and Noble, 1971), 97; Harold Wilensky, *The Welfare State and Equality* (Berkeley: University of California Press, 1975), 24–26.

60. Company-financed fringe benefits had been put on the union bargaining agenda during World War II, initially when such schemes were given important tax advantages (1942), and then more forcefully when the War Labor Board exempted the cost of "fringe" benefits from the government's wage ceiling in a politically adroit maneuver designed to derail union efforts to break the Little Steel formula (1944). See Sumner Slichter et al., *The Impact of Collective Bargaining on Management* (Washington, D.C.: Brookings Institution, 1960), 372–76; Donna Allen, *Fringe Benefits: Wages or Social Obligation?* (Ithaca, N.Y.: Cornell University Press, 1964), 99–152; and Beth Stevens, "Blurring the Boundaries: How the Federal Government Has Influenced Welfare Benefits in the Private Sector," in Margaret Weir, Ann Shola Orloff, and Theda Skocpol, *The Politics of Social Policy in the United States* (Princeton, N.J.: Princeton University Press, 1988), 123–48.

61. Dubofsky and Van Tine, *John L. Lewis*, 454–72; Edward Berkowitz and Kim McQuaid, *Creating the Welfare State: A Political Economy of Twentieth-Century Reform* (New York: New York University Press, 1980), 137. The draft and the lure of higher paying urban jobs also confronted Lewis with a dramatically older work force in the coal fields. Average age rose from 32 to 45 during the war, with over 11,000 men aged 65 or over still working in 1944.

62. *Proceedings of the Eighth Constitutional Convention of the CIO*, Atlantic City, N.J., November 18–22, 1946, 186–87.

63. Peter Drucker, *The Unseen Revolution: How Pension Fund Socialism Came to America* (New York: W. W. Norton, 1976), 5–10; Ruth Glazer, "Welfare Discussion Down-to-Earth," *Labor and the Nation*, Spring 1950, 30–36; author's interview with Nelson Crunkshank, former AFL director of social insurance activities, July 18, 1984; Martha Derthick, *Policymaking for Social Security* (Washington, D.C.: Brookings Institution, 1979), 110–31. According to Crunkshank and Derthick, the AFL soon proved a stronger advocate of some social wage expenditures than did the CIO because its influential craft unions found pension and health insurance systems difficult to establish in multiemployer industries.

64. By the early 1970s private pension plans covered more than 30 million workers and amounted to almost $900 billion (U.S. Department of Commerce, *Statistical Abstract of the U.S.*, [Washington, D.C.: Government Printing Office, 1975], 286).

65. "Harold Levinson, "Pattern Bargaining: A Case Study of the Automobile Workers," *Quarterly Journal of Economics*, Spring 1959, 299.

66. Even at their greatest popularity in the late 1970s, only about 60 percent of all *union* contracts contained a COLA provision. See Louis Uchitelle, "A Labor Fight Looms over the COLA Concession," *New York Times*, June 14, 1987, p. E5. For a more extensive account of wage differentials within the working class see Paul Blumberg, *Inequality in an Age of Decline* (New York: Oxford University Press, 1980), 65–107.

67. For additional discussion of these important issues, see Robert Gordon, Richard Edwards, and Michael Reich, *Segmented Work, Divided Workers* (New York: Cambridge University Press, 1982), 165–227; Jill Bernstein, "Employee Benefits in the Welfare State: Great Britain and the United States since World War II" (Ph.D. diss., Columbia University, 1980), 579; Hugh Mosley, "Corporate Benefits and the Underdevelopment of the American Welfare State," *Contemporary Crisis* 5 (1981): 139–54; Stevens, "Blurring the Boundaries," 145–48; and Dunlop, *Labor and the American Community*, 208–14.

6 Cold War—Warm Hearth: Politics and the Family in Postwar America

ELAINE TYLER MAY

IN THE summer of 1959, a young couple married and spent their honeymoon in a bomb shelter. *Life* magazine featured the "sheltered honeymoon," with photographs of the duo smiling on their lawn, surrounded by canned goods and supplies. Another photo showed them descending twelve feet underground into the twenty-two-ton, eight-by-eleven-foot shelter of steel and concrete where they would spend the next two weeks. The article quipped that "fallout can be fun," and described the newlyweds' adventure—with obviously erotic undertones—as fourteen days of "unbroken togetherness."[1] As the couple embarked on family life, all they had to enhance their honeymoon were some consumer goods, their sexuality, and total privacy. This is a powerful image of the nuclear family in the nuclear age: isolated, sexually charged, cushioned by abundance, and protected against impending doom by the wonders of modern technology.

The stunt itself was little more than a publicity device; yet seen in retrospect it takes on symbolic significance. For in the early years of the cold war, amid a world of uncertainties brought about by World War II and its aftermath, the home seemed to offer a secure, private nest removed from the dangers of the outside world. The message was ambivalent, however, for the family also seemed particularly vulnerable. It needed heavy protection against the intrusions of forces outside itself. The image of family togetherness within the safety of the thick-walled shelter may have been a reassuring one to Americans at the time, for along with prosperity, World War II left new unsettling realities in its wake. The self-contained home held out the promise of security in an insecure world. At the same time, it also

153

offered a vision of abundance and fulfillment. As the cold war began, young postwar Americans were homeward bound.

Demographic indicators show that Americans were more eager than ever to establish families. The bomb-shelter honeymooners were part of a cohort of Americans who brought down the age at marriage for both men and women, and quickly brought the birth rate to a twentieth-century high after more than a hundred years of steady decline, producing the "baby boom." These young adults established a trend of early marriage and relatively large families that lasted for more than two decades and caused a major but temporary reversal of long-term demographic patterns. From the 1940s through the early 1960s, Americans married at a higher rate and at a younger age than their European counterparts. Less noted but equally significant, the men and women who formed families between 1940 and 1960 also reduced the divorce rate after a postwar peak; their marriages remained intact to a greater extent than did those of couples who married in earlier as well as later decades. Although the United States maintained its dubious distinction of having the highest divorce rate in the world, the temporary decline in divorce did not occur to the same extent in Europe. Contrary to fears of the experts, the roles of breadwinner and homemaker were not abandoned; they were embraced.[2]

Why did postwar Americans turn to marriage and parenthood with such enthusiasm and commitment? Scholars and observers frequently point to the postwar family boom as the inevitable result of a return to peace and prosperity. They argue that depression-weary Americans were eager to "return to normalcy" by turning the fruits of abundance toward home and hearth. There is, of course, some truth to this point; Americans were indeed eager to put the disruptions of hardship and war behind them. But prosperity followed other wars in our history, notably World War I, with no similar rush into marriage and childbearing. Peace and affluence alone are inadequate to explain the many complexities of the postwar domestic explosion. The demographic trends went far beyond what was expected from a return to peace. Indeed, nothing on the surface of postwar America explains the rush of young Americans into marriage, parenthood, and traditional gender roles.[3]

It might have been otherwise. The depression had brought about widespread challenges to traditional gender roles that could have led to a restructured home. The war intensified these challenges, and pointed the way toward radical alterations in the institutions of work and family life. Wartime brought thousands of women into the paid labor force as men left to enter the armed forces. After the war, expanding job and educational opportunities, as well as the increasing availability of birth control, might well have led to delayed marriages, fewer children, or individuals opting out of family life altogether. Indeed, many moralists, social scientists, educators, and other professionals at the time feared that these changes would pose serious threats to the continuation of the American family. Yet the evidence overwhelmingly indicates that postwar American society experienced a surge in family life and a reaffirmation of domesticity resting on distinct roles for women and men in the home.[4]

The rush began in the early 1940s and continued for two decades. But then it stopped. The family explosion represented a temporary disruption of long-term trends. It lasted only until the baby-boom children came of age, challenged their inherited gender roles, and began to reverse the demographic patterns. Their parents, having grown up during the depression and the war, had begun their families during years of prosperity. These children, however, grew up amid affluence during the cold war; they reached adulthood during the sixties and seventies, creating the counterculture and a new women's liberation movement. In vast numbers, they rejected the political assumptions of the cold war, along with the family and sexual codes of their parents. The baby-boom generation, in fact, brought the American birth rate to an all-time low and the divorce rate to an unprecedented high—both trends in excess of what demographers would have predicted based on twentieth-century patterns.[5]

Observers often point to the 1950s as the last gasp of time-honored family life before the sixties generation made a major break from the past. But the comparison is shortsighted. In many ways, the youth of the sixties resembled their grandparents more than they did their parents. Their grandparents had come of age in the first decades of the twentieth century; like many of their baby-boom grandchildren, they challenged the sexual norms of their day, pushed the divorce rate up and the birth rate down, and created a unique youth culture, complete with music, dancing, movies, and other new forms of urban amusements. They also behaved in similar ways politically, developing a powerful feminist movement, strong grass-roots activism on behalf of social justice, and a proliferation of radical movements to challenge the status quo. Against the backdrop of their grandparents, then, the baby boomers provide some historical continuity. The generation in between—with its strong domestic ideology, pervasive consensus politics, and peculiar demographic behavior—stands out as different.[6]

It is important to note that observers normally explain the political activism and the demographic behavior of the baby-boom gener-

ation as the effects of affluence and the result of expanding opportunities for women in education and employment. Yet precisely those
conditions obtained twenty years earlier, at the peak of the domestic
revival. The circumstances are similar, yet the responses are quite different. What accounts for this time lag? How can we explain the endorsement of "traditional" family roles by young adults in the postwar years and the widespread challenge to those roles when their
children, the baby boomers, came of age? Answering these questions
requires entering the minds of the women and men who married and
raised children during these years. The families they formed were
shaped by the historical and political circumstances that framed their
lives.

The context of the cold war points to previously unrecognized
connections between political and familial values. Diplomatic historians paint one portrait of a world torn by strife, and a standoff between two superpowers who seem to hold the fate of the globe in
their hands. Sociologists and demographers provide a different picture of a private world of affluence, suburban sprawl, and the baby
boom. These visions rarely connect, and we are left with a peculiar
notion of domestic tranquility in the midst of the cold war that has
not been fully explained or fully challenged.[7] In this exploration,
public policy and political ideology are brought to bear on the study
of private life, allowing us to see the family as existing within the
larger political culture, not outside of it. The approach enables us to
see the cold war ideology *and* the domestic revival as two sides of the
same coin: postwar Americans' intense need to feel liberated from
the past as well as secure in the future.

The power of this ideological duality, as well as its fundamental
irony, are most apparent in the anti-Communist hysteria that swept
the nation in the postwar years. It is well to recall that McCarthyism
was directed against perceived internal dangers, not external enemies. The Soviet Union loomed in the distance as an abstract symbol
of what we might become if we became "soft." Anti-Communist cru-
saders called upon Americans to strengthen their moral fiber in order to preserve both freedom and security. The paradox of anticommunism, however, was precisely in that double-edged goal, for the
freedom of modern life itself seemed to undermine security. Mc-
Carthyism was fueled in large measure by suspicion of the new secularism, materialism, bureaucratic collectivism, and consumerism that
represented not only the achievement but also the potential "decadence" of New Deal liberalism.

Cosmopolitan urban culture represented a threat to national security akin to the danger of communism itself; indeed, the two were

often conflated in anti-Communist rhetoric. If American democracy resided in adherence to a deeply rooted work ethic tied to a belief in upward mobility as the reward for the frugal and virtuous, then the appeal of mass purchasing, sexual temptations in the world of amusements, and even the "cushion" of the welfare state could serve to unravel that essential virtue. Many feared that the restraints imposed by the watchful eyes of small-town neighbors would dissolve in the anonymous cities. The domestic ideology emerged as a buffer against those disturbing tendencies. Rootless Americans struggled against what they perceived as internal decay; the family seemed to offer a psychological fortress that would, presumably, protect them against themselves. Family life, bolstered by scientific expertise and wholesome abundance, might ward off the hazards of the age.[8]

This challenge prompted Americans to create a family-centered culture that took shape in the early years of the cold war. This "cold war culture" was more than the internal reverberations of foreign policy, and it went beyond the explicit manifestations of anti-Communist hysteria such as McCarthyism and the Red Scare. It took shape amid the legacy of depression and war and the anxieties surrounding the development of atomic weapons. It reflected the aspirations as well as the fears of the era, as Americans faced the promises as well as the perils of postwar life. Prosperity had returned, but would there be a postwar slump that would lead to another depression, as there had been after World War I? Would men returning from war be able to find secure positions in the postwar economy? Women such as the proverbial "Rosie the Riveter" had proved themselves competent in previously all-male blue-collar jobs, but what would happen to their families if they continued to work? Science had brought us atomic energy, but would it ultimately serve humanity or destroy it? The family was at the center of these concerns, and the domestic ideology taking shape at the time provided a major response to them.[9] The legendary fifties family, complete with appliances, a station wagon, a backyard bar-b-que, and tricycles scattered along the sidewalk, represented something new. It was not, as common wisdom tells us, the last gasp of "traditional" family life with roots deep in the past. Rather, it was the first wholehearted effort to create a home that would fulfill virtually all of its members' personal needs through an energized and expressive personal life.

One of the most explicit descriptions of this modern domestic ideal was articulated, significantly, by a major politician in an international forum at the peak of the cold war. In 1959, Vice-President Richard M. Nixon traveled to the Soviet Union to engage in what would become one of the most noted verbal sparring matches of the century. In a lengthy and often heated debate with Soviet premier Nikita Khrushchev at the opening of the American National Exhibition in Moscow, Nixon extolled the virtues of the American way of life, as his opponent promoted the Communist system. What is remarkable about this exchange is its focus. The two leaders did not discuss missiles, bombs, or even modes of government. Rather, they argued over the relative merits of American and Soviet washing machines, televisions, and electric ranges. According to the American vice-president, the essence of the good life provided by democracy was contained within the walls of the suburban home.

For Nixon, American superiority rested on a utopian ideal of the home, complete with modern appliances and distinct gender roles. He proclaimed that the "model home," with a male breadwinner and a full-time female homemaker, and adorned with a wide array of consumer goods, represented the essence of American freedom. Nixon insisted that American superiority in the cold war rested not on weapons but on the secure, abundant family life available in modern suburban homes, "within the price range of the average U.S. worker." Houses became almost sacred structures, adorned and worshiped by their inhabitants. Here women would achieve their glory, and men would display their success. Consumerism was not an end in itself, but rather the means for achieving a classless ideal of individuality, leisure, and upward mobility.

With such sentiments about gender and politics widely shared, Nixon's remarks in Moscow struck a responsive chord among Americans at the time. He returned from Moscow a national hero. The visit was hailed as a major political triumph; popular journals extolled his diplomatic skills in this face-to-face confrontation with the Russian leader. Many observers credit this trip with establishing Nixon's political future. Clearly, Americans did not find the kitchen debate trivial. The appliance-laden ranch-style home epitomized the expansive, secure life-style postwar Americans wanted. Within the protective walls of the modern home, worrisome developments like sexual liberalism, women's emancipation, and affluence would lead not to decadence but to wholesome family life. Sex would enhance marriage; emancipated women would professionalize homemaking; affluence would put an end to material deprivation. Suburbia would serve as a bulwark against communism and class conflict, for, according to the widely shared belief articulated by Nixon, it offered a piece of the American dream for everyone. Although Nixon vastly exaggerated the availability of the suburban home, one cannot deny the fact that he described a particular type of domestic life that had become a reality for many Americans, and a viable aspiration for many more.[10]

What gave rise to the widespread endorsement of this familial consensus in the cold war era? The depression and war laid the foundations for a commitment to a stable home life, but they also opened the way for what might have become a radical restructuring of the family. The yearning for family stability gained momentum and reached fruition after the war; but the potential for restructuring did not. Instead, that potential withered, as a powerful ideology of domesticity became imprinted on the fabric of everyday life. Traditional gender roles revived just when they might have died a natural death, and became, ironically, a central feature of the "modern" middle-class home.

Since the 1960s, much attention has focused on the plight of women in the fifties. But at the time, critical observers of middle-class life considered homemakers to be emancipated and men to be oppressed. Much of the most insightful writing examined the dehumanizing situation that forced middle-class men, at least in their public roles, to be "other-directed" "organization men," caught in a mass, impersonal white-collar world. The loss of autonomy was real. As large corporations grew, swallowing smaller enterprises, the numbers of self-employed men in small businesses shrank dramatically. David Riesman recognized that the corporate structure forced middle-class men into deadening, highly structured peer interactions; he argued that only in the intimate aspects of life could a man truly be free.[11] Industrial laborers were even less likely to derive intrinsic satisfactions from the job itself; blue-collar and white-collar employees shared a sense of alienation and subordination in the postwar corporate work force.[12] Both Reisman and William Whyte saw the suburbs as extensions of the corporate world, with their emphasis on conformity. Yet at the same time, suburban home ownership and consumerism offered compensations for organized work life.

For women, who held jobs in greater numbers than ever before, employment was likely to be even more menial and subordinate. Surveys of full-time homemakers indicated that they appreciated their independence from supervision and control over their work, and had no desire to give up their autonomy in the home for wage labor. Educated middle-class women whose career opportunities were severely limited hoped that the home would become not a confining place of drudgery, but a liberating arena of fulfillment through professionalized homemaking, meaningful childrearing, and satisfying sexuality.[13]

While the home seemed to offer the best hope for freedom, it also appeared to be a fragile institution, in many ways subject to forces beyond its control. Economic hardship had torn families asunder, and war had scattered men far from home and thrust women into the public world of work. The postwar years did little to alleviate fears that similar disruptions might occur again. In spite of widespread affluence, many believed that reconversion to a peacetime economy would lead to another depression. Peace itself was also problematic, since international tension was a palpable reality. The explosion of the first atomic bombs over Hiroshima and Nagasaki marked not only the end of World War II but also the beginning of the cold war. At any moment, the cold war could turn hot. The policy of containment abroad faced its first major challenge in 1949 with the Chinese revolution. That same year, the Russians exploded their first atomic bomb. The nation was again jolted out of its sense of fragile security when the Korean War broke out in 1950, sending American men abroad to fight once again. Many shared President Truman's belief that World War III was at hand.[14]

Insightful analysts of the nuclear age, such as Paul Boyer and Robert J. Lifton, have explored the psychic impact of the atomic bomb. Boyer's study of the first five years after Hiroshima shows that American responses went through dramatic shifts. Initial reactions juxtaposed the thrill of atomic empowerment and the terror of annihilation. The atomic scientists were among the first to organize against the bomb, calling for international control of atomic energy. Others followed suit in expressing their moral qualms. But by the end of the 1940s, opposition had given way to proclamations of faith in the bomb as the protector of American security. As support grew for more and bigger bombs, arguments for international control waned, and the country prepared for the possibility of nuclear war. Psychologists were strangely silent on the issue of atomic fear, and by the early fifties the nation seemed to be almost apathetic. Boyer suggests that nuclear fear did not evaporate, but may well have been buried in the national consciousness. Boyer echoes Robert J. Lifton in suggesting that denial and silence may have reflected deep-seated horror rather than complacence; indeed, in 1959 two out of three Americans listed the possibility of nuclear war as the nation's most urgent problem.[15]

Lifton argues that the atomic bomb forced people to question one of their most deeply held beliefs: that scientific discoveries would yield progress. Atomic energy presented a fundamental contradiction: science had developed the potential for total technological mastery as well as total technological devastation. Lifton describes "nuclear numbing" as the result of the overwhelming reality of the bomb's existence. He points to unrealistic but reassuring civil defense strategies as efforts on the part of government officials to tame the fear, or "domesticate" the threat. Lifton does not see this numbing, or domestication, as evidence of indifference, but rather of the powerful psychic hold the fear of nuclear annihilation had on the nation's subconscious.[16]

Americans were well poised to embrace domesticity in the midst of the terrors of the atomic age. A home filled with children would provide a feeling of warmth and security against the cold forces of disruption and alienation. Children would also provide a connection to the future, and a means to replenish a world depleted by war deaths. Although baby-boom parents were not likely to express conscious desires to repopulate the country, the deaths of hundreds of thousands of GIs in World War II could not have been far below the surface of postwar consciousness. The view of childbearing as a duty was painfully true for Jewish parents, after six million of their kin were snuffed out in Europe. But they were not alone. As one Jewish woman recalled of her conscious decision to bear four children, "After the Holocaust, we felt obligated to have lots of babies. But it was easy because everyone was doing it—non-Jews, too."[17] In secure postwar homes with plenty of children, American women and men might be able to ward off their nightmares and live out their dreams.

In the face of prevailing fears, Americans moved toward the promise of the good life with an awareness of its vulnerability. The family seemed to be one place left where people could control their own destinies, and maybe even shape the future. Of course, nobody actually argued that stable family life could prevent nuclear annihilation. But the home did represent a source of meaning and security in a world run amok. If atomic bombs threatened life, marriage and reproduction affirmed life. Young marriage and lots of babies offered one way for Americans to thumb their noses at doomsday predictions. Commenting on the trend toward young marriages, *Parents Magazine* noted in 1958, "Youngsters want to grasp what little security they can in a world gone frighteningly insecure. The youngsters feel they will cultivate the one security that's possible—their own gardens, their own . . . home and families."[18]

Thoughts of the family rooted in time-honored traditions may have allayed fears of vulnerability. Nevertheless, the "traditional" family was quickly becoming a relic of the past. Much of what had previously provided family security became unhinged. For many Americans, the postwar years brought rootlessness. Those who moved from farms to cities lost a way of life familiar to them and rooted in the land itself. Children of immigrants moved from familiar ethnic neighborhoods with extended kin and community ties in order to form nuclear families in the homogeneous suburbs, and invested them with extremely high hopes.[19] Suburban homes offered freedom from kinship obligations, along with material comforts that had not been available on the farm or in the ethnic urban ghetto. As William Whyte noted about the promoters of the Illinois suburb he studied, "At first they had advertised Park Forest as housing. Now they began advertising happiness." But consumer goods would not replace community, and young mobile nuclear families could easily find themselves adrift. Whyte noted the "rootlessness" of the new suburban residents. Newcomers devoted themselves to creating communities out of neighborhoods comprised largely of transients: "In suburbia, organization man is trying, quite consciously, to develop a new kind of roots to replace what he left behind."[20]

Young adults aged twenty-five to thirty-five were among the most mobile members of the society, comprising 12.4 percent of all migrants but only 7.5 percent of the population. Higher education also prompted mobility; fully 45.5 percent of those who had one year of college or more lived outside their home states, compared with 27.3 percent of high school graduates. Overwhelmingly, these young, educated migrants worked for large organizations: three-fourths of all clients of long-distance movers—those affluent enough to afford the service—worked for corporations, the government, or the armed services, with corporate employees the most numerous. In their new communities, they immediately forged ties with other young transients. As Whyte noted, "The fact that they all left home can be more important in bonding them than the kind of home they left is in separating them." In the new community, they endeavored to forge ties that would be as rewarding and secure as the ones left behind, without the restraints of the old neighborhood.[21]

Postwar Americans struggled with this transition. The popular culture was filled with stories about young adults shifting their allegiances from the old ethnic ties to the new nuclear family ideal. When working-class situation comedies shifted from radio to television, ethnic kin networks and multigenerational households faded as the stories increasingly revolved around the nuclear family.[22] One of the most successful films of the 1950s was *Marty*, winner of the Academy Award for Best Motion Picture. In this enormously popular film, the main character, a young man living with his mother, sustains a deep commitment to the ethnic family in which he was reared. The sympathy of the audience stays with Marty as he first demonstrates tremendous family loyalty, allowing his mother to bring her cranky aging sister to live with them and doing his filial duty as the good son.

As the story unfolds, Marty falls in love, and to the horror of his mother and his aunt, decides to marry his sweetheart and move away from the old neighborhood. Far from his family and their obligations, the young couple can embark upon a new life freed from the constraints of the older generation. By the film's end, the audience has made the transition, along with the main character, from loyalty to the community of ethnic kinship to the suburban ideal of the emancipated nuclear family.[23]

The film ends there, providing no clues as to what would replace the loving kinship network portrayed so favorably at the beginning of the story. New suburbanites would need to figure that out for themselves. One way this could be achieved was through conformity to a new, modern, consumer-oriented way of life. William Whyte called the suburbs the "new melting pot" where migrants from ethnic neighborhoods in the cities moved up into the middle class. Kin and ethnic ties were often forsaken as suburban residents formed new communities grounded in shared experiences of home ownership and childrearing.[24]

Young suburbanites were great joiners, forging new ties and creating new institutions to replace the old. Park Forest, Illinois, had sixty-six adult organizations, making it a "hotbed of Participation." Church and synagogue membership reached new heights in the postwar years, expanding its functions from prayer and charity to include recreation, youth programs, and social events. Church membership rose from 64.5 million in 1940 to 114.5 million in 1960—from 50 percent to 63 percent of the entire population (a hundred years earlier only 20 percent of all Americans belonged to churches). In 1958, 97 percent of all those polled said they believed in God. Religious affiliation became associated with the "American way of life." Although many observers have commented upon the superficiality and lack of spiritual depth in much of this religious activity, there is no question that churches and synagogues provided social arenas for suburbanites, replacing to some extent the communal life previously supplied by kin or neighborhood.[25]

Still, these were tenuous alliances among uprooted people. As William Whyte observed, suburbs offered shallow roots rather than deep ones. With so much mobility in and out of neighborhoods, and with success associated with moving on to something better, middle-class nuclear families could not depend upon the stability of their communities. Much as they endeavored to form ties with their neighbors and conform to each other's life-styles, they were still largely on their own. So the nuclear family, ultimately, relied upon itself. As promising as the new vision of home life appeared, it depended heavily on the staunch commitment of its members to sustain it. The world could not be trusted to provide security, nor could the newly forged suburban community. What mattered was that family members remained bound to each other, and to the modern, emancipated home they intended to create.

To help them in this effort, increasing numbers of women and men turned to scientific expertise. Inherited folkways would be of little help to young people looking toward a radically new vision of family life. The wisdom of earlier generations seemed to be increasingly irrelevant for young adults trying self-consciously to avoid the paths of their parents. As they turned away from "old-fashioned" ways, they embraced the advice of experts in the rapidly expanding fields of social science, medicine, and psychology. After all, science was changing the world. Was it not reasonable to expect it to change the home as well?

Postwar America was the era of the expert. Armed with scientific techniques and presumably inhabiting a world above popular passions, the experts had brought the country into the atomic age. Physicists developed the bomb; strategists created the cold war; scientific managers built the military-industrial complex. It was now up to the experts to make the unmanageable manageable. As the readers of *Look* magazine were assured, there was no reason to worry about radioactivity, for if ever it became necessary to understand its dangers, "the experts will be ready to tell you." Science and technology seemed to have invaded virtually every aspect of life, from the most public to the most private. Americans were looking to professionals to tell them how to manage their lives. The tremendous popularity of treatises such as Dr. Benjamin Spock's *Baby and Child Care* reflects a reluctance to trust the shared wisdom of kin and community. Norman Vincent Peale's *The Power of Positive Thinking* provided readers with religiously inspired scientific formulas for success. Both of these best-selling authors stressed the centrality of the family in their prescriptions for a better future.[26]

The popularity of these kinds of books attests to the faith in expertise that prevailed at the time. One recent study by a team of sociologists examined the attitudes and habits of over four thousand Americans in 1957 and found that reliance on expertise was one of the most striking developments of the postwar years. Long-term individual therapy reached unprecedented popularity in the mid-1950s; 14 percent of the population said they had sought the help of professionals—counselors, social workers, psychiatrists, and the like—at some point in their lives. The authors concluded,

Experts took over the role of psychic healer, but they also assumed a much broader and more important role in directing the behavior, goals, and ideals of normal people. They became the teachers and norm setters who would tell people how to approach and live life. . . . They would provide advice and counsel about raising and responding to children, how to behave in marriage, and what to see in that relationship. . . . Science moved in because people needed and wanted guidance.

A survey taken in the mid-fifties confirms these findings. Respondents frequently mentioned the experts they had read, used therapeutic jargon in their answers to questions, and even footnoted authorities in anonymous questionnaires. One out of six had consulted a professional for marital or emotional problems. Yet fewer than one-third that number considered their personal problems to be severe. It seems evident that people were quick to seek professional help. Clearly, when the experts spoke, postwar Americans listened.[27]

In spite of public perceptions of aloofness and objectivity, professionals themselves were not far removed from the uncertainties of the day, and they groped for appropriate ways to conceptualize and resolve them. Like other postwar Americans, experts feared the possibility of social disintegration during the cold war era. As participants in the cold war consensus, they offered solutions to the difficulties of the age that would not disrupt the status quo. Professionals helped to focus and formulate the domestic ideology. For these experts, public dangers merged with private ones, and the family appeared besieged as never before. The noted anthropologist Margaret Mead articulated this problem in a 1949 article addressed to social workers. The methods of the past, she wrote, offered "an inadequate model on which to build procedures in the atomic age." Children were now born into a world unfamiliar even to their parents, "a world suddenly shrunk into one unit, in which radio and television and comics and the threat of the atomic bomb are everyday realities." For the coming generation, she wrote, "our miracles are commonplace." The task for the helping professions—psychologists, family counselors, social workers—would be especially complicated, because conditions had changed so drastically. For each adult in the new age faced "the task of trying to keep a world he [*sic*] never knew and never dreamed steady until we can rear a generation at home in it."[28]

Political activism was not likely to keep the world steady. Instead of resistance, the experts advocated adaptation as a means of feeling "at home." The solution they offered was a new vision of family life. The modern home would offer the best means of making the inherited values of the past relevant to the uncertainties of the present and future. Experts fostered an individualist approach to family life that would appeal to postwar Americans who felt cut off from the past as they forged into a world both promising and threatening. The new home had to be fortified largely from within. Couples embarking on marriage were determined to strengthen the nuclear family through "togetherness." With the guidance of experts, successful breadwinners would provide economic support for professionalized homemakers, and together they would create the home of their dreams.

Testimonies drawn from a survey of six hundred husbands and wives during the 1950s reveal the rewards as well as the disappointments resulting from these fervent efforts to create the ideal home. The respondents were among the cohort of Americans who began their families during the early 1940s, establishing the patterns and setting the trends that were to take hold of the nation for the next two decades. Their hopes for happy and stable marriages took shape during the depression, while many couples among their parents' peers struggled with disruption and hardship. They entered marriage as World War II thrust the nation into another major crisis, wreaking further havoc upon families. They raised children as the cold war took shape, with its cloud of international tension and impending doom. Yet at the same time, they were fiercely committed to the families they formed, determined to weather the storms of crises.[29]

These women and men were hopeful that family life in the postwar era would be secure and liberated from the hardships of the past. They believed that affluence, consumer goods, satisfying sex, and children would enhance and strengthen their families, enabling them to steer clear of potential disruptions. As they pursued their quest for the good life at home, they adhered to traditional gender roles and prized marital stability highly. Very few of them divorced. They represented a segment of the predominantly Protestant white population that was relatively well-educated and generally lived a comfortable middle-class life. In other words, they were among those Americans who would be most likely to fit the normative patterns. If any Americans had the ability to achieve the dream of a secure, affluent, and happy domestic life, it would have been these prosperous young adults.

These women and men were among the first to establish families according to the domestic ideology taking shape at the time. Their children would be among the oldest of the baby-boom generation. By the time their families were well established in the 1950s, they easily could have been the models for the American way of life Nixon extolled in Moscow. Relatively affluent, more highly educated than the average, they were among those Americans who were best able to take advantage of postwar prosperity. They looked toward the home, rather than the public world, for personal fulfillment. No wonder that when they were asked what they felt they sacrificed in life as a result of their decision to marry and raise a family, a decision that required an enormous investment of time, energy, and resources, an overwhelming majority of both men and women replied "nothing." Their priorities were clear.[30]

One of the most striking characteristics of these respondents was their apparent willingness to give up autonomy and independence for the sake of marriage and family. Although the 1950s marked the beginning of the glamorization of bachelorhood, most of the men expressed a remarkable lack of nostalgia for the unencumbered freedom of a single life. Typical were the comments of one husband who said he gave up "nothing but bad habits" when he married, or another who said he relinquished "the empty, aimless, lonely life of a bachelor. I cannot think of anything I really wanted to do or have that have been sacrificed because of marriage." Many of these men had been married for over a decade, and had seen their share of troubles. Particularly poignant was the comment of a man with an alchoholic wife whom he described as sexually "frigid." Brushing aside these obvious difficulties, he wrote, "Aside from the natural adjustment, I have given up only some of my personal independence. But I have gained so much more: children, home, etc. that I ought to answer . . . 'nothing at all.' "[31]

Women were equally quick to dismiss any sacrifices they may have made when they married. Few expressed any regret at having devoted themselves to the homemaker role—a choice that effectively ruled out other lifelong occupational avenues. Although 13 percent mentioned a "career" as something sacrificed, most claimed that they gained rather than lost in the bargain. One wife indicated the way in which early marriage affected the development of her adult identity. Stating that she sacrificed "nothing" when she married, she continued, "Marriage has opened up far more avenues of interest than I ever would have had without it . . . I was a very young and formative age when we were married and I think I have changed greatly over the years. . . . I cannot conceive of life without him."[32]

Many of the wives who said they abandoned a career were quick to minimize its importance. One said she gave up a "career—but much preferred marriage," suggesting that pursuing both at the same time was not a viable option. Many defined their domestic role as a career in itself. As one woman wrote of her choice to relinquish an outside profession: "I think I have probably contributed more to the world in the life I have lived." Another mentioned her sacrifices of "financial independence. Freedom to choose a career. However, these have been replaced by the experience of being a mother and a help to other parents and children. Therefore the new career is equally as good or better than the old." Both men and women stressed the responsibilities of married life as a source of personal fulfillment rather than sacrifice. One man remarked that "a few fishing trips and hunting trips are about all I have given up. These not to keep peace in the family, but because the time was better (and more profitably) spent at home."[33]

Further evidence of the enormous commitment to family life appears in response to the question, "What has marriage brought you that you could not have gained without your marriage?" While the most common responses of both men and women included family, children, love, and companionship, other typical answers included a sense of purpose, success, and security. It is interesting to note that respondents claimed that these elements of life would not have been possible without marriage. Women indicated that marriage gave them "a sense of responsibility I wouldn't have had had I remained single," or a feeling of "usefulness I have had for others dear to me." One said marriage gave her a "happy, full, complete life; children, feeling of serving some purpose in life other than making money." Another remarked, "I'm not the 'career girl' type. I like being home and having a family. . . . Working with my husband for our home and family brings a satisfaction that working alone could not."[34]

Men were equally emphatic about the satisfactions brought about by family responsibility. Responding in their own words to an open-ended question, nearly one-fourth of all the men in the sample claimed that their marriages gave them a sense of purpose in life and a reason for striving. Aside from love and children, no other single reward of marriage was mentioned by so many of the husbands. Numerous comments pointed to marriage as the source of "the incentive to succeed and save for the future of my family," "above all, a purpose in the scheme of life," or "a motivation for intensive effort that would otherwise have been lacking." One confessed, "Being somewhat lazy to begin with the family and my wife's ambition have made me more eager to succeed businesswise and financially." A contented husband wrote of the "million treasures" contained in his family; another said that marriage offered "freedom from the boredom and futility of bachelorhood."

Others linked family life to civic virtues by claiming that marriage strengthened their patriotism and morals, instilling in them "responsibility, community spirit, respect for children and family life, reverence for a Supreme Being, humility, love of country." Summing up the feelings of many in his generation, one husband said that marriage "increased my horizons, defined my goals and purposes in life, strengthened my convictions, raised my intellectual standards and stimulated my incentive to provide moral, spiritual, and material support; it has rewarded me with a realistic sense of family and security I never experienced during the first 24 years of my life."[35]

The modern home would provide not only virtue and security, but also liberation and expressiveness. Most of the survey respondents agreed with the widely expressed belief that "wholesome sex relations are the cornerstone of marriage." Sexual expertise was one of several skills required of modern marital partners; as one historian has noted, by the 1940s experts had fully articulated the "cult of mutual orgasm." The respondents repeatedly noted that sexual attraction was a major reason they married their particular partners, while sexual compatibility and satisfaction were deemed essential elements in a marriage. One man wrote about his future wife, "I like particularly her size and form. . . . She attracts me strongly, physically." Others wrote about the centrality of "sex desire" in their relationships, and how important it was that they were "passionately attracted to each other." Women as well as men were likely to mention the "great appeal physically" of their partners. In essence, sexual liberation was expected to occur *within* marriage, along with shared leisure, affluence, and recreation. The modern home was a place to feel good.[36]

These comments express a strong commitment to a new and expanded vision of family life, one focused inwardly on parents and children, and bolstered by affluence and sex. The respondents claimed to have found their personal identities and achieved their individual goals largely through their families. Yet on some level the superlatives ring a bit hollow—as if these women and men were trying to convince themselves that the families they had created fulfilled all their deepest wishes. For the extensive responses they provided to other questions in the survey reveal evidence of disappointment, dashed hopes, and lowered expectations. Many of the respondents who gave their marriages high ratings had actually resigned themselves to a great deal of misery.

As postwar Americans endeavored to live in tune with the prevailing domestic ideology, they found that there were costs involved in the effort. The dividends required a heavy investment of self. For some, the costs were well worth the benefits; for others, the costs turned out to be too high. Ida and George Butler were among those who felt the costs were worth it. After more than a decade of marriage, they both claimed that they were satisfied with the life they had built together. When they first embarked on married life, they brought high hopes to their union. Ida wrote that George "very nearly measures up to my ideal Prince Charming." George, in turn, noted Ida's attractiveness, common sense, and similar ideas on home life and sex. He was glad she was "not the 'high stepping' type," but had "experience in cooking and housekeeping." For this down-to-earth couple, the home contained their sexuality, her career ambitions, his success drive, and their desires for material and emotional comforts.

Yet like all things worth a struggle, it did not come easy. Ida's choices reflect the constraints that faced postwar women. She sacrificed her plans for "a professional career—I would [have] liked to have been a doctor—but we both agreed that I should finish college which I did." Following her marriage, "there were obstacles" to her continuing to pursue a career in medicine. It was nearly impossible to combine a professional life with a family. For one thing, the children were primarily her responsibility. "My husband works very hard in his business and has many hobbies and friends. The care and problems of children seem to overwhelm him and he admits being an 'only' child ill prepared him for the pull and tug of family life. We work closely together on discipline and policies but he is serious minded and great joy and fun with the children is lacking."

If Prince Charming's shining armor tarnished a bit with the years, Ida was not one to complain. She had reasons for feeling contented with the family she helped to build. "I think a *stability* which runs through my life is important. I cannot recall any divorce or separation in my immediate family—We are a rural—close-to-the-soil group and I was brought up 'to take the bitter with the sweet'—'marry-off not on (your family)'—'you make your own bed—now lie in it' philosophy so it would not occur to me 'to run home to mother.' " Although marriage was not her first career choice, it eventually became her central occupation: "Marriage is my career—I chose it and now it is up to me to see that I do the job successfully in spite of the stresses and strains of life." She felt that the sacrifices she made were outweighed by the gains: "children—a nice home—companionship—sex—many friends." Her husband George also claimed to be "completely satisfied" with the marriage. He wrote that it brought him an "understanding of other people's problems, 'give and take,' love and devotion." He felt that he sacrificed "nothing but so-called personal freedom." Her medical career and his "so-called personal freedom" seemed to be small prices to pay for the stable family life they created together.[37]

For men and women like George and Ida Butler, the gains were worth the sacrifices. But their claims of satisfaction carried a note of resignation. Combining a profession with a family seemed an unrealistic goal for Ida; combining personal freedom with the role of provider seemed equally out of reach for George. They both felt they faced an either/or situation, and they opted for their family roles. At first glance, this case appears rather unremarkable: two people who made a commitment to marriage and made the best of it. But the Butlers' choices and priorities take on larger significance when we keep in mind that they were part of a generation that was unique in its commitment to family life. The costs and benefits articulated by the Butlers, and their willingness to settle for somewhat less than they bargained for, were conditions they shared with their middle-class peers.

While the Butlers emphasized the benefits of family life, Joseph and Emily Burns emphasized the costs. For this couple, the legacy of depression and war stood out in bold relief as the backdrop to the cold war family. Joseph Burns looked toward marriage with the hope that it would yield the "model home" where affluence, intimacy, and security would prevail. But for him, the worrisome state of the world was inescapable, even in the family. Although he was ultimately disappointed by the failure of his family to match the substantial emotional stake he invested in it, he nevertheless articulated the way in which the world situation contributed to the intense familism of the postwar years.

At the time of his engagement in 1939, Joseph Burns had high expectations for his future marriage. He noted the reasons he chose his fiancée: he could trust and respect her, her "past life has been admirable," she did not drink or smoke, and "she is pleasing to the eye." If anything made him uneasy about their prospects for future happiness, it was the fear of another depression: "If the stock market takes another drop so that business will be all shot, I would feel skeptical as to the outcome of the social status of the citizens of U.S." The depression had already made him wary of the world situation, but his disillusionment would be complete by the time World War II had come and gone.

Looking back over his life from the vantage point of the 1950s, Joseph Burns reflected:

> As I review the thoughts that were mine at the time of marriage and as they are now, would like to give an explanation that should be considered. . . . A young couple, much in love, are looking forward to a happy life in a world that has been held up to them by elders as a beautiful world. Children are brought up by their parents to love God and other

children, honesty is a must, the obedience to the Ten Commandments necessary, follow the golden rule, etc. With such training I started out my life only to find out the whole thing is a farce. Blundering politicians lusting for power and self glory have defiled what is clean and right, honesty is just a word in the dictionary, Love of God; who really believes in God? Love of neighbor . . . get him before he gets you. Well I agree it does sound cynical but let us face the facts. Mankind has been slowly degenerating, especially since 1914 and today what do we have to look forward to? Civil defense tests, compulsory military training, cold wars, fear of the atomic bomb, what about the diseases that plague man, the mental case outlook? Did you [sic] grandfather have these fears? no! I submit these things to show how a marriage can be vitally affected as was ours and therefore many of my ideals, desires and most of all my goal has been substantially affected in the past 17 years.

Joseph Burns's cynicism toward the wider world made him place even higher hopes on the potential of the family to provide a buffer. When world events intruded into that private world, he was devastated: "On December 7 1941 the question burned in my mind; how can (so called) Christian nations tear each other apart again?" Joseph resolved his personal anguish in a unique manner: he became a Witness of Jehovah. But he continued to cling to the family for his sense of security in a chaotic world. Although he claimed that the world situation had dashed his ideals, he still rated his marriage happier than average, and said it gave him "the opportunity to think and reason." As far as what he sacrificed for his marriage, he wrote, "Whatever was given up, which probably would have been material possessions, has been offset by the things gained because of marriage."

For Joseph Burns, his rage at the world was tempered by life within his family, even if it did not live up to his ideal. He still believed that the family provided him with security and satisfaction, and fulfilled at least some of the hopes he originally brought to it. But his wife Emily had a different view of their marriage. She was less satisfied with the marriage than her husband. While Joseph found in family life some buffer against the world, Emily found little comfort in life with Joseph. Although his religious conversion was at the center of her dissatisfaction, her testimony raises other issues as well. She complained about her husband's pessimism, coldness ("Webster's Collegiate Dict. 2d definition"), aloofness, and lack of a love of beauty. Although she would not have married the same person if she had it to do over again, she never considered divorce. As she explained it, "The above may seem inconsistent but [I would] definitely [marry the] *same* person, if [my] husband's change of religion had not affected his daily life—attitude toward wife, children, home, friends, and world. Unless I completely become absorbed in it (his religion), we are coming to a parting of the ways since I'm an outsider in my own home."

Aside from this major rift over her husband's conversion, Emily was also quite specific about the costs and benefits of her marriage. She enumerated her sacrifices as follows:

1. Way of life (an easy one)
2. All friends of long duration; close relationship
3. Independence and personal freedom
4. What seemed to contribute to my personality
5. Financial independence
6. goals in this life
7. Idea as to size of family
8. Personal achievements—type changed
9. Close relationship with brother and mother and grandmother
10. Probably too many already listed.

Her complaints add up to much more than religious incompatibility. They suggest some of the costs of adhering to the domestic ideology that took shape in the postwar era: an emphasis on the nuclear family at the expense of other relatives and friends, and loss of personal freedom, financial independence, "goals," and "personal achievements." For this woman, like Ida Butler and others of their generation, marriage and family life led to a narrowing of options and activities. But it was a bargain she accepted because it appeared to be the best route toward achieving other goals in life. She continued by enumerating the benefits she gained in marriage with as much logical precision as she listed the sacrifices. Even though she, like her husband, was rather cynical, her list reveals why she chose the domestic path:

1. The desire to give up all for the love of one
2. The placing of self last.
3. A harmonious relationship until religion entered to change this.
4. Two ideal children even tho' boy is cold and indifferent like father. (Have strong religious ties in common).
5. A comfortable home independent of others.
6. Personal satisfaction if all turns out well.
7. Personal satisfaction in establishing a home.

In the above listing, Emily Burns mentioned practically all the major subjective compensations that made marriage such an important commitment for so many women at the time. Yet it was a qualified list. Her dissatisfaction was obvious even as she enumerated her gains. So she struggled to improve her situation as best she could.

While her husband used the last space in the questionnaire to brood over the world situation and explain his turn toward religion, Emily used it to reaffirm her faith in the potential for happiness in marriage. She wrote to Kelly and his research team: "Honestly wish this survey will help future generations to maintain happiness throughout marriage and that your book will become more than cold facts and figures. We have enough such now!" At the same time, she revealed a submerged feminist impulse that also surfaced in numerous testimonies of her peers. To help her formulate these ideas and influence her husband, she turned to experts: "Have tried to arouse interest in the woman's point of view by reading parts of Dr. Marie Carmichael Stopes' works pertaining to marriage, to my husband. He says, 'Oh she is just a woman what does she know about it!' and 'how can such things (marriage relationship) be learned from a book?' I have ideas on marriage and when I see the same ideas expressed in print by a supposedly person of authority [*sic*], at least I can see that I am not the only woman or person who thinks 'such and such.' " Recognizing that her rebellion against female subordination was not lost upon her husband, and realizing that he was unsympathetic, she predicted, "Because of a developing—hard, slightly independent attitude on my part, believe my husband's report on me will be anything but favorable. 'Amen.' "

Joseph and Emily Burns, in spite of their numerous complaints, stayed together. Through all their disillusionment and anger, they never wavered in their commitment to their imperfect relationship. They both insisted that their marriage was worth the struggle. With everything outside the home so uncertain, they continued to seek their satsifaction in life from the family they built together. Emily chafed against the limits to her freedom; but instead of shedding the home, she turned to experts to bolster her status within the family. Joseph turned to the home to provide solace from the miseries that surrounded him in the public world. He articulated the impact of the depression, war, and cold war on his family ideals, while Emily enumerated the costs as well as the gains of her marriage. Both invested a great deal of their personal identities in their domestic roles; neither was willing to abandon them. Even if the home did not fulfill their dreams for an emancipated, carefree life, it still provided more satisfaction and security than they would be likely to find elsewhere. As Emily explained it, marriage provided "a comfortable home independent of others . . . personal satisfaction if all turns out well . . . personal satisfaction in establishing a home." For all their struggles and strains, Joseph and Emily Burns created something together that met their needs. In 1980, they were still married to each other.[38]

Unhappy as they each claimed to be, Emily and Joseph Burns still rated their marriage as satisfactory. Like the Butlers, the Burnses demonstrate the powerful determination, and the considerable sacrifice, that went into the creation of the postwar family. Even if the result did not fully live up to the hopes brought to it, these husbands and wives never seriously considered bailing out. Keeping in mind the fact that this generation brought down the divorce rate, it is important to consider the limited options and alternatives these men and women faced. It was not a perfect life, but it was secure and predictable. Forging an independent life outside the home carried enormous risks of emotional and economic bankruptcy, along with social ostracism. As each of these couples sealed the psychological boundary around their family, they also in large measure sealed their fates within it. No wonder it was their deepest wish to build a warm hearth against the cold war.

The cold war consensus, politically as well as domestically, did not sustain itself beyond this single generation. The politics of the 1930s, 1940s, and 1950s had helped to shape the postwar home. In turn, the postwar home had a direct bearing on the politics of the 1960s. Much of what sparked the social and political movements forged by the baby-boom children as they came of age stemmed from a rejection of the values of postwar domesticity and the cold war itself. The children were keenly aware of the disappointments of their parents— that the domestic ideal had not fully lived up to its promise. Unlike their depression- and war-bred parents, they were less security-minded and less willing to tolerate the restraints and dissatisfactions experienced by their elders. Yet they did not wholly give up on the dream of a more liberated and expressive life; they simply looked for the fulfillment of that promise elsewhere. This new quest took more overtly political forms, since much of their energy poured out of the family into public life. In many ways, then, the children's effort to gain what their parents had failed to achieve in the way of true liberation gave rise to the New Left, the antiwar movement, the counterculture, and the new feminism. As a result, by the late 1960s they had shattered the political and familial consensus that had prevailed since the 1940s.

In the years since the 1960s, politics and personal life have remained intertwined. The lines remain drawn around the same sets of values. Militant cold warriors still call for the virtues of "traditional domesticity"; critics on the Left challenge the assumptions of the cold war and champion gender equality inside and outside the home. Issues of personal life, such as abortion and day care, have landed squarely in the center of hot political debates. Although it is unclear which side will ultimately prevail, there can be no doubt that public and private life continue to exert a powerful influence on each other.

NOTES

1. "Their Sheltered Honeymoon," *Life*, August 10, 1959, 51–52.

2. For an excellent discussion of demographic trends, see Andrew Cherlin, *Marriage, Divorce, Remarriage* (Cambridge: Harvard University Press, 1981), 6–32; for comparisons with European demographic patterns, see Hugh Carter and Paul C. Glick, *Marriage and Divorce: A Social and Economic Study* (Cambridge: Harvard University Press, 1976), pp. 22–24 on marriage rates, and p. 31 on divorce rates. For the rise in the marriage rate in the United States after 1940, see p. 41.

3. In the historical literature, almost all references to the boom in family life after the war refer to the return to peace and prosperity. Recent investigations point to the legacy of depression as well. Andrew Cherlin provides an excellent summary of scholarly explanations of postwar demographic trends, in which he offers an insightful critique. See Cherlin, *Marriage*, 33–44.

4. Recently, scholars have begun to uncover the contradictions inherent in postwar culture, particularly the potential for radically altered gender relations that did not materialize. For an insightful analysis, see Wini Breines, "The 1950s: Gender and Some Social Science," *Sociological Inquiry* 56, no. 1 (Winter 1986): 69–92. Literature on worries about postwar family life is abundant. Examples run from guidebooks, such as Judson T. Landis and Mary G. Landis, *Building a Successful Marriage* (New York: Prentice Hall, 1948), to texts such as Reuben Hill and Howard Baker, eds., *Marriage and the Family* (Boston: D. C. Heath, 1942). These sources express widespread fears about the future of the family, particularly following the disruptions in gender roles brought about by the war.

5. Cherlin, *Marriage*, 1–5.

6. See, for example, a study in progress by Battille Memorial Institute's Health and Population Research Center in Seattle, described by Nadine Brozan of the *New York Times* in "What's New about Women Really Isn't," *Minneapolis Star and Tribune*, September 1, 1986, pp. 1C, 2C.

7. Much of the recent scholarship on the cold war era has begun the process of integration: the cultural impact of the atomic bomb in Paul Boyer's excellent study, *By the Bomb's Early Light: American Thought and Culture at the Dawn of the Atomic Age* (New York: Pantheon, 1985); the overlapping of political and scientific momentum documented in Martin Sherwin, *A World Destroyed: The Atomic Bomb and the Grand Alliance* (New York: Alfred A. Knopf, 1975); the interweaving of social, economic, and political concerns in texts covering the era, such as Godfrey Hodgson, *America In Our Time: From World War II to Nixon, What Happened and Why* (New York: Random House, 1976), Lawrence S. Wittner, *Cold War America: From Hiroshima to Watergate* (New

York: Praeger, 1974), James Gilbert, *Another Chance: Postwar America, 1945–1985* (New York: Alfred A. Knopf, 1981; 2d ed., Chicago: Dorsey Press, 1986), and William Chafe, *The Unfinished Journey: America since World War II* (New York: Oxford University Press, 1986). A few scholars have begun addressing the problems of the 1950s in new ways; see, for example, Leo P. Ribuffo's essay "Abusing the Fifties," *Worldview*, November 1973, 143–47. Specific work on women in the 1950s is beginning to emerge, such as Eugenia Kaledin, *Mothers and More: American Women in the 1950s* (Boston: Twayne Publishers, 1984), and Leila J. Rupp and Verta Taylor, *Survival in the Doldrums: The American Women's Rights Movement, 1945 to the 1960s* (New York: Oxford University Press, 1987). For opposing views on the postwar era, see, for example, Marty Jezer, *The Dark Ages: Life in the United States, 1945–1960* (Boston: South End Press, 1982), which provides a critical appraisal, and William O'Neill, *American High: The Years of Confidence, 1945–1960* (New York: Free Press, 1986), which offers a more celebratory one. The connection, more specifically, between sex and politics has been explored in some depth by John D'Emilio in "The Homosexual Menace: The Politics of Sexuality in Cold War America" (Paper presented at the Organization of American Historians annual meeting, Philadelphia, April 1982), and D'Emilio, *Sexual Politics, Sexual Communities: The Making of a Homosexual Minority in the United States, 1940–1970* (Chicago: University of Chicago Press, 1983). Recent studies of the family and demographic trends after World War II offer valuable insights, although they limit their analyses to particular facets of family life. For example, Andrew Cherlin, whose *Marriage, Divorce, Remarriage* offers the most succinct discussion of the demographic trends since World War II, does not provide a detailed discussion relating the data to larger cultural or political trends. Richard Easterlin, in *Birth and Fortune: The Impact of Numbers on Personal Welfare* (New York: Basic Books, 1981), explains demographic swings in terms of the relative economic well-being of each generation; but he does not consider the unique historical circumstances that affected each in different ways. Glen Elder tries to unravel these patterns in his sociological masterpiece, *Children of the Great Depression: Social Change in Life Experience* (Chicago: University of Chicago Press, 1974), by examining the long-term effects of the depression on the people who grew up in that era. But Elder slights the profound impact of the later historical developments that faced this cohort in early adulthood, specifically the changes in men's and women's lives brought about by the war and the cold war. Christopher Lasch, in his insightful book *Haven in a Heartless World: The Family Besieged* (New York: Basic Books, 1977), portrays the modern family besieged by outside institutions that strip it of its vital functions of educating and socializing children. But Lasch does not explore the motivations of family members themselves, who were active participants in the shift toward reliance on outside experts. Barbara Ehrenreich's *The Hearts of Men* (Garden City, N. Y.: Doubleday, 1983) takes a provocative look at the revolt against the breadwinner ethic of the 1950s that shaped domestic gender roles, but leaves unanswered the question of why so many postwar men and women embraced those roles in the first place.

8. For an insightful discussion of the anti-Communist preoccupation with "deviant" behavior as a source of national weakness and vulnerability, see D'Emilio, *Sexual Politics, Sexual Communities*, 40–53; for a collection of essays that explore the paradoxical nature of the postwar years, see Lary May, ed., *Promise and Peril: Explorations in Postwar American Culture* (Chicago: University of Chicago Press, forthcoming).

9. Feminist scholarship has done a great deal to break down the academic barriers between public and private life, by demonstrating that the personal is political. The feminist scholarship that has influenced this work is too voluminous to list here; I discuss its impact on the writing of American history in "Expanding the Past: Recent Scholarship on Women in Politics and Work," *Reviews in American History* 10, no. 4 (December 1982): 216–33. A few pathbreaking historical studies have particular relevance for their insights into the relationship between gender, family, and politics. Those works include Linda Kerber, *Women of the Republic: Intellect and Ideology in Revolutionary America* (Chapel Hill: University of North Carolina Press, 1980); Nancy Cott, *The Bonds of Womanhood: "Women's Sphere in New England, 1780–1835* (New Haven: Yale University Press, 1977); Cott, *The Grounding of Modern Feminism* (New Haven: Yale University Press, 1987); Sara Evans, *Personal Politics: The Roots of Women's Liberation in the Civil Rights Movement and the New Left* (New York: Alfred A. Knopf, 1979); Estelle Freedman, *Their Sisters' Keepers: Women's Prison Reform in America, 1830–1930* (Ann Arbor: University of Michigan Press, 1980); Linda Gordon, *Woman's Body, Woman's Right: A Social History of Birth Control in America* (New York: Grossman, 1976); Mari Jo Buhle, *Women in American Socialism, 1870–1920* (Urbana: University of Illinois Press, 1981); Mary Ryan, *Cradle of the Middle Class: The Family in Oneida County, New York, 1790–1865* (New York: Cambridge University Press, 1981); and D'Emilio, *Sexual Politics, Sexual Communities*, among others. Methodologically, this study utilizes the interdisciplinary techniques pioneered by social historians in recent years, and draws upon the work of symbolic anthropologists, historical sociologists, and social psychologists. Insights from these fields are derived from studies such as Robert J. Lifton, *The Broken Connection: On Death and the Continuity of Life* (New York: Simon and Schuster, 1979); Clifford Geertz, *The Interpretation of Cultures* (New York: Basic Books, 1973); Glen H. Elder, Jr., *Children of the Great Depression: Social Change in Life Experience* (Chicago: University of Chicago Press, 1974); Robert N. Bellah et al., *Habits of the Heart: Individualism and Commitment in American Life* (Berkeley and Los Angeles: University of California Press, 1985). Theoretical issues pertaining to the relationship between the state, the structure of the economy, and the family in advanced capitalist systems have been explored by insightful scholars in recent years. Studies with particular relevance to this investigation include Jurgen Habermas, *Legitimation Crisis*, trans. Thomas McCarthy (Boston: Beacon Press, 1975); and Joel Kovel, "Rationalization and the Family," *Telos* 37 (Fall 1978): 5–21.

10. Quotes from the debate between Vice-President Richard Nixon and Soviet premier Nikita Khrushchev in Moscow are drawn from "The Two Worlds: A Day-Long Debate," *New York Times*, July 25, 1959, 1, 3; "When Nixon Took On Khrushchev," a report on the meeting that contains the text of Nixon's address at the opening of the American National Exhibition in Moscow on July 24, 1959, printed in "Setting Russia Straight on Facts about the U.S.," *U.S. News and World Report*, August 3, 1959, 36–39, 70–72; "Encounter," *Newsweek*, August 3, 1959, 15–19. (Khrushchev spoke in Russian with a translator. See brief excerpt in The Archives Project, Inc., *The Atomic Cafe*, documentary film, 1982, Thorn Emi Video.)

11. C. Wright Mills, *White Collar: The American Middle Classes* (New York: Oxford University Press, 1956); William H. Whyte, *The Organization Man* (New York: Simon and Schuster, 1956); David Riesman, *The Lonely Crowd: A Study of the Changing American Character* (New Haven: Yale University Press, 1950); George Lipsitz, *Class and Culture in Cold War America: "A Rainbow at Midnight"* (South Hadley, Mass.: J. F. Bergin, 1982), 7; quote is from Whyte, *Organization Man*, 267. No widely read examination of women's oppression in the 1950s appeared until 1963, when Betty Friedan published *The Feminine Mystique* (New York: Dell, 1963).

12. Lipsitz, *Class and Culture*, 88–95.

13. The survey of housewives is reported in Lipsitz, *Class and Culture*, 94; attitudes of middle-class housewives are drawn from testimonies of wives in E. Lowell Kelly, Kelly Longitudinal Study, Henry Murray Research Center, Radcliffe College, Cambridge, Mass., open-ended questions, 1955 survey. Hereafter, this study is abbreviated as KLS.

14. On the beginning of the cold war, see Sherwin, *A World Destroyed*; see also John Lewis Gaddis, *Strategies of Containment: A Critical Appraisal of Postwar American National Security* (New York: Oxford University Press, 1982), chap. 4; Chafe, *Unfinished Journey*, 248–51.

15. Boyer, *By the Bomb's Early Light*; Lifton, *Broken Connection*. Poll data is in Boyer, *By the Bomb's Early Light*, 355. On the unrealistic nature of civil defense strategies, see the excellent documentary by The Archives Project, Inc., *The Atomic Cafe*.

16. Lifton, *Broken Connection*, 338.

17. Conversation with Jewish writer Ruth F. Brin, April 11, 1987, Minneapolis, Minn.

18. Mildred Gilman, "Why They Can't Wait to Wed," *Parents Magazine*, November 1958, 46.

19. Judith Smith shows that this process began before 1940, and would intensify after the war; see her *Family Connections: A History of Italian and Jewish Immigrant Lives in Providence Rhode Island, 1900–1940* (Albany: State University of New York Press, 1985), 107–23. See also Kenneth Jackson, *Crabgrass Frontier: The Suburbanization of the United States* (New York: Oxford University Press, 1985).

20. Whyte, *Organization Man*, 284.

21. Ibid., 268–70; quote is on p. 270.

22. George Lipsitz, "The Meaning of Memory: Family, Class, and Ethnicity in Early Network Television Programs," *Cultural Anthropology* 1, no. 4 (November 1986): 355–87; the discussion of shifting themes is on p. 356.

23. *Marty*, 1955, screenplay by Paddy Chayefsky, first written for TV in 1953. For an excellent analysis of both the TV and film versions in their cultural settings, see Judith E. Smith, "Ethnicity, Class, and Sexuality: Popular Conceptions of Gender in *Marty*," paper in progress, 1987.

24. Whyte, *Organization Man*, 300.

25. William O'Neill, *American High: The Years of Confidence, 1945–1960* (New York: Free Press, 1986), 212–15; Chafe, *Unfinished Journey*, 120–21; Whyte, *Organization Man*, 287, 380. For an excellent discussion of the roll of the suburban synagogue in the community life of upwardly mobile assimilating Jews, see Riv-Ellen Prell, *Recreating Judaism in America: An Anthropology of Contemporary Prayer* (Detroit: Wayne State University Press, forthcoming).

26. The cult of the professional, of course, did not emerge suddenly after World War II. For its nineteenth-century origins, see, for example, Burton J. Bledstein, *The Culture of Professionalism: The Middle Class and the Development of Higher Education in America* (New York, 1976). The rise of professional intervention in family life is documented in Lasch, *Haven in a Heartless World*. In the postwar years, rational expertise was institutionalized in new ways. See Terrence Ball, "The Politics of Social Science," in L. May, ed., *Promise and Peril*. Eisenhower's presidency epitomized this trend; see Robert Griffith, "Dwight D. Eisenhower and the Corporate Commonwealth," *American Historical Review* 87, no. 1 (February 1982): 87–122, and Joseph Veroff, Richard A. Kulka, and Elizabeth Douvan, *Mental Health in America: Patterns of Help-seeking from 1957 to 1976* (New York: Basic Books, 1981), 8, 10, 226. For the professionalization of motherhood through expertise see Nancy Pottishman Weiss, "Mother, the Invention of Necessity: Dr. Benjamin Spock's *Baby and Child Care*," *American Quarterly* 29, no. 5 (Winter 1977): 519–46. On Peale, see Donald Meyer, *The Positive Thinkers: A Study of the American Quest for Health, Wealth, and Personal Power from Mary Baker Eddy to Norman Vincent Peale* (Garden City, N.Y.: Doubleday, 1965).

27. Joseph Veroff, Richard A. Kulka, and Elizabeth Douvan, *The Inner American: A Self-Portrait from 1957 to 1976* (New York: Basic Books, 1981), 194; aggregate data, KLS.

28. Margaret Mead, "Problems of the Atomic Age," *The Survey*, July 1949, 385. It is worth noting that both Peale and Spock were supporters of the cold war consensus, one from the Right and one from the Left. An interesting discussion of Spock as struggling to come to terms with an unsettling world is in William Graebner, "The Unstable World of Benjamin Spock: Social Engineering in a Democratic Culture, 1917–1950," *Journal of American History* 67, no. 3 (December 1980): 612–29. For a social scientist's criticism of social science at the time, see Robert S. Lynd, *Knowledge for What? The Place of Social Science in American Culture* (Princeton: Princeton University Press, 1948). Perhaps the most eloquent expression of the expert's discomfort with the impact of scientific expertise comes from J. Robert Oppenheimer him-

self, in his "Speech to the Association of Los Alamos Scientists," Los Alamos, November 2, 1945, in which he stated that the development of the atomic bomb has led to a situation where "the very existence of science is threatened, and its value is threatened." The speech is found in Alice Kimball Smith and Charles Weiner, *Robert Oppenheimer: Letters and Recollections* (Cambridge: Harvard University Press, 1980), 315–25; the quote is on p. 316. Paul Boyer provides an excellent discussion of the scientists' activism after the war in *By the Bomb's Early Light*, pt. 3.

29. KLS.

30. Responses to open-ended question no. B.V.7., 1955 survey, KLS: "Looking back over your life, what did you have to sacrifice or give up because of your marriage?"

31. Ibid. For a discussion of the rebellion against the breadwinner role, the glorification of bachelorhood, and the rise of the Playboy culture, see Ehrenreich, *Hearts of Men.*

32. Responses to question no. B.V.7., KLS.

33. Ibid.

34. Responses to open-ended question no. B.V.8., 1955 survey, KLS: "Looking back over your life, what has marriage brought you that you could not have gained without your marriage?"

35. Ibid.

36. Anna W. Wolf, "Will Your Child Have a Happy Marriage?" *Woman's Home Companion*, April 1948, 132–33; Michael Gordon, "From an Unfortunate Necessity to a Cult of Mutual Orgasm: Sex in American Marital Educational Literature, 1830–1940," in James M. Henslin and Edward Sagarin, eds., *The Sociology of Sex* (New York: Schocken Books, 1978), 59–83; Cases 229, 14, 296, 49, 18, 67, KLS.

37. Case 158, KLS. All names used are fictitious; the Kelly respondents were identified in the survey only by number.

38. Case 290, KLS.

PART II

The New Deal Political Order:
Decline and Fall,
1960–1980

7   *Was the Great Society a Lost Opportunity?*

Ira Katznelson

Some five weeks after the assassination of his predecessor, President Johnson received the report of the Task Force on Manpower Conservation. This committee of four included the secretary of labor, who chaired it, the secretary of health, education and welfare, the secretary of defense, and the head of the Selective Service. The report focused on men rejected by the draft. It found "that one-third of the nation's youth would, on examination, be found unqualified for military service," and, second, "that poverty was the principal reason these young men failed to meet those physical and mental standards." In receiving the report, President Johnson announced (three days before he did so more widely in his first State of the Union address), "I shall shortly present to Congress a program designed to attack the roots of poverty in our cities and rural areas. . . . This war on poverty . . . will not be won overnight."[1]

The principal drafter of the document was an assistant secretary of labor, Daniel Patrick Moynihan. At the end of the decade, when he was assistant to President Nixon for urban affairs, he wrote a stinging critique of the war he helped initiate. "The great failing of the Johnson Administration," he wrote, "was that an immense opportunity to institute more or less permanent social changes—a fixed full employment program, a measure of income maintenance—was lost while energies were expended in ways that very probably hastened the end of the brief period when such options were open, that is to say the three years from the assassination of Kennedy to the election of the Ninety-first Congress."[2]

Was the Great Society a lost opportunity? Moynihan's appraisal was that of a disaffected liberal Democrat. Here, I wish to broaden this question in order to evaluate the character and legacy of the Great Society from the vantage point of its implications for the reform impulse and coalition that originated in the New Deal. I argue that the "opportunity" to achieve the social democratic potential of the New Deal was compromised not in the 1960s but in the 1940s. By social democracy I mean the attempts by labor and socialist movements in Western capitalist democracies to work through their electoral and representational political systems to achieve two principal goals: first, to effect interventions in markets that in the short run mitigate unequal distributional patterns, in the medium run promote more basic public controls over markets, and in the long run bring about a shift in social organization from capitalism to socialism; and, second, to secure the solidarity of their working-class base while reaching out for the allies they need to achieve majorities in elections and legislatures. The New Deal presented the possibility that such a strategic orientation, at least insofar as it concerned governmental activity to organize markets and mitigate market outcomes, might be feasible even in the United States, which had lacked such efforts. It is my central contention that key features of partisan politics and policy-making in the 1940s, a decade of war and reconversion, shaped the character of the Great Society's determinate limits (as well as its impressive achievements) more decisively than short-term causes. In turn, the Great Society significantly diminished subsequent prospects for a social democratic trajectory in American politics. The domestic policy choices made by the Johnson administration within the framework of the constraints inherited from the 1940s hastened major changes in the character of political debate, policy choice, and partisanship that haunt the Democratic party two decades later.

Underpinning my argument is a perspective on the dilemmas of social democracy drawn from the scholarship of Adam Przeworski and Gosta Esping-Andersen on the history and prospects of European social democracy. In schematic form, these authors propose that the relationship between social democratic parties, left-wing public policies, and working-class formation—that is, between politics and its social basis—as Esping-Andersen writes, "is historically indeterminate. This is so for the simple reason that none of the social forces that shape it is predetermined." Politics, policies, political change, and political support all go hand in hand. For their aims to be secured, social democratic parties must not only win elections and secure legislative successes to demonstrate they can make a difference. Even more, they need a program that effectively reinforces the commitment of supporters to social democratic policies and goals. This positively reinforcing spiral of reform and social transformation hinges in large measure on the character of the policies social democratic political parties succeed in passing and implementing, and on the effects of these policies in organizing and reorganizing the social basis of politics; as Przeworski puts the point, "Not all reforms are conducive to new reforms."[3]

The contraction of political space for the Left in American politics in the 1940s redefined the social forces undergirding social democratic possibilities in the Democratic party, and changed the locus of political debate from questions of social organization and class relations to issues of technical economics and interest group politics. These alterations to the political landscape defined the features the Democratic party took into the Eisenhower era; in so doing, they set the terms for the modest reform efforts of the Kennedy administration and the more assertive reformist attempt to utilize the state in the Johnson years. The Great Society, in turn, reinforced and exaggerated features of American politics that had only begun to appear in the 1940s: the reduction of labor to an interest group; the centrality of race; and an economist's definition of public policy and political choice. In this way, the Great Society's immense reform effort embodied Janus-like facings: it decisively broadened the social base of the Democratic party by incorporating blacks both within and outside of the South, yet it contracted the party's social base by contributing to the disaffections of an ever-narrowing labor movement; it substantially expanded the policy themes of American politics, but it did so in a way that simultaneously ruled out a politics of more vigorous intervention in the marketplace. The Great Society, in short, is best understood in terms of a larger dynamic of reform in the postwar era that undercut, more than it reinforced, the prospects for an American social democratic politics. The subsequent turn to the Right that culminated in the election of President Reagan on an explicit pro-market, anti-state platform with significant working-class support thus was facilitated by the way the Great Society embedded the trajectory of the 1940s.

Most explanations of the meaning of the Great Society, and the War on Poverty that nestled within it, begin, appropriately enough, with an assessment of its considerable ambition—the extraordinary range of its reformist efforts in social insurance and medical care, and the War on poverty's unprecedented and rhetorically unconditional assault on poverty. Ironically, many accounts of the Great Society consider and choose between very short term and situational alternative explanations of the immediate causes of this program such as the electoral pressures of managing urban black and white ethnic political coalitions, the Kennedy administration's need to find an innovative domestic program, or the particular composition of policy-planning committees within the administration.[4] I have no quarrel with these themes: they are not so much wrong as insufficient.

When analyses of the Great Society transcend this narrow, time-bound perspective, they most frequently tell the story of the Great Society in three quite distinctive narratives. The first is a teleological tale that locates the Kennedy-Johnson presidencies in an unfolding elaboration of the engagement of the Democratic party with social reform: from the New Deal, with its roots in progressivism and perhaps Jacksonianism, to the Fair Deal, and, after the interregnum of Eisenhower, to the New Frontier and Great Society. In this version, the panoply of legislative achievements in the middle 1960s demonstrated a deep affinity with earlier extensions of the role of government and signified the continuing political efficacy of the New Deal coalition. Transcending the boundaries of North and South, and of white ethnicity and race, the Great Society was rooted in the reformist stream of American political life. This is the version of events found in the speeches of Democratic party politicians, in the scholarly expositions of James Sundquist, and in the hagiographic treatment of the Kennedy administration by Arthur Schlesinger, Jr.[5]

The second version views the Great Society quite differently, as less the product of a revived political coalition than as the achievement of a new social group of policy intellectuals. The Great Society signified the coming of age of a new knowledge class, and its networks, institutions, and policy thinking. The larger questions of social organization and ideology had been resolved earlier. What now remained was a knowledge-based assault on persisting, yet manageable, problems of race and poverty. The Great Society thus represented social science and policy analysis ascendant.[6]

The third version perceives political and knowledge elites anticipating and responding to the tumult of the disorderly politics of the 1960s whose most destabilizing characteristic was the powerful and unpredictable insertion of race into the core of American political life. The massive migration of blacks from South to North during and after World War II radically altered the demography of politics and labor markets: and in the period following *Brown v. Board of Education*, blacks challenged the limits of political and social citizenship both in a civil rights movement dedicated to principles of nonviolence and in the bloody ghetto rebellions of the middle and late 1960s. The Great Society, in this narrative, was one of the markers of a profound racial revolution.[7]

Instead of selecting between these three most common narratives, or some combination of them, I should like to alter the angle of vision of each by elongating the time horizons of our consideration. This shift of just a few degrees can bring the Great Society as object of analysis into better focus. If we insert the story of the 1940s into each of the three main narratives about the Great Society, they alter decisively.

I

"By the end of 1937," Richard Hofstadter has written, "it was clear that something had been added to the social base of reformism. The demands of a large and powerful labor movement, coupled with the interests of the unemployed, gave the later New Deal a social-democratic tinge that had never been present before in American reform movements."[8] To be sure, this proto-social democracy was a contested matter; just the same, it was part of the contest for the Democratic party. Even after a more conservative Congress was elected in 1938, the social democratic–labor wing of the party continued to define an important pole of political possibility.

It had many resources: the support of the president, at least in speech; the support of the labor movement and the rank and file (the labor vote for Roosevelt after 1936 was higher than corresponding electoral support in Europe for the social democrats): the votes of most farmers; concrete electoral cooperation between the labor movement and ethnic political machines; centers of bureaucratic strength within the state in such agencies as the National Resources Planning Board and the Department of Labor, committed to planning and vigorous interventions in the marketplace; and an intellectual climate in the knowledge community that considered a host of ideas drawn from the socialist movements, the planning profession, and the interventionist wing of Keynesian economics.

By the end of the 1940s, none of these features of a proto-social democracy held up.

In spite of the hopes, and fears, of such analysts as C. Wright Mills, Daniel Bell, and Charles Lindblom, labor lost its radical edge and movement characteristics to become a congeries of trade unions out for the best possible deal.[9] The NRPB was dissolved. The Department of Labor lost its capacity to intervene in manpower policy. The emergence of race onto the political agenda, and the failure of the CIO to unionize successfully in the postwar South, deeply divided the Democratic party, inhibited its legislative room for maneuver, and began to challenge the capacities of the Northern urban machines to appeal simultaneously to their white ethnic and growing black constituencies. And, perhaps most important, the range of debate among the policy-interested intelligentsia both changed and narrowed to a combination of pluralist political theory and the neoclassic synthesis in economics. Together, these developments sharply contracted the range and prospects of the progressive wing of the Democratic party.[10]

At the beginning of this decade, the key political divide appeared to be between business and labor. Business threatened the social and economic order because of its potential for disinvestment, and labor, because of its capacity to disrupt capitalism at the point of production. The tensions between business and labor were intensified by uncertainties about whether prosperity and liberalism could go hand in hand in a democratic capitalist order. In this situation, labor as a political actor appeared to teeter between being an anticapitalist insurgent force and the most important presence in the left wing of the Democratic party in favor of significant planning and an intrusive version of Keynesianism.

That labor had the ability to lead a social democratic breakthrough in American politics that could build on the achievements of the New Deal and radicalize them was a commonplace of the early 1940s, one that appeared to be affirmed during World War II by such achievements as the organization by the CIO of Ford and Bethlehem steel, the growth in the size of organized labor, the incorporation within labor's embrace of the previously unorganized female and black members of the labor force, and an extraordinary wave of strikes in the aftermath of the war.[11] Further, during the New Deal, the labor movement broke with its traditional abjuration of partisan politics and integrated itself into the Democratic party through the instrumentality of the Non-Partisan League in 1936 and the Political Action Committee of the CIO in 1944, which, at the time, was widely thought to ensure a leftward tilt within the party.

Writing in 1944 as a committed social democrat, Daniel Bell warned that indicators of labor strength had an illusory quality. "The war has given labor its great numerical strength," he argued, "yet sapped it of its real strength" because of the price it exacted by way of integration into the dominant institutions and assumptions of the society. The quasi-corporatism of the war was a conservative version of statism, he insisted; after the war, he predicted, the leadership of the labor movement would be compelled to discipline its work force and limit its political horizons. He proved right. Inflation, not massive unemployment, emerged as the central and much more manageable threat of the reconversion period. It was "managed" in part by privately negotiated and relatively lucrative union contracts in basic industry. Meanwhile, a Keynesian program of government spending helped ensure that the bottom did not fall out of the demand side of the economy. An assault on the prerogatives of labor during the massive strike wave that followed the war culminated in the passage of the Taft-Hartley Act, which simultaneously produced a contraction of labor's ability to organize new workers and signified the acceptance by conservatives of the institution of collective bargaining within the limits of the act. Labor's inability to organize in the South, and the schisms between the non-Communist and Communist Left, further narrowed the scope of action of the labor movement.[12] For these and other reasons, by the end of the 1940s labor's vision and potential contracted. This reorientation was remarkably successful; arguably, labor was the most potent of the host of interest groups active in American politics. At the same time, its most militant organizational tools had been lost to Taft-Hartley, and its position within the Democratic party was that of one of a number of important constituents. It seems telling that David Truman could write his magisterial text *The Governmental Process* at the end of the decade and subsume his treatment of labor within such chapters as those concerning the genesis of interest groups, interest groups and political parties, and the web of relationships in the administrative process.[13]

This shift from labor as political opposition to labor as an interest group was paralleled by a remarkable transformation in the nature of public debate within what might be called, broadly, the policy community. At the beginning of the decade, these discussions were dominated by the discourse of political economy—the attempt "to understand economic events and arrangements in the framework of a comprehensive social theory, or at least as part of a social totality." Works as diverse as Joseph Schumpeter's *Capitalism, Socialism, and Democracy*, Karl Polanyi's *The Great Transformation*, and Friedrich Hayek's *The Road to Serfdom*, all of which were written and published in the first half of the decade, wrestled with the question of whether the tight ties between private property and market organization, on the one hand, and state ownership and bureaucratic management, on the other hand, were immutable; or, whether a "third way" could (or could not) be found to maximize the chances for prosperity *and* liberty in the postdepression, postwar world. At the end of the 1940s, by contrast, policy disputes were the province of economics, the attempt "to study the 'economic' in isolation from the 'social,' not by ignoring the latter but by taking it as a given." In political economy, however, the economy cannot be disentangled from society, history, and considerations of social organization and human nature.[14]

Social organization and human nature were now to be taken for granted, either as givens or as exogenous variables. Even the radical impulses of Keynes were domesticated in a new synthesis of neoclassic economics and Keynesianism. Keynes had viewed his *General Theory* of 1936 as representing a radical rupture with the then current economic theory, particularly in its treatment of the pricing of capital assets and capitalist financial institutions (in that these elements produce a theory of instability, whereas, by contrast, the neoclassic tradition emphasizes market stability and tendencies toward equilibrium). Yet shortly after its publication, mainstream economists truncated Keynes and assimilated it into pre-Keynesian equilibrium analysis. Within the neoclassic synthesis that developed the capitalist economy was viewed as timeless. The synthesis did not allow for internal mechanisms of destabilization. The result, Hyman Minsky writes, was "the reduction of the Keynesian Revolution to a banality."[15]

The neoclassic synthesis that became dominant within American economics by the end of the Truman years ruled out precisely those questions which had been basic to the policy debates of the early 1940s, and to the possibilities of a class-based social democratic politics within the Democratic party. Indeed, the shift to a domesticated Keynesianism as the given of policy debates went hand in hand with a labor movement content with enlarging its share of national wealth incrementally in negotiations with employers limited to wages, fringe benefits, and working conditions—private accords buttressed by government policies aimed at maintaining a level of aggregate demand consistent with a high demand for labor. Taken together, the collapse of the labor movement as a potentially social democratic force and the evaporation of the theoretical and academic bases for left-wing policy-making within American politics, demoralized the American Left, and put it in a position where it lacked a "third way" between an assertive, internationalist, capitalism and the socialism of Soviet-type societies. Given this set of actually existing alternatives, Democrats on the Left joined the tight confines of the liberalism of the cold war. "By 1950," Daniel Bell judged, "American socialism as a political and social fact was simply a matter for history alone";[16] an American society based on class divisions had been supplanted by an interest-group society of voluntary associations. In short, in the 1940s, economics replaced political economy, and pluralism supplanted the politics of class.

To these two basic changes in the political landscape must be added a third: the introduction of what proved to be the solvent of race into the Democratic party coalition. The New Deal, in spite of a small number of token gestures, had had little to offer blacks in particular, and as such left the segregationist social organization of the South unchallenged. Within the Congress, the president's programs in the first and second New Deal passed with the support of all regional wings of the party.

During the 1920s, the Democratic party had widened its regional base beyond the South, and was transformed from a primarily rural to an urban-based electoral organization. Faced with the calamity of the depression, the white South subsumed its distinctive regional interests and supported the New Deal. At its convention of 1936, the party revoked its rule that required the approval of two-thirds of the delegates to designate the presidential nominee. This provision had been instituted to protect regional interests. Now, party leaders argued, it was no longer needed because the Democrats had become a genuinely national party.[17] The tacit quid pro quo showed a high degree of tolerance for the racial civilization of the South by the party as a whole. This accommodation manifested itself in the absence of civil rights legislation, and the high degree of discretion left to the states in setting rules and benefit levels for most public assistance programs, including the Aid to Dependent Children provisions of the Social Security Act.

Writing in 1949, V. O. Key observed that "whatever phase of the Southern political process one seeks to understand," including the politics of cotton, free trade, agrarian poverty and social relations, "sooner or later the trail of inquiry leads to the Negro."[18] By that date, the partisan consistency support for the Democrats in the eleven former states of the Confederacy that had protected the system of white supremacy from national interference no longer could do so. With the voting realignments of the Roosevelt years, the South became only one element, and a minority one at that, in the coalitional structure of the Democratic party. With the massive migration of blacks to the North during World War II, their insertion into the urban-based politics of the North, and their integration into the mass production industries and the labor movement, questions of civil rights could no longer be contained as a regional matter. The character of the racial civilization of the South was placed on the national political agenda. With this, the solidarity of the Democratic party as an electoral vehicle and as a national force promoting the assertive use of the federal government to organize and reshape the market economy was compromised. The Dixiecrat rebellion of 1948 was only the most visible indicator of this change that had been manifest on a daily basis in the emergence of a blocking coalition of conservative Republicans and Southern Democrats in the Congress. In particular, any proposal that extended the planning capacity of the central state was seen, not without reason, as a direct challenge to the white supremacist arrangements of the South. For Republicans, an anti-statist position on such debates in the reconversion period as whether to decentralize or nationalize the Federal Employment Service or pass a Full Employment Act was primarily a stance against government intervention in the marketplace: for southerners, these votes were a hedge against the prospect of basic social reform.[19]

The shifts from the politics of class to the politics of pluralism, from political economy to economics, and from the omission to the inclusion of race on the national political agenda proved mutually reinforcing. Taken together, these developments starkly reduced the prospects of strong social democratic–type intervention in the marketplace. Instead, they promoted a less intrusive set of public policies: less of a state capacity to directly plan and organize markets, and more of a state capacity to shape markets by fiscal policies focusing on spending levels and the promotion of adequate aggregate demand. This "fiscalization" of public policy went hand in hand with the strengthening of the Bureau of the Budget (and an enhanced role for economists within it), the creation of the Council of Economic Advisors, and the enhancement of what Peri Arnold calls the managerial presidency. By contrast, more assertive bureaucratic agencies such as the National Resources Planning Board and the Department of Labor either were eliminated entirely or were stripped of key interventionist functions.[20] In turn, this new policy terrain reinforced the ascendancy of economics within the policy community, made it possible for the Democratic party to postpone the day of reckoning on civil rights, and confirmed the labor movement's truncated goals by facilitating the successful pursuit of Keynesian policies designed to underpin high wage settlements in the mass production industries.

With this interactive set of political, social-knowledge, and policy elements, what remained of the social democratic option for the Democratic party closed off. The Democratic party that remained competitive on the national scene during and immediately after the Eisenhower years conceded this in its discourse and practices. In the interregnum between the administrations of Truman and Kennedy the party's political formula did not alter, but it did undergo a developmental process. Each of the three main features of this formula that came to be defined in the late 1940s proved to have a powerful directionality. In the 1950s, labor narrowed its focus even more, race moved to the center of political life, and the hegemony of the neoclassic synthesis appeared complete.

This inheritance circumscribed and informed the character of the Great Society; in turn, the Johnson program reinforced, even exaggerated, each of its elements. The labor movement's confining self-definition was evinced by its concern only for the Great Society's extension of social insurance; by contrast, labor was almost totally disinterested in the War on Poverty. In spite of its early, and accurate, rhetoric to the effect that most poor people were white, these anti-poverty efforts reinforced the emergence of race as a centerpiece of national politics just at the moment when class-based issues seemed settled.[21] With regard to social knowledge, it was mainly economists working within the limits of their profession's consensus, rather than other kinds of policy professionals or more heterodox practitioners, who defined the contours and content of President Johnson's domestic initiatives.[22]

II

Listen to Lyndon Johnson. In the midst of the presidential campaign of 1964, Johnson spoke to a business audience in Hartford, Connecticut. His theme was the current "period of prosperity that has never been equaled before in the annals of history of this country," and the challenge of communism to this achievement. "I am proud to say to you that we are standing up, we are resisting, and we are trying to halt the envelopment of freedom anywhere in the world." He quickly moved on to a characterization of the basis of this resistance: democratic government built on the base of "the free enterprise system." This successful economic order is one of a partnership between "capitalists," "managers," "workers," and "government." It is the partnership of these four elements, he held, that provides the basis for a democratic system of government capable of resisting the spread of communism. The speech concluded with a discussion, and a defense, of his budget policies and macroeconomic management.[23]

The president's rhetoric is revealing of the self-satisfied context that informed the Great Society as a moment of political and social reform and of the Democratic party patrimony the Johnson administration brought to its domestic policies. Assertive yet reserved, reformist yet conservative, the Johnson program was the direct descendant of the substantive formula of the late Fair Deal that joined together the fiscal direction of markets by a neoclassic-Keynesian economic synthesis and a robust interest group politics at home to anti-Communist containment abroad. In the 1960s, the War on Poverty and the war in Vietnam were twin aspects of public policy rooted in precisely this coherent world view.[24]

Within the constraints first established in the 1940s, the Johnson administration produced a broad and assertive domestic program in the grief-stricken aftermath of the murder of President Kennedy and the landslide victories of November 1964. Because of these constraints, the judgment of Pat Moynihan at the end of the 1960s rings half-true: if the Great Society was a missed opportunity for social democratic reform, the reasons are to be found mainly in the road not taken two decades earlier.

If a missed opportunity, the Great Society still marked one of this century's most vigorous moments of utilization of the state to shape markets and mitigate their distributional outcomes. President Johnson's Great Society, and the War on Poverty within it, built on initiatives begun in the Kennedy years that focused on juvenile delinquency. In 1964, the president soon proposed, and Congress approved, the most sweeping domestic legislative program since the New Deal. For a remarkable moment, the country's domestic politics focused sympathetically and constructively on the least advantaged, and the United States seemed prepared to override its historical reticence in finding a role for the state in mitigation of the distributive patterns of the market.

The War on Poverty was only one feature of what Johnson came to call his program for the Great Society, but this rubric alone captured a host of new programs for poor people: the Job Corps that focused on remedial programs for teenagers in residential settings to make them employable; the Neighborhood Youth Corps that provided training and work experience to adolescents who were in school or who had dropped out; the Manpower Development and Training Act that retrained unemployed workers; Head Start that provided preschool education; Upward Bound that helped talented high school students to prepare for college; the Teacher Corps, Title I of the Education and Secondary Education Act, and school lunch programs to improve schooling at the elementary and secondary levels; Foodstamps, begun in the Kennedy administration, to supplement the budgets of the poor; Medicaid and neighborhood health centers to address the maldistribution of medical care in a fee-for-service system; Legal Services to partially equalize the availability of this service; Model Cities, a program to coordinate and concentrate urban development efforts in selected poverty areas; and, of course, Community Action. This most controversial feature of the War on Poverty was based on the provision in the Economic Opportunity Act of 1964 that stipulated "the maximum feasible participation of the residents of the areas and the members of groups served" in the design and decisions of community action agencies. The federal government contracted with these nongovernmental, community-based groups to administer federal antipoverty efforts and to develop local antipoverty programs in their areas. More broadly, the Great Society label encompassed fundamental civil rights legislation, Medicare for all Americans over the age of sixty-five, and enhancements to Social Security, among other programs.

The Great Society inaugurated a considerable shift in the construction of the federal budget. Military spending declined as a share of the whole, even during the Vietnam War; social welfare expenditures increased. Total public expenditures on social insurance and income transfer assistance programs doubled to $61 billion in the second half of the 1960s (rising from 4.6 percent to 6.1 percent of GNP). The most dramatic period of expansion spanned the fiscal years 1965–67, when the annual rate of increase, even after taking inflation into account, averaged about 15 percent; later, the pressures of Vietnam reduced the rate of growth in these programs to about 10 percent each year in real terms. These changes in the pattern of federal programs made a difference. Though it is difficult to separate out the effects of economic expansion and the effects of antipoverty programs on the reduction of poverty, the steep decline from the nearly one in five Americans who were poor by the official measure when the War on Poverty was declared to just over one in ten by 1973 at minimum represents a provocative correlation between governmental efforts and effects. Health care, hunger, unemployment, delinquency, manpower training, community action, legal services, educational initiatives, and antidiscrimination legislation, moreover, defined an interrelated cluster of concerns that altered the boundary line between the state and the marketplace and that redefined the content of citizenship to include an enhanced social component.

In these ways, the Great Society revived some of the social democratic impulses of the New Deal and Fair Deal. The capacities of the state were mobilized to alter the abilities of its least-advantaged citizens to effectively participate and compete in labor markets and to mitigate the effects of market distributions. The aim, and the result, was a more equitable and less harsh society. Even the hardheaded assessment of the radical critique of the history of American social policy by Michael Katz concluded that the expansion of the role of government by the Great Society tilted decisively toward social democracy, and invigorated the social basis of reform:[25]

> First, it vastly increased the proportion of the most disadvantaged Americans assisted by their government; it virtually guaranteed them a minimally adequate diet and health care; and it lifted a significant fraction of them, especially the elderly, out of extreme poverty. Second, it mobilized the power of the federal government behind the civil rights movement

and thereby helped reduce discrimination and increase the accessibility of jobs to minorities. Third, the OEO's emphasis on community action nourished and intensified the growing citizen's movement, or grass-roots revolution, that already has reshaped urban politics and launched a new generation of leaders into government and social service. Fourth, it altered the relations between citizens and the state by making the federal government the most important source of income for a large fraction of the population. . . . Fifth, all of the above point unequivocally in at least one direction: the federal government has the resources and the administrative capacity with which to stimulate and sustain progressive social change.

My own formulation is both similar and different—similar because I too think the Great Society represented a vigorous and creative use of the state to affect distributional patterns of class and race, but different, too, because this intervention was undertaken within already established narrow limits, and it thus had the paradoxical effect of weakening, more than it strengthened, the prospects for further reform.

Katz, like most sympathetic commentators who look back at least half wistfully at the Johnson domestic program in the age of Reagan, stresses the Great Society's willingness to utilize the state in unprecedented ways for social ends, but he downplays its other side: a non-ideological (self-consciously technical, trans-ideological) orientation to reform grounded in a very high degree of self-satisfaction with the country's economy and society. The Great Society was not an organic part of a larger vision or politics of the Left. It certainly lacked any of the anticapitalist or even critical content of its European social democratic counterparts. With the exception of Medicare, its politics did not promise any significant changes in the life conditions of the majority of Americans, or even the majority of supporters of the Democratic party. Substantively, it stopped well short of attempts to reorganize and modify the marketplace. It entirely left alone the organization of work, the patterns of investment, and the role of the business class. It did not call into question either the larger contours and rationality of the American political economy or the tools, a version of Keynesianism, that had been elaborated over the course of a quarter-century to manage the macroeconomic issues of growth, employment, and inflation. If at the heart of the Great Society was a *war* on poverty, this was a quite timid call to arms, with the enemy identified circumspectly.

The most compelling characteristic of the Great Society was that it was a program of mainstream economists and technicians who conceded from the start the framework of ideas and practices of the larger political economy. It sought to correct inequities and problems on the margin of a thriving system of production and consumption. If, for working people, as Arthur Stinchcombe observes, "Social Democracy is almost always compromise of basic principles for concrete advantages, while capitalist compromise is almost always an expedient to save the basic features of the system by bargaining away some concrete advantages,"[26] the Great Society entailed a constricted version of this trade-off.

Writing in an attempt to put "the Great Society in perspective," Brookings Institution scholar Henry Aaron observed that "none of the ideas embodied in the Great Society or the War on Poverty was really new. All had been foreshadowed in the New Deal or Fair Deal."[27] This is partially, but not precisely, my point. For the ideas available in the period of the New Deal and Fair Deal were very capacious. They included national and regional economic planning and a highly interventionist Keynesianism as well as the public policies actually adopted or the policy discourse that came to prevail by the late 1940s. It is incontestable that the Great Society had ties of continuity with earlier periods of Democratic party reform: the key issue is how earlier outcomes of the contest within the Democratic party of competing reformist possibilities tacitly impressed assumptions and limits on the Johnson initiatives.

III

It is useful to contrast the New Deal and the Great Society. The New Deal was concerned, in the short and medium term, to restore the economy to a path of positive performance, and, in the medium and long term, to create a system of social insurance that would secure individuals against the vicissitudes of the labor market, and, in so doing, cushion the markets against themselves. At a time of great class-based turmoil, the New Deal, more than any previous American reform program, understood poverty as anchored in class relations as it aimed to put the working class back to work. And yet, its antipoverty measures were conceived as emergency efforts to deal with the temporary crisis of capitalism: they did not attempt a basic redistribution of wealth and income between the classes. Moreover, Roosevelt's program had nothing distinctive to offer to blacks except insofar as the New Deal promised renewed economic growth and prosperity for all.

The Great Society, by contrast, presumed such prosperity and a formula to secure it. Postwar economic development and growth in the United States, as elsewhere in the West in the 1960s, was robust and unprecedented. Economists grew confident they had reduced the business cycle to manageable proportions and to the dimensions of a technical problem. Broadly, supply and demand seemed to be in a high-employment equilibrium, and the societal relations of class appeared to be based more on harmony than on conflict.[28] In this context, poverty was conceived of by the Great Society not as a matter of class relations even in the limited terms of the New Deal, but principally as a matter of race. The twin paths of civil rights legislation on public accommodations and voting rights and the War on Poverty were explicitly linked by President Johnson in his commencement address at Howard University in June 1965. There, he spoke of the special "burden that a dark skin can add to the search for a productive place in Society," of the fact that "unemployment strikes most swiftly and broadly at the Negro," of the need for a multicentered solution that goes beyond antidiscrimination legislation to questions of jobs, income, and housing.[29]

Features of the Great Society could trace a direct lineage back to the New Deal; part of the Johnson program extended the social insurance provisions of the Social Security Act, especially as they concerned medical care for the elderly. But unlike the New Deal, the Great Society moved beyond the economy in general to the specificities of antipoverty policies, beyond social insurance to a host of noninsurance programs directed at the poor, and beyond class orientations to poverty to a confrontation with the intertwined questions of race and inequality.

In a penetrating essay that takes up the origins of the Great Society, Hugh Heclo notes the absence of an antipoverty legacy of the New Deal, as well as the lack of a popular ground swell in favor of such initiatives. Where, then, did the Great Society root itself? Following John Kingdon's work on agendas, Heclo argues that there was a fortuitous, and felicitous, conjuncture of three elements: the emergence of poverty, often connected to race relations, as a "problem" in the media and in public consciousness; the need of Presidents Kennedy and Johnson to find subjects for innovation; and, perhaps most important, the availability of a stream of policy proposals with a distinctive, and politically palatable, perspective on poverty by different kinds of policy experts.[30]

This policy perspective that constituted the kit bag of ideas available to the Democratic presidents of the 1960s was principally that of economists who were concerned with human capital and incentives to opportunity, and of sociologists and social work professionals who had developed theories of blocked opportunity. Joined together, this package of orientations to policy had a coherent analysis and prescriptive perspective: its central intent was the integration of the poor into the growth economy and the social insurance state from which they had been excluded both for reasons of economic structure and individual behavior. Since the revitalization of the economy alone could not perform this feat of integration, the intervention of the state was required to incorporate all Americans into market mechanisms and into the public programs of collective insurance that went hand in hand with these labor markets.

Broadly speaking, this intervention took two new forms. The first (in what might be dubbed the Great Society of the economists) attempted to eliminate unemployment that was understood to be structural. From the start, economists had a high involvement in the formulation and implementation of the War on Poverty, and from the outset they impressed upon the programs a distinctive logic and theory of poverty, and thus of the kinds of interventions that were called for. "The strategy adopted," Robert Haveman has observed in his study of the relationship of the Great Society and the social sciences,[31]

> was premised on the view that the problem was ultimately one of low labor market productivity. The poor were viewed as being in that state because they did not work enough, or because they did not work hard enough, or because their meager skills and qualifications were insufficient to raise them out of poverty even if they did work hard. This condition was in turn attributed to several factors—the lagging state of the economy, the characteristics of the poor, and discrimination against them by those who controlled access to jobs or goods and services.

The remedies of the economists could not be changes in programs of income transfers since the productivity characteristics of the poor would be left untouched. Thus, there was a need for policies targeted at the poor to improve their skills and behavioral traits, and thus their capacity to compete. These various programs, from the Job Corps to manpower training, would have to meet the rigorous tests of cost-benefit analysis. Thus, from the outset, the Office of Economic Opportunity convened an enormous amount of poverty research, and its economics-oriented staff was one of the first in Washington to adopt in the domestic arena the cost-effectiveness measures that Secretary of Defense McNamara had brought with him from Ford.

The second form of intervention (what might be called the Great Society of the social policy experts), sought to change the institutionalized linkages between the poor and the state. It did so because it saw institutional barriers to the participation of poor people in the mainstream institutions of the economy and the polity, and because it believed that community activity of a grass-roots kind could effect behavioral changes in the poor as well. From this perspective, a host of behavioral pathologies afflicted the poor, including female-headed families, teenage pregnancy, very high dropout rates from secondary schooling, crime, ill-formed work habits, weak collective organization for self-help, and inattention to political matters. In addressing remedies, a number of different strands of thinking and action in social work, community organization, and social policy thinking intersected.

As a profession, social work has been torn from the start between a casework orientation, focusing on individual and family pathology, and a penchant for structural social reform. Its history has oscillated between these orientations.[32] In 1960, two members of the social work faculty at Columbia University published a landmark book that promised to overcome this duality. In *Delinquency and Opportunity*, Richard Cloward and Lloyd Ohlin joined structure and agency together by propounding a theory that understood the delinquency of teenagers as the product of insufficient opportunity to conform to societal norms; thus they proposed that the key to intervention be the provision of a mix of social and psychological resources to induce more conformity.[33] This work directly influenced important demonstration activities of the Ford Foundation in New York City and President Kennedy's Committee on Juvenile Delinquency. These were the precursors of the War on Poverty's controversial program of community action, and its goals of the "maximum feasible participation" of poor people.[34]

What is striking, but scarcely noticed, is the close affinity between the War on Poverty of the economists and the War on Poverty of the social worker–social policy experts. Neither perspective understood poverty in terms of basic conflicts of interest; the central issue was not one of redistribution or of conflicting goals between the poor and the better-off. After all, the bounty of economic growth could suffice for everyone, and all Americans shared in a set of values, if only they could achieve them. Both groups of experts sought to enhance economic opportunity at the interface of structure and behavior. The basic structures of American Society were satisfactory; they needed adjustment, fine-tuning, enhanced access. The keys were manpower training, more grass-roots democracy, and a rigorous cost-benefit approach to the new programs.

The appeal of this rhetorical and policy construct for reform politicians at the national level in search of an innovative agenda is manifest. This was a program that displaced challenges to political authority to the local level and that did not threaten the central features of American capitalism, the distribution of goods and services, or prevailing ideological predispositions. It favored equality of opportunity rather than equality of results.[35] It was not relief or the hated idea of the dole. Nor did it pose a challenge to the class compromise that underpinned the quasi-Keynesian growth of a big-government, social insurance state.[36] It gave Democratic party leaders the chance to solidify their base in the black ghettos of the North and in the poorer areas of the rural South without disrupting their existing ties to white ethnic political machines or to the elite-dominated system of the Old South. Or, at the time, so it seemed.

The congressional Democratic party supported this program in overwhelming numbers across regional and ideological lines. But not without some uneasy moments. After the overwhelming passage of the Economic Opportunity Act of 1964 in the Senate, a group of Southern opponents appeared in the House, led by Howard Smith, the chairman of the Rules Committee, who feared the creation of OEO would hasten racial integration. The administration protected the bill by conceding a veto to the governor of any state of any programs of community action not affiliated with institutions of higher education, and by allowing participation of private groups only if they had already displayed a "concern" for poverty, a clause meant to exclude such civil rights organizations as the NAACP. In the end, sixty of the one hundred Southern Democrats supported the bill, providing its margin of victory.[37] At the same time, the fragility of Southern support was made clear; should race relations come to drive the issue of poverty, the cross-regional character of Democratic party support for Johnson's domestic agenda would cease.[38] Later, the same would prove to be the case for politicians from white ethnic areas of the North and Midwest. But at the time of passage, the labor movement and big-city mayors like Richard Daley backed the president. And why not? The war on poverty he had inaugurated seemed to be on the periphery of their concerns.[39]

The robustness of this program and the remarkable acquiescence of the Congress in it during the early part of Johnson's administration presented more than the appearance of assertive reform; the Great Society pushed to its limits the possibilities inherent in the political formula of the late 1940s to utilize the state as a counterpoint to markets. But precisely because of this combination of vigor and limits, the cumulative result was a continuation of a negative spiral in the relationship between the social base and public policies of social democratic reform.

These central characteristics of the Great Society—its vigorous use of the state in a conservative way; the importance of policy intellectuals in the making and administering of the programs; the complementarity of the perspectives of economists, social policy experts, and politicians; its lack of challenge to prevailing patterns of authority, production, distribution, labor relations, or programs of social insurance; the relative inattention of the labor movement; and the partial overlap with issues of civil rights and race relations—were shaped decisively in the Democratic party, in the knowledge community, and in the labor movement of the 1940s. By the end of that decade, a host of decisions and developments had removed a wide range of interventionist, social democratic possibilities from the political agenda, possibilities that had remained live prospects within the range of ordinary politics at the end of the second New Deal. It was this reduction of political space, this closure of the agenda, and the deepening of distinctive patterns of politics and policy, that most shaped the character of the Great Society—what it was, and what it was not.

The reinforcement of the limited role of the labor movement, the identification of the party with blacks, rather than with cross-race, class-based policies, and the enhancement of the complacent orientation of the party's Keynesian economists who viewed the problems of employment, inflation, growth, and financial stability as merely technical rather than structural, left the Democrats very vulnerable to assaults from the Right in the 1970s. In the North, the party became dependent on a narrowly defined labor movement vulnerable to domestic disinvestment and stagflation, as well as on urban political organizations, the residues of the once robust political machines that had incorporated white ethnics into Democratic party politics and that had been bypassed by the War on Poverty's Community Action programs as mechanisms of mobilizing racial minorities in cities that were increasingly black and brown. The white South defected. Overall, the Democratic party electorate in presidential elections became more poor and less white. Locked into the limited analyses of neoclassic Keynesianism, the Democrats were unable to deal convincingly with the emergent economic instabilities, low growth, and inflation of the Ford and Carter years. Moreover, in the absence of either an engaged working-class social base in support of social democratic programs or realistic prospects for social democratic policies, the party embraced interest group pluralism as the only coherent strategy available. As a result, it found itself vulnerable to charges that it was nothing more than a holding company for special interests.[40]

Thus, a central effect of the Great Society was its reinforcement of the tendencies of the 1940s, and with it, at the very moment of the most vigorous domestic reforms since the first term of Franklin Roosevelt, the exhaustion of the social democratic promise of the New Deal and the reinforcement of the centrifugal forces within the Democratic party.

Each of the standard scholarly narratives about the Great Society stands up well: there were continuities with earlier Democratic party reform efforts, and both race relations and the knowledge community provided key elements that shaped Johnson's program. It has been the burden of this essay to show that these narratives stand up best, however, when they are intertwined, and when their time horizons are elongated. When this is done it becomes clear that the "lost opportunity," lamented by Moynihan, for a more assertive social democratic program no longer existed in the early 1960s, as it had only two decades earlier. And yet, the Great Society did not lack for significance. It reminds us, as Katz asserts, that even within the limitations of American politics the current failures of the federal government are more matters of will than the absence of a potential institutional capacity. "In this recognition, there is at least some small cheer for dark days."[41] At the same time, if the aspiration to renew the reform impulse is to have practical meaning, we must also come to understand how it was the Great Society reinforced just those aspects of the trajectory of the late 1940s which continue to present obstacles to the achievement of an American version of social democracy.

NOTES

1. Cited in John C. Donovan, *The Politics of Poverty* (New York: Pegasus, 1967), 26.

2. Daniel P. Moynihan, *Maximum Feasible Misunderstanding: Community Action in the War on Poverty* (New York: Free Press, 1969), 193.

3. Adam Przeworski, *Capitalism and Social Democracy* (Cambridge: Cambridge University Press, 1985); Gosta Esping-Andersen, *Politics against Markets: The Social Democratic Road to Power* (Princeton: Princeton University Press, 1985). The quotations are from Esping-Andersen, p. 26, and Przeworski, p. 242. Esping-Andersen's comparison of the Scandinavian social democratic experiences argues that policies that have a universalistic cast tend to vitalize working-class politics, while more particularistic policies tend to demobilize working-class politics and decompose social democratic parties. This process of negative reinforcement has wreaked havoc on the Democratic party and its relatively meager social democratic prospects. For a treatment of the United States along these lines, see Alan Wolfe, "Sociology, Liberalism, and the Radical Right," *New Left Review* 128 (July–August 1981).

Of course, the extent to which the American Democratic party deserves to be included within the family of social democratic parties is a contested matter. The most judicious formula, even as it begs some questions, is David Greenstone's:

In the early and mid-1960's, the American labor movement's role in the national Democratic party represented a *partial* equivalence to the Social Democratic (formerly socialist) party–trade union alliances in much of Western Europe. This equivalence obtained with respect to its activities as a party campaign (and lobbying) organization, its influence as a party faction, and its welfare-state policy objectives. (J. David Greenstone, *Labor in American Politics* [New York: Alfred A. Knopf, 1969], 361–62)

I briefly discuss this issue, while citing Greenstone, in my essay "Considerations on Social Democracy in the United States," *Comparative Politics* 11 (October 1978). In this essay, I am rather more concerned with identifying the distinctive qualities of the reform–public policy–social base interknitting in the American regime, utilizing the perspective developed by Przeworski and Esping-Andersen, than with speaking to the question of similarities and differences between the Democratic party and European social democracy.

4. When scholarly treatments of the massive agenda of the Johnson administration take a longer view, it is when they move on to studies of its implementation or to assessments of success and failure in actually dealing with poverty, race, and the underclass. Important examples include Moynihan, *Maximum Feasible Misunderstanding*; Henry J. Aaron, *Politics and the Professors: The Great Society in Perspective* (Washington, D.C.: Brookings Institution, 1978); Sar Levitan and Robert Taggart, *The Promise of Greatness: The Social Programs of the Last Decade and Their Major Achievements* (Cambridge: Harvard University Press, 1976); Sar Levitan, *The Great Society's Poor Law* (Baltimore: Johns Hopkins University Press, 1969); Peter Marris and Martin Rein, *Dilemmas of Social Reform: Poverty and Community Action in the United States* (Chicago: Aldine, 1967); Jeffrey L. Pressman and Aaron B. Wildavsky, *Implementation* (Berkeley and Los Angeles: University of California Press, 1973); Frances Fox Piven and Richard Cloward, *Regulating the Poor: The Functions of Public Welfare* (New York: Pantheon Books, 1971); John E. Schwartz, *America's Hidden Success: A Reassessment of Twenty Years of Public Policy* (New York: W. W. Norton, 1983); Charles Murray, *Losing Ground: American Social Policy, 1950–1980* (New York: Basic Books, 1984); Sheldon Danziger and Daniel H. Weinberg, eds., *Fighting Poverty: What Works and What Doesn't* (Cambridge: Harvard University Press, 1986); Marshall Kaplan and Peggy Cuciti, eds., *The Great Society and its Legacy: Twenty Years of U.S. Social Policy* (Durham, N.C.: Duke University Press, 1986); William Julius Wilson, *The Truly Disadvantaged: The Inner City, the Underclass, and Public Policy* (Chicago: University of Chicago Press, 1987); Ken Auletta, *The Underclass* (New York: Random House, 1982); Lawrence Mead, *Beyond Entitlement: The Social Obligations of Citizenship* (New York: Free Press, 1986); J. L. Sundquist, ed., *On Fighting Poverty: Perspective from Experience* (New York: Basic Books, 1969); and, David Zarefsky, *President Johnson's War on Poverty: Rhetoric and History* (Birmingham: University of Alabama Press, 1986).

5. James L. Sundquist, *Politics and Policy: The Eisenhower, Kennedy, and Johnson Years* (Washington, D.C.: Brookings Institution, 1968); Arthur M. Schlesinger, Jr., *A Thousand Days: John F. Kennedy in the White House* (Boston: Houghton Mifflin, 1965). See especially Schlesinger's discussion of the con-

tinuities in personnel between the Fair Deal and Great Frontier concerns with poverty on pp. 1009–10.

6. This perspective is closely associated with Moynihan, and the phrase he coined, "The Professionalization of Reform." In addition to *Maximum Feasible Misunderstanding*, also see his "The Professors and the Poor," *Commentary* 46 (August 1968). The role of the knowledge community in shaping and evaluating the reforms of the Johnson years is also discussed in Aaron, *Politics and the Professors*, and in Robert H. Haveman, *Poverty Policy and Poverty Research: The Great Society and the Social Sciences* (Madison: University of Wisconsin Press, 1987). Also see the special issue edited by Eli Ginsburg and Robert M. Solow, "The Great Society: Lessons for the Future," *The Public Interest* 34 (Winter 1974).

7. Piven and Cloward, *Regulating the Poor*, cast the Great Society in these terms. Also see Robert Allen, *Black Awakening in Capitalist America* (New York: Doubleday Anchor, 1970); J. David Greenstone and Paul E. Peterson, *Race and Authority in Urban Politics: Community Participation and the War on Poverty* (New York: Russell Sage Foundation, 1973); and Peter Orleans and William Russell Ellis, Jr., eds., *Race, Change and Urban Society* (Beverly Hills, Calif.: Sage Publications, 1971).

8. Richard Hofstadter, *The Age of Reform* (New York: Vintage Books, 1955), 308. I have been influenced by the argument sketched in Maurizio Vaudagna, "The New Deal and European Social Democracy," unpublished manuscript, 1983.

9. Charles Lindblom, *Unions and Capitalism* (New Haven: Yale University Press, 1949); C. Wright Mills, *The New Men of Power* (New York: Harcourt Brace, 1948); Daniel Bell, "The Capitalism of the Proletariat: A Theory of American Trade Unionism," in *The End of Ideology* (New York: Free Press, 1960).

10. This is hardly the place either for a comprehensive treatment of the 1940s or for a causal account of what happened. These subjects are an important part of a project I am currently undertaking on the changing political agenda of American politics since the New Deal, with assistance from the Ford Foundation. Here, I will limit myself to a schematic description. Unfortunately, though there is a great deal of literature that covers the 1940s, there is little to recommend. A basic overview is provided in Alonzo Hamby, *Beyond the New Deal: Harry S. Truman and American Liberalism* (New York: Columbia University Press, 1973).

11. "For the number of strikers, their weight in industry and the duration of struggle," Preis observes, "the 1945–46 strike wave in the U.S. surpassed anything of its kind in any capitalist country, including the British General Strike of 1926" (Art Preis, *Labor's Giant Step* [New York: Pioneer Publishers, 1964], 276).

12. Daniel Bell, "The Coming Tragedy of American Labor," *Politics*, March 1944, cited in Howard Brick, *Daniel Bell and the Decline of Intellectual Radicalism: Social Theory and Political Reconciliation in the 1940's* (Madison: University of Wisconsin Press, 1966), 92–93. Much of the American Left within

and without the labor movement in this period consisted of the Communist party and its allied organizations. The decline of the Left in this period can be understood in full measure only in light of the deep schism between the Communists and the social democrats and liberals on the left, and when the situation of the Left is assessed in the larger context of the cold war and the anti-Communist mood, bordering on hysteria, at home. The links between domestic and foreign policy concerns were brought home to the labor movement by the visit of Secretary of State Marshall to the CIO convention of 1947, where he made a plea for support of foreign aid and for the expulsion of "subversives" from the ranks of labor. During the purge of communists from the CIO unions in 1949, the issue of support for the Marshall Plan was the central issue. From that period forward, the labor movement played an active role in promoting non-Communist, and anti-Communist, labor movements abroad.

13. See Greenstone, *Labor in American Politics*; Karen Orren, "Union Politics and Postwar Liberalism in the United States, 1946–1979," in *Studies in American Political Development: An Annual* (New Haven: Yale University Press, 1986); Christopher L. Tomlins, *The State and the Unions: Labor Relations, Law, and the Organized Labor Movement in America, 1880–1960* (Cambridge: Cambridge University Press, 1985); David B. Truman, *The Governmental Process* (New York: Alfred A. Knopf, 1951).

14. F. H. Hahn, "Recognizing the Limits," *Times Literary Supplement*, December 6, 1985, p. 1399. See Joseph A. Schumpeter, *Capitalism, Socialism, and Democracy* (New York: Harper & Row, 1942); Karl Polanyi, *The Great Transformation: The Political and Economic Origins of Our Time* (New York: Rinehart & Co., 1944); Friedrich Hayek, *The Road to Serfdom* (London: Routledge, 1944).

15. On this basis the discourse of economics, he has argued tellingly, was directed into a very narrow trough between the late 1940s and the 1970s:

> During the 1970's American economists engaged in what might have been taken to be a serious controversy between Keynesians and monetarists. . . . In truth, the differences were minor—as the competing camps used the same economic theory. Furthermore, the public policy prescriptions do not really differ. . . . In this debate, monetarists emphasized that changes in the money supply destabilize the economy, and Keynesians argued that fiscal variables can be used to stabilize the economy. . . . Both schools hold that the business cycle can be banished from the capitalist world; and neither school allows for any within-the-system disequilibriating forces that lead to business cycles. . . . The view that the dynamics of capitalism lead to business cycles that may be thoroughly destructive is foreign to their economic theory. (Hyman P. Minsky, *Stabilizing an Unstable Economy* [New Haven: Yale University Press, 1986], 138, 102)

16. Cited in Brick, *Daniel Bell*, 189.

17. The chair of the Rules Committee at that convention, Senator Clark of Missouri, declared confidently that "the Democratic Party is no longer a sectional party; it has become a great national party" (cited in Robert A. Garson, *The Democratic Party and the Politics of Sectionalism, 1941–1948* [Baton Rouge: Louisiana State University Press, 1974], 7).

18. V. O. Key, *Southern Politics* (New York: Alfred A. Knopf, 1949), 5.

19. Useful discussions include Garson, *The Democratic Party and the Politics of Sectionalism*; David B. Truman, *The Congressional Party: A Case Study* (New York: John Wiley, 1959); Barbara Sinclair, *The Congressional Realignment, 1925–1978* (Austin: University of Texas Press, 1982); Barbara Sinclair, "From Party Voting to Regional Fragmentation: The House of Representatives from 1933–1956," *American Politics Quarterly* 6, no. 2 (1978).

20. For an important discussion, see Peri E. Arnold, *Making the Managerial Presidency* (Princeton: Princeton University Press, 1986), esp. chaps. 4 and 5.

21. Labor did align with the civil rights movement to the extent specific unions had a significant black membership. Useful discussions of race and the Great Society include Gary Orfield, "Race and the Liberal Agenda: The Loss of the Integrationist Dream, 1965–1974," University of Chicago, Department of Political Science, unpublished manuscript, 1986; and Michael K. Brown and Steven P. Erie, "Blacks and the Legacy of the Great Society: The Economic and Political Impact of Federal Social Policy," *Public Policy* 3 (Summer 1981).

22. For treatments of the role of economists in policy-making, see Robert H. Nelson, "The Economics Profession and the Making of Public Policy," *Journal of Economic Literature* 25 (March 1987); Alice Rivlin, "Economics and the Political Process," *American Economics Review* 77 (March 1987); Ronald King, "Macroeconomics and Presidential Policy: A Review Essay," *Western Political Quarterly* 40 (March 1987).

23. Reprinted in Marvin E. Gettleman and David Mermelstein, eds., *The Failure of American Liberalism: After the Great Society* (New York: Vintage Books, 1971), 124–28.

24. Although I think the links between domestic and foreign policy in the Johnson years to be fertile ground, I do not explore it further in this essay. Rather, I wish to show how some central aspects of partisanship and public policy-making in the 1940s shaped the character of the most assertive moment of domestic social reform since the second New Deal. For a discussion of the domestic-foreign policy linkage, see Mary Sperling McAuliffe, *Crisis on the Left: Cold War Politics and American Liberals, 1947–1954* (Amherst: University of Massachusetts Press, 1978).

25. Michael Katz, *In the Shadow of the Poorhouse: A Social History of Welfare in America* (New York: Basic Books, 1986), 271–72.

26. Arthur L. Stinchcombe, *Stratification and Organization: Selected Papers* (Cambridge: Cambridge University Press, 1986), 71.

27. Aaron, *Politics and the Professors*, 26.

28. A fine overview is provided in Herman Van der Wee, *Prosperity and Upheaval: The World Economy, 1945–1980* (London: Penguin Books, 1987).

29. Congressional Quarterly, *Congress and the Nation* (Washington, D.C.: Congressional Quarterly, Inc., 1969), 2:397.

30. Hugh Heclo, "The Political Foundations of Anti-Poverty Policy," in Danziger and Weinberg, *Fighting Poverty*. This perspective is consistent with

the treatment of the War on Poverty by Polsby as an example of one distinctive genre of policy innovation characterized by a short time-span between policy proposals and enactment, a fusion of various stages of policy formulation and adoption, and a relatively low degree of partisanship or conflict associated with the legislation (Nelson W. Polsby, *Political Innovation in America: The Politics of Policy Initiation* [New Haven: Yale University Press, 1984], chap. 5).

31. Haveman, *Poverty Policy and Poverty Research*, 14–15; also see, Sar A. Levitan and Irving H. Siegel, eds., *Dimensions of Manpower Policy: Programs & Research* (Baltimore: Johns Hopkins University Press, 1966). I have found instructive as a discussion of the policy perspectives of economists the paper by Peter VanDoren, "Is Welfare Economics Sufficient for Policy Prescription?" (paper presented to the Annual Meeting of the Midwest Political Science Association, April 1987).

32. For a fine history, see John H. Ehrenreich, *The Altruistic Imagination: A History of Social Work and Social Policy in the United States* (Ithaca: Cornell University Press, 1985).

33. Richard A. Cloward and Lloyd E. Ohlin, *Delinquency and Opportunity: A Theory of Delinquent Gangs* (New York: Free Press, 1960).

34. For discussions, see Marris and Rein, *Dilemmas of Social Reform*, and Moynihan, *Maximum Feasible Understanding*.

35. For important discussions, see Jennifer Hochschild. *What's Fair? American Beliefs about Distributive Justice* (Cambridge: Harvard University Press, 1981); and Sidney Verba and Garry R. Orren, *Equality in America: The View from the Top* (Cambridge: Harvard University Press, 1985).

36. See Przeworski, *Capitalism and Social Democracy*, chap. 5.

37. Polsby, *Political Innovation in America*, 142. Yet another concession by the administration was the pledge that Adam Yarmolinsky, thought to be an intrusive liberal, would not be part of the Office of Economic Opportunity to be headed by Sargent Shriver. Yarmolinsky had been brought into government by McNamara at Defense. and was widely expected to be Shriver's deputy. Opposition to Yarmolinsk/ centered in the delegations from North Carolina and South Carolina (see Zarefsky, *President Johnson's War on Poverty*, 55).

38. For a relevant discussion, see Stanley Kelley, Jr., "Democracy and the New Deal Party System," Project on the Federal Social Role, Working Paper no. 10, 1986.

39. In June 1983, Walter Heller, the chair of the Council of Economic Advisors, addressed the annual convention of the Communications Workers of America. Thinking this a supportive audience, he tried out the idea of a comprehensive assault on poverty. Levitan reports:

> His address hammered at a double theme: the need for a tax cut and for policies "to open more exits from poverty." Although the minutes of the convention indicate that Heller received the predictable applause at the end of his address, CWA President Joseph Beirne, in thanking Heller for his address, indicated his support for the tax cut but made no reference to the antipoverty program. Heller's own reaction was that the union members were interested in the tax cut but that he had

lost his audience when he spoke about poverty. (Levitan, *The Great Society's Poor Law*, pp. 15–16)

40. A lucid treatment of these changes is Thomas Byrne Edsall, *The New Politics of Inequality* (New York: W. W. Norton, 1984). A strong case for cross-racial class-based social democratic politics and policies is made in Wilson, *The Truly Disadvantaged*. In his memoir of the early Reagan administration, former budget director David Stockman presents the analysis of the Democratic party as an assemblage of special interests, and, interestingly, says that he came to this view by a reading of Theodore Lowi's *The End of Liberalism*. Stockman wrote,

> The interest group liberalism I had learned about at Harvard, which had been my answer to Marxism, was getting out of hand. I decided to go back and reread what in hindsight must be considered one of the more seminal works of modern American political science, *The End of Liberalism* by Theodore Lowi. His theory was that interest group pluralism had radically transformed American governance. . . .
>
> After the New Deal, the line dividing state and society came tumbling down like the walls of Jericho. Interest groups appropriated its authority, and the uses of state power were defined not by the Constitution but by whatever claims the organized interest groups could successfully impose on the system. . . . Might had become Right. Public policy was not a high-minded nor even an ideological endeavor, but simply a potpourri of parochial claims proffered by private interests parading in governmental dress. Much of the vast enterprise of American government was invalid, suspect, malodorous. Its projects and ministrations were not spawned by higher principles, broad idealism, or even humanitarian sentimentality; they were simply the flotsam and jetsam of a flagrantly promiscuous politics, the booty and spoils of the organized thievery conducted within the desecrated halls of government. (David Stockman, *The Triumph of Politics: Why the Reagan Revolution Failed* [New York: Harper & Row, 1986])

Lacking an overall conception to guide its interventionist use of the state, and without a mobilized social base, the Democratic party stood quite naked before such attacks as that of Stockman.

41. Katz, *In the Shadow of the Poorhouse*, 272.

8 The Failure and Success of the New Radicalism

MAURICE ISSERMAN AND
MICHAEL KAZIN

As easy it was to tell black from white
It was all that easy to tell wrong from right
And our choices were few and the thought never hit
That the one road we travelled would ever shatter and split.

—"Bob Dylan's Dream,"
from *The Freewheelin' Bob Dylan*

I

So WROTE Bob Dylan, not yet twenty-two years old, in what was in 1963 a prophetic—or at least prematurely nostalgic—elegy for the illusions of youthful commitment. Shatter and split the new radicalism certainly did, in the space of only a decade and in a way that left many of its adherents embittered and its historical reputation in tatters. After Ronald Reagan's two victories at the polls, the sixties, viewed at the time as the beginning of a new era of reform, seem instead a short interregnum amid the larger rightward shift in American politics that began during Franklin Roosevelt's troubled second term and continued through the 1980s. What difference, if any, did the decade of cultural and political upheaval encapsulated by the rise and fall of the New Left make?

Though the origins of the New Left can be traced back at least to the mid-1950s, radicalism only began to reemerge as a significant undercurrent on American campuses in 1960 when a heretofore obscure group called the Student League for Industrial Democracy (SLID) renamed itself Students for a Democratic Society (SDS). Under the leadership of two recent University of Michigan graduates, Al Haber and Tom Hayden, SDS became a small but increasingly influential network of campus activists. At its official founding convention,

held in Port Huron, Michigan, in 1962, SDS adopted a manifesto declaring that the ideas and organizational forms familiar to earlier
generations of Marxian radicals were outmoded. The "Port Huron
Statement" dedicated SDS to the achievement of "participatory democracy" inside its own movement and within the larger society. Initially engaged on a wide variety of fronts, from civil rights to nuclear
disarmament to university reform, by the mid-1960s, many SDS
founders had left the campuses to concentrate on community organizing in the slums of northern cities. Ironically, just as SDS leaders
began to forsake the campus, the Berkeley Free Speech Movement in
the fall of 1964 and the Vietnam teach-in movement in the spring of
1965 signaled the growing responsiveness of college students to radical ideas.

The steady escalation of the war in Vietnam from the spring of
1965 up to the spring of 1968 spurred the growth of both a broadly
based antiwar movement and of the campus New Left, and led the
latter to adopt increasingly militant rhetoric and tactics. By the fall of
1967 the New Left had moved "from dissent to resistance." Teach-ins
and silent vigils gave way to the seizure of campus buildings and disruptive street demonstrations. Under new and younger leadership
SDS continued to grow, and eventually some of its original leaders,
like Tom Hayden and Rennie Davis, were attracted back to antiwar
organizing from the slums of Newark and Chicago.

In the aftermath of the bloody confrontations at the Chicago
Democratic convention in the summer of 1968, and the indictment
of Hayden, Davis, and six others for "conspiracy," most New Leftists
abandoned whatever hopes they still cherished of reforming the existing political system. Declaring themselves allies and disciples of
third-world Communist revolutionaries like Mao Zedong and Che
Guevara, SDS leaders now conceived their principal role as one of
"bringing the war home" to the "imperialist mother country." In
1969, SDS collapsed as small, self-proclaimed revolutionary vanguards
squabbled over control of the organization, but the ranks of student
radicals continued to increase through the 1969–70 school year. Polls
showed that as many as three quarters of a million students identified
themselves as adherents of the New Left. The national student strike
that SDSers had long dreamed of but had never been able to pull off
became a reality in the spring of 1970. Spontaneously organized in
response to the invasion of Cambodia and the killing of four students
at Kent State University, it effectively paralyzed the nation's university system.[1]

The American writer John Dos Passos, describing the revolutionary exaltation and illusion of 1919 in his novel, *Three Soldiers*, de-

clared: "Any spring is a time of overturn, but then Lenin was alive, the Seattle general strike had seemed the beginning of the flood instead of the beginning of the ebb."[2] It soon became apparent to despairing New Leftists that the spring of 1970 marked a similar "beginning of the ebb." Former SDS president Carl Oglesby was one among many who took to the hills (literally, in his case) at the start of the new decade. As Oglesby would say in a bittersweet reflection years later: "There were a lot of good, righteous people showing up in places like Vermont and New Hampshire in those days. Lots of parties, great reefer, good acid. Lovely friends . . . I remember it with great fondness. It was almost the best part of the struggle. The best part of the struggle was the surrender."[3]

When the sixties were over, it seemed to many former activists that they had accomplished nothing. The "participatory democracy" the New Left sought in its early years remained a utopian dream; the "revolutionary youth movement" it built in its waning years had collapsed; the tiny "new communist parties" that one-time New Leftists tried to organize in the 1970s only illustrated once again the wisdom of Marx's comments in *The Eighteenth Brumaire* on the way history repeated turns tragedy into farce.[4]

Yet in surveying the ruins of these successive political failures, it is striking that while "nothing" was accomplished by the New Left in its short life, everything was different afterward. If the years that followed the 1960s did not live up to the hopeful vision of the future sketched out in the Port Huron Statement, still they did not mark a return to the previous status quo. America certainly became a more politically and culturally contentious society because of what happened in the 1960s—and in some respects it also became a more just, open, and egalitarian one. On the coldest, darkest, and most reactionary days of the Reagan ascendancy, there was more radical belief and activity to be seen in the United States than was present anytime in the 1950s. As an organizational presence the New Left had vanished, but as a force in American political culture its impact continued to be felt.

The New Left was shaped by and came to embody a profound dislocation in American culture, and, in the end, it had more impact on the ideas that Americans had about themselves and their society than on structures of power that governed their lives. Young radicals articulated a critique of "everyday life" in the United States, which was, in time, taken up by millions of people who had little notion of where those ideas originated. In the course of the sixties and seventies, many Americans came to recognize and reject the prevalence of racial and sexual discrimination, to ask new questions about the legitimacy of established institutions and authority, and to oppose military adventures abroad. To understand the New Left's role in this transition, historians need both to explore the organizational dynamics of radical groups like SDS and to analyze the ways in which American culture shaped the young radicals who emerged to challenge the received wisdom of their society.

II

The late 1980s saw a revival of interest in both the ephemera and the history of the 1960s. Tie-dyed shirts, peace symbols, Beatles music, and one-time Yippie leader Abbie Hoffman all resurfaced on college campuses. Many students, while knowing little about the politics of the New Left, admired sixties protesters for being, as the credulous young character in a "Doonesbury" cartoon put it, "larger than life, bonded and driven by commitment, putting their lives on the line for a great cause."[5]

Popular interest in and memories of the New Left often seem preoccupied with celebrities, fashion, and life-styles. The most accessible sources of information available on the sixties to young people in the eighties—"classic rock" radio shows and Hollywood movies— were hardly designed to facilitate serious historical inquiry. In the 1983 film *The Big Chill*, director Lawrence Kasdan offered a vision of the sixties as a time of embarrassing idealism that produced enough good songs to fill out a sound track but otherwise bequeathed nothing of continuing relevance. The film depicted a group of supposed New Left veterans who gather to mourn the passing of one of their own. Although a brief reference is made to one of the characters having been seriously wounded in Vietnam, no one in the film seems at all interested in reflecting on the war or any of the other causes that moved them in their youth, let alone in making connections between their former beliefs and the world around them in the 1980s. Not once in a long, emotional weekend do any of them abandon their self-absorption long enough to mention the words "Ronald Reagan," "nuclear war," or "Central America."[6]

The Big Chill did, however, contain a kernel of truth. "Politics," as conventionally defined, was only of secondary importance in the rise of the new radicalism of the 1960s. The emergence and celebration of generationally defined life-styles preceded the appearance of the New Left and, for most Americans throughout the 1960s, continued to overshadow the fate of organizations, candidates, and causes. As contemporary observers and historians have since agreed, the phenomenon of the "baby boom" determined the contours of the sixties' dizzying pace of change. Between 1945 and 1946, the birth rate in the United States leaped 20 percent. Thereafter, it continued to climb, peaking in 1957 when over four million babies were born in a single year. The impact of this unexpected development, which reversed a century-long decline in the birth rate, had effects everywhere—from the spread of suburbia to the transformation of the university system. At each stage of its life, the baby-boom generation has proven to be a voracious consumer of material goods, from diapers and cribs to microwave ovens and video cassette recorders. It has also shown an enormous capacity to absorb new forms of entertainment, new images, and new ideas about politics and society.[7]

Starting with the Davy Crockett fad of the early 1950s, cultural entrepreneurs seeking to tap the disposable income controlled by the nation's young perfected their pitch and inadvertently helped shape a distinctive generational consciousness. Hollywood soon learned to gear its offerings to the tastes of the new generation. While ostensibly condemning juvenile delinquency, such movies as *The Wild One* and *Rebel without a Cause* in effect established actors like Marlon Brando and James Dean as icons of youthful rebellion. Elvis Presley's fusion of country music and rhythm and blues combined with the frank sensuality of his stage presence signaled the arrival of a new musical era; major record producers were quick to take note and seek imitators. To a far greater extent than their parents, baby boomers grew up surrounded by and at home in a world of mass culture and mass consumption. And it was precisely because they were so deeply imbued with the promise and assumptions of that world—believing the advertisers who told them that a time of unending affluence and total freedom of choice was at hand—that they were willing, at least for a few years, to forego the quest for economic security and its material tokens that obsessed the older generation. The purveyors of mass culture were thus unintentionally acting as the gravediggers of a depression-inspired and cold war–reinforced conservative cultural consensus.[8]

As a college education became the norm rather than a privilege, millions of young people found themselves in a new socially determined developmental stage that extended adolescence into the middle twenties or even later. By the early 1960s, "youth communities" had sprung up on the outskirts of college campuses, often in the cheap housing available on the edge of black ghettos. There, surrounded by their peers, largely freed from adult supervision and spared for the time being the responsibilities of career, family, and mortgage, young people began to experiment with new manners, mores, stimulants, sexual behavior, and, in due time, forms of political expression.

"Beat" poets, artists, jazz musicians, and folksingers, though less commercially exploitable than Presley and his imitators, soon carved out their own niche on the margins of college communities as well as in such urban enclaves as New York's Greenwich Village and North Beach in San Francisco. Jack Kerouac's novel *On the Road*, a free-form chronicle of cultural alienation, became a best-seller when it appeared in 1957 and has never been out of print. Kerouac's protagonist, though displaying no discernible political sympathies, was thoroughly disenchanted with mainstream American values and sought refuge among and enlightenment from America's dispossessed and despised classes—tramps, winos, migrant farm laborers, black musicians. Norman Mailer's controversial essay "The White Negro," also published in 1957, celebrated white hipsters who "drifted out at night looking for action with a black man's code to fit their facts." Mailer predicted that "a time of violence, new hysteria, confusion and rebellion" would soon come along to "replace the time of conformity." The roots of the coming counterculture could be seen in the growing tendency among young whites to view black culture as a vibrant, sexually and emotionally honest alternative to what was regarded as the hypocrisy of the dominant culture. As Mailer noted, "in this wedding of the white and the black it was the Negro who brought the cultural dowry."[9] Elvis Presley's first hit, "You Ain't Nothin' But a Hound Dog," was a "cover" version of a song first recorded by blues singer Willie Mae "Big Mama" Thornton. For some whites it would prove a short step from idolizing and imitating such black musicians as Thornton, Charlie Parker, and Chuck Berry, to doing the same with black civil rights activists like Robert Moses and Stokely Carmichael.

At precisely the moment when the first wave of the baby boom reached the college campuses, the southern civil rights movement exploded into newspaper headlines and the nation's consciousness through the use of an innovative strategy of mass, nonviolent civil disobedience. The 1960 southern sit-in movement, which attracted fifty thousand participants in the space of a few months, was sparked by four black college freshmen in Greensboro, North Carolina, who decided on their own to challenge the segregation of a Woolworth's lunch counter. Rennie Davis, a founder of SDS who was a sophomore at Oberlin College in 1960, recalled: "Here were four students from Greensboro who were suddenly all over *Life* magazine. There was a feeling that they were us and we were them, and a recognition that they were expressing something we were feeling as well and they'd won the attention of the country."[10]

For sympathetic college students, the civil rights movement blended the appeal of "making history" with the potential for testing one's own sense of personal "authenticity" through an existential (and for those who joined the freedom rides or the voter registration campaigns in the South, quite genuine) brush with danger. In her book *Personal Politics*, historian Sara Evans described the compelling example set by the young black volunteers of the Student Non-Violent Coordinating Committee: "Eating, sleeping, working side by side day after day, SNCC activists created a way of life more than a set of ideas."[11] Thus, in the early 1960s, the sort of quixotic identification with outcasts and outsiders offered by *On the Road* and "The White Negro" acquired a compelling moral and political relevance. A new style of bohemianism that embodied a cultural stance derived from the Beats, and a political critique inspired by the black freedom movement attracted a growing following among college-age white Americans.

The superheated ideological atmosphere of 1950s cold war America played an important role in shaping the political outlook of college students at the start of the new decade. They had grown up in a political culture that stressed the division of the world into absolute good and absolute evil, freedom versus totalitarianism. The cold war was justified in much the same terms that had been used in the recent victorious struggle against the Axis powers. Yet, beneath the surface agreement among conservatives and liberals on the need to contain the Soviet threat, certain ambiguities still lurked. For many Americans, the cold war summoned up an uncritical identification with the emerging national security state. But some others, loyal to the liberatory and antiracist beliefs that had fueled the war against fascism, tendered their support for the "free world" on a more conditional basis.

Consider the wide appeal that the classic World War II film *Casablanca* developed on college campuses by the early 1960s. *Casablanca* portrayed America as a redemptive force in a world too long dominated by brutal and amoral power relations, a beacon of light to refugees who had fled Nazi-occupied Europe and impatiently awaited the "plane to Lisbon" (and thence to New York). In the course of the film, Humphrey Bogart's character, saloonkeeper Rick Blaine, discards his cynical go-it-alone veneer to reveal his romantic idealism. Victor Laszlo, the European resistance leader, challenges Rick to recognize that "each of us has a destiny, for good or for evil." Rick responds by choosing to fight the good war (as would the United States days later, the film being set in early December 1941). But suppose the United States had chosen to back the likes of the sinister Nazi leader, Major Strasser, rather than Victor Laszlo? What would Rick's choice have been then? His conduct was the product of individual moral choice rather than unwavering patriotic allegiance—and what was freely given could, by implication, be just as freely withheld or withdrawn.[12]

World War II also taught a lesson about the unspeakable horrors that could be committed by an advanced bureaucratic state that had lost its moral bearings. The Israeli capture and trial of former SS Obersturmbannführer Adolf Eichmann in 1960–61 revived memories of the postwar Nuremburg trials; while Hannah Arendt's 1963 book *Eichmann in Jerusalem* made the "banality of evil" a commonplace of educated liberal discourse. Arendt argued that European Jews were the victims of a monstrous system that depended on the acquiescence of ordinary human beings. Eichmann had served so efficiently as a cog in the Nazi death machine not out of personal depravity or exceptional sadism but because of a lack of imagination: he proved incapable of comprehending the evil of his own actions. Among the conclusions Arendt drew from her meditation on the "banality of evil" was a surprisingly optimistic one. She no longer contended that totalitarianism was capable of stamping out every vestige of independent thought and resistance among its subject populations: "Under conditions of terror most people will comply but some people will not. . . . No more is required, and no more can reasonably be asked, for this planet to remain a place fit for human habitation."[13]

Norman Mailer in his 1957 essay "The White Negro" had already begun to refer to American society as "totalitarian"; in the decade that followed, a lot of loose talk would be heard on the Left comparing Nazi Germany and the United States. But one need not have subscribed to such misleading analogies to be drawn to the moral imagery and lessons provided by the Nuremburg trials. In fact, if resisters to evil could be found even under the extreme conditions of Nazi oppression, could less be expected of those who enjoyed the protections of liberal democracy? Joan Libby, a Mount Holyoke College student and antiwar activist in the mid-1960s, became an organizer for the National Moratorium Committee in 1969. Her parents disapproved of her antiwar activities, and she found herself relying on the Nuremburg analogy in her arguments with them:

> Both my parents were Jewish, and one of the things I had had to learn about, of course, was the Holocaust, and one of the lessons in that always is that you shouldn't stand by and think somebody else is going to do it.

That's a serious lesson, I think, for susceptible young people like myself—
a powerful one. It becomes sort of an imperative. There's always a double-edged sword when you bring people up with the notion that you
should take [moral] positions on things. You never know where they'll
come out.[14]

In 1961, John F. Kennedy had sounded the call for a selfless ded-
ication to the (vaguely defined) national cause, significantly posed in
terms of individual choice: "Ask not what your country can do for
you, ask what you can do for your country." The same spirit of self-
sacrificing idealism that led many students to volunteer for the Peace
Corps led others to the civil rights movement. Many young white volunteers felt that their civil rights activism was sanctioned from on
high (although SNCC's black field workers never shared that particular
illusion, knowing how unresponsive the Justice Department was to
their requests for protection against racist attacks). A succession of
emotional and political blows followed, with the cumulative effect of
redirecting the spirit of idealism away from the official agenda being
set in Washington: there was fear of nuclear annihilation during the
Cuban missile crisis in October 1962, indignation over the brutal
treatment of civil rights demonstrators in Birmingham in the spring
of 1963, shock at Kennedy's assassination that fall, distrust the following summer as a result of the Democratic convention's "compromise" that prevented the seating of Fannie Lou Hamer and other
black delegates from the Mississippi Freedom Democratic Party, and
dismay over the escalation of the war in Vietnam in the spring of
1965.

In the early-to-mid 1960s, an essential prop of the old order gave
way in the minds of tens of thousands of young people. In more
jaded times, like those which followed the Vietnam War and the Watergate scandal, disbelief in the official pronouncements of American
foreign-policy makers would lead primarily to cynicism and apathy;
but, in the 1960s, when the fervor of cold war liberalism was still a
potent force, such disillusionment was often the prelude to an intensely moralistic conversion to political activism.

Bob Dylan's rapid rise to fame was emblematic of the newly
emerging cultural and political sensibility. Dylan's first album, a combination of folk and blues interpretations and his own ironic ballads,
was released in February 1962. It sold an unremarkable five thousand copies in its first year. But Dylan's second album, released in
May of 1963, found a broad new audience. *The Freewheelin' Bob Dylan*,
which featured protest songs like "Blowin' in the Wind," "Masters of
War," and "A Hard Rain's A Gonna Fall," sold 200,000 copies by July

1963. The following month, Peter, Paul and Mary released a single of Dylan's "Blowin' in the Wind" that sold over 300,000 copies in less than two weeks, making it the first protest song ever to grace the hit parade.[15]

Where were Dylan's new fans coming from, and what message did they seek in his music? "Blowin' in the Wind" was simultaneously a song about coming-of-age ("How many roads must a man walk down / Before you call him a man?") and about moral choice ("Yes, 'n' how many times can a man turn his head / Pretending he just doesn't see?"), as well as a promise that those who understood its message would soon help redeem the nation ("The answer, my friend, is blowin' in the wind / The answer is blowin' in the wind").[16] Young Americans in the 1960s were not the first generation to feel that they were more sensitive to hypocrisy and injustice than their elders. But due to the structural and ideological framework that had emerged in postwar America, they were primed for an opening to the Left in the early 1960s. The demographic bulge, the delayed entry into the adult world, the encouragement of generational consciousness by advertisers, the cultural identification with outsiders and marginal groups, the inspirational example of the civil rights movement, and the paradoxical influence of cold war liberalism were the raw materials from which a mass New Left would be fashioned over the next few years.

III

The chief organizational beneficiary of these trends would be SDS. As the war and the protests it inspired escalated in the mid-1960s, SDS grew rapidly. This occurred despite the fact that, after organizing the first antiwar march on Washington in April 1965, its leaders disdained sponsorship of any more such events because they did not address the root issue of an imperialist foreign policy—"stopping the seventh Vietnam from now," as one slogan put it.[17] But the policies SDS leaders chose to embrace or reject had little to do with the organization's growth. As Steve Max, an early leader of the group, recalled in a recent interview: "The progression in SDS was to be more and more movement and less and less organization. It was a situation of a movement looking for a place to happen."[18]

There were national headlines in the spring of 1965 when SDS's antiwar march attracted some twenty thousand participants. By the end of that school year, the SDS National Office (NO) was receiving a flood of letters from individuals and groups eager to affiliate, from places like Dodge City Community College in Kansas not previously known as loci of radical activity. It was no longer necessary for SDS to organize chapters: they organized themselves.[19] Many recruits were members of preexisting local groups who sought access to the resources and prestige that only a national organization could provide.

A typical communication arrived at the NO in November 1965 from a student at Ventura College (near Los Angeles) inquiring about the possibility of affiliating his local "Free Students for America" (FSFA) with SDS:

> What I have read and heard of your group leads me to believe we think much in the same direction. The basic aims of the F.S.F.A. are the removal of all American troops from Viet Nam, the use of aid rather than soldiers to combat the growth of totalitarian governments throughout the world, the affirmation of the right of any individual not to kill and not to be forced to serve in any military organization.

The Ventura "Free Students" wanted to join SDS because "we feel there is considerably more creative power in the unity of many groups than there is in many separate groups." The NO's response was favorable, including only the proviso that if the "Free Students" became an official SDS chapter they would have to agree to admit nonpacifists.[20]

The NO set up a system of campus "travelers" and regional offices, but these did little more than service existing chapters, distribute literature, and make an occasional statement to the media. New members were seldom "converted" to SDS ideology. If the SDS "old guard" had had its way, the organization would have functioned chiefly as a recruiting pool for future community organizers. Instead, reflecting the loosely formulated set of ideas, concerns, and political priorities that new members brought with them into the national organization, SDS chapters increasingly focused their efforts on resisting the war in Vietnam. Students did not become activists because they joined SDS; they joined SDS because they were already activists.[21]

The SDS annual national conventions were important mainly as places where SDSers from around the country could make contacts and share experiences. Labored efforts to chart a coordinated national strategy (like an abortive "Ten Days to Shake the Empire" plan in 1968) were almost universally ignored by local chapters. To the extent that people in SDS chapters learned to speak a common language and pursue a common political agenda, they did so through a process of osmosis rather than central direction.

Just at the moment when it began to develop a significant national presence, SDS lost the ability to set its own agenda. Starting in 1965, SDS's concerns and the pace of its development were largely reactions to decisions being made in the White House and the Pentagon. The escalation of the Vietnam War thus simultaneously strengthened and weakened SDS. In the matter of a few months, it transformed the group from a small network of activists, most of whom knew one another, into a national movement with hundreds of chapters—and an organizational infrastructure that never managed to make the transition. And while the war galvanized protesters, it also bred frustration and extremism in their ranks. Vietnam was a particularly volatile issue around which to build a mass movement. No partial victories or breathing spaces could be won: the movement would either force the government to end the war, or it would fail. As a result the peace movement, with the New Left at its core, constantly swung back and forth between near-millennial expectations and dark and angry despair.[22]

As the political climate changed after 1965, so did the New Left's cultural style. The new members who flooded into SDS (dubbed the "prairie power" contingent because so many of them came from places other than the usual urban centers of radical strength) were less likely to share the theoretical sophistication or intellectual ambitions of the group's founding generation. The new breed tended to be unschooled in and impatient with radical doctrine, intensely moralistic, suspicious of "elitism" and "bureaucracy," and immersed in the new cultural currents running through college towns.[23]

In January 1966, three members of the newly organized SDS chapter at the University of Oklahoma were among those arrested in a marijuana raid on a private party in Norman. Newspapers throughout the country picked up the story, linking SDS with pot-smoking. The Norman police chief unabashedly revealed to local reporters that his suspicions of the students had been aroused by their politics as much as their alleged drug use: "Several of these people have been active in the Society [SDS]. . . . One of them had a receipt showing he had just joined the SDS." High bail was set for all the defendants, and two of them were locked up incommunicado in a state mental hospital for observation because of their long hair.[24]

Jeff Shero, an SDS campus traveler and leading exponent of "prairie power" within the organization, visited Norman soon after the bust. He reported back to the NO that the police had assembled prescription drugs and antiwar literature for sensationalized photographs. Local newspapers reported that a book on "homosexuality" was found in the raided apartment. They neglected to mention the name of the book's author—Sigmund Freud. Shero was both indignant and amused at the crudity of the official antics, but he concluded that the affair had not done SDS any real political harm. "The chapter probably isn't irreparably damaged," he wrote to the NO.

"Chapter people were mixed as to the effect of the raid, some actually thought it would be beneficial."[25]

Steve Max and a few other "old guard" leaders of SDS had a different reaction. Speaking in a tone that reflected the assumptions of his earlier involvement with the Communist youth movement, Max regarded it a matter of "Socialist discipline" that "unless the organization votes to carry on a Legalize marijuana through a civil disobedience campaign, then our members ought not place themselves and the organization in a position where they can be put out of commission so easily." He wanted the Norman chapter suspended until it had, through some unspecified procedure, reformed itself. In a subsequent letter, he reiterated, "If we don't start to draw the line someplace we are going to wind up with a federation of dope rings instead of a national political organization."[26]

But sentiment in the hinterland seemed to run in a completely opposite direction. One member from Ohio reported to the NO that news of the Norman arrests "strikes home in the Ohio area since a number of people including three friends have been arrested on charges involving pot." Although he realized that SDS might have good reasons to avoid involvement in a campaign to legalize pot-smoking, "nevertheless, I think this area is another expression of the lack of individual freedom in the society for an individual desiring to control his own life without interference."[27]

The Norman SDS chapter was not suspended. Moreover, within a few years, SDS would not simply regard the use of drugs as a question of individual choice but would endorse it as yet another emblem of the revolutionary disaffection of the young. "Our whole life is a defiance of Amerika," the newspaper of the Weatherman SDS faction exulted in 1969. "It's moving in the streets, digging sounds, smoking dope . . . fighting pigs." By the late sixties, marijuana and LSD were circulating freely at national SDS conventions.[28]

Underlying the ability and willingness of so many young radicals, along with others of their generation, to experiment with new "lifestyles" (including drugs) was the economic prosperity of the postwar era. New Leftists took affluence for granted and despised its corrupting influence, unlike the Socialists and Communists of the 1930s who denounced capitalism for its inability to provide the minimum decencies of life to the poor. The great revolutionary drama of the New York theater in the 1930s had been Clifford Odets's *Waiting for Lefty*, which ended with the "workers" in the cast and the audience joining together in chanting "Strike, strike, strike!"

Perhaps the closest equivalent to Odets's work in the 1960s was the popular play by Peter Brooks, *The Persecution and Assassination of*

Jean Paul Marat as Performed by the Inmates of the Asylum of Charenton under the Direction of the Marquis de Sade (or, as it was more commonly known, *Marat/Sade*), which suggested that conventional politics, even conventional revolutionary politics, was exhausted as a force for change. The final scene in *Marat/Sade* provoked the same kind of audience empathy as the climax of *Waiting for Lefty*, although this time the identification was not with striking workers but with rioting lunatics in an insane asylum, who sang "We want a revolution . . . NOW!" The song went on to become a kind of unofficial anthem of the Columbia strike in the spring of 1968.[29]

Julian Beck's "Living Theater," which toured campuses during the late 1960s, went a step further than *Marat/Sade* by dispensing with scripts altogether. In a typical Living Theater production, the "actors" challenged the audience to join them on stage in disrobing, smoking marijuana, and milling around in a kind of pseudo-liberated confusion. A student who participated in a building seizure at the University of Chicago in 1969 saw a direct link between the decision by the local SDS chapter to take over the building and a visit shortly before by the Living Theater:

> The idea was to liberate yourself from the confining conventions of life, and to celebrate the irrational side of your nature, kind of let yourself go. . . . At a place like the University of Chicago, this was really the opposite of every message that you'd been getting from the moment you stepped into the place. . . . This was the counterculture coming to us, and it stirred people up and made us feel like doing something dramatic.[30]

Earlier generations of radicals had derided capitalism as an anarchic, irrational system; the new radicals scorned the system because it was *too* rational, based on a soul-destroying set of technological and bureaucratic imperatives that stifled individual expression. From university reform, where the slogan was "I am a human being, do not fold, spindle or mutilate," to draft resistance, where the buttons read "Not with my life, you don't," the New Left championed a form of radical individualism that was authentically American in derivation and flavor—ironically, all too "American" for the organizational well-being of the movement. For this deeply rooted individualism prepared the way for the development of a movement cult of "confrontation."

In the Communist, Socialist, and Trotskyist movements of the 1930s, young radicals had prided themselves on their analytic abilities, their skill in debate, their command of the intricacies of Marxist theory. In contrast, a kind of emotional and moral plain-speaking was the preferred rhetorical style among SDS leaders. Authenticity, usually described as "commitment," was the political and personal value New Leftists were most eager to display, a quality that could best be established by the willingness to "put your body on the line." Overcoming any lingering squeamishness about breaking the law (and plate-glass windows) was the ultimate "gut-check" that alone could establish whether you were "part of the problem or part of the solution."

The political deficiencies of this personal stance were not lost on some SDSers, though they found themselves powerless to correct the situation. As early as 1965, Lee Webb, former SDS national secretary, complained in an internal document that "SDS influences its membership to become more militant rather than more radical. . . . Calls to fight the draft, stop a troop train, burn a draft card, avoid all forms of liberalism, have become . . . the substitute for intellectual analysis and understanding."[31] Late sixties SDS rhetoric, composed of equal parts Maoist jargon and black street rap, communicated little but the angry alienation of its practitioners. Nevertheless, it had a very potent appeal to the already-converted or would-be recruits in defining the cultural terrain of the movement—if you spoke the language, you were already a revolutionary. "Brothers," a high school student wrote to the NO in the late 1960s, "I sympathize with the movement and its goals. But information on what's going on is hard to come by in rural, conservative western Pennsylvania. Dig?"[32]

By the late 1960s, SDS had grown to as many as a hundred thousand loosely affiliated members, while tens of thousands more could be counted as supporters of the movement. But off-campus, the New Left's activities, and the increasingly outrageous and opaque language in which they were justified, found few supporters. Ronald Reagan spoke for many Americans when he declared in the midst of the People's Park disorders in Berkeley in 1969 (which left one spectator dead from police buckshot), "If it's a blood bath they want, let it be now."[33] The ferocity with which authorities sought to crack down on campus protest only exacerbated the appeal of extreme rhetoric and doctrines within SDS. In the summer of 1969 the organization splintered, with one small faction led by the Progressive Labor Party (PLP) heading for the factories, and another small faction led by Weatherman heading for the "underground." Neither the PLP nor Weatherman enlisted more than a tiny fraction of SDS members under their banners, but Weatherman's cultural style—which included a fervent if erratic promotion of drugs, sex, and rock and roll—gave it a measure of influence on campuses that the dour dogmatists in the PLP were never able to match. In the early 1970s underground newspapers gave extensive coverage to Weatherman's bombings and "communiqués"; posters in college dorms invited Bernardine Dohrn and other Weatherman fugitives to seek shelter.³⁴

IV

The demise of sds did not retard the flowering of cultural radicalism. From campus towns to the "youth ghettos" of big cities and even to American military bases in Vietnam, a diffuse set of "countercultural" ideas, symbols, and behaviors circulated. "Liberation" was easy to achieve, since it was defined as the practice of a communal, playful, and sensual life-style. While they often ignored or explicitly rejected the politics advocated by "power-tripping" radicals, those immersed in the counterculture embraced beliefs the earlier New Left had first popularized. Alternative, participatory communities based on decentralized, small-scale technology and an ethic of loving mutuality had all been prefigured by the Port Huron Statement, the civil rights movement, and sds's community-organizing projects. Garbed in apolitical dress, this vision continued to attract believers (many of them from working-class backgrounds) who never would have considered attending an sds meeting. In the mid-1970s, pollster Daniel Yankelovich called attention to the ways in which new attitudes toward authority, sexual morality, and self-fulfillment had spread from elite college campuses to much of the younger population: "Indeed," he wrote, "we are amazed by the rapidity with which this process is now taking place."³⁵

As the sixties ended, some radical leaders withdrew from the increasingly fractious realm of left-wing politics to join rural communes or mystical cults, or to embrace various "new age" therapies. The well-publicized voyage of Jerry Rubin from yippie revolutionary to yuppie networker is the best known, if not most representative, example of this process. Paul Potter, a former sds president, was less self-serving and more reflective when he recorded his own painful withdrawal from the movement in his 1971 book *A Name for Ourselves.* Potter reaffirmed his belief in the values and concerns that had initially led him to the New Left, but rejected organized politics as a means of achieving a better world:

> I am less involved in changing America. . . . This does not mean that I am less angry or upset or horrified by this country than before. If anything, I am more profoundly and intuitively aware, day to day, of what an ugly society this is and how desperately it needs change. But my information comes less and less from the papers—more and more from my own experience with it.³⁶

Potter now sought to be "in touch with children," agonized about his lingering desire for power, and found solace in daily rituals. His lover Leni Wildflower (whose adopted surname represented a symbolic break with her Old Left parents) contributed an angry foreword to *A Name for Ourselves*:

> I am trying desperately to peel away the layers of lies—trying to pull back the skin of society, school, family. The expectations which somewhere along the line got internalized. The desire to "be something," the pretty deep conviction that I am *nothing* . . . And in the middle of my quest there are all these men laying their power-ego-identity trips on me.[37]

The emergence of a new feminist movement had the paradoxical effect of drawing many New Left women into more active political participation while hastening the political withdrawal of many men. In the late 1960s and early 1970s few male leaders of the New Left escaped being taken to task for sexism by women in the movement. What more decisive step could men take to indicate repentance for past misdeeds than to abdicate any further claim to leadership? With the movement foundering, the "politically correct" decision often served to rationalize personal inclinations. Coinciding with the decline of the antiwar movement, a widespread and decentralized network of women's "consciousness raising" groups, health clinics, bookstores, newspapers, publishing houses, and similar enterprises emerged, giving new meaning to the original New Left call for a "beloved community."

V

"The sixties are over," literary critic Morris Dickstein wrote in 1977, "but they remain the watershed of our recent cultural history; they continue to affect the ambiance of our lives in innumerable ways."[38] The passage of more than a decade and Ronald Reagan's two terms in office have not lessened the truth of that observation. In the 1980s, the conservative victors found it politically convenient to lump together the vestiges of New Deal–Great Society liberalism with the memory of the New Left to justify reversing both the social legislation and the "moral permissiveness" associated with the sixties. They were quite successful in cutting back or abolishing domestic programs that had no wealthy or powerful constituency. But as the New Right's plaintive refrain "Let Reagan be Reagan" indicated, conservatives did not have everything their own way in the 1980s. The right was forced to govern within a cultural environment that, in significant ways, limited what it could accomplish. Conservatives had to repackage many of their ideas and policies to appeal to a public that had caught a "democratic distemper" and was unwilling to defer automatically to its new governors.[39]

The movements and events of the 1960s generated an attitudinal penumbra that glimmered long after SDS and SNCC had been eclipsed. Chastened by the collapse of "the movement," many pragmatic radicals entered the left wing of the Democratic party, helping transform its stance on foreign policy and producing at least a strong rhetorical commitment to equal rights for all disadvantaged groups. In the 1970s and 1980s, erstwhile New Leftists taking a few steps toward the center met and worked alongside liberals disenchanted with cold war shibboleths who were moving gradually to the Left. The activist Left largely shed traditional Marxist concerns for issues centering on the workplace and economic growth, groping instead for a new synthesis of environmentalism, feminism, antimilitarism, and interracial solidarity.

Right-wing movements also sought to exploit the mood of morally committed idealism that sixties radicals had done so much to create; in some instances, they proved more successful than their left-wing counterparts. The impulse to expose and attack illegitimate authority was turned against legislators who tried to "solve problems by throwing money at them," against a Democratic president who could neither free American hostages nor punish their captors, and against liberal judges perceived as protecting muggers, drug-pushers, or pornographers. At the same time, a vigorous libertarian spirit, itself a legacy of the sixties, acted as a countervailing force, preventing the New Right from imposing its version of morality on law and society. America's political culture in the 1980s thus contained enough contradictory impulses to baffle the pundits who assumed that Reagan's electoral victories represented a fundamental rightward shift.

American politics in the past decade has actually been characterized by the existence of a deep divide between two camps: one, a broad but disorganized Left, has attempted to defend and develop ideas, issues, and "life-styles" that emerged in the sixties; the other, an equally diverse but far better organized Right, has built its own influence around popular revulsion from those same images and practices. New Leftists thus succeeded in transforming American politics—though not according to the sanguine script laid out at Port Huron. The continued influence of the movements of the 1960s has been most pronounced in five aspects of contemporary American society: intellectual life, perceptions of race and of gender, foreign policy, and the language of politics itself.

According to the mythology promoted by *The Big Chill*, sixties radicals had all "sold out" by the 1980s. The main characters in that film made their living by peddling running shoes or dope, writing trashy stories for *People* magazine, or starring in a trashy action series on television. In real life, no doubt, some came to such ends. But thousands of others took up jobs and professions that did not represent a break with their earlier political aspirations. They became social workers, union and community organizers, public school teachers, Legal Services lawyers, or doctors involved in occupational or neighborhood health programs. A recent study of the political attitudes held by aging "veterans of the protest movement" discovered that a majority retained the ideological predilections of their youth.[40]

Significantly, many former radicals made careers in the "information industry," as academics, journalists, and media specialists. Conservative social scientists have done much viewing-with-alarm of this phenomenon. They blame a left-wing "new class" for undermining the public's faith in both domestic institutions and U.S. foreign policy. Opinion surveys of the "media elite" conducted by Robert Lichter and Stanley Rothman in the late 1970s found that print and electronic journalists and filmmakers overwhelmingly endorsed "strong affirmative action for blacks," as well as women's right to abortions; a near-majority agreed that the "U.S. exploits the Third World and causes poverty." Writing in *Partisan Review* in 1986, sociologist Paul Hollander condemned the Left's alleged "domination of the public political discourse" on campus, complaining that while its adherents may work "within the system," they are "without any sense of allegiance towards it." Prominent neoconservatives like Norman Podhoretz, Midge Decter, and Hilton Kramer sound similar alarms about the radical fifth columnists they believe have debauched American culture.[41]

While these attacks on the "new class" suffer from hyperbole, they do gesture at a truth about contemporary thought. Radicals probably played a larger role in the universities and the media in the 1980s than at any previous time in American history. In the fields of history and literature, the most innovative scholars have been those who sympathetically illuminate the lives and thought of subaltern groups and "deconstruct" the works and reputations of famous writers and other authorities. Different schools of Marxism, feminism, and radical linguistic theory infuse this work, which, in the spirit of the New Left, questions not just established ideas (for that is the perpetual task of good scholarship) but the methods used to create them and the consequences that flow from their application in society. Far from having cloistered themselves, as some left-wing critics have charged, radical scholars have shown considerable concern for making their views available to a nonacademic audience. Radical perspectives, albeit somewhat diluted ones, find their way into a surprising number of mainstream venues, from National Public Radio programming to the op-ed pages of the *New York Times* and the *Wall Street Journal*, to the Smithsonian's National Museum of American History, to historical sites like Harpers Ferry and Colonial Williamsburg (where blacksmiths in period dress pepper their narratives with insights culled from recent literature about slavery and abolitionism by such radical scholars as John Blassingame, Eugene Genovese, and Eric Foner).[42]

None of this, to be sure, represents a left-wing cultural coup d'état. In the media, there is little evidence that the private views of reporters control the message being transmitted on the page and screen. In academia, radical assistant professors are as preoccupied with the scramble for tenure as colleagues on their right—and lack access to the patronage and sources of alternate employment that well-funded right-wing think tanks and the Reagan administration offered to a generation of young conservative intellectuals.[43] Still, the contention in the media and the university over basic questions of ideology stands in sharp contrast with the intellectual scene of the 1950s when radical journalist I. F. Stone had to start his own shoestring newsletter to publish his acute exposés of government policies; while academic mavericks like Paul Baran and C. Wright Mills nurtured their ideas largely in isolation from their colleagues.

Since the 1960s, the politics of race has been a major battleground between Left and Right. On the one hand, "new class" individuals and institutions exhibit a heightened level of racial sensitivity. The study of the history and culture of minority groups is a staple of public education, at least in urban areas. Black history was the subject of the most popular television event of the 1970s ("Roots"), while a black family served as the model of domesticity on the most popular situation comedy of the 1980s ("The Cosby Show"), and Oprah Winfrey, black hostess of the most popular daytime television talk show, portrayed her own career as the product of struggles by Sojourner Truth, Harriet Tubman, and Fannie Lou Hamer.[44]

Millions of middle-class whites have joined with blacks in establishing a firm line demarcating acceptable from unacceptable public conduct and expression regarding race. Together they have succeeded in delegitimating beliefs that were the norm among white Americans only a generation earlier. Since the mid-1970s, any nationally prominent public figure who has castigated blacks as a people, even with humorous intent, has quickly lost reputation, employment, or both. Consider the firings of agriculture secretary Earl Butz in 1975 for telling a racist joke; of baseball executive Al Campanis in

1987 for questioning, on a television show commemorating the anniversary of Jackie Robinson's major league debut, whether blacks had "the necessities" to make good managers; and of network football commentator Jimmy "the Greek" Snyder for claiming that blacks were bred by slaveholders to be faster and stronger than whites and for wanting to reserve front-office jobs for the latter. A record of hostility to the civil rights movement, even in the absence of evidence of personal racial prejudice, can also destroy careers. Judge Robert Bork's nomination to the Supreme Court was fatally damaged by the revelation that he had described the public accommodations section of the 1964 Civil Rights Act as embodying "a principle of unsurpassed ugliness," while Arizona governor Evan Meacham inspired a powerful impeachment movement when he refused to recognize Martin Luther King's birthday as a state holiday. The black leader, who, in his lifetime, was harassed by the FBI, mistrusted by the presidents he dealt with, and openly despised by millions of whites, is today a national icon.[45]

But the new consensus on racial equality is far from universal. The Boston busing riots of the mid-1970s, the 1986 assault on three blacks who had the misfortune of having their car break down in the white Howard Beach neighborhood of New York City, and other events have revealed a bitter fraction of white working-class America that lashes out against those regarded as threats to its homes, jobs, and personal safety. Moreover, in the 1980s, students on major college campuses like Dartmouth, Penn State, and the University of Massachusetts (Amherst) engaged in racial slurs and, on a few occasions, even violence, demonstrating that segregation (albeit of an informal, interpersonal kind) still plagued these overwhelmingly white institutions. By opposing affirmative action (in the name of "equal opportunity") and welfare programs, conservative politicians have both contributed to and benefited from such conflicts.

Meanwhile, many middle-class whites share the perception that a black "underclass" has become fatally trapped within a nexus of family dissolution, drug abuse, and crime, past all reasonable hope of salvation. Radicals and liberals won an important victory when they transformed the public language and imagery of race. But at a time when racial inequality has become primarily a question of access to wealth and secure employment, they have, for the most part, fallen into a puzzled, if not indifferent, silence about issues more complicated than Jimmy the Greek's notions of slavery.[46]

Attitudes about women and women's issues have undergone a similar change, taking a large cultural step forward while suffering a political step back, or at least sideward, in the struggle for equality of the sexes. The central ideological tenet of the new feminist movement was the idea that "the personal is political." The most intimate and seemingly mundane details of private life—housework and childcare, among many others—were seen as fundamentally linked to social power. In the late 1960s and early 1970s, feminists struck an enormously rich vein of anger and insight about personal issues that American radical movements had never systematically addressed before.

The mass media, initially inclined to dismiss the new feminists with the trivializing designation "bra-burners," by the mid-1970s made a dramatic about-face in their treatment of many of the movement's concerns. Notions like "equal pay for equal work" were easily assimilated into public discourse; today most young middle-class women routinely expect to have access to the same careers and to receive the same compensation as men. What is surprising, in retrospect, is how quickly other, more highly charged, issues—rape, abortion, family violence, incest—began to attract respectful coverage in the daily press and on television. Talk shows routinely broadcast heated discussions about sexuality, day care, and birth control. "Sexism" itself has become so common a concept that even so unreflective a Reaganite as Fawn Hall immediately made use of the phrase to respond to Senator Howell Heflin's accusation that she had stuffed classified documents into her underwear in order to smuggle them out of Oliver North's office.

Feminists have succeeded in establishing a new "common sense" about gender roles among the urban middle class—and beyond. By the mid-1980s, according to a synthesis of opinion polls, a majority of Americans agreed with positions that, at the end of the 1960s, were the province of radical feminists. They supported federally subsidized day-care centers, sex education for the young, and the idea that men and women should share housework and child rearing equally.[47] Women from constituencies that the New Left had tended to write off—the white working class, the Catholic church, the suburbs—came to embrace feminist ideas and proposals in the course of the 1970s even though many still feel constrained to preface their new beliefs with the disclaimer, "I'm no women's libber, but . . ." It was as if American society had been waiting for decades, with mounting nervousness and impatience, for some group to have the courage to come along and state the obvious about the problems between the sexes.

But, here too, not everyone was converted. The New Right accepted the challenge of "personal politics" and responded by organizing its own network of women activists. Phyllis Schlafly's Eagle Forum, the right-to-life movement, and similar groups proved quite adept at stirring, articulating, and channeling fears about the destruction of the male-headed "traditional family." In tandem with rising conservative politicians, they were able to block passage of the Equal Rights Amendment (despite the support the ERA consistently received in national polls). As a result, organized feminism stalled and began to be described, even by some Democrats, as merely another "special interest."[48]

The legacy of the sixties has continued to play an explicit role in framing popular attitudes toward military intervention abroad. Despite the appeals of President Reagan and other supporters of the Nicaraguan Contras, Americans have consistently opposed policies designed to overthrow the Sandinista government by a margin of roughly 2 to 1.[49] That sentiment is routinely expressed as fear of stumbling into "another Vietnam"—a phrase worth examining. Understandably, Americans remember the war as a time of futile bloodletting. Many oppose U.S. intervention in Central America out of a sense of pragmatic isolationism; if the conquest of Nicaragua looked to be as effortless as that of Grenada, the public opinion polls would almost certainly look different.

For many Americans, however, the lesson of Vietnam goes beyond the need to avoid unwinnable wars. A plurality of Americans agrees retrospectively with the judgment that the antiwar movement proclaimed in the 1960s. In a May 1985 poll, taken at a moment when Reagan's popularity was as yet untarnished by the Iran-Contra affair, 38 percent agreed that U.S. involvement in Vietnam had been both "wrong and immoral." Only 34 percent concurred with the president's description of the war as a "noble cause."[50]

Such an opinion, like that in any sphere of public controversy, reflects both conclusions drawn from immediate experience and the cumulative influence of mass-mediated images and attitudes. The popularity, not to say domination, of liberal, antiwar politics in Hollywood since the 1960s has resulted in treatments of Vietnam that are harshly critical of the premises that underlay U.S. policy. "MASH," the highest-rated television series of the late 1970s, conveyed an implicitly pacifist message through characters who mocked conventional military authority and held no particular grudge against the Communist enemy. The 1978 film *Coming Home* depicted its hero, a disabled antiwar veteran, besting his sexual and political rival, another veteran who had returned home with his body intact but his mind mangled with militarist rage. The prize the two competed for was the love of a strong female character played by Jane Fonda. Oliver Stone's 1987 production *Platoon*, which won the Academy Award for Best Picture, portrayed the war as seen through the eyes of a young infantryman. Even as he fights a desperate battle for personal survival, the protagonist comes to reject the mindless brutality of the war as represented by a sinister, scar-faced sergeant (a rejection symbolized, according to the truest Hollywood convention, by the hero killing the bad guy).[51]

But attitudes toward and images of the war remain a contested terrain in Hollywood, as they do for the larger public. Michael Cimino's *The Deer Hunter,* which won the Oscar for Best Picture the same year that *Coming Home* picked up the prizes for Best Actor and Actress, depicted Vietnamese culture as an evil, decadent force that bewildered and corrupted white ethnic GI's before killing them. Eight years later, Sylvester Stallone, in *Rambo: First Blood, Part II,* took revenge, like a bare-chested, overmuscled Western sheriff, on the Vietnamese outlaws who had once defeated him. By asking, "Do we get to win this time?" and then blasting away in the affirmative, Rambo was also attacking cowardly bureaucrats back home who had reputedly scuttled the patriotic cause. In the summer of 1987, Oliver North gained a brief but intense popularity when he enacted what might be called "Mr. Rambo Goes to Washington," in which yet another battle-hardened warrior stood up to a pack of pusillanimous civilians.[52] Vietnam remains a nightmare legacy from the sixties that Americans repeatedly put behind them and yet obsessively continue to relive.

The politics of the two major parties also reflect the impact of sixties radicalism. The most direct influence appears within the Democratic party. In many areas, local Democratic activists began to move left during the 1968 presidential campaign and, in time, found their forces strengthened by an infusion of former New Leftists. By the 1980s, left Democrats represented a variety of "single-issue" movements—black, Chicano, feminist, environmentalist, peace, gay and lesbian, and elderly—as much as they did the party apparatus itself. Such organizations as the National Organization for Women, the Sierra Club, and SANE saw their memberships swell in the early 1980s and developed increasingly professional and intermittently powerful lobbies in Washington. Liberal and radical Democratic activists helped transform Jesse Jackson into a serious candidate for president, promoted Geraldine Ferraro's vice-presidential nomination in 1984, and set the anti-interventionist tenor of the party's foreign policy debates. To the dismay of many party officials in the South, and those elsewhere nostalgic for the days of Jim Farley and Richard Daley, "New Politics"–style Democrats increasingly supply the financial backing, political energy, and moral élan that keeps the party organization afloat.[53]

Yet what gives life to one side also provides opportunity for the other. Since the 1960s, conservative Republicans have lured away traditional Democratic voters by portraying the GOP as the only safe haven for the white ethnic working class against the onslaught of the civil rights movement and the political and social insurgencies it spawned. After taking a Watergate-induced pause in the mid-1970s, this backlash intensified, as millions of white northern voters joined southerners in rejecting the presidential candidates of their own party whom they perceived as apostles of weakness abroad and captives of single-issue "special interests" at home. Meanwhile, the New Right was using the specter of a hedonistic, God-denying counterculture to raise funds and recruit activists. Thus both parties, each in its own way, still lived off energy generated in the 1960s.[54]

Notions of "personal politics" took on a new meaning in the late 1980s as a series of prominent political figures fell victim to revelations about private moral transgressions. Circumstantial evidence of adultery derailed front-runner Gary Hart's 1988 presidential campaign, while the Supreme Court nomination of the conservative jurist Douglas Ginsburg collapsed amid reports that he had occasionally used marijuana. A libertarian impulse favoring open discussion of previously taboo subjects meshed with a lurid soap-opera-and-supermarket-tabloid-fed curiosity about the misdeeds of the highly placed. The unlucky offenders were punished not so much for having strayed from standards of behavior that relatively few American adults under the age of forty-five had themselves upheld, as for their lack of "authenticity": Hart's self-portrait of himself as a dedicated family man and Ginsburg's "law-and-order" stance were revealed as shams.[55]

A final way in which the sixties have influenced American politics can be seen in the use of "populist" stances by politicians of all persuasions. The past quarter-century has been a fertile breeding ground for expressions of discontent that defy old categories of "liberal" and "conservative." Advocates of desegregation and all-white community schools, feminists and right-to-lifers, the New Left and the George Wallace presidential campaign, agreed on very little; but all railed against "the establishment" in the interests of the common folk. And from a disgruntled public, the majority of which, according to polls taken since the early 1970s, consistently feels "alienated from the power structure," come new waves of anti-elitist anger that invigorates such movements.[56] In fact, the very language of these opinion surveys again demonstrates how conventional some New Left terminology has become.

Populism, of course, has long been a staple of American political discourse. Ignatius Donnelly, Huey Long, and Saul Alinksy were winning votes or building movements out of such material long before young radicals moved to urban slums in the early 1960s. The unique contribution of the new radicals was to broaden the scope of the populist critique, challenging the legitimacy of cultural as well as political and economic power structures.

In ways both trivial and serious, the example, language, and actions of sixties radicals offered millions of Americans a way to express the discontent generated by the triple debacle of Vietnam, Watergate, and seventies stagflation. Often it was the New Left's style rather than its politics that wound up being recycled in the 1970s and 1980s. Some otherwise law abiding "right-to-life" demonstrators risked arrest blockading abortion clinics while singing, in paraphrase of John Lennon, "All we are saying / is give life a chance." Campus conservatives distributed leaflets accusing Gulf Oil of "corporate murder" because the firm does business with the pro-Soviet government of Angola.[57] New Leftists succeeded in exposing the bankrupt policies of the liberal state in the 1960s. But that very success activated right-wing critics of liberalism who championed a "counterculture" of their own, based on biblical injunctions, the patriarchal family, and the economic homilies of nineteenth-century capitalism.

The contradictory legacy of the sixties thus provides evidence of both the failures and successes of the new radicalism—"failures" that were sometimes unavoidable, and sometimes self-inflicted, and "successes" that usually were unrecognized and were often the opposite of what was intended. Richard Hofstadter wrote in *The Age of Reform* that while it may be "feasible and desirable to formulate ideal programs of reform, it is asking too much to expect that history will move . . . in a straight line to realize them."[58] Despite the best efforts of the Reagan administration and the New Right, the 1980s did not represent a return to the "normalcy" of the 1950s. Young radicals never became serious contenders for state power, but the issues they raised and the language in which those issues were dramatized became the normal fare of American politics.

Whether scorned as pro-Communistic and nihilistic or smothered in bland nostalgia, the New Left's reputation in the late 1980s was not all that its founders might have hoped for. But the message of the young radicals had certainly been received.

Notes

The epigraph from "Bob Dylan's Dream" © 1963 Warner Bros. Inc. and a portion of "Blowin' in the Wind" on p. 221, © 1962 Warner Bros. Inc., are used by permission. All rights reserved.

1. Recent books considering the history of the New Left include Kirkpatrick Sale, *SDS* (New York: Random House, 1973); Sara Evans, *Personal Politics: The Roots of Women's Liberation in the Civil Rights Movement and the New Left* (New York: Knopf, 1979); Todd Gitlin, *The Whole World is Watching: Mass Media in the Making and Unmaking of the New Left* (Berkeley: University of California Press, 1980); Gitlin, *The Sixties: Years of Hope, Days of Rage* (New York: Bantam Books, 1987); Clayborne Carson, *In Struggle: SNCC and the Black Awakening of the 1960s* (Cambridge: Harvard University Press, 1981); Wini Breines, *Community and Organization in the New Left, 1962–1968: The Great Refusal* (New York: Praeger, 1982); James Miller, *"Democracy Is in the Streets": From Port Huron to the Siege of Chicago* (New York: Simon and Schuster, 1987); George Katsiaficas, *The Imagination of the New Left: A Global Analysis of 1968* (Boston: South End Press, 1987); Hans Koning, *Nineteen Sixty-Eight: A Personal Report* (New York: Norton, 1987); David Caute, *The Year of the Barricades: A Journey through 1968* (New York: Harper and Row, 1988); David Farber, *Chicago '68* (Chicago: University of Chicago Press, 1988); Ronald Fraser, *1968: A Student Generation in Revolt* (New York: Pantheon, 1988); Tom Hayden, *Reunion: A Memoir* (New York: Random House, 1988); and Maurice Isserman, *If I Had a Hammer . . . The Death of the Old Left and the Birth of the New Left* (New York: Basic Books, 1987).

2. John Dos Passos, *Three Soldiers* (New York: Modern Library, 1932), p. v.

3. Quoted in Joan Morrison and Robert K. Morrison, *From Camelot to Kent State* (New York: Times Books, 1987), 307.

4. The New Left has yet to produce a literature of disillusionment comparable in quality or quantity to that turned out by ex-Communists in the 1950s, but for some initial forays see David Horowitz and Peter Collier, "Who Killed the Spirit of '68," *Encounter* 65 (October 1985): 69–73; and Jeffrey Herf, "The New Left and its Fading Aura," *Partisan Review* 53, no. 2 (1986): 242–52. Ronald Radosh claimed in a review of Todd Gitlin's memoir/history *The Sixties* that "the New Left became as much of an agent for the Vietnamese and Cubans as had the earlier generation of Communists for the Soviet Union" (*Wall Street Journal*, November 5, 1987). Horowitz, Herf, Radosh, and others staged a "Second Thoughts" conference in October 1987 to criticize their former views. See Todd Gitlin and Michael Kazin, "The Rise and Rapid Decline of the New Ex-Left: Two Thoughts Forward, One Thought Back" *Tikkun*, January–February 1988, 49–52.

5. Garry Trudeau, *Doonesbury Deluxe* (New York, 1987). For recent evocations of sixties nostalgia, see David E. Pitt, "To '68 Leader, Columbia is Still Lively," *New York Times*, March 28, 1987; and Patricia Leigh Brown, "A New Generation Shares the 60's," *New York Times*, July 11, 1987.

6. Todd Gitlin commented on the absence of all political references in *The Big Chill* in a 1984 interview with one of the authors.

7. Landon Y. Jones analyzes the demographic mysteries of the postwar era in *Great Expectations: America and the Baby Boom Generation* (New York: Coward, McCann, and Geoghegan, 1980), 11–35.

8. Jones, *Great Expectations*, 61–76; Marty Jezer, *The Dark Ages: Life in the*

United States, 1945–1960 (Boston: South End Press, 1982), 235–50; Maurice Isserman, "Davy Crockett Nears 30," *New York Times*, September 29, 1984; William L. O'Neill, *American High: The Years of Confidence, 1945–1960* (New York: Free Press, 1986), 266–69; and Simon Frith, *Sound Effects: Youth, Leisure, and the Politics of Rock 'n', Roll* (New York: Pantheon, 1981), 12–38.

9. Jack Kerouac, *On the Road* (New York: Viking, 1957); Norman Mailer, "The White Negro," *Dissent* 4 (Summer 1957): 276–92; Dennis McNally, *Desolate Angel: Jack Kerouac, the Beat Generation and America* (New York: Random House, 1979); and Christopher Brookeman's chapter "Norman Mailer and Mass America" in his *American Culture and Society since the 1930s* (London: MacMillan, 1984), 150–70.

10. Quoted in Milton Viorst, *Fire in the Streets: America in the 1960s* (New York: Simon and Schuster, 1979), 176. On the sit-ins, see Carson, *In Struggle*, 9–18.

11. Evans, *Personal Politics*, 42.

12. Rick Blaine's service in the Republican cause in the Spanish Civil War is also alluded to in the film. Although the full political significance of that detail was probably better understood by audiences in 1943 than in the 1960s, it is clear that Rick is not solely or even primarily concerned with his own country's battles.

13. Hannah Arendt, *Eichmann in Jerusalem: A Report on the Banality of Evil* (New York: Viking, 1963), 233.

14. Quoted in Morrison and Morrison, *From Camelot to Kent State*, 138.

15. Robert Shelton, *No Direction Home: The Life and Music of Bob Dylan* (New York: William Morrow, 1986), 129–40, 173–78, 183; Wayne Hampton, *Guerrilla Minstrels: John Lennon, Joe Hill, Woody Guthrie, Bob Dylan* (Knoxville, Tenn.: University of Tennessee Press, 1986), 155, 165.

16. Bob Dylan, *Lyrics, 1962–1985* (New York: Knopf, 1985), 53.

17. Sale, *SDS*, 250–51.

18. Interview with Steve Max, May 14, 1986.

19. Breines, *Community and Organization*, 70. For the formation of Dodge City Community College sds, see letter from Bill Burrows to no, January 11, 1965, Reel 21, sds Papers (microfilm of holdings in Wisconsin State Historical Society collection).

20. Letter from Timothy Tyndall to no, November 23, 1965, Reel 21, sds Papers.

21. For example, in December 1965, a student affiliated with a high school antiwar group in Sanger, California, wrote to the no: "Gentlemen, Our chief concern is the war in Vietnam and we have been circulating leaflets and petitions protesting our government's actions there. However, we are experiencing difficulties. We lack material to print and distribute. Could you please remedy this situation" (Rick Lehman to no, December 7, 1965, Reel 21, sds Papers).

22. "The violence in Vietnam seemed to elicit a similar air of violence in the United States, an appetite for extremes: people felt that history was accelerating, time was running out, great issues were reaching a point of final

decision" (Thomas Powers, *Vietnam: The War at Home* [1973; reprint, Boston: G. K. Hall, 1984], 200).

23. Sale, *SDS*, 279–85; Miller, *"Democracy,"* 240–42.

24. *New York Post*, January 10, 1966; *New Left Notes*, January 21, 1966.

25. Letter from Jeff Shero to National Administrative Committee (NAC), January 19, 1966, Reel 20, SDS Papers.

26. Letter from Steve Max to NAC, January 17, 1966; Max to "Paul" [Booth?] [n.d., January 1966?]; C. Clark Kissinger to "NICNACers" [n.d., January 1966?], Reel 20, SDS Papers.

27. Letter from "Wulf" [Ohio SDSer] to NO, February 9, 1966, Reel 25, SDS Papers.

28. *Fire* 1 (November 21, 1969). The ready availability and use of drugs at SDS conventions were noted, on separate occasions, by both authors.

29. Lionel Abel offered a perceptive analysis of *Marat/Sade* and its audience in *Dissent* 13 (March–April 1966): 164–69.

30. Quoted in Morrison and Morrison, *From Camelot to Kent State*, 236. Popular films like *King of Hearts* and novels like Ken Kesey's *One Flew over the Cuckoo's Nest* offered similar messages.

31. Lee Webb, "Conference Working Paper and Suggested Priorities for the NC" [n.d., late 1965?], Reel 20, SDS Papers.

32. Letter from Craig Fisher to NO [n.d., 1968?], Reel 21, SDS Papers.

33. Ronald Reagan, quoted in Robert Justin Goldstein, *Political Repression in Modern America, 1870 to the Present* (Cambridge: Scheinkman, 1978), 511.

34. Abe Peck, *Uncovering the Sixties: The Life and Times of the Underground Press* (New York: Pantheon, 1985), 228–29.

35. Daniel Yankelovich, *The New Morality: A Profile of American Youth in the 70's* (New York: McGraw Hill, 1974), 11.

36. Paul Potter, *A Name for Ourselves* (Boston: Little, Brown, 1971), 215.

37. Ibid., p. xvi.

38. Morris Dickstein, *Gates of Eden: American Culture in the Sixties* (New York: Basic Books, 1977), 213.

39. The phrase "democratic distemper" was used in Michel Crozier, Samuel P. Huntington, and Joji Watanuki, *The Crisis of Democracy: Report on the Governability of Democracies to the Trilateral Commission* (New York: New York University Press, 1975).

40. R. Kent Jennings, "Residues of a Movement: The Aging of the American Protest Generation," *American Political Science Quarterly* (June 1987): 367–82. Also see Ellen Perley Frank, "The Real 'Big Chill' in Michigan," *Nation*, October 31, 1987, 480–82. John Sayles, whose film *The Return of the Secaucus Seven* also portrayed a reunion of New Left veterans, offered a more informed and sympathetic portrait than *The Big Chill*. It is interesting to note how different the post-sixties careers of his characters were from those in *The Big Chill*: among the "seven" were two public high school teachers, a drug counselor, a folksinger, the speechwriter for a liberal senator, and a female medical student hoping to become an obstetrician.

41. S. Robert Lichter and Stanley Rothman, "Media and Business Elites," *Public Opinion* (October–November 1981): 42–46, 59–60; Paul Hollander, "The Survival of the Adversary Culture," *Partisan Review* 53 (1986): 345–57. For useful works on the phenomenon of the "new class" written from other than neoconservative perspectives, see Alain Touraine, *Post-Industrial Society* (New York: Random House, 1971); Daniel Bell, *Cultural Contradictions of Capitalism* (New York: Basic Books, 1976); Claus Offe, "New Social Movements: Challenging the Boundaries of Institutional Politics," *Social Research* 52 (Winter 1985): 817–68; and Peter Clecak, " 'The Movement' and Its Legacy," *Social Research* 48 (Autumn 1981): 521–56.

42. In the spring of 1988, the National Museum of American History displayed exhibits on Japanese internment during World War II (as its recognition of the Constitution's bicentennial), black migration to cities during and after World War I, and the imagery of workers. In the planning stages were a presentation of female activism during the Progressive era and a redesign of the popular First Ladies exhibit to emphasize the insights of recent feminist scholarship. On changes at the Smithsonian, see Barbara Gamarekian, "Smithsonian Recognizes Influence beyond White," *New York Times*, June 17, 1988, p. B6. For an analysis of radical contributions to the burgeoning field of public history, see Susan Porter Benson, Stephen Brier, and Roy Rosenzweig, eds., *Presenting the Past: Essays on History and the Public* (Philadelphia: Temple University Press, 1986).

43. A more skeptical view of the role and prospects of academic radicals is offered in Russell Jacoby, *The Last Intellectuals: American Culture in the Age of Academe* (New York: Basic Books, 1987).

44. Oprah Winfrey was interviewed on National Public Radio's "Morning Edition," September 30, 1987.

45. Daniel Golden, "Bork Affair Reflects Attitudinal Changes," *Boston Globe*, October 11, 1987.

46. See William J. Wilson, *The Declining Significance of Race* (Chicago: University of Chicago Press, 1978); and Wilson, *The Truly Disadvantaged: The Inner City, the Underclass, and Public Policy* (Chicago: University of Chicago Press, 1987). For a good statistical survey of the problem, see Andrew Hacker, "American Apartheid," *New York Review of Books*, December 2, 1987, 26–33.

47. Louis Harris, *Inside America* (New York: Vintage, 1987), 83–84, 87, 95–96, 99–100; E. J. Dionne, "Poll Finds Reagan Support Down," *New York Times*, December 1, 1987, 1. Interviews with "focus groups" of white Democrats who voted for Reagan in 1984 found a "preponderant concern with equality and opportunity" for women in the workplace and agreement "that women were discriminated against at work." However, the participants also viewed blacks as a privileged group and themselves as the victims of unjust policies to help the minority at the expense of the majority (Stanley Greenberg of The Analysis Group, "Report on Democratic Defection, Prepared for the Michigan House Democratic Campaign Committee," April 15, 1985; copy in authors' possession).

48. Jane J. Mansbridge, *Why We Lost the ERA* (Chicago: University of Chicago Press, 1986); on poll results, see 201–18.

49. Jefferson Morley, "The Paradox of North's Popularity," *Nation*, August 15/22, 1987.

50. Ibid.

51. William Adams has perceptive things to say about Oliver Stone's movie in "Platoon: Of Heroes and Demons," *Dissent* 34 (Summer 1987): 383–86.

52. "Americans have fallen in love with Oliver North because they see him as a two-fisted John Wayne in a Marine uniform who beat the stuffing out of the bureaucracy—a man of action who made mincemeat of pompous, prying politicians with his honest, forthright answers" (*National Enquirer*, July 28, 1987, 2).

53. To take just one group influential in Democratic party politics, NOW had 150,000 members in 1987, roughly five times its membership of a decade earlier, despite losses suffered after the defeat of the ERA. The Sierra Club, Nuclear Freeze movement, and American Civil Liberties Union enjoyed similar growth spurts during Reagan's first term in office.

54. On party dynamics, see Kevin Phillips, *Post-Conservative America* (New York: Random House, 1982); and William Schneider, "The New Shape of American Politics," *Atlantic Monthly*, January 1987, 39–54.

55. In the aftermath of the Ginsburg affair, several other leading political figures announced that they too had used marijuana in their early days—and suffered no loss of popularity as a result. Also see Todd Gitlin and Ruth Rosen, "Give the 60's Generation a Break," *New York Times*, November 14, 1987.

56. Harris, *Inside America*, 33–38.

57. The CBS Evening News, September 13, 1987. One of the demonstrators told a reporter that "what we need is another revolution in this country." The anti-Gulf leaflet was written and distributed by "Students for America" in the spring of 1987.

58. Richard Hofstadter, *The Age of Reform: From Bryan to FDR* (New York: Knopf, 1955), 19.

9 The Rise of the "Silent Majority"

JONATHAN RIEDER

INTRODUCTION: POPULIST CONSERVATISM

*T*HE New Deal collapsed in the 1960s. Baldly put, in need of qualification, this is the key truth, the essential condition, of our recent political life. The popular coalition that sustained the New Deal through postwar prosperity and McCarthyism burst into its constituent shards. The early years of the decade sounded a note of high liberal promise. By the end of the decade, liberalism was in full rout, with the Democratic party embroiled in internal warfare and the Republicans ascendant. At the time, Lyndon Johnson's defeat of Barry Goldwater in 1964 was widely interpreted as proof that a conservative ideologue could not achieve victory in America. In truth, the outlines of Reagan's popular victory may be glimpsed in shadowy form in the Goldwater debacle.

The travail of the Democrats, and its corollary, the Right's return from the fringes of national political life, involved many things. Most tangibly, this coming unstuck of the New Deal alliance could be seen at the level of architecture, of broken form: millions of voters, pried loose from their habitual loyalty to the Democratic Party, were now a volatile force, surging through the electoral system without the channeling restraints of party attachment. This does not mean that they immediately underwent some ideologically profound conversion; it does mean that they were now available for courting.[1] And the Republicans courted them. In the presidential elections from 1968 through 1984, the Democrats won only once, and that was in 1976 with a candidate who disavowed New Deal themes, embraced budget balancing, and ran against a Republican party discredited by Watergate.

No less important than this institutional volatility was the middling status of the voters who helped produce it. Of course, certain segments of that vast and eclectic American middle, split in countless ways by region and income, religion and ethnicity, had warmed to the Republicans for a long time. But now in the 1960s and its aftermath, conservatives and Republicans found a responsive audience among once-Democratic constituencies: southerners, ethnic Catholics in the Northeast and Midwest, blue-collar workers, union members, even a sprinkling of lower-middle-class Jews. Out of this maelstrom of defection there emerged a new social formation, Middle America.

Middle America did not really exist as a popular term before the 1960s. In part, it emerged out of the center's own efforts to name itself. But it also emerged from the efforts of others to capture and beguile it, most notably from the oratorical flourishes of Republicans, reactionaries, and conservatives who had their own ideological projects in mind.

The rhetorical foil to this middle, "limousine liberalism," another coinage of the time, sought to convince the middling classes that liberalism was a special enthusiasm of the well-born and well-placed, that the Democrats decreasingly spoke to and for the vast middle. The reborn right, then, was a populist right, at least in its oratory. This too must be qualified. But it offers an important insight into the Right's recovery, and its vulnerability and fleeting tenure.

Beyond the novel language, the new formation and broken architecture, something more basic was at work in this political upheaval. The language took, because it jibed with the resentments of so many ordinary Americans. The forms broke because they could no longer contain the surging passions of betrayal and resistance. What drew the disparate segments of the middle together was its restorationist impulse, its unhappiness with the directions of change in American life. If there was any single source of displeasure that shook the New Deal coalition to its core, it was the civil rights revolution. Race, however, was only the earliest and most powerful spur to these defections. Later, the Vietnam War cleaved through the Democratic party and hacked it into bits. Other issues like law and order, the revolution in morals, and a corrosive inflation added to disaffection. Whatever the mélange of separate complaints that fed the stream of resentment and complaint, this much is clear: the consequences were immense. At least for a time, they rearranged the basic categories of American political life.

PRELUDE: THE PROBLEM OF THE RIGHT

Despite a variety of demographic, economic, and institutional changes in American life between 1932 and 1960, it was still possible to argue in the early 1960s that little had changed in thirty years, and that the New Deal remained essentially intact, with some erosions and qualifications.[2] Even at the height of the New Deal, the Democratic majority contained certain vulnerabilities. One potential strain involved the ambiguity of the "liberalism" that sustained the New Deal electorally, and the limited sense in which various working-class fractions could be described as liberal. While Roosevelt had a penchant for high-flown rhetoric, and progressive forces fashioned an idiom of transcendent social purpose, many workers, naturally enough, liked the New Deal mainly for the benefits it bestowed. For them, the New Deal did not represent universalism as much as the particularism of household provision.

Ethnic commitments, and the foreign policy concerns they generated during World War II, further weakened the unity of the New Deal coalition. Above all, isolationism fed a fierce alienation from Democratic liberal internationalism. The Irish opposed Roosevelt's war policy as pro-British intervention. His condemnation of Italy's attack on France—"The hand that held the dagger has plunged it into the back of its neighbor"—stirred public outcry in America's Little Italys. And now for a second time, American entry into a world war risked compromising the good reputation of German-Americans. In the years after the war, these grievances would give rise to a "politics of revenge," to borrow Samuel Lubell's famous phrase, against the Democrats. Similarly, ethnic Catholics from the occupied countries of Eastern Europe—including many Lithuanian, Polish, and Czech Democrats—responded to charges that the party of Roosevelt was soft on communism and had sold out their ancestral homelands at Yalta.

Finally, the progressive policies of the national Democratic party rested anomalously on a racist electoral base of Southern Democrats, who constituted an enclave of white supremacy within the party. However much Southern workers and farmers prized the social legislation of the New Deal, the Southern Democratic party was, by any reckoning, a reactionary force. As a result of the one-party character of the South, the Democratic party contained many "natural" Republicans, awaiting release.

All these vulnerabilities of the Democrats—and others—could be detected at the very start of the New Deal, but they remained low-level tensions that flared episodically. The reactionary right, that remnant of the pre-1929 order that never forgave the New Deal and its "creeping Socialism" for subverting the individualistic verities of "true Americanism," retained its presence in the Midwestern branch of the Republican party. The Right also survived as a force in Congress. As an influence on national policy, however, it was essentially demobilized, and took recourse in a sulking desire for vengeance. It had to accept a bitter truth: the "modern" Republican party was no longer an agency of reactionary restoration. Mainstream Republicans, too, had faced facts: there was no electoral market for ending state benevolence. The conservatism they could muster consisted of a recognition that the innovations of the New Deal were part of the fabric of American life—had become the past that was to be saved. The rejectionists of the Right—not content with modest trimming—wanted domestic rollback. They were thus truly radical in colloquial parlance. They were radical in another sense: they had ceased to be popular. The masses of ordinary working men and women, at least on average, belonged to the Democrats.[3]

The Right did not cease to imagine the people, and to imagine them as its allies, or its potential allies. It developed a theory of a natural majority, hidden and kept from it. Anticipating the turn of 1960s conservatism toward majoritarian themes, some conservative intellectuals like Willmoore Kendall lauded the "virtuous people."[4] And still the Right kept seeking ways to return to power. The Truman victory of 1948 underscored the popularity of the New Deal's social policies. Any attack on the Democrats would thus have to be oblique, could not be a headlong defense of "liberty against socialism."[5] The Right had to fight for a popular following on the more auspicious terrain of foreign policy.

More than any other figure, Sen. Joseph McCarthy offered the right a brief flurry of hope. He developed all the plaints of the nationalist right and added new twists: the sellout of Yalta, the weak moral fiber of New Dealers and their penchant for humiliating appeasement, the loss of Eastern Europe and China, the enfoldment of subversives into the heart of the New Deal. The time was ripe to expand the market for these classic themes. Global developments in the postwar years had deepened the public's anxiety about foreign affairs. Moreover, the implacable anticommunism of the Catholic church, and the problem of the captive nations, sustained a ferocious conservatism among many Catholic Democrats. Presumably, in appealing to these more plebeian constituencies, McCarthy's tough, swaggering style and his pseudo-populist diatribes would prove helpful. His famous Wheeling, West Virginia, speech was laced with seeming class resentment. "It is not the less fortunate, or members of minority groups who have been selling this nation out, but rather those who have had all the benefits the wealthiest nation on earth has had to offer. . . . This is glaringly true of the State Department. There the bright young men who are born with silver spoons in their mouth are the ones who have been worst."[6]

For various reasons, McCarthyism did not rescue the Right. The gap between McCarthy's core constituencies and his popular support never closed. As Michael Rogin has argued, McCarthyism "reflected the specific traumas of conservative Republican activists—internal Communist subversion, the New Deal, centralized government, left-wing intellectuals, and the corrupting influences of a cosmopolitan society."[7] The market for these themes remained confined to the Right's traditional base among the provincial petite bourgeoisie. Among his ethnic plebeian supporters, McCarthy tapped rather straightforward worries about Korea, the cold war, and communism. On these issues, however, the two parties did not fundamentally differ. Democrats and Republicans alike shared in the anti-Communist consensus; the marginal difference between soft and hard forms of anticommunism was insufficient to stir the public at large.

If anticommunism failed to realign the parties, McCarthy accomplished two things of moment for this discussion. First, his success in the polls with Catholic ethnics prefigured "one of the right's basic post-war strategies for a return to power—the Catholic/ethnic/blue-collar strategy."[8] The ethnic response to McCarthy heartened Catholic conservatives like L. Brent Bozell and William Buckley and highlighted the folly of what Buckley called "the university crowd." It appeared that openings to the ethnic working class might be welcome, and more: the status resentments of petit-bourgeois elites in the hinterland toward the Eastern Establishment offered an idiom with which to seduce ethnic Democrats. As a result, the Right's commitment to a rhetoric of plebeian contempt for things effete and patrician deepened. All in all, McCarthy hurried the movement of the Right toward a conservatism conspicuously more majoritarian than previously.

The second effect of McCarthyism was on the liberal imagination. Simply put, the red scare revealed a dimension of the people that was frightening. It seemed as if a demonic volk was rising up to assault established institutions and civil liberties with its plebiscitary passion. In American historiography, the reconsideration of populism as an ethnocentric movement fueled by wish fulfillment and status humiliation underlined this change of heart among many liberals. In less academic quarters, McCarthyism highlighted the festering ethnic tension within the Democratic party, in which Jewish liberals decried Catholic authoritarianism and Catholics reciprocated with charges of Jewish bolshevism. These mutual recriminations marked more than ethnic squabbling; they indicated an important vein of Catholic conservatism within the Democratic party, as well as the ideological schisms it was capable of provoking.

McCarthyism broke through the civil rhetorical settlement that kept animosity suppressed and backstage. Once McCarthyism was defeated, those tensions were driven underground, to be whispered sotto voce. But the stylistic war between plebeian and patrician continued as a latent undertheme in the struggle between conservatism and liberalism. During the 1960s it resurfaced with dramatic intensity.

Southern Insurgency

An ideological party of right-wing reaction could not rouse the middle-income classes from their self-absorbed, acquisitive mood in the 1950s. The right's broadsides against the Warren Court and sociological jurisprudence fell on deaf ears. That same indifference befell the Right's apocalyptic vision of communism, its pure form of laissez-faire, its indictment of the permissive society. Nor did the public show much appetite for a more respectable corporate-style conservatism. Despite the running down of liberal energies, depression-vintage tensions between the classes, while muted and diminishing, remained. Lower- and working-class Americans supported welfare state measures more vigorously than did upper-middle- and upper-class voters, and they linked their economic fate to the Democratic party. In addition, ingrained Democratic loyalty, no matter how ritualized, tended to keep the electorate from considering more conservative alternatives. Even when Democrats did vote for a particular Republican, say for Eisenhower, they did not alter their basic political identities and sympathies.[9]

Even the inertia of old partisan habits did not survive the social crisis that erupted across America between 1960 and 1972. The exodus of habitual Democrats from the party began earliest in the South. In the presidential election of 1948, Truman's initiatives on civil rights spurred a Dixiecrat secession led by Strom Thurmond. The quickening assault on white supremacy by Supreme Court decisions, the civil rights movement, and Democratic liberals eventually led to the collapse of the Democratic party in the white South. In the early 1960s, Republican strategists developed Operation Dixie, the precursor to the Southern Strategy that envisioned a new Republican majority founded on the conservatism of the West, the South, and the heartland. By 1980, the Republicans had essentially fulfilled this vision of political geography.[10]

Racial resentment was not the sole cause of these defections, nor was it only a cause. It also was a condition for defections on other grounds. Anything that broke the hold of Democratic loyalty, as only the racial liberalism of the national party could, freed conservative-leaning Democrats to embrace the Republican party. Already in the 1950s, a stream of upper-middle-class business and professional types had begun to flow to the Republicans. In metropolitan areas like Shreveport, Augusta, and Jackson, Donald Strong concluded, "They're acting like Yankees! The prosperous folk of Richmond, Charleston, and Dallas voted just like their economic counterparts in Syracuse, Indianapolis, and Cleveland."[11] In a sense, racial turmoil in the South did not overthrow the class axis of the New Deal but simply completed it, albeit on terms favorable to Republicans.[12]

The emotional edge of Southern defections in the 1960s came from more tawdry racial passions. The effort to dismantle the South's caste system catalyzed a politics of massive resistance that redounded to the Republicans' benefit. Barry Goldwater, the Republican candidate in 1964, seemed a good bet to capitalize on white resistance. His defense of states rights came from a Jeffersonian fear of federal power, not from heartfelt racialist ideology, but the South did not mind. One of eight senators who had voted against the Civil Rights Act of 1964, he appealed directly to segregationists alienated by Johnson's civil rights efforts. Although Goldwater's reactionary politics were repudiated in a Democratic victory of landslide proportions, he won stunning victories in the Deep South. Unlike the Republicanism of the 1950s, his support was distributed across the classes, among lower-income whites as well as those in the upper social strata.[13]

Goldwater's brand of reactionary Republicanism met the requirements of preserving the racial order, but it had its shortcomings. In the absence of racial struggle, it was too steeped in Sunbelt individualism to entice disprivileged Southern workers and farmers, especially up-country whites in the Deep South outside the Black Belt counties. For those elements, George Wallace was the true talisman of order. As governor of Alabama, Wallace defied a court order to integrate the University of Alabama, placing himself in front of federal marshals and vowing, "I will never submit to an order of the federal court ordering the integration of the schools." He quickly became a hero of Southern nullification. Wallace frankly defended the Southern way of life: "I don't believe in the social and educational mixing of the races."[14]

Heir to one strain of the Southern populist tradition, Wallace heralded "this average man on the street, this man in the textile mill, this man in the steel mill, this barber, this beautician, the policeman on the beat, they're the ones, and the little businessman—I think those are the mass of people that are going to support a change on the domestic scene."[15] A former Golden Gloves boxer with a tough and gritty mien, Wallace jabbed at the fancy people, the Eastern Establishment, the cultural sophisticates who allegedly disdained the values of the common people. "We are going to show them in November that the average American is sick and tired of all those over-educated Ivory-tower folks with pointed heads looking down their noses at us."[16] As rebuttal to such imputed slights, he proffered a raw version of linguistic democracy: "Being from Alabama, we didn't know what it means when the head recapitulator of Maryland said that they were going to recapitulate the vote. . . . We still don't know what recapitulate means, but I'll tell you this, when anyone says he is going to recapitulate on you, you better watch out, because they're fixing to do something to you."[17] As Kevin Phillips put it, "Wallace was the personification of the poor white Deep South. His Dixie crowds roared every time Wallace brandished a *New York Times* clipping which sneered at his wife's dime store job."[18]

Wallace matched his rhetoric with a vigorous economic liberalism. As a state legislator and as governor he championed progressive legislation in housing and health. His electoral vehicle, the American Independent party, affirmed a classical New Deal position on social policy. It called for increases in Social Security and affirmed the government's obligation to ensure health care for the economically vulnerable. Despite the South's long-standing hostility to organized labor and the pervasive regional support for the right-to-work laws, the AIP applauded "the great trade organizations" and the right to collective bargaining.

As the 1960s unfolded, Wallace's average men and women in the street fumed over other grievances besides race, and Wallace ministered to them as well. The Vietnam War expanded, and the country, and the Democratic party, divided into camps of hawks and doves. In addition, protests against the war raised emotional debates about the limits of dissent, the meaning of patriotism, and the loyalty of demonstrators. Speaking to those who chafed at the ambiguities of limited war, Wallace, and his running mate Curtis Lemay, prescribed a solution in the manly mode: do not cut and run; bomb the Communists back to the Stone Age. Wallace's calls for using the same forcefulness against domestic enemies drew an equally sympathetic hearing. In good Southern fashion, Wallace's supporters prized military courage and sacrifice. As they saw it, patriotism demanded a simple, unreflective loyalty. They did not cotton to abstract notions of the right of dissent, especially when the people doing the protesting were privileged college students exempt from the draft who donned scruffy, hippy garb and waved Vietcong flags. As a result, they cheered when

Wallace cast protesters beyond the pale of the loyally opposed, rendering them as shameful cowards and traitors.[19]

This struggle over patriotism reflected a broader cultural struggle between the forces of moral tradition and modernist liberation. Both were lodged in the Democratic party. Wallace's followers were disproportionately unlettered and provincial; they clung to fundamentalist and Baptist forms of faith. As they peered out at America in the 1960s, they saw an upsurge of sexual immorality, the decline of the work ethic, disrespect for authority. Demands for women's liberation threatened to blur the primal distinctions between men and women. Worse still, for some, they evoked a satanic violation of biblical prescriptions. The mobilization of fundamentalist Christians was only in its infancy, but throughout the 1970s, Supreme Court decisions on abortion and the tax status of religious schools shook fundamentalist ministers out of their quiescence. As Democratic platforms heralded the Equal Rights Amendment, a politicized ministry, and the larger New Right movement that prodded it, discovered in Wallace supporters a responsive audience for their fulminations against moral decline.

For all these racial, moral, and patriotic infamies, Wallace offered relief. He promised to restore law and order to America, and would not let squeamishness or finicky concerns about due process stand in the way. "Hell, we got too much dignity in government," Wallace told his true believers. "What we need is some *meanness*. You elect one of those steel-workers guvnuh, you talk about a revolution—damn, there'd be shootin' and tearin' down and burnin' up and killin' and bloodlettin' sho *nuff*."[20] His stump oratory was tinged with hints of retaliatory violence against traitors and wreckers. He excelled at using the hecklers who showed up at his rallies, baiting them and driving his supporters to a higher pitch of emotion. In Marshall Frady's words, "Wallace had invoked, had discovered a dark, silent, brooding mass of people whom no one—the newspapers, the political leaders, the intellectuals—no one but Wallace had suspected were there."[21]

The power of this populist conservative movement of the Southern middling classes showed itself in the 1968 presidential election. The force of racial reaction and populist passion blasted away the Democratic hold on the South. Classical New Deal Democrat Hubert Humphrey took only 30 percent of the vote; in the Deep South, a rising number of black votes barely pushed him to the 20-percent level. But this was no obvious Valhalla for the Republicans. Their effort to build on the Goldwater breakthrough ran smack into Wallace and his American Independent party. Wallace and Republican candidate Richard Nixon split the rest of the Southern vote down the middle, each taking 34 percent. Wallace won the Deep South. Nixon and the Republicans won the Outer South. Nixon held the more privileged, better educated, economic conservatives. Less often were Nixon voters members of pietistic Protestant sects, and they did not evince the high levels of commitment to segregation.[22]

The Wallace candidacy ultimately posed a far graver threat to the Democrats than to the Republicans. He made painfully clear that reactionary politics might prove attractive to economically liberal, disprivileged southerners, whether in the party or generally alienated from politics and outside the party system altogether. Wallace provided a niche for middling Democrats who disliked the racial and foreign policies of the Democrats and were in the process of cutting their ties to the ancestral party. In the absence of Wallace in the 1972 election, Republicans were the ones to gain. Richard Nixon trounced liberal Democrat George McGovern with ease, sweeping every state in the Deep South, the Southern rim, and the border states.

For the Republicans, Wallace-style conservatism showed the dangers of a right-wing resurgence that drew its force from plebeian racial animosity, frustrated nationalism, and cultural restoration. The opportunities were obvious, and they continued the movement of Republican rhetoric, candidates, and strategists toward the apotheosis of "middle America." To budding New Right theorists, the Wallace voters were the key to a transformed Republicanism centered on populist themes and lower-middle-class resentment. As they refigured their genealogy, the lineage ran from Andrew Jackson and William Jennings Bryan through Joseph McCarthy and George Wallace to Ronald Reagan and Jerry Falwell.[23]

But populist conservatism had its limits. No matter how much the Right tried to encompass Wallace and Goldwater within the same category, they did not fit. Wallace's attack on bureaucrats and liberals, his revilement of an intrusive national state, formed a contingent opposition to specific bureaucrats and judicials who were transforming the Southern way. The "conservatism" of Wallace voters was spotty and suspect in other respects. "Country and Western Marxism," Chilton Williamson dubbed it in the *National Review*.[24] "To the Nashville Station" was how Kevin Phillips captured the ambiguous drift of the "conservative" movement.[25] Wallace's people did not feel at home in a Republican party that still was the organ of establishment conservatism. In 1976, Carter constructed a biracial populist coalition in the South; in 1982, in the midst of the recession, Southern workers flocked back to the Democrats. Finally, Wallace came at the midpoint of racial transition. Once the shocks of the 1960s were through, racial politics lost their corrosive edge. The gradual coming of black power to the South, and the growing acceptance among whites that the civil rights revolution could not—and in many cases, should not—be reversed, marked a change of heart in the 1970s.[26]

The evolution of the South reminds us of the imperfect relationship between shifts in votes for political parties and shifts in underlying sentiment. The upheavals of race, war, and morality did not simply create conservative temptations; rather, they exploded the Democratic container that had kept them within the party. Once the genie escaped, it would be hard to put it back. Southern Democrats had always been at odds with many of the policies of the national party, but they believed it represented their feelings. "The tumultuous sixties eroded this myopic perception. As issues became more salient and politics intruded on more individuals, there was a heightened awareness of discrepancies between what the parties stood for as opposed to what they were believed to stand for."[27] The loss of Democratic dominance, and the emergence of a truly competitive two-party system in the South, permitted an indigenous conservatism on a variety of issues—race, sexual morality, civil liberties, religion, and foreign policy—to achieve expression.

REVOLT IN THE NORTH

At the start of the 1960s, the bitter passions of race seemed very much a Southern affair. The ferocity of resistance could still be considered a regional aberration. It soon became clear that the North could not achieve immunity from the struggle for racial justice. The complex forces that kept blacks subordinate in the North lacked the clarity of the evil of the Southern caste system, which also meant that the limits of liberal reform, and the ambiguous entanglement of race, ethnicity, and class, surfaced more quickly in the North.

The racial discontent that marked the 1969 mayoral race in New York City and the behavior of blue-collar ethnic Democrats in a Philadelphia industrial suburb in 1968 struck Walter Dean Burnham as a historic break with New Deal routine. Far more ominous than the break itself was its character—a proto-fascist revolt of the little man, animated by fearful resentment.[28] This was populism with a vengeance, literally; it was not the populism of optimistic reform but the populism of Poujade and the petite bourgeoisie. That the Weimar analogy could issue forth from one of America's savviest electoral analysts marked just how far the country, and the North most spectacularly, had traveled toward racial conflict in barely half a decade. New York City, crucible of New Deal liberalism and bastion of Jewish tolerance, seemed a paradoxically apt symbol of this unhappy development, and more than a few conservatives savored that fact.

The most flamboyant indication of the threat of the civil rights movement to the Democratic party in the North occurred during the presidential primaries in 1964, when George Wallace did amazingly well—between 30 percent and 45 percent of the vote—in strongly Democratic blue-collar precincts in Milwaukee, Baltimore, and Cleveland. Wallace had not minced words. His boast that he would make race the basis of politics across the nation credited his own powers too fulsomely, but the general point held.[29] Wallace prefigured things to come, in more eclectic, and less reactionary, form. In the congressional elections of 1966, white backlash against Great Society liberalism was in full force throughout the country. As the decade advanced, backlash spread from the working class to the middle class, from Catholic enclaves to Jewish ones, from the provincial, vindictive reaches of the center up into its more genteel, democratic quarters.

The motives behind resistance may be so transparent as to require little accounting. Unabashed racism played its considerable part. And as Burnham indicates, the frustrations of a squeezed lower-middle class could easily yield to the most vindictive and paranoid intimations.

Accurate as far as it goes, the diagnosis of racism or populism fails to grasp the complexity of racial resentment. Backlash was a disorderly affair that contained democratic, populist, genteel, conspiratorial, racist, humanistic, pragmatic, and meritocratic impulses. Simply put, the middle was too diverse, the grievances it suffered too varied, to be captured in a single category.

Escalation in part followed from certain structural limitations of liberal reform. Blacks in the North still had much work to do in achieving basic constitutional rights and fighting white supremacy, but class issues—of poverty, of jobs, of inequality—prevailed over strictly caste ones, and demanded other solutions. A stance of racial neutrality, of equal opportunity, would not immediately benefit the members of the lumpen classes, especially during a time of economic transition. As black demands ran up against the limits of liberalism, frustration spurred the search for alternatives: affirmative action, community control of schools, welfare rights, racial quotas, model cities programs, busing, reparations, political mobilization of the black masses, black pride. Each of these remedies surpassed the existing level of moral legitimacy and political acceptability.

Opposition to compensatory efforts sprang from the self-interest of vulnerable whites, whose hold on middle-class status was precarious. Integration threatened white ethnic monopolies on labor markets, the civil service, unions, and municipal power. More specifically, for disprivileged whites in high-tax states like California and New York, the fiscal levies of a spiraling welfare bill seemed like confiscatory exactions on their meager resources. Busing for racial integration heightened primal anxieties about children's safety and futures. Philadelphia plans in the construction industry, like court-ordered affirmative action programs elsewhere, often reserved a certain percentage of jobs for blacks, thereby reducing the number of jobs available for whites.

Such policies gradually yielded a diffuse sense among many traditional Democratic ethnic workers that they had become the victims of "reverse discrimination." This was more than a proxy for racist animosity. Unemployed carpenters might yell, "Those quotas and Philadelphia plans made us angry. They should create plans to help both sides. Create jobs, but don't take from one to give the other and create bitterness." Former supporters of the early civil rights movement argued that blacks wanted to get ahead, "they *should* get ahead. But not on my kid's back. Blacks are taking advantage." As the lament suggests, "reverse discrimination" also formed an ethical critique of the remedies advanced by liberals, the judiciary, and blacks. As well as a psychic economy and a political economy of backlash, there was a moral economy of backlash.[30]

Policies that seemed to give special privileges to blacks and exempt them from the rigors of competition scandalized whites. This is not to say that Northern Democratic workers were pristine Lockeans. Even more than the Protestant working and middle classes of the South and Sunbelt, Jewish and Catholic Democrats came from familistic and communal cultures, and had benefited greatly from the welfare state. But they were also partisans of earning, self-reliance, and the work ethic. Their own historic experience, and the mythologies that surrounded it, sustained a great faith in, even a romance of, bootstrapping. Even whites sympathetic to black suffering often responded to compensatory policies with indignation, an emotion born of violated justice. One spokesman for aggrieved white ethnics rejected the claim by an NAACP official that whites had to pay the price for all those years of slavery: "But I ask you, who will pay the Jews for two thousands years of slavery? Who will compensate the Italians for all the ditches they dug?"[31]

The whole tenor and turn of the black movement after the mid-1960s offended no less than the remedies it championed. Its militancy, the increasingly forceful and even violent tone of its demands, the spread of black nationalism through the Northern ghettos—these frightened and offended provincial workers, many of whom little understood the historical brutalization of blacks in America and the assaults on culture and identity that accompanied it. The Watts riot of 1965, during which images of blacks crying "Burn, baby, burn" flickered across white television sets, marked a turning point in the white perception of the black movement. In a great reversal, white support for black demands, which had been steadily growing through the early 1960s, dropped precipitously. The proportion of whites who believed the civil rights movement was proceeding too fast rose in tandem.[32]

This spiral upward in black anger and militancy had a certain ironic quality that escaped white workers. Every display of white reluctance and meanness frustrated the desire of blacks for moderation, and disillusionment then pushed them toward higher levels of militancy, and eventually black nationalism. If the universal vision of integration gave way to the particularism of racial separatism, defensive whites unwittingly helped call forth the very nationalist excess they reviled.

In ways that Americans did not always appreciate, these apparent arguments about race and remedy were often displaced conflicts of class. In the minds of many white ethnics, ghetto rioting fused with the street crime practiced by a dispirited segment of the black underclass. The white view that quotas were a way to get ahead without paying one's dues merged with popular resentment of welfare "giveaways" to poor blacks. The dislike of welfare drew force from a broader perception of the ghetto as a place of incivility, where the cult of pleasure triumphed over all moral restraint and striving. Little in their culture focused the attention of provincial ethnic Democrats on the sociological causes of drug addiction, illegitimate births, male sexual irresponsibility, and female-headed households. Their moral traditionalism stoked contempt for transgression, which added a powerful overlay of virtue and vice to the fundamental cleavage of race and class already dividing two crucial elements of the Democratic coalition.

The final ingredient in this volatile mix of race, morality, ethnicity, and class was proximity. The historical patterns of migration and settlement were such that millions of Northern Democratic workers lived near black ghettos, and the black underclass loomed as a powerful physical presence. Integration was not a remote abstraction. It was freighted with a vivid and brutal particularity. When white ethnics of modest means thought about integration of schools and neighborhoods, they did not envision encounters with blacks in general but with the quite specific blacks who lived near them, who seemed morally and physically dangerous. Countless ethnic neighborhoods had undergone rapid racial change, and many of those formerly white enclaves had become seamy ghettos. To hard-pressed workers, whose major investment was tied up in their home and community, the prospect of integrated schools and residences raised the prospect of jeopardy, racial engulfment, tipping.[33]

None of the tangible threats of the underclass unsettled whites as much as crime. Black street crime soared in the 1960s, and as black protest devolved into ghetto rioting, both fortified the white perception that poor blacks were a malevolent lot who resorted to illegitimate means to get what they wanted. "Crime in the streets" catapulted to the very top of the list of pressing issues by the mid-1960s, and created a market for conservative politicians who would restore "law and order." Demagogues often inflamed popular fears about crime. The phrase functioned for some as a code word for racism; when would-be avengers recited the phrase, some listeners heard a commitment to satisfy their fantasies of reprisals against blacks. But the phrase also spoke to more practical fears of physical safety shared by the racially generous and vindictive alike.

As James Sundquist has well summarized, fear of crime tended to blend with a host of other moral anxieties: "In the public's perception, all these things merged. Ghetto riots, campus riots, street crime, anti-Vietnam marches, poor people's marches, drugs, pornography, welfarism, rising taxes, all had a common thread: the breakdown of family and social discipline, of order, of concepts of duty, of respect for law, of public and private morality."[34] If Northern ethnic Democrats were not Bible-thumping pietists after the fashion of Southern fundamentalists and evangelicals, they were moral traditionalists. Just as they affirmed the verities of patriotic duty, they grieved over flagrant homosexuality, the apparent decline in respect for authority, the feminist revolution with its blurring of the boundaries between men's and women's places. On all these issues, many middle-income Democrats saw liberal fellow Democrats as their moral adversaries.

Each of the varied issues that grew up around the controversies of race (especially), life-style, and foreign policy became points of complaint and conflict with their own consequences. Together, they had a cumulative effect that was more diffuse but no less critical. They added to a growing sense of alienation among many white Democrats of modest means who felt betrayed by the direction of change. The political system seemed unfairly stacked against them. Increasingly, they saw other factions dominating the Democratic party with an agenda that did not include room for white ethnic concerns.

No small part of this sense of danger and dispossession flowed from the perception by the middle-income classes of a growing chasm between themselves and the regnant version of liberalism. This sense of difference transformed the folk imagery of liberalism. In the popular mind, liberalism acquired a variety of invidious connotations. No longer did it suggest a vision of transcendent justice or the support of vulnerable working people. Liberalism meant taking the side of blacks, no matter what; dismissing middle-class plaints as racism; handcuffing the police; transferring resources and sympathy from a vulnerable middle class to minorities; rationalizing rioting and dependency and other moral afflictions as "caused" by the environment or as justifiable response to oppression. Liberalism appeared to them as a force inimical to the working and lower-middle classes, assaulting their communities, their sense of fairness, their livelihood, their children, their physical safety, their values.

THE DEMOCRATS IN DISARRAY

By the late 1960s, the issues of race, Vietnam, and life-style had changed the political climate of the entire nation, not just of the South. Restive forces had broken free of the party restraints that once enveloped them. With that institutional breakdown, there emerged a new civic culture, or, more precisely, a culture of incivility. Tension between rival groups now yielded to outright feuding, and unabashed denunciation replaced private grumbling.

One sign of the grass-roots revolt against liberalism was the emergence of new champions of the white working and lower-middle classes. Republicans saw a chance here to expand their sway, but conservative Democrats abounded who articulated the passions of provincial reaction. Mario Procaccino in New York City, Mayor Sam Yorty in Los Angeles, Frank Rizzo in Philadelphia, and Louise Day Hicks in Boston developed a politics that was essentially the geopolitics of local community. They spoke to white concerns about busing, tipping neighborhoods, crime in the streets, scatter-site low-income housing, judicial leniency, the safety of schools, white flight, and the death penalty. The style of the politics was even more striking than its substantive themes. These leaders affected a vulgar speaking style that was unembarrassed in its vow to protect white interests; no genteel inhibitions kept them from lambasting black leaders and "limousine liberals." Unafraid of appearing tough and racist, at times they reveled in their "bad-boy," outlaw identity, embodied in their willingness to resort to disrespectable, illegal, even violent, means to protect white power.

For all the vividness of these local saviors, developments in the cities were only a microcosm of the organizational implosion of the Democratic party at the national level. The mobilization of blacks, programmatic liberals, antiwar protesters, and women brought volatile new forces into the party that disturbed the existing balance of power. As the white Democratic electorate split into reactionary, traditionalist, and left-liberal wings, disputes about race and Vietnam produced intense feuding between liberal, "regular," and conservative elites. Antiwar Democrats, who demanded withdrawal from Vietnam, squared off against hawkish boosters of the war—cold war liberals, powerful unionists, and machine leaders. Speaking for many New Deal traditionalists, Hubert Humphrey during the 1972 Democratic primaries tagged George McGovern as a proponent of the three A's: "Acid, Abortion, and Amnesty."

These fraction fights reflected a power struggle for the control of the Democratic party that was glaringly visible at the Democratic conventions of the time.[35] In 1968, the Democrats met in Chicago, home base of machine titan Mayor Richard Daley, spokesman for his city's embattled white ethnics and supporter of the war effort. The convention was a raucous affair, punctuated by a police riot against antiwar demonstrators and the national press. Despite the primary strength of insurgents like Robert Kennedy and Gene McCarthy, the regulars kept their hold on the party, but only momentarily. Angry reformers managed to rewrite the party rules, adding quotas that ensured the future participation of women, blacks, and the young. These rule changes produced a significant yield in 1972. Even as rank-and-file Democrats were moving to the right, party activists and delegates were increasingly liberal. Defrocking the old elites, the liberals radically reduced the influence of white ethnics, Democratic mayors, organized labor, and party leaders in the industrial Northeast.

The Democrats' disquiet was an open invitation to their rivals. From the moment of its appearance, Republicans sought to capitalize on popular grievance. A party whose image was dominated by country-club Republicanism, Eastern Establishment patricians, and corporate conservatism could not sharpen those resentments into a barbed electoral weapon. But the institutional work of transforming the Republican party into a vehicle for such a mission had been proceeding for some time. The efforts of conservative strategists to move the party toward a Sunbelt strategy in the early 1960s was part of this effort to oust liberal Republicans and seize control of the party. As the 1960s unfolded, they came to see that the Southern Strategy might have Northern applications.[36]

Organizational succession was necessary to produce a version of populist conservatism, but it was only a condition of success, not a guarantee. To refashion Republican identity around more populist-sounding themes also required cultural work, the refinement of a new kind of political rhetoric. In 1964, even as he plied the waters of the Southern Strategy, Goldwater had targeted his appeal to "the Silent Americans" at Northern ethnic workers. Although he had some success with Northern Catholics in racially tense urban precincts in the Midwest and Northeast, Goldwater's opening to Northern ethnics mainly went unheeded. The appeal was premature. The racial and social crisis had not advanced sufficiently to weaken party ties and make the demand for law and order resonate. The question thus remained for conservatives, how to entice Democratic ethnics, whose material circumstances and cultural traditions sustained a rival sensibility, with the language of Republican fundamentalism? Narrative trickery alone would not build a market among traditional Democratic constituencies, and neither would self-congratulatory calls to silent and forgotten Americans.

What doctrinal grudges, cultural alienation, and finely honed argument had not yet achieved for conservatives, the turbulence of the times finally accomplished. In the years after the Goldwater debacle, the idiom of populist conservatism was repeated and refined, and always with growing resonance. The idiom acquired high and low, genteel and vulgar, incarnations. Not only Republicans mouthed its pieties. Wallace spouted his vindictive variant. Democrats experimented with their versions in local and state elections. It was the core of Ronald Reagan's oratory, and his successful gubernatorial bid. At the end of the decade, this language even entered the presidency as its official motif.

Elections during this period frequently seemed like cockfights or slugfests; the voters affirmed not the goal of corrective equilibrium but their own irreconcilable desires. In 1968, the country was racked by antiwar protest, political assassination, and urban conflagration. Throughout the campaign, Republican candidate Richard Nixon appealed to the middle, ever mindful of the chance to reap a windfall among working- and middle-class Catholics. Garry Wills has well described Nixon's ingenious appeal to the middle-American belief in striving. "Nixon's success was not offered in Maimi as a theme for mere self-congratulations. It was a pledge to others, a pledge that he would not rob them of the fruits of their success."[37] Nixon declared, "In a time when the national focus is concentrated upon the unemployed, the impoverished and the dispossessed, the working Americans have become the forgotten Americans. In a time when the national rostrums and forums are given over to shouters and protestors and demonstrators, they have become the silent Americans. Yet they have a legitimate grievance that should be rectified and a just cause that should prevail."[38]

Democrats and Republicans alike could not afford to ignore the threat of George Wallace, who had taken his campaign beyond the South and turned it into a national social movement on the American Independent party line. As the election neared, it seemed as if Wallace might deny both major parties a majority. Democratic unionists were shocked to find strong support for him among Democratic workers in usually loyal unions. "The death of his old adversary, Martin Luther King, came like a miracle. The riots it touched off meant that the 1968 campaign would be fought on Wallace's chosen ground. The theme would be his theme: law and order."[39] This time, in contrast with 1964, Wallace did not run as an unreconstructed segregationist but couched his racialist concerns in more sublimated form.

Wallace's support in the polls of 23 percent fell by half on election day; his stronger showing in the South was balanced by a lower figure in the other regions. Countless workers who admired Wallace or saw him as a fitting vehicle for their protest shied from wasting their vote on a third-party chimera. Despite that, Wallace did well among Catholics in northeastern locales where racial violence had recently erupted. Among New Jersey Catholics, he took between 10 and 15 percent of the vote. In New York City, Wallace captured almost 10 percent of the vote in Catholic assembly districts, reaching 15 percent in lower-middle-class Irish districts; he drew support from Italian and Irish policemen, firemen, bus drivers, and sanitation workers. Wallace ran strongly in blue-collar ethnic strongholds in racially polarized Flint, Michigan, Cleveland, Ohio, and Gary, Indiana.[40]

Nixon also made inroads in traditionally Democratic working- and middle-class communities. Nixon's appeal was pure simplicity: he heralded a less malevolent version of Wallace's crusade against 1960s liberalism. If Wallace offered rollback, Nixon suggested containment. As Richard Scammon and Benjamin Wattenberg observed, Nixon was the only candidate of the three whose supporters wanted to maintain Negro progress at its current levels rather than slow it down or speed it up.[41]

The power of the racial and social issues did not abate during Nixon's presidency. In the face of continuing black and antiwar dissent, Nixon and his vice-president, Spiro Agnew, went on the attack. As Jonathan Schell recounted it, the president was building a political consensus around the Silent Majority. Increasingly, he believed the principal institutions of American life—including the Supreme Court, Congress, the foundations, television, and the press, all of them in sway to the left-liberal ideology—"were impeding his communion with the new majority, and were thereby thwarting the majority's will." The task, then, was "to clear away this noisy, willful minority impediment."[42] The appeal to Middle America took on a more vindictive edge, as the line between the virtuous middle and demonic outsiders—blacks, liberals, antiwar protesters—was drawn with increasing sharpness. Vice-president Agnew's 1970 address to Delaware Republicans captured this moral cosmos of purity and danger:

> The elite consist of the raised-eyebrow cynics, the anti-intellectual intellectuals, the pampered egotists who sneer at honesty, thrift, hard work, prudence, common decency, and self-denial. In their lust to divorce themselves from the ordinary mortals, they embrace confrontation as a substitute for debate and willingly wrench the Bill of Rights to cloak criminal and psychotic conduct it was never intended to cover. They consider this self-alienation to be true sophistication.
>
> Innocently or not, this haughty clique has brought on a permissiveness that in turn has resulted in a shockingly warped sense of values.[43]

Nineteen seventy-two marked the culmination of the party system of the 1960s. The Democratic nominating process produced in George McGovern a candidate who came to personify all the forces that were anathema to the interests and ideals of the middle-income classes. His pledge to get down on his hands and knees to obtain peace from North Vietnam violated popular taboos on humiliating appeasement. He supported busing, amnesty for draft evaders, and abortion rights, all the while repudiating the death penalty. His widely misinterpreted plan for a Demogrant, a plan to give every American family one thousand dollars, reinforced an impression of fiscal extravagance.

Nixon defeated McGovern in a rout, as the Democrat won only the single state of Massachusetts. Among countless conservative Democratic leaders, including many champions of alienated working-class ethnics, the seeming "radicalism" of the "prairie populist" sparked rebellious rump committees of Democrats and Independents for Nixon. The Teamsters', Longshoremen's, and Construction Workers' unions rallied to the president. As always, ideological preferences alone did not produce the pattern of defection; Nixon's stimulation of a preelection economic boom also motivated Democrats to leave their party. In addition, the rate of defection from the Democrats was a function of conservative views on Vietnam, the use of force to quell college demonstrations, amnesty for draft dodgers, and legalization of marijuana. Nixon received a majority of white working-class votes.

And of the preponderantly Democratic voters attracted to Wallace in 1968, nearly 80 percent voted for Nixon.[44]

CONCLUSION

Caught up in the frenzies of the late 1960s and early 1970s, one could easily foresee the makings of a populist conservative majority. More than a few citizens, including some of the nation's most sober pundits, believed that the country had crossed some primal threshold, that the old rules and assumptions they relied on to produce a sense of order no longer obtained, and they experienced a tremulous sense of unsettlement. As liberals saw it, something mean and violent had been aroused in the white middling classes. With democracy at bay, slogans like "the genius of American politics" and "American exceptionalism" seemed wildly sanguine. Some even talked of an American Weimar or the "Europeanization" of American politics. America had entered one of those "moments of madness" captured by Aristide Zolberg, when possibilities barely imagined suddenly crash through the surface of ordinary life and achieve riotous expression.

And yet the more remarkable thing, as striking as the fact that such frenzies materialized at all, is how quickly they seemed to give way. By the middle of the 1970s, Americans were in the grip of an entirely new set of concerns. With Carter's 1976 victory, and the oratory of moral reassurance that accompanied it, it was possible once more to talk of American elections not as cockfights but as self-regulating mechanisms for damping down passion, composing differences, and achieving harmony. In reality, things were infinitely more complicated than this imagery of ordained equilibrium suggests. Notwithstanding the Carter win and Democratic victories in the 1974 congressional elections, life had not returned to some former status quo that would automatically favor the Democrats and halt their decline. On the contrary, Carter's handling of the economy and foreign affairs would generate popular demands for action in both realms that Reagan successfully exploited in 1980. Nor did Carter reassemble a once-proud Democratic majority. As Gary Orren wrote, Carter's electoral coalition "was composed of something old, something borrowed, and something new."[45] Suspended between the old order and a new one whose shape had yet to be revealed, the mid-1970s offered an odd interim in American politics.

Factors internal to the middle-income classes, the leanings and taboos that shaped their political wishes, partially accounted for the failure of the Republicans to convert the victory of 1972 into that ever-phantom realignment. In the North no less than in the South, the conservatism of the middle-income classes was ambiguous. True enough, many Democrats of modest means would never again feel the same loyalty to any political party, let alone to the Democrats, that they once had given to the party of Roosevelt. Still, as a general rule, they could not find it in themselves to enlist in the Republican party. The Right gained their votes more than it gained their hearts.

Despite all its bathos about silent and moral majorities, the Right's "populism" never entirely converged with the people's. After all, there is a big difference between speaking populist words and offering populist policies. Throughout American history, at least since the time of Jackson, political movements of all persuasions have been forced to talk the language of the people, but they have managed to infuse that common lingo with very different meanings. As Michael Paul Rogin points out, appeals to the people "could attack the status quo; they could also defend it . . . 'populistic' appeals could be made not only by the generally deprived but also by local or national elites that opposed government action."[46]

At least through the 1970s, the Republicans' cramped version of populism consisted mainly of their efforts to flatter the middle, to affirm its values and assuage its sense of neglect and slight. Those efforts, however, were always hedged by the Right's ideological purity and the conservative interests which that purity served. The words sought to cover the gap of interest and belief that separated the Right and restive Democrats. As a result, even as it pursued Middle America, it never quite captured it, or, more precisely, enough of it.

If the Right's populism was narrow and stillborn, that was so mainly relative to the reluctant conservatism of the people that populism was aimed at. Classical Republican fulminations about big government went down well with working people, to the degree white workers resented certain policies and programs that struck them as particularistic or unwholesome benefits for blacks. Such policies and programs, however, represented a small proportion of the total federal budget. The people's nervousness about government thus stopped far short of unmitigated hostility to the welfare state. On the contrary, the middle's well-being depended on an array of entitlements they were loath to surrender. The same lack of coincidence between the Republicans' popular constituencies and disaffected Democrats existed on other issues. Many traditional Democrats shared in a diffuse sense of grievance over moral breakdown, but on the whole they did not embrace the religious Right's desire to install a Republic of Virtue in America.

The intense conservatism displayed by many down-home Democrats during the 1960s was an artifact of their own dialectical need to respond to what appeared to be certain extreme moral and racial dangers. Once the challenges were removed, or at least had diminished, the people could only fall upon their own internal differences and their dissent from the program of the moral zealots. It became apparent that many members of the middle had evolved a good deal in their thinking about moral tolerance and racial justice. If during the 1960s the alignment of issues cast them as opponents of change, the traditionalism they affirmed was a selective, vital, "modernizing" one. William Schneider has summarized, "Most voters have no problem with the Democratic Party's speaking out for the interests of women, blacks, and working people; that is its traditional role as advocate for the disadvantaged and victims of discrimination. But speaking out for the interests of feminists, labor unions, and civil rights organizations is something else. That is not populism. That is interest group liberalism."[47]

The apparent evanescence of the New American Majority that Nixon assembled in 1972 derived from external forces as much as from internal dispositions of the middling classes. Just as external events called Middle America forth, just as surely did history dissolve it. This involved the waning of the passions of race and Vietnam that had divided the nation for a decade, and the ascension of rather more urgent issues. In the 1970s, American voters were increasingly preoccupied with economic concerns. The old Keynesian magic disappeared, and double-digit inflation combined with rising unemployment to produce the neologism of stagflation. America's "humiliation" by emboldened third-world oil powers, who cut America off from its foreign sources of fuel, pointed to the uncertainties of the new global economic and geopolitical order. No longer could the United States enforce the international prerogatives that once guaranteed the nation's economic growth. The rise of OPEC symbolized a more general vulnerability of the American economy in the face of competition from all corners of the world. Finally, the constitutional crisis of Watergate toppled Nixon, titular head of the New American Majority. Whether Watergate derailed or merely postponed the movement toward a Republican majority was heatedly debated, but the short-run consequence was clear: it discredited the Republican party.

The crafting of a new culture of the Right, one more self-consciously grounded in appeals to the working and lower-middle classes, did not occur full-blown, overnight. If the Right discovered the people, it did so by fits and starts, and required a good deal of mental labor. To arrive where it eventually did in 1980, it first had to suffer electoral loss and reap electoral gain. It also needed luck, the

complicity of Democrats, the accident of history, organizational resources, and, more than anything else, the vagaries of the economy.
During the Reagan years, some parts of the Right reduced all of this
complexity to a mandate for their restorationist aims. They had discovered the people, and the people who deserted them during the
New Deal had finally come to their senses, or so they thought. Emboldened by these false inferences, the Right sought to radically re-
construct moral, judicial, economic, and global life. The American
people rejected this effort. What the Right then discovered was not
the people but its own misreading of them. Its vision of the middle,
it turned out, was no more nuanced than the demonic vision of many
liberals. "The people," Middle America, Silent Majority—these were
abstractions, good for polemic and exhortation, but each was too vacuous to grasp the rival, elusive, and lambent impulses that composed
it.

NOTES

1. Indeed, the much heralded "realignment" never arrived. Defections
from the Republican party also increased, leaving a growing pool of independents. Hence, one best characterizes this volatility in partisanship as "decomposition." See Walter Dean Burnham, *Critical Elections and the Mainsprings of
American Politics* (New York: W. W. Norton, 1970), 91–193; Norman H. Nie,
Sidney Verba, and John R. Petrocik, *The Changing American Voter*, enlarged
ed. (Cambridge: Harvard University Press, 1979); James Sundquist, *Dynamics
of the Party System: Alignment and Realignment of Political Parties in the United
States*, rev. ed. (Washington, D.C.: Brookings Institution, 1983); Martin P.
Wattenberg, *The Decline of American Political Parties, 1952–1980* (Cambridge:
Harvard University Press, 1984).

2. The classic statement is Angus Campbell, Philip E. Converse, Warren
E. Miller, and Donald E. Stokes, *The American Voter* (New York: John Wiley,
1960).

3. On the marginality of the right and its "remnant identity," see George
H. Nash, *The Conservative Intellectual Movement in America since 1945* (New
York: Basic Books, 1976).

4. Ibid., chap. 8.

5. The phrase is from Michael Miles, *The Odyssey of the American Right*
(New York: Oxford University Press, 1980), 124.

6. Quoted in ibid., 143.

7. Michael Paul Rogin, *The Intellectuals and McCarthy: The Radical Specter*
(Cambridge: MIT Press, 1967), 216.

8. Miles, *Odyssey of the American Right*, 145.

9. See Nie, Verba, and Petrocik, *The Changing American Voter*, 29, 40–41.

10. William Schneider, "Democrats and Republicans, Liberals and Con-

servatives," in Seymour Martin Lipset, ed., *Party Coalitions in the 1980s* (San Francisco: Institute for Contemporary Studies, 1981), 179–231.

11. Quoted in Sundquist, *Dynamics of the Party System*, 281.

12. Ibid., chap. 12, also stresses this point.

13. Ibid., 358.

14. Quoted in Seymour Martin Lipset and Earl Raab, *The Politics of Unreason: Right-Wing Extremism in America, 1790–1977*, 2d ed. (Chicago: University of Chicago Press, 1978).

15. Ibid., 349.

16. Ibid., 350.

17. Ibid., 349.

18. Kevin Phillips, *The Emerging Republican Majority* (Garden City, N.Y.: Doubleday, 1970), 238.

19. For evidence on the militant anticommunism of Wallace supporters, see James McEvoy III, *Radicals or Conservatives? The Contemporary American Right* (Chicago: Rand McNally, 1971).

20. Cited in Marshall Frady, *Wallace*, enlarged ed. (New York: New American Library, 1975), 9.

21. Ibid., 177.

22. For the factors that distinguished Nixon and Wallace voters, see Lipset and Raab, *The Politics of Unreason*, chap. 10.

23. See William A. Rusher, *The Making of the New Majority Party* (New York: Sheed and Ward, 1975); Richard Viguerie, *The New Right: We're Ready to Lead* (Falls Church, Va.: Viguerie Co., 1980); and Robert W. Whitaker, *The New Right Papers* (New York: St. Martin's Press, 1982).

24. Chilton Williamson, Jr., "Country and Western Marxism," *National Review*, June 9, 1978, 711.

25. Kevin Phillips, *Post-Conservative America: People, Politics, and Ideology in a Time of Crisis* (New York: Random House, 1982), 31.

26. On the complexities of evolving Southern politics, see Sundquist, *Dynamics of the Party System*, 368–75; Jack Bass and Walter DeVries, *The Transformation of Southern Politics: Social Change and Political Consequence since 1945* (New York: Basic Books, 1976); and Earl Black and Merle Black, *Politics and Society in the South* (Cambridge: Harvard University Press, 1987).

27. Nie, Verba, and Petrocik, *The Changing American Voter*, 269.

28. Burnham, *Critical Elections*, 189.

29. See *George C. Wallace and the Politics of Powerlessness: The Wallace Campaigns for the Presidency, 1964–1976* (New Brunswick, N.J.: Transaction Books, 1981), chaps. 4–6.

30. For the importance of conceptions of justice in shaping ethnic reaction, see Nathan Glazer and Daniel P. Moynihan, "New York City in 1970," in *Behind the Melting Pot: The Negroes, Puerto Ricans, Jews, Italians, and Irish of New York City*, 2d ed. (Cambridge: MIT Press, 1970), p. lv; also see Jonathan Rieder, *Canarsie: The Jews and Italians of Brooklyn against Liberalism* (Cambridge: Harvard University Press, 1985), chap. 4.

31. Cited in Rieder, *Canarsie*, 112.

32. Richard Hamilton concluded from his survey research, "The adoption of the Black Power rhetoric had the added consequence of frightening large numbers of persons who were either in sympathy or, at minimum, favorably inclined to the goals of integration and improving the condition of blacks" (*Class and Politics in the United States* [New York: John Wiley, 1972], 551).

33. See Rieder, *Canarsie*, chap. 3, 6–7.

34. See Sundquist, *Dynamics of the Party System*, 383.

35. See Lewis Chester, Godfrey Hodgson, and Bruce Page, *An American Melodrama: The Presidential Campaign of 1968* (New York: Viking, 1969), 503–604; and Byron Shafer, *Quiet Revolution: The Struggle for the Democratic Party and the Shaping of Post-Reform Politics* (New York: Russell Sage Foundation, 1983).

36. See the interesting, if highly partisan, account by F. Clifton White, *Suite 3505: The Story of the Draft Goldwater Movement* (New Rochelle, N.Y.: Arlington House, 1967).

37. Quoted in Garry Wills, *Nixon Agonistes: The Crisis of the Self-Made Man* (Boston: Houghton Mifflin, 1970), 310.

38. Quoted in ibid., 287.

39. Quoted in Chester, Hodgson, and Page, *An American Melodrama*, 262.

40. See Phillips, *The Emerging Republican Majority*, 79, 170–74, 352.

41. Richard Scammon and Ben J. Wattenberg, *The Real Majority* (New York: Coward-McCann, 1970), 100.

42. Jonathan Schell, *The Time of Illusion: An Historical and Reflective Account of the Nixon Era* (New York: Random House, 1975), 78.

43. Spiro Agnew, Address, Delaware Republican Dinner, October 14, 1970, in Murray Friedman, *Overcoming Middle Class Rage* (Philadelphia: Westminster Press, 1971), 317–18.

44. See Sundquist, *Dynamics of the Party System*, 394.

45. "Candidate Style and Voter Alignment in 1976," in Seymour Martin Lipset, ed., *Emerging Coalitions in American Politics* (San Francisco: Institute for Contemporary Studies, 1978), 173.

46. Rogin, *The Intellectuals and McCarthy*, 50.

47. "What the Democrats Must Do," *New Republic*, March 11, 1985, 16–20.

10   The Changing Shape of Power: A Realignment in Public Policy

Thomas Byrne Edsall

*T*HE PAST twenty years in America have been marked by two central political developments. The first is the continuing erosion of the political representation of the economic interests of those in the bottom half of the income distribution. The second is the growing dominance of the political process by a network of elites that includes fund-raisers, the leadership of interest groups, specialists in the technology and manipulation of elections, and an army of Washington lobbyists and law firms—elites that augment and often overshadow political officeholders and the candidates for office themselves.

This shift in the balance of power has not been accompanied by realignment of the electorate, although the shape and relative strength of the Republican and Democratic parties have changed dramatically.

Twice during the past twenty years, the Republican party has had the opportunity to gain majority status: in the early 1970s, and again after the 1980 election. The first opportunity emerged when the fragile Democratic coalition was fractured by the independent presidential bid of Alabama governor George C. Wallace in 1968. The Democratic party then amplified its own vulnerability four years later with the nomination of Sen. George S. McGovern, Democrat of South Dakota, whose candidacy alienated a spectrum of traditional Democrats from Detroit to Atlanta. This potential Republican opportunity crumbled, however, when the web of scandals known as Watergate produced across-the-board setbacks for the GOP in campaigns ranging from city council contests to the presidency in the elections of 1974 and 1976.

The period from 1978 to 1981 offered even more fertile terrain for the Republican party. Not only had Democratic loyalties dating back to the depression of the 1930s been further weakened during the presidency of Jimmy Carter, with the emergence of simultaneous inflation and high unemployment, but the candidacy of Ronald Reagan provided the Republican party with its first substantial opportunity to heal the fissures that had relegated the GOP to minority status for two generations. In Reagan, the party long identified with the rich found a leader equipped to bridge divisions between the country club and the fundamentalist church, between the executives of the Fortune 500 and the membership of the National Rifle Association. Just as Watergate halted Republican momentum in the early 1970s, however, the severe recession of 1981–82 put the brakes on what had the earmarks of a potential Republican takeover, for the first time since 1954, of both branches of Congress. In the first two years of the Reagan administration, the Republican party captured the Senate by a six-vote margin and, with a gain of thirty-two House seats, acquired de facto control of the House in an alliance with southern Democratic conservatives. The recession, however, resulted in the return of twenty-six House seats to the Democrats in 1982, and with those seats went the chance to establish Republican dominance of the federal government.

As the two parties have gained and lost strength, the underlying alteration of the balance of political power over the past decade has continued in a shift of power among the rich, the poor, and the middle class; among blacks and whites; among regions in the country; and among such major competitors for the federal dollar as the defense and social services sectors.

The past twenty years have, in effect, produced a policy realignment in the absence of a political realignment. The major beneficiaries of this policy realignment are the affluent, while those in the bottom half of the income distribution, particularly those whose lives are the most economically marginal, have reaped the fewest rewards or have experienced declines in their standard of living.

A major factor contributing to this development is the decline of political parties: In the United States, as well as in most democratic countries, parties perform the function of representing major interests and classes. As parties erode, the groups that suffer most are those with the fewest resources to protect themselves. In other words, the continued collapse of the broad representation role of political parties in the United States has direct consequences for the distribution of income.[1]

As the role of parties in mobilizing voters has declined, much of the control over both election strategy and issue selection—key functions in defining the national agenda—has shifted to a small, often interlocking, network of campaign specialists, fund-raisers, and lobbyists. While this element of politics is among the most difficult to quantify, there are some rough measures. For example, there are approximately thirty Republican and Democratic consultants and pollsters, almost all based in Washington, who at this writing are the principal strategists in almost every presidential and competitive Senate race, in addition to playing significant roles in gubernatorial, House, and local referenda contests.[2]

At another level, the years from 1974 to 1984 show a steady growth in the financial dependence of House and Senate candidates on political action committees (PACs), vehicles through which money is transferred from organized interest groups to elected officeholders. In that decade, the PAC share of the total cost of House campaigns went from 17 percent to 36 percent, while individual contributions fell from 73 percent to 47 percent, with the remainder coming from parties, loans, and other sources. For House Democratic incumbents, 1984 marked the first year in which PACs were the single most important source of cash; they provided 47 percent of the total, compared with 45 percent from individuals.[3]

This shift has, in turn, magnified the influence of a group of lobbyists who organize Washington fund-raisers for House and Senate incumbents, among whom are Thomas Hale Boggs, Jr., whose clients include the Trial Lawyers Association, the Chicago Board of Options Exchange, and Chrysler; Edward H. Forgotson, whose clients include Enserch Corp., the Hospital Corp. of America, and the Texas Oil and Gas Corp.; Robert J. Keefe, whose clients include Westinghouse and the American Medical Association; and J. D. Williams, whose clients include General Electric Co. and the National Realty Committee. The Washington consulting-lobbying firm of Black, Manafort, Stone, Kelly and Atwater provides perhaps the best example of the range of political and special interests one firm can represent. In 1987, one partner, Charles Black, managed the presidential bid of Rep. Jack Kemp (R—N.Y.); another, Lee Atwater, managed the campaign of Vice-President George Bush; and a third, Peter Kelly, was a principal fund-raiser for the campaign of Sen. Albert Gore (D—Tenn.). At the same time, the firm's clients have included the Dominican Republic, the anti-Communist insurgency in Angola run by Jonas Savimbi, Salomon Brothers, the government of Barbados, the Natural Gas Supply Association, and, briefly, the Marcos government in the Philippines. In addition, the firm has served as principal political consultant to the Senate campaigns of Phil Gramm (R—Tex.), Jesse Helms (R—N.C.), and Paula Hawkins (formerly R—Fla.).

A few general indicators of the scope of lobbying and political party bureaucracies point to the sizable influence small elites can exercise over public policy. In 1986, there were almost 10,000 people employed as registered Washington lobbyists, with 3,500 of these serving as officers of 1,800 trade and professional organizations, including labor unions; another 1,300 were employed by individual corporations, and approximately 1,000 represented organizations ranging from the National Right to Life Association to the Sierra Club. The six major political party committees headquartered in Washington now employ roughly 1,200 people. The creation and expansion of such ideological think tanks as the Heritage Foundation, the Center for National Policy, the Urban Institute, the American Enterprise Institute, the Cato Institute, and the Hoover Institution have established whole networks of influential public policy entrepreneurs specializing in media relations and in targeted position papers. Within a general framework of increasingly monopolized American mass media—both print and electronic—the growth of the Gannett and Los Angeles Times–Mirror chains are examples of an ever greater concentration of power within the media, just as the acquisition of NBC by General Electric has functioned to submerge a major network within the larger goals of the nation's sixth biggest corporation. Staffers acquiring expertise and influence on Capitol Hill, in the executive branch, and throughout the regulatory apparatus routinely travel to the private sector—and sometimes back again—through the so-called revolving door. In effect, an entire class of public and private specialists in the determination of government policy and political strategy has been created—a process replicated in miniature at the state level.

The rise to authority of elites independent of the electorate at large, empowered to make decisions without taking into direct account the economic interests of voters, is part of a much larger shift in the balance of power involving changed voting patterns, the decline of organized labor, a restructuring of the employment marketplace, and a transformed system of political competition. This power shift, in turn, has produced a policy realignment most apparent in the alteration of both the *pre-tax* distribution of income and the *after-tax* distribution of income. In both cases, the distribution has become increasingly regressive. The alteration of the pretax distribution of income is the subject of a broad debate in which there are those, particularly critics on the left, who argue that growing regressivity emerges from government policies encouraging weakened union representation and a proliferation of low-wage service industry jobs. On the other side, more conservative analysts contend that changes

TABLE 10.1

SHARES OF PRE-TAX HOUSEHOLD INCOME, BY INCOME DISTRIBUTION

Income Group	*Year*	
	1980 (%)	*1985* (%)
Quintile[a]		
Bottom	4.1	3.9
Second	10.2	9.7
Third	16.8	16.3
Fourth	24.8	24.4
Top	44.2	45.7
Top 5%	16.5	17.6

Sources: Bureau of the Census, *Estimating After-Tax Money Income Distribution*, Series P-23, no. 126, issued August 1983; and ibid., *Household After-Tax Income: 1985*, Series P-23, no. 151, issued June 1987.

[a] A quintile is a block of 20% of the population.

in the pre-tax distribution result from natural alterations of the marketplace and the workplace, as the United States adjusts to a changing economic and demographic environment.[4] The figures in table 10.1, derived from Census Bureau data, indicate changes in the distribution of pretax household income from 1980 through 1985, the most recent year for which data from the census is available.

The data clearly show a growing disparity in the distribution of income. Of the five quintiles, all but those in the top 20 percent have seen their share of household income decline. In addition, most of the gains of the top 20 percent have, in fact, been concentrated in the top 5 percent of the income distribution. The gain of 1.1 percent for the top 5 percent translates into a total of $38.8 billion (in 1987 dollars) more for this segment of the population than if the income distribution had remained constant after 1980.[5] These regressive trends were, moreover, intensified by the tax policies enacted between 1980 and 1985, as demonstrated in table 10.2, based on Census Bureau data.

What had been a $38.8 billion improvement in the status of the top 5 percent in pre-tax income over these six years becomes a $49.5 billion gain in after-tax income, while the bottom 80 percent of the population saw larger losses in its share of after-tax income between 1980 and 1985 than it had seen in the case of pre-tax income. These

TABLE 10.2

SHARES OF AFTER-TAX HOUSEHOLD INCOME, BY INCOME DISTRIBUTION

| | Year | |
Income Group	1980 (%)	1985 (%)
Quintile[a]		
Bottom	4.9	4.6
Second	11.6	11.0
Third	17.9	17.2
Fourth	25.1	24.7
Top	40.6	42.6
Top 5%	14.1	15.5

Sources: Bureau of the Census, *Estimating After-Tax Money Income Distribution*, Series P-23, no. 126, issued August 1983; and ibid., *Household After-Tax Income: 1985*, Series P-23, no. 151, issued June 1987.

[a] A quintile is a block of 20% of the population.

findings are even more sharply delineated in a November 1987 study by the Congressional Budget Office showing that from 1977 to 1988, 70 percent of the population experienced very modest increases in after-tax income or, for those in the bottom 40 percent, net drops, when changes over that period in the federal income tax, the Social Security tax, corporate tax, and excise taxes are taken into account. In contrast, those in the seventy-first to ninetieth percentiles experienced a modest improvement, and those in the top 10 percent significantly improved their standard of living. For those at the very top, the gains have been enormous. Table 10.3, developed from Congressional Budget Office data, shows that distribution.

What these tables point to is a major redistribution of economic power in the private marketplace and of political power in the public sector, which, in turn, has been reflected in very concrete terms in family income patterns. One of the major characteristics, then, of the post–New Deal period in American politics has been a reversal of the progressive redistribution of income that underlay the policies of the administrations of Franklin Roosevelt and Harry Truman.

In the competition between the defense and social welfare sectors, the outcome of a parallel, although more recent, shift in the balance of power can be seen in the years from 1980 through 1987. During this period, the share of the federal budget going to national defense grew from 22.7 percent in 1980 to 28.4 percent in 1987. At the same

TABLE 10.3
CHANGES IN ESTIMATED AVERAGE AFTER-TAX FAMILY INCOME,
BY INCOME DISTRIBUTION
(IN 1987 DOLLARS)

Income Group	1977 Average Income ($)	1988 Average Income ($)	Percentage Change (+ or −)	Dollar Change (+ or −)
Decile[a]				
First (poor)	3,528	3,157	− 10.5	− 371
Second	7,084	6,990	− 1.3	− 94
Third	10,740	10,614	− 1.2	− 126
Fourth	14,323	14,266	− 0.4	− 57
Fifth	18,043	18,076	+ 0.2	+ 33
Sixth	22,009	22,259	+ 1.1	+ 250
Seventh	26,240	27,038	+ 3.0	+ 798
Eighth	31,568	33,282	+ 5.4	+ 1,718
Ninth	39,236	42,323	+ 7.9	+ 3,087
Tenth (rich)	70,459	89,783	+ 27.4	+ 19,324
Top 5%	90,756	124,651	+ 37.3	+ 33,895
Top 1%	174,498	303,900	+ 74.2	+ 129,402
All groups	22,184	26,494	+ 9.6	+ 2,310

Source: Congressional Budget Offices, *The Changing Distribution of Federal Taxes: 1975–1990*, October 1987.

[a] A decile is a block of 10% of the population.

time, the share of federal dollars collectively going to education, training, employment, social services, health, income security, and housing dropped from 25.5 percent in 1980 to 18.3 percent in 1987.[6]

In many respects, these policy changes reflect the rising strength of the Republican party. In terms of tax policy and the balance of spending between defense and social programs, the Republican party under Ronald Reagan has been the driving force pushing the country to the right. During the past ten years, the Republican party has made substantial gains in the competition for the allegiance of voters, gaining near parity by 1987, reducing what had been a 20- to 25-point Democratic advantage in terms of self-identification to a six- or seven-point edge.[7]

The income distribution trends and the shifts in budget priorities began, however, before the Republican party took over the presidency and the U.S. Senate in 1980. The emergence of a vital, competitive Republican party is less a cause of the changed balance of power in the country than a reflection of the underlying forces at work in the post–New Deal phase of American politics.

Together, these forces—which include the deterioration of organized labor, the continued presence of divisive racial conflict, the shift from manufacturing to service industries, the slowing rates of economic growth, the threat of international competition to domestic production, the replacement of political organization with political technology, and the growing class-skew of voter turnout—have severely undermined the capacity of those in the bottom half of the income distribution to form an effective political coalition.

In tracing the erosion of the left wing of the Democratic party in the United States, it is difficult to overestimate the importance of the collapse of the labor movement. In 1970, the continuing growth in the number of labor union members came to a halt. Unions represented 20.7 million workers that year, or 27.9 percent of the nonagricultural work force. Through 1980, the number of workers represented by unions remained roughly the same, dropping slightly to 20.1 million employees by 1980. At the same time, however, the total work force had grown, so that the percentage of workers who were represented by unions fell to 23 percent in 1980. With the election of Ronald Reagan, however, the decline of organized labor began to accelerate sharply, a process encouraged by Reagan's firing of 11,500 striking PATCO air traffic controllers, and by the appointment of pro-management officials to the National Labor Relations Board and to the Department of Labor. From 1980 to 1986, not only did the share of the work force represented by unions drop from 23 percent to 17.5 percent, but the number of workers in unions began to fall precipitously for the first time in fifty years, dropping by 3.1 million men and women, from 20.1 million to 17 million, in 1986. During the first half of the 1980s, almost all the decline in union membership was among whites employed in private industry.[8]

The decline of organized labor dovetailed with a continuing shift from traditional manufacturing, mining, and construction employment to work in the technology and service industries. From 1970 to 1986, the number of jobs in goods-producing industries, which lend themselves to unionization, grew only from 23.8 million to 24.9 million, while employment in the service industries, which are much more resistant to labor organizing, shot up from 47.3 million to 75.2 million.[9]

The difficulties of organized labor were compounded by the unexpected decision on the part of many of the major corporations in the early 1970s to abandon what had been a form of tacit détente between labor and management, in which Fortune 500 companies kept labor peace through agreements amounting to a form of profit sharing by means of automatic cost-of-living pay hikes. Faced with growing competition from foreign producers—in 1968, car imports exceeded exports for the first time in the nation's history, an unmistakable signal that domestic producers of all goods faced serious foreign competition—major American companies dropped the fundamentally cordial relations that had characterized the largest part of postwar union negotiations. Catching the leaders of organized labor entirely unprepared, these corporations adopted a tough, adversarial approach regarding both pay and fringe benefits, willing to break union shops and to relocate facilities either abroad or in nonunion communities in the South and Southwest.[10]

The decline of organized labor was particularly damaging to the Democratic party because unions represent one of the few remaining institutional links between working-class voters and the Democratic party. The decline of political parties has resulted in the end of the clubhouse tie between the party of Franklin Delano Roosevelt and the blue-collar voters of row- and tract-house neighborhoods throughout the Northeast and Midwest. In addition, it is among these white, blue-collar workers that the racial conflicts within the Democratic party have been the most divisive. Interviews[11] with whites in Dearborn, Michigan, the west-side suburbs of Birmingham, Chicago, Atlanta, and New Orleans—all communities that have suffered major industrial layoffs and that are either part of or adjoin cities now run by Democratic black mayors—reveal voters who are disenchanted with the unions that failed to protect their jobs, and with a local Democratic party no longer controlled by whites. Race, which previously severed the tie between the white South and the Democratic party, has, in cities with black mayors, served to produce white Republican voting, not only for president but for local offices that once were unchallenged Democratic bastions.[12]

These developments, in the 1970s, contributed significantly to the creation of a vacuum of power within the Democratic party, allowing the party to be taken over, in part, by its most articulate and procedurally sophisticated wing: affluent, liberal reformers. This faction capitalized first on the public outcry against police violence at the Chicago presidential convention in 1968, and then on the Watergate scandals in the mid-1970s, to force priority consideration of a series of reforms involving campaign finance, the presidential nominating process, the congressional seniority system, the congressional code of ethics—and an expansion of the federal role in regulating the environment, through creation of the Environmental Protection Agency and new water- and air-pollution standards. The strength of this wing of the Democratic party subsided during the 1980s, although its leverage within the party has been institutionalized through the creation of a host of primaries and caucuses in the presidential selection process, giving disproportionate influence to middle- and upper-middle-class voters and interests in a party that claims to represent the nation's working and lower-middle classes. The turnout in primaries and in caucuses is skewed in favor of the affluent and upper-middle class.[13] In addition, these delegate selection processes have been contributing factors in the acceleration of the decline of political organizations in working-class communities.

The Democratic agenda set in the 1970s by the reform wing of the party was, however, more important for what it omitted and neglected than for what was included. The ascendancy of the reformers took place just when the fissures within the Democratic party had become most apparent. In 1968, 9.9 million mostly Democratic voters turned to George C. Wallace, the segregationist-populist governor of Alabama, and they strayed off the Democratic reservation in 1972 when Nixon beat McGovern by a margin of 47.2 million votes to 29.2 million. The cultural and ideological gulf that had steadily widened between these voters and the wings of the Democratic party supporting the antiwar movement, gay rights, women's rights, and civil rights had reached such proportions in the early and mid 1970s that rapprochement between warring factions was difficult, if not impossible.

The rise to prominence within the Democratic party of a well-to-do liberal-reform wing worked in other ways to compound the divisions in the party. Relatively comfortable in their own lives, reformers failed to recognize the growing pressure of marginal tax rates on working- and lower-middle-class voters. The progressive rate system of the federal income tax remained effectively unchanged from the early 1950s through the 1970s, so that the series of sharply rising marginal tax rates that had originally been designed to affect only the upper-middle class and rich, began to directly impinge on regular Democratic voters whose wages had been forced up by inflation.[14] By neglecting to adjust the marginal rate system to account for inflation, in combination with repeated raising of the highly regressive Social Security tax, Democrats effectively encouraged the tax revolt of the 1970s which, in turn, provided a critically important source of support to the conservative movement and to the rise of the Republican party.

The pressures of the tax system on traditional Democratic voting blocks were aggravated by the sudden halt in 1973 of what had been steadily rising median family incomes since the end of World War II. Family income in 1981 dollars rose from $12,341 in 1947, to $17,259 in 1960, to $23,111 in 1970, and it topped out at $24,663 in 1973—a level that was not exceeded at least through 1986.[15] Of all the blows

to the Democratic coalition in the 1960s and 1970s, the stagnation of
family income had the potential to inflict the most severe long-range
damage. It undermined the party's basic claim that the system of government established in the years following the New Deal promised
continued growth and the prospect for a better life for each new generation.

On the Republican side, the same developments that debilitated
the Democratic coalition served to strengthen ascendant constituencies of the Right. For a brief period in the late 1970s and early
1980s, the constituencies and interests underpinning the Republican
party had the potential to establish a new conservative majority in the
electorate. The tax revolt, the rise of the religious right, the mobilization of much of the business community in support of the Republican party, renewed public support for defense spending, the politi-
cal-financial mobilization of the affluent, and the development of a
conservative economic theory promising growth through lower
taxes—all combined to empower the political right to a degree unprecedented since the 1920s.

Proposed tax cuts provided an essential common ground for the
right-of-center coalition that provided the core of the Reagan revolution. The combination of corporate tax reductions and individual
tax cuts embodied in the 1981 tax bill served to unify a divided business community by providing a shared legislative goal, to strengthen
the commitment of the affluent to the Republican party, and to attract white working- and lower-middle-class former Democrats who
had seen their paychecks eaten away by inflation-driven higher marginal rates. The tax cut theme was adopted as a central element of
the speeches of such religious-right figures as the Rev. Jerry Falwell
of the Moral Majority, Ed McAteer of the Religious Roundtable, and
the Rev. Marion G. (Pat) Robertson of the Christian Broadcast Network.

The sustained attacks by Democratic reformers on traditional political organizations, and their demands for changes in the financing
of campaigns, meshed perfectly with the techniques developed by the
Right in the acquisition of power. The deterioration of old-guard organizations, which were effectively taken out of the presidential nomination process by the reforms of the early 1970s, accelerated the
shift toward a political system dominated by technology—a highly sophisticated mix of detailed polling, focus groups, targeted direct
mail, and television and radio commercials precisely tailored in response to the flood of information concerning public attitudes.

The shift to expensive technology, in turn, elevated fund-raising
from a critically important factor in campaigns, to the dominant fac-

TABLE 10.4
AMOUNT OF MONEY RAISED BY THE THREE MAJOR COMMITTEES
OF THE REPUBLICAN AND DEMOCRATIC PARTIES
(IN MILLIONS OF DOLLARS)

	Election Cycle				
	1985–86	1983–84	1981–82	1979–80	1977–78
Democrats raised	61.8	98.5	39.3	37.2	26.4
Republicans raised	252.4	297.9	215.0	169.5	84.5

Source: Federal Election Commission report issued May 31, 1987.

tor. The sharp escalation of the importance of money gave the Republican party a decided advantage over the Democratic party. Campaign contributors are overwhelmingly concentrated among the upper-middle class and the rich, just the groups among whom Republican allegiance is strongest.[16] The key institutions in the development of campaign technology, and in transferring such technology to candidates, are the six national party committees—the Democratic and Republican National, Senatorial, and Congressional campaign committees. It is at this level that the disparity between the parties has been most apparent. As shown in table 10.4, in the decade between the 1977–78 and 1985–86 election cycles, the Republican party maintained a decisive edge over the Democratic party.

The Republican party fund-raising advantage was, in many ways, encouraged by the campaign finance reforms enacted by a Democratic Congress in 1974. These reforms placed a $1,000 limit on individual contributions to any candidate for federal office, while allowing contributions of up to $20,000 to political party committees. For the Democratic party, which had depended on large contributions in excess of the new legal limits,[17] the 1974 law became a tourniquet, stemming the flow of vital cash resources. For the Republican party, in contrast, the campaign reforms of the mid-1970s served as an invitation to capitalize on the new technology of direct mail, in order to convert the pro-Republican tilt of the affluent into a full-fledged commitment of money from literally millions of donors. By 1984, the Republican National Committee had built a donor base of 1.6 million people, a number almost matched by the National Republican Congressional Committee.[18] In effect, the combination of the rise of regulated money in campaigns and the decline in the role of traditional neighborhood-based clubs and organizations was functioning to reduce the participation of working- and lower-middle-class voters in the political process, while encouraging the direct-mail mobilization of the affluent.

This growing political tilt in favor of the affluent is further reflected in voting turnout patterns over the past twenty years. During this period, the class-skewing of voting in favor of the affluent has grown significantly. In the presidential election year of 1964, the self-reported turnout among members of professions associated with the middle and upper classes was 83.2 percent, compared with 66.1 percent among those employed in manual jobs, including skilled crafts, a difference of 17.1 points; by 1980, the spread between the two had grown to 25 points, 73 percent to 48 percent. In the off-year election of 1966, the percentage-point spread in terms of voter turnout between middle-to-upper-class job holders and those employed in manual jobs was 18.1 percent; by 1978, this had grown to a 23.8-percent spread.[19] While overall turnout has been declining, the drop has been most severe among those in the bottom third of the income distribution.

For the Republican party, these turnout trends were a political bonanza, accentuated by trends in the correlation between income and both voting and partisan commitment. Through the 1950s, 1960s, and into the early 1970s, the sharp class divisions that characterized the depression-era New Deal coalition structure gave way to diffuse voting patterns with relatively little correlation between income and allegiance to the Democratic or Republican party. By 1980 and 1982, with the election of Reagan and then the enactment of the budget and tax bills of 1981, the correlation between income and voting began to reemerge with a vengeance. By 1982, the single most important determinant of probable voting, aside from membership in either the Republican or Democratic party, became income, with the Democratic margin steadily declining as one moved up the ladder.[20] The changes in partisan allegiance are shown in table 10.5. The numbers in the table are the percentage-point Democratic advantage in the income group (+) or the Democratic disadvantage (−). Thus, for example, the very poor were 18 points more Democratic than Republican in 1956, and 36 points more Democratic than Republican in 1984.

In other words, the Reagan years polarized the electorate along sharp income lines. While income made almost no difference in the partisan loyalties of 90 percent of the population in 1956, by 1984 income became one of the sharpest dividing lines between Democrats and Republicans. In 1956, the very poor were only 5 percentage points more likely to be Democratic than the upper-middle class, and 40 points more likely than the affluent top 10 percent of the income

TABLE 10.5
DEMOCRATIC PARTY ALLEGIANCE, BY INCOME, 1956 AND 1984

Income Group	Percentage-Point Advantage (+) or Disadvantage (−)	
	1956	1984
Very poor (bottom 10%)	+ 18	+ 36
Working and lower-middle class (11–30%)	+ 22	+ 29
Middle class (31–60%)	+ 17	+ 6
Upper-middle class (61–90%)	+ 13	0
Affluent (91–100%)	− 22	− 33

Source: Martin B. Wattenberg, "The Hollow Realignment: Partisan Change in a Candidate-Centered Era" (Paper delivered at the 1985 annual meeting of the American Political Science Association, based on data from the National Election Studies).

distribution. By 1984, however, the spread between the poor and the upper-middle class reached 36 points, and between the poor and affluent, 69 points. These income correlations with partisan allegiance were replicated, in part, by actual voting patterns, as shown in table 10.6.

These figures accurately describe an electorate polarized by income, but what they mask are the effects of black and white voter participation on the figures. The civil rights movement, and civil rights legislation enacted in the 1960s, enfranchised millions of blacks who, in 1956, were barred from voting. During the twenty-eight years from 1956 to 1984, roughly 4.2 million blacks entered the electorate.[21] During the same period, blacks' allegiance to the Democratic party, which in 1956 held their loyalty by a 34-percentage-point edge, increased to provide an overwhelming 72-percentage-point Democratic edge in 1984.[22] This infusion of black Democratic support sharply increased the low-income tilt of the party: in 1984, the median family income for whites was $28,674, while for blacks it was $15,982.[23]

The Reagan revolution was, at its core, a revolution led by the affluent. The class polarization of voters reflected in tables 10.5 and 10.6 cut across the country, but nowhere were the trends stronger than in the South, where a realignment in miniature took place among the white elite. In the 1950s, Democratic allegiance in the

TABLE 10.6
REPUBLICAN PERCENTAGE OF PRESIDENTIAL VOTE, BY INCOME, 1956 AND 1984

Income Group	Eisenhower, 1956 (%)	Reagan, 1984 (%)
Very poor (bottom 10%)	59	36
Working and lower-middle class (11–30%)	56	43
Middle class (31–60%)	58	57
Upper-middle class (61–90%)	57	64
Affluent (91–100%)	75	75

Source: Martin P. Wattenberg, "The Hollow Realignment: Partisan Change in a Candidate-Centered Era" (Paper delivered at the 1985 annual meeting of the American Political Science Association, based on data from the National Election Studies).

South was strongest among the most well-to-do whites, for whom the Democratic party was the vehicle for maintaining the pre–civil rights social structure of the Confederate states. These voters gave the Democratic party their support by a 5 to 1 margin, higher than that of any other income group in the South. By the 1980s, in the aftermath of a civil rights movement supported by the Democratic party, these same voters had become the most Republican in the South. "The class cleavage had reversed itself," John R. Petrocik, of UCLA, noted.[24] Whites, particularly white men, have become increasingly Republican as blacks have become the most consistent source of Democratic votes. In the five presidential elections from 1968 to 1984, only one Democrat, Jimmy Carter, received more than 40 percent of the white vote, and by 1984, white, male Protestants voted for Reagan over Mondale by a margin of 74 to 26.[25]

The Reagan revolution would, however, have been a political failure if it had not gained extensive support from voters outside the upper-middle class. In addition to the deep inroads made in previously Democratic working-class communities in northern urban areas, perhaps the single most important source of new support for the Republican party has been the religious Right.

In a far shorter period, voters identifying themselves as born-again Christians radically shifted their voting in presidential elections. Between 1976 and 1984, these voters went from casting a 56-to-44 margin for the Democratic candidate, Jimmy Carter, to one of the highest levels of support of any group for the reelection of President Reagan in 1984: 81 to 19, according to *New York Times/*CBS exit polls. This shift represents, in effect, a gain of eight million voters for the GOP.

As a political resource, support among born-again Christians represents not only a loyal core of voters, but a growing core. In contrast with such mainline churches as the United Methodist Church, the United Church of Christ, and the United Presbyterians, which experienced membership losses from 1970 to 1980, the fundamentalist, evangelical, and charismatic churches have seen their congregations grow at an explosive rate: the Southern Baptist Convention by 16 percent, the Assemblies of God by 70 percent, and Seventh Day Adventists by 36 percent.[26]

The Republican party has, in turn, been the major beneficiary of an internal power struggle taking place within the Southern Baptist Convention, now the largest Protestant denomination. During a ten-year fight, the denomination has been taken over by its conservative wing, believers in the "absolute inerrancy" of the Bible. This wing of the denomination, in turn, has been a leading force within the broader religious Right, as such pastors as Adrian Rogers, James T. Draper, Jr., and Charles F. Stanley—all outspoken conservatives—have won the denomination's presidency. The move to the right has been reflected in the ranks of the denomination, producing what amounts to a realignment of the ministry of the Southern Baptist Convention. James L. Guth, of Furman University, found that in just three years, surveys of Southern Baptist ministers showed a remarkable shift from a strong majority in 1981 favoring the Democratic party, 41 to 29, to nearly 70 percent in 1984 favoring the GOP, 66 to 26.[27]

The growth of Republican strength is not, however, confined to evangelical and charismatic Christians, and the party appears to be developing a much broader religious base as part of its core constituency. In one of the most interesting recent analyses[28] of voting trends, Frederick T. Steeper, of Market Opinion Research, and John Petrocik, of UCLA, have found that since 1976, one of the sharpest partisan cleavages emerging among white voters in the electorate is between those who attend church regularly and those who never go to church.[29] This represents a major change from past findings. In the period from 1952 to 1960, there was no statistical difference between the Democratic and Republican loyalties of white churchgoers and nonchurchgoers. By the elections of 1972 and 1976, a modest difference began to appear, with nonchurchgoers 7 percentage points more likely to be Democrats than regular churchgoers. By 1986, however, the spread had grown to a striking 35-point difference, with regular churchgoers identifying themselves as Republicans by a 22-point margin, and with nonchurchgoers identifying themselves as Democrats by a 13-point edge. The partisan spread between churchgoers and nonchurchgoers was most extreme among white Northern Protestants (51 points) and Catholics (52 points). These findings dovetail with studies showing that the memberships of such Establishment, nonevangelical denominations as the Methodists, Episcopalians, Lutherans, and Presbyterians were significantly more supportive of the election of Ronald Reagan than the electorate at large.[30]

The changing shape of the electorate has provided the Republican party with a base of support that has not proved adequate to produce a realignment. It has, however, proven sufficient to establish the GOP as the favored party in presidential elections, and as a full-fledged competitor in any Senate or gubernatorial contest in the nation, despite the erosion of some support. Since the election of 1980, many of the constituencies that provided vitality and strength to the Republican party have floundered or split. The right-wing PACs—the National Conservative Political Action Committee, the Free-Congress PAC, the Conservative Victory Fund, the Christian Voice Moral Government Fund—had all fallen on hard times by the end of 1987, and were no longer significant participants in the political process. In addition, after the 1986 election, when the GOP lost the Senate, the flow of cash to the major Republican committees began to slow significantly, lessening the financial advantage of the GOP over the Democratic party.[31] The business community, which had been unified behind the 1981 budget and tax bills, splintered into warring factions over the 1986 Tax Reform Act, over monetary policy in the wake of the October 1987 stock market debacle, and over the continuing debate concerning protectionist trade legislation.[32] Perhaps most important, after successfully polarizing the two parties along issues of taxation, defense, and domestic spending, the Reagan administration failed to expand its agenda in the mid-1980s to produce the kind of issues that divide the electorate, and separate the parties one from the other in ways essential to genuine realignment.[33] This failure to maintain a polarizing agenda was in sharp contrast with the Conservative party in England, where Prime Minister Margaret Thatcher vowed, "Our third election victory was only a staging post on a much longer journey. . . . Whose blood would run faster at the prospect of five years of consolidation?" as she outlined initiatives on education, property taxation, and home ownership designed to strengthen the grip of the Conservative party on Britain immediately upon winning a third term.[34] Furthermore, the coalition of the Right in the United States faces the prospect of divisive struggles on foreign policy, particularly conflicts over arms control policies that pit Republican centrists against the deeply anti-Communist conservative wing of the party; and it faces as well continuing conflicts over party policy on "social issues," between GOP party regulars and the growing political army of fundamentalist Christians—in addition to conflicts between these two factions over the control of local party structures. Perhaps most important, however, is the inherent difficulty for a party that receives its strongest levels of support from the affluent in directing effective economic appeals to the lower-middle class and the working class.

Despite conflicts and a certain loss of ideological and programmatic vitality, the development of a Republican party whose core supporters are concentrated among the affluent and among the religious gives the party a continuing advantage in low-turnout elections in which money plays a central role. Not only do the affluent vote in the highest percentages, and provide the best target for fund-raising solicitations; in a political universe where the strength of such Democratic institutions as the union hall and the political clubhouse are steadily declining, the neighborhood church provides one of the few remaining means—outside of television—of contacting and mobilizing voters.

Cumulatively, developments over the past twenty years—the deterioration of the labor movement; economically polarized partisanship; the skewing of turnout patterns by income; stagnation of the median family income; the rising importance of political money; the emergence of a Republican core composed of the well-to-do and the religious; the globalization of the economy; and competition from foreign producers—have combined to disperse constituencies and groups seeking to push the country to the left, and to consolidate those on the right. The consequences of that shift are most readily seen in the figures in table 10.3, which show that 80 percent of the population has experienced a net loss in after-tax income between 1977 and 1988, while the top 5 percent has seen average family income grow by $26,134, and the top 1 percent, by $117,222.

In the long run the prospects are for the maintenance of a strong, conservative Republican party, continuing to set the national agenda on basic distributional issues, no matter which party holds the White House. Barring a major economic catastrophe, or a large-scale inter-

national conflict, the basic shift from manufacturing to service industry jobs is likely to continue to undermine the political left in this
country, not only for the reasons outlined earlier in this essay, but
also by weakening economically—and therefore politically—those in
the bottom 40 percent of the income distribution.

In the thirty-year period spanning 1949 to 1979, the number of
manufacturing jobs grew by an average of three million a decade,
from 17.6 million in 1949, to 20.4 million in 1959, to 24.4 million in
1969, and finally to a high of 26.5 million in 1979. This growth in no
way kept pace with the increase in service industry jobs, which shot
up from 26.2 million in 1949 to 63.4 million in 1979,[35] but the continuing, if modest, manufacturing expansion provided a partial cushion in an economy going through a major restructuring—a restructuring involving the loss of 950,000 jobs in steel and other metals
industries, automobiles, food production, and textiles from 1972 to
1986.[36] From 1979 to 1986, however, the absolute number of manufacturing jobs began to decline, dropping from 26.5 million to 24.9
million, a loss of 1.6 million jobs.[37]

These employment shifts have been particularly damaging to
blacks and Hispanics. From 1970 to 1984, in major northern cities,
there has been a massive decline in the number of jobs requiring relatively little education—the kind of jobs that provide entry into the
employment marketplace for the poor—and a sharp increase in the
number of jobs requiring at least some higher education. "Demographic and employment trends have produced a serious mismatch
between the skills of inner-city blacks and the opportunities available
to them . . . substantial job losses have occurred in the very industries
in which urban minorities have the greatest access, and substantial
employment gains have occurred in the higher-education-requisite
industries that are beyond the reach of most minority workers," according to William Julius Wilson, of the University of Chicago[38] (see
table 10.7).

While blacks and Hispanics will, at least for the time being, disproportionately bear the burden of this shift in job requirements, the
altered structure of the marketplace will work to the disadvantage of
the poorly educated of all races. In 1985, there were 30.6 million
whites over the age of twenty-five without a high school education—
five times the number of blacks without high school degrees (5.9 million) and seven times the number of poorly educated Hispanics (4.4
million).[39] These job market trends will intensify throughout the rest
of this century. According to estimates by the Department of Labor,[40]
21.4 million jobs will be created between 1986 and the year 2000, all
of which will be in service industries or government, as losses in tra-

TABLE 10.7

CHANGES IN THE COMBINED NUMBER OF JOBS, BY EMPLOYEE EDUCATION LEVEL,
IN NEW YORK, PHILADELPHIA, BOSTON, BALTIMORE, ST. LOUIS, ATLANTA,
HOUSTON, DENVER, AND SAN FRANCISCO, 1970 AND 1984

	Number of Jobs		
Mean level of employee education	*1970*	*1984*	*Change, 1970–84*
Less than high school	3,068,000	2,385,000	−683,000
Some higher education	2,023,000	2,745,000	+722,000

Source: Computed from William Julius Wilson, *The Truly Disadvantaged: The Inner City, the Underclass, and Public Policy* (Chicago: University of Chicago Press, 1987), table 2.6, p. 40. The table, in turn, is taken from John D. Kasarda, "The Regional and Urban Redistribution of People and Jobs in the U.S." (Paper presented to the National Research Council Committee on National Urban Policy, National Academy of Sciences, 1986).

ditional goods manufacturing industries are unlikely to be fully offset by gains in the technology manufacturing sector. In terms of educational requirements, there will be a significant increase in the proportion of jobs requiring at least one year of college education, no change in the proportion of jobs requiring a high school degree, and a sharp decline in the percentage of jobs requiring no high school education.[41]

In effect, trends in the job market through the next ten years will in all likelihood exacerbate the regressive distribution of income that has taken place over the past decade. Under American democracy, those who are unemployed or marginally employed are weakest politically. The decline of traditional political organizations and unions has made significantly more difficult the political mobilization of the working poor, the working class, and the legions of white-collar workers making from $10,000 to $25,000 a year—a universe roughly containing 24.6 million white households, 3.4 million black households, and 2 million Hispanic households.[42] Within this group, providing a political voice becomes even more difficult for those workers with poor educations who have been dispersed from manufacturing employment into cycles of marginal work.[43] While most of those who have lost manufacturing jobs have found full-time employment, such workers have, in the main, seen wages fall and fringe benefits, often including medical coverage, decline or disappear, leaving them even further outside of the American mainstream and even less well equipped to ensure adequate educational levels for their children. When combined with the declining voter turnout rates associated with falling income, these workers have fallen into what amounts to a new political underclass.

The major forces at work in the last two decades of the post–New Deal period are, then, cumulatively functioning to weaken the influence and power of those in the bottom half of the income distribution, while strengthening the authority of those in the upper half, and particularly the authority of those at elite levels. Trends in political competition and pressures in the private marketplace have combined to create a whipsaw action, reversing New Deal policies that empowered the labor movement and reduced disparities between rich and poor. Recent forces, both in the marketplace and in the political arena, have not produced a realignment of the electorate, but, in terms of outcomes, there has been a realignment in public policy— with few forces, short of a downturn in the business cycle, working against the continuing development of a political and economic system in which the dominant pressures will be toward increased regressivity in the distribution of money and in the ability to influence the outcome of political decisions.

NOTES

1. In reaching these conclusions, I am indebted to a number of scholars and students of politics. The most important of these are V. O. Key, for his discussion of the role of political parties in *Southern Politics in State and Nation* (New York: Alfred A. Knopf, 1949); Samuel Lubell, *The Future of American Politics*, rev. ed. (New York: Doubleday/Anchor Books, 1955); Walter Dean Burnham, *Critical Elections and the Mainsprings of American Politics* (New York: W. W. Norton, 1970); and Burnham, *The Current Crisis in American Politics* (New York: Oxford University Press, 1982) (Burnham's recent work has also discussed the abilities of elites to manipulate policy in the absence of popular political support); David S. Broder, *The Party's Over: The Failure of American Politics* (New York: Harper & Row, 1972); and Nelson W. Polsby, *The Consequences of Party Reform* (New York: Oxford University Press, 1983).

2. A list of the most influential political consultants and pollsters would include, on the Republican side, Lee Atwater, Charles Black, and Roger Stone, of Black, Manafort, Stone, and Atwater; Robert Teeter, of Market Opinion Research; Richard Wirthlin, of the Wirthlin Co.; Lance Tarrance, of Tarrance, Hill, Newport & Ryan; Rich Bond, of Bond & Company; Bob Goodman, of The Goodman Agency, Inc.; Stu Spencer, of Spencer-Roberts; Susan Bryant and Vince Breglio, of RSM Incorporated; Ed Rollins, of Russo, Watts and Rollins; Lyn Nofziger, of Nofziger & Bragg; Doug Bailey and John Deardourff of Bailey, Deardourff, Sipple & Assoc.; and Linda DiVall, of American Viewpoint.

On the Democratic side are Peter Hart and Geoff Garin, of Peter Hart

Research Associates; Harrison Hickman and Paul Maslin, of Hickman-Maslin Research; Bill Hamilton and Greg Schneiders, of Hamilton, Frederick and Schneiders; Robert Squier, of The Communications Company; Frank Greer, of Greer and Associates; David Doak and Robert Shrum, of Doak, Shrum & Associates; Ray Strother, of Raymond D. Strother Limited; Patrick Caddell, of Cambridge Survey Research; David Garth, of The Garth Group; and John Marttila and Thomas Kiley, of Marttila and Kiley.

3. Report from the Democratic Study Group, "Troubling Trends in Election Financing—Grassroots Money Shrinks as PAC Money Grows," October 22, 1985, Washington, D.C.

4. Among the participants in this debate are James L. Medoff of Harvard University; Peter F. Drucker of Claremont Graduate School; Richard B. Freeman, of Harvard University; Barry Bluestone of the University of Massachusetts—Boston; Bennett Harrison, of MIT; Marvin H. Kosters, of the American Enterprise Institute; Warren T. Brookes, syndicated columnist appearing in the *Washington Times*; Robert Lawrence, of the Brookings Institution; Lester C. Thurow, of MIT; Robert J. Samuelson, syndicated columnist appearing in the *Washington Post*; Robert Kuttner, of the *New Republic*; and Janet Norwood, U.S. Commissioner of Labor Statistics.

5. "Economic Report of the President," January 1987, table B-24, p. 272.

6. Historical Tables, Budget of the United States Government, Fiscal Year 1987, table 3.1, "Outlays by Superfunction and Function: 1940–1991."

7. Data presented by Richard Wirthlin, president of The Wirthlin Group polling firm, at the American Political Science Association meetings in Chicago, August 1987. Similar findings are contained in the results of public opinion polls by the *Washington Post*/ABC and the *New York Times*/CBS, and in a paper, "Trends in Partisan Realignment, 1976–1986: A Decade in Waiting," by Barbara G. Farah and Helmut Norpoth, presented at the 1986 APSA meeting in Washington, D.C.

8. Department of Labor, Bureau of Labor Statistics, "Employment and Earnings," January 1987.

9. "Economic Report of the President," January 1987, table B-40, pp. 290, 291.

10. Among the most interesting analyses of the political consequences of international competition can be found in *The Hidden Election*, ed. Thomas Ferguson and Joel Rogers (New York: Pantheon, 1981); in Rogers and Ferguson, *Right Turn: The Decline of the Democrats and the Future of American Politics* (New York: Hill and Wang, 1986); and in Joshua Cohen and Joel Rogers, " 'Reaganism' after Reagan," scheduled to appear in the forthcoming *The Socialist Register, 1988*, ed. Ralph Miliband and Leo Panitch (London: Merlin Press).

11. The *Washington Post* has conducted interviews in all of these areas. In addition to the author of this essay, other *Post* reporters who have shared reports of their findings include David Broder, Haynes Johnson, Ed Walsh, Paul Taylor, Milton Coleman, Bill Peterson, and James Dickenson.

12. In Chicago, for example, the election of the late Harold Washington

to the mayoralty is, in the view of local Republican and Democratic leaders, the reason the city's 7th and 24th state senate seats are now held by Republicans. Similarly, in Philadelphia, the GOP now dominates the entire Northeast quadrant and has picked up legislative seats in the low-income river wards. Districts on the west side of Birmingham having the highest percentage of union workers in Alabama now elect Republicans to the state legislature, and in 1986 voted overwhelmingly for Guy Hunt, the state's first GOP governor since Reconstruction.

13. For evidence of the disproportionate influence of the upper-middle class in primaries, see pp. 12 and 13 of the report to the Democratic National Committee, "Democratic Party's Commission on Openness, Participation, and Party Building: Reforms for a Stronger Democratic Party," Washington, D.C., 1978; and Polsby, *Consequences of Party Reform.* The income bias is, if anything, probably stronger in caucus states; see Edsall, *Washington Post,* August 14, 1987, p. A1; and E. J. Dionne, Jr., *New York Times,* November 1, 1987, 36.

14. The most detailed account of this process is in a paper by Eugene Steuerle and Michael Hartzmark, "Individual Income Taxation, 1947–1979," Office of Tax Analysis, Department of the Treasury.

15. "Economic Report of the President," February 1983, table B-27, p. 194; and press release, Bureau of the Census, July 30, 1987, "Median Family Income Up Significantly, Poverty Rate Drops Slightly, Census Bureau Reports."

16. Gary C. Jacobson, *Money in Congressional Elections* (New Haven: Yale University Press, 1980), 65.

17. Herbert E. Alexander, in *Financing the 1964 Election,* Citizens' Research Foundation, Princeton, N.J., May 1966, points out that the 1964 election, with Barry Goldwater as the GOP nominee, marked a major shift in Republican financing toward the relatively small (under $500) donor. That year, 69 percent of the money received by the Democratic party came from contributors of $500 or more, while only 28 percent of the Republican money came from these large givers (p. 86).

18. Edsall, *Washington Post,* "Money, Technology Revive GOP Force," June 17, 1984, and "Donors, Voters Pinpointed; GOP Purchasing Technological Edge," June 18, 1984.

19. Based on Bureau of the Census figures as reported in Walter Dean Burnham, "The Turnout Problem," in *Elections American Style,* ed. A. James Reichley (Washington, D.C.: Brookings Institution, 1987).

20. Interview in August 1982 with Linda Divall, then the political director of the National Republican Congressional committee and now a GOP pollster, and numerous subsequent interviews with Robert Teeter, president of Market Opinion Research, a Republican polling firm.

21. Based on figures supplied by K. F. Brimak, research director, Voter Education Project, Inc., Atlanta, Ga.

22. Wattenberg, "Hollow Realignment."

23. "Economic Report of the President," January 1987, table B-29, p. 278.

24. Edsall, *Washington Post*, June 14, 1987, p. H1. Petrocik, a political scientist, has worked extensively with the Republican polling firm Market Opinion Research tracing the changing shape of the two party coalitions.

25. *Washington Post*, November 11, 1984, p. H1.

26. A. James Reichley, *Religion in American Life* (Washington, D.C.: Brookings Intitution, 1985).

27. James L. Guth, "Political Converts: Partisan Realignment Among Southern Baptist Ministers," in the magazine *Election Politics* (Winter 1985–86) published by the Institute for Government and Politics, Washington, D.C.

28. Frederick T. Steeper and John Petrocik, "New Coalitions in 1988," a version of which is to appear in the magazine *Public Opinion*, American Enterprise Institute, Washington, D.C.

29. The study was confined to Catholics, union members, southerners, and northern Protestants, all of them white.

30. Reichley, *Religion in American Life*, 275.

31. Edsall, *Washington Post*, July 17, 1987, p. A1.

32. Alan Murray, *Wall Street Journal*, March 25, 1987, 1.

33. For one of the best explanations of the importance of substantive issues in a realignment, see David W. Brady, *Critical Elections and Congressional Policy Making* (Stanford, Calif.: Stanford University Press, 1988).

34. Howell Raines, *New York Times*, October 11, 1987, 3.

35. "Economic Report of the President," January 1987, table B-40, pp. 290, 291.

36. Department of Labor, Bureau of Labor Statistics, "BLS Previews the Economy of the Year 2000," June 1987, table 4.

37. "Economic Report of the President," January 1987, table B-40.

38. William Julius Wilson, *The Truly Disadvantaged: The Inner City, the Underclass, and Public Policy* (Chicago: University of Chicago Press, 1987), 102.

39. Bureau of the Census, *Statistical Abstract of the United States* (Washington, D.C., 1987), table 198, "Years of School Completed by Race, Spanish Origin, and Sex: 1960 to 1985," p. 121.

40. Department of Labor, Bureau of Labor Statistics, "BLS Previews the Economy of the Year 2000."

41. Ibid.

42. Bureau of the Census, *Statistical Abstract of the United States*, 1987, table 722, "Money Income of Households—Percent Distribution by Income Level in Constant 1985 Dollars, by Race and Spanish Origin of Households: 1970 to 1985," p. 431.

43. While future employment prospects suggest that blacks and Hispanics will face the most difficulty in finding work, income figures indicate that whites have experienced more downward mobility as a result of recent economic dislocations than either blacks or Hispanics. From 1970 to 1985, the poorest category of white households—those with incomes of $20,000 or less (in constant 1985 dollars)—has grown from 40.9 to 42.2 percent, while for

blacks, it has remained effectively the same (62.9 and 63 percent, respectively), and for Hispanics, the percentage has fallen from 56.6 percent in 1970 to 55.6 percent in 1985. All groups have experienced a decline in the number of middle-income ($20,000 to $35,000) households, and an increase in the percentage of upper-income households ($35,000 and above), but the increases have been proportionally larger for blacks and Hispanics than for whites (see ibid., table 722, "Money Income of Households," p. 431).

EPILOGUE

IN THE lexicon of American politics, "liberal" now bears the opprobrium once reserved for "communist." Try as he might, Michael Dukakis could not escape its odious stigma. George Bush, in an election at one time predicted to be a cliffhanger, ended up stampeding to a victory that, rhetorically at least, represented a national repudiation of liberalism. One can scarcely ask for a more convincing demonstration that the political order inaugurated by the New Deal has ended.

Yet we are living through a time of great political ambiguity, when everything is less clear than it seems. On the hustings, Ronald Reagan and George Bush decried the baneful effects of intrusive and centralized government many times over. The assault was not merely verbal. If the New Deal ushered in a Reformation in American political life, then arguably the reign of Ronald Reagan constituted a Counter-Reformation. So long as the conservative politics of resentment remained confined to Congress, it could never mount a frontal assault on the institutional foundations of the New Deal order. The Reagan presidency changed all that. It opened wide the portals of executive and administrative leverage to ideologues of the Right. As presidential advisors, cabinet members, and national security operatives, as executors of federal policy on the environment and health and safety, from posts on the Civil Rights Commission and the NLRB to the hallowed sanctuaries of the federal judiciary, the Counter-Reformation fastened its hold on the levers of power and implemented its social policies. And yet, over the past eight years the "administrative state" has continued to thread its way through the fabric of national life. Indeed, in its build-up of the military-industrial complex and in its determination to use the state to enforce private morality on such issues as abortion, Reaganism has actually given the administrative state new vigor. It also seems clear that on some quintessentially Democratic issues, like protection of the environment, a broad mandate for strong governmental action is taking shape. And while

Dukakis was swamped, Democrats, not a few of them conspicuous members of the "L-tribe," actually added to their numbers in Congress and in state houses across the country.

Indeed, during the same presidential year when some were declaring a liberal to be practically *non compos mentis*, others saw signs of a recrystallizing New Deal coalition. Jesse Jackson vividly articulated the concerns for social justice and broadly distributed economic welfare that gave moral force to the New Deal order at its height. Remarkably, after a decade and more during which the politics of racism and resentment threatened the major achievements of the welfare state, a black minister and civil rights leader captured the imagination of a sizable segment of disaffected white voters—blue collar workers in the rust belt, rural and small town folk for whom the politics of Reaganism paid poor dividends, urban liberals struck by the absence of moral vision among Jackson's opponents. Everyone was caught by surprise. The "Rainbow Coalition" was never as multicolored as its apostles envisioned, but neither was it as monochromatic as its more cynical observers claimed. Is there simmering, beneath the surface of the "conservative populism" analyzed by Jonathan Rieder, a radical antagonism to the new politics of inequality examined by Thomas Byrne Edsall? Richard Gephardt's early primary successes with economic nationalist themes and Michael Dukakis's belated embrace of the "I'm on your side" message in the desperate days of his campaign suggest that more might have been made of the brewing popular anger over class inequality.

But little in Dukakis's background prepared him to parlay such sentiments into widespread appeal. If Dukakis is the heir of any political tradition, it is hardly the "class-conscious" liberalism presided over by FDR. Rather he is most closely identified, not least of all by himself, with the politics of managerial expertise, that version of postwar liberal elitism discussed by Ira Katznelson in his anatomy of the Great Society. In a process that began in the late 1930s, according to Steve Fraser, and was all but completed by the late 1940s, say Alan Brinkley and Nelson Lichtenstein, practitioners of technocratic liberalism more or less banished the rhetoric and much of the reality of class conflict that made the second New Deal such a watershed in modern American history. Michael Dukakis is fluent in this language of "disinterested" managerialism. But, as compared with his predecessors, he spoke it at a far less auspicious moment.

The Democratic party, to begin with, is a shadow of its former self. Its various presidential aspirants were less spokesmen of coherent constituencies of a political party than free-lancers in search of an image and some social base. Of course, the Democratic party was not much more robust an organism in 1932 when it captured the presidency. But then whole new subspecies of the immigrant working class suddenly enlarged the electorate and were simultaneously mobilized by a new labor movement and a program that, at least on its face, promised wide-ranging, egalitarian economic reform. Today, newly enfranchised blacks, Hispanics, and Asians similarly swell the ranks of potential voters, but they do not have the numbers or coherence necessary to trigger a mass mobilization; nor do they possess trade union, middle-class, or policymaking allies with anything resembling the daring or the programmatic coherence of the new elite that came to power in the days of the second New Deal.

It has become a commonplace to note the sorry state of the trade union movement as it declines in numbers, economic strength, and political influence. The heirs of the CIO display little inclination to assume the organizational and political risks involved in initiating a mass movement of the unorganized—a failure of nerve and imagination that began, as Nelson Lichtenstein has shown, in the immediate postwar period. Moreover, no one in the Dukakis "brains trust" was disposed to welcome that sort of mass mobilization in any event. Once the primary season ended, the Dukakis camp tried to segregate Jesse Jackson and his incendiary talk of wealth and poverty, power and oppression, inside the ghettoes of American politics, while offering reassurances, in the form of a Texas land baron, that underneath all the partisan paraphernalia we are all Reagan Democrats now. Technocratic liberalism, always prone to inflate its achievements in the realm of social engineering, may have outsmarted itself. As it so self-assuredly offered the American people "competence" in place of an ideological vision rooted in the concerns of family and community, it allowed a preppy, Eastern Establishment Republican to transform himself into a flag-waving booster of "mainstream" American values.

A more clever set of media pyrotechnics alone, however, could hardly have resuscitated the New Deal coalition. History conspired against that. The *sine qua non* of the New Deal, that which legitimated its programmatic experiments as well as its moral-ideological combativeness, was the Great Depression. Moreover, as the essays by Michael A. Bernstein, Thomas Ferguson, and Steve Fraser variously indicated, the Depression fissured the worlds of industry, finance, and commerce, creating among portions of those normally conservative circles an urgent desire for substantial, even structural, economic and political reform. Today, of course, the country suffers no such calamity; not yet anyway. Michael Dukakis sometimes pretended that the budget deficit was the same thing as the Great Depression. But of course it is not; nor does it generate the same degree of political upheaval, even if today's extravagant borrowing is arguably a harbinger of tomorrow's collapse. For that reason, perhaps, it is harder to detect a rising segment of American business with the same potential for reconciling the often competing claims of capital and labor. Still, no one can be sure what waits just beyond the technological and economic horizon. Perhaps a future Michael Bernstein will identify a constellation of emergent industries poised to lead a new epoch of capital accumulation, full employment, and mass consumption. America's precarious position in today's system of global trade and production suggests an urgency about this overshadowed by the megalomerger mania that has preoccupied Wall Street during the Reagan years.

And what ideas, in the nation's future political economy, will take on the critical role of those articulated so brilliantly by John Maynard Keynes? Keynesianism, when it first burst on the scene, was part of a bold attack on entrenched centers of wealth and political influence. But by the end of World War II policy-making circles were committed to a "commercial Keynesianism," which effectively foreclosed earlier proposals for more fundamental rearrangements of the economic system. Instead of interrogating power, Keynesian economists became its servitors. When their kit bag of remedies failed amidst the economic firestorms of the 1970s, the Democratic party suddenly appeared mentally exhausted.

Since then, the only departure from neo-Keynesian orthodoxy has been the startling recapture of the mind and soul of the Republican party by an old orthodoxy: the moral and commercial axioms of the nineteenth century's free market ideology. This commercial egoism, when added to all the other disabilities from which it suffered, was enough to do in the New Deal order. Yet, as Thomas Edsall points out, it hardly prepared the ground for a basic political realignment of the sort many once predicted.

The old order is dead. Nothing with the same combination of programmatic coherence, ideological credibility, and mass political appeal has arisen to take its place. We live inside a political parenthesis. Who and what will define the future of the American "commonwealth" remain open questions. Indeed, after eight years dedicated to the pursuit of private interests the very concept of "commonwealth" is scarcely credible. The year 1988 recorded the lowest voter turnout in any presidential election since 1924.

For this descent into the purely private, the New Deal order must take some of the credit. Elaine Tyler May's essay reminds us that, at the dawn of the Cold War, domestic political stability, and even the global posture of the United States was premised on the retreat from a troubling public world into the comforting private world of family and personal consumption. The emphasis on individual expressiveness, on the pursuit of "authenticity," could have momentous political consequences. Maurice Isserman and Michael Kazin point out that it fueled the "new radicalism's" 1960s assault on the fundamental principles of the New Deal order. But in the more cynical days of the 1970s, it too easily rationalized a retreat from politics altogether, especially among those who felt that the "system" was impervious to change.

Liberals must also bear some responsibility for the resurfacing of the insidious rhetoric of anticommunism in George Bush's campaign speeches. Anticommunism, these last forty years, has not only vented the anticapitalist frustrations of those middling sorts who felt offended and excluded by the liberal consensus, but has also been the ideological *sanctum sanctorum* of the postwar liberal elite. In McCarthy's heyday, liberals did as much as conservatives to make the phrase "card-carrying member of the Communist party" the most devastating attack on a politician's honor and integrity. So there is a nasty sort of historical justice at work when "conservative populists" obdurately decry "limousine liberals" for their membership in such "dishonorable" and "immoral" organizations as the ACLU. Finally, it is the irony of our times that today those most likely to champion the social and economic generosity of the old order are precisely those marginalized populations—blacks and other minorities, women, new immigrants—whose historic weakness barred them from the social compact of 1936. *Sic transit gloria mundi.*

CONTRIBUTORS

MICHAEL A. BERNSTEIN is Associate Professor of History at the University of California–San Diego. He is the author of *The Great Depression: Delayed Recovery and Economic Change in America, 1929–1939*. He is presently at work on *American Economics in the American Century: The State and Modern Economic Thought*, a study of the economics profession in the twentieth century.

ALAN BRINKLEY is Professor of History at the City University of New York Graduate School. He is the author of *Voices of Protest: Huey Long, Father Coughlin, and the Great Depression*. He is currently working on *The Transformation of American Liberalism, 1937–1945*.

THOMAS BYRNE EDSALL is a political reporter for the *Washington Post*. He is the author of *The New Politics of Inequality: How Political Power Shapes Economic Policy* and *Power and Money: Writings about Politics*, and is the co-editor of the forthcoming *The Reagan Legacy*.

THOMAS FERGUSON is Professor of Political Science and Fellow in the McCormack Institute for Public Policy, University of Massachusetts–Boston. He is the co-author of *Right Turn: The Decline of the Democrats and the Future of American Politics*. He is finishing *Critical Realignment: The Fall of the House of Morgan and the Origins of the New Deal*.

STEVE FRASER is Senior Editor at Basic Books. He is the author of several articles on labor and American politics. He is presently working on *Sidney Hillman: Labor's Machiavelli*.

GARY GERSTLE is Assistant Professor of History at Princeton University. He is the author of the forthcoming *Working-Class Americanism: The Politics of Labor in a Textile City, 1914–1960*.

MAURICE ISSERMAN is Visiting Assistant Professor of History at Mount Holyoke College. He is the author of *Which Side Were You On?: The American Communist Party during the Second World War* and *If I Had a Hammer: The Death of the Old Left and the Birth of the New Left*. At present, he is working on a book about the decline and fall of the New Left.

IRA KATZNELSON is Henry A. and Louise Loeb Professor of Political and Social Science and Dean of the Graduate Faculty at the New School for Social Research. He is the author of *City Trenches: Urban Politics and the Patterning of Class in the United States,* and is co-author of *Schooling for All: Class, Race, and the Decline of the Democratic Ideal.* He is currently working on a manuscript concerned with American social and economic policy in the 1940s and 1970s.

MICHAEL KAZIN is Assistant Professor of History at American University. He is the author of *Barons of Labor: The San Francisco Building Trades and Union Power in the Progressive Era.* He is presently working on *Language of Discontent: The Persistence of Populism in Twentieth Century America.*

NELSON LICHTENSTEIN is Associate Professor of History at Catholic University. He is the author of *Labor's War at Home: The CIO in World War II,* and is co-editor of *On the Line: Essays in the History of Auto Work.* He is now writing a biography of Walter Reuther.

ELAINE TYLER MAY is Associate Professor of American Studies at the University of Minnesota. She is the author of *Great Expectations: Marriage and Divorce in Post-Victorian America* and *Homeward Bound: American Families in the Cold War Era.* At present, she is working on a study of infertility from the colonial era to the present, tentatively entitled "Childlessness in America: A Social and Cultural History."

JONATHAN RIEDER is Associate Professor of Sociology at Yale University. He is the author of *Canarsie: The Jews and Italians of Brooklyn against Liberalism.* He is currently working on a book about moral argument in contemporary American politics.

INDEX

Aaron, Henry, 199
Abt, John, 71
Acheson, Dean, 22
Addes, George, 72
Administrative Process (Landis), 92
Age of Reform (Hofstadter), 237
Agnew, Spiro, 261, 262
Agricultural Adjustment Act, 4
Aid to Dependent Children, 193
aircraft industry, 37, 48
Aircraft Production Board, 126
Aldrich, Winthrop, 14–16, 19, 20, 23
Alinksy, Saul, 236
Amalgamated Clothing Workers (ACW),
   77
American Enterprise Institute, 272
American Federation of Labor (AFL), 19,
   66, 68, 71, 74, 131, 136
American Independent party, 250, 251,
   261
American Plan, 10
American Retail Federation, 23
America Self-Contained (Crowther), 21
American Standard of Living (ASL), 57
American Steel and Wire Company, 38
American Woolen, 76
anticommunism, 73, 137, 139, 156–57,
   195, 207–8n.12, 247, 286
antimonopoly movement, 56, 89–92,
   114–15n.14
antitrust laws. *See* antimonopoly move-
   ment
Arendt, Hannah, 219
Arnold, Peri, 194
Arnold, Thurman, xiv, 88, 89–91, 92,
   94, 104, 110
Assemblies of God, 284
associational economy, 88

Astor, Vincent, 9, 15
Atwater, Lee, 271, 289–90n.2
Auburn automobiles, 40
Auchincloss, Gordon, 15
automobile industry, 37, 39–41, 43, 46,
   74, 143, 144, 287
Automotive Industrial Workers Association, 72
aviation industry. *See* aircraft industry

baby boom, 154–55, 175, 215–16, 217
Bailey, Doug, 289–90n.2
Baldwin, Beanie, 83n.38
bankers: and bank reform, 15–16, 68;
   and Democratic party, 11; interna-
   tional, 8; and Republican party, 7, 11–
   13
Bank of America, 11, 20, 22
Baran, Paul, 231
Baruch, Bernard, 102, 119n.51
Beat generation, 217, 218
Beck, Julian, 225
Bell, Daniel, 189, 190, 192
Bendix, 16
Benedum, J. L., 23
Berkeley Free Speech Movement, 213
Berle, Adoph A., 18, 70
Berry, Chuck, 217
Beyer, Otto, 60
big business, 5, 6, 24
Big Chill (film), 215, 229
Birdseye, Clarence, 42
Bitter, Van, 136
Black, Charles, 271, 289–90n.2
Black Legion, 72
Black, Manafort, Stone, Kelly and Atwa-
   ter, 271

blacks: and CIO, 73; and civil rights, xviii, 135, 136, 209n.21, 217–18, 220, 231–32; and Democratic party, 192–93, 203, 204, 282; employment of, 287–88; and Great Society, 187, 188; militancy of, 255–56; and New Deal, 199
Blassingame, John, 231
Bluestone, Barry, 290n.4
Boggs, Thomas Hale, Jr., 271
Bond, Rich, 289–90n.2
Borah, William, 91
Bork, Robert, 232
Bowles, Chester, 111, 125, 127
Boyer, Paul, 160
Bozell, L. Brent, 247
Brains Trust, 14, 87
Brandeis, Louis D., xiii, 26–27n.16, 55, 59, 69, 91, 114–15n.14
Brando, Marlon, 216
Breglio, Vince, 289–90n.2
Broder, David, 290n.11
Brookes, Warren T., 290n.4
Brooks, Peter, 224
Brophy, John, 62
Brown v. Board of Education, 188
Bryan, William Jennings, 252
Bryant, Susan, 289–90n.2
Buckley, William, 247
budget: balanced, 95–96, 107; and defense spending, 274; and Great Society, 197
building materials industry, 44, 45
Bunker, Ellsworth, 23
Bureau of the Budget, 194
Burnham, Walter Dean, 24n.2, 253
Burns, Emily, 171–75
Burns, Joseph, 171–75
Bush, George, 271
Butler, George, 169–71
Butler, Ida, 169–71
Butz, Earl, 231
Byrnes, James F., 118–19n.48

Caddell, Patrick, 289–90n.2
Cambodia, invasion of, 213
Campanis, Al, 231
campus protests. *See* student revolts
capitalism: and new radicalism, 225; political, 5; and role of government, 87, 105. *See also* capitalists

Capitalism, Socialism, and Democracy (Schumpeter), 191
capitalists: and Democratic party, xi–xii, 6, 13, 22–23; and New Deal, xi–xii, xiii, 88–89. *See also* capitalism
Carmichael, Stokely, 217
Carmody, John, 71
Carter, Jimmy, 204, 252, 263, 270, 283, 284
Casablanca (film), 218–19
Catchings, Waddill, 62
Catholics: as Democrats, xi, 246, 247; liberal, 73
Cato Institute, 272
Catton, Bruce, 103
cellophane, development of, 53n.21
Center for National Policy, 272
Chase, Stuart, 99
Chase National Bank, 14–15, 23, 24
Chemical Foundation, 21
chemical industry, 37, 44, 46, 48
Chicago Democratic convention (1968), 213, 259, 277
Christian Broadcast Network, 279
Christian Voice Moral Government Fund, 285
Chrysler Corporation, 40, 72
Cimino, Michael, 235
CIO News, 128
Civil Rights Act of 1964, 232, 249
civil rights movement, xviii, 135, 136, 145, 194, 209n.21, 217–18, 220, 227, 231–32, 244. *See also* blacks
Clayton, William, 22
Clifford, Clark, 130
Cloward, Richard, 202
Cohen, Benjamin, 56, 62, 69, 75, 88, 110, 116n.31
Coleman, Milton, 290n.11
collective bargaining, 61, 71, 76–77, 132, 140–41
Columbia University, 225
Coming Home (film), 234, 235
Committee for Economic Development, 129
Committee for the Nation, 17, 20
Committee on Juvenile Delinquency, 202
Communist party, 72, 139, 207–8n.12
Community Action, 196, 202, 204
Congress of Industrial Organization (CIO): and AFL, 74; and Communism,

72–73; and corporatism, 126, 128; and Democratic party, 127, 137–38, 140, 190; development of, 61–62, 67, 68, 123, 135; and government intervention, 70, 76, 78; need for, 65; and New Deal, 76, 78; and third party, 56; views of, 70, 76, 78, 126–27, 128, 190. *See also* Operation Dixie

Conservative Victory Fund, 285

consumerism, xvi–xvii, 34, 35–36, 94, 98, 158

Conway, Carle, 76

Cooke, Morris, xiii, 56, 60, 61, 62, 64, 71, 77

Corcoran, Thomas, 56, 62, 69, 75, 87–88, 110

corporatism, xv, 126, 128, 146–47n.6

"Cosby Show" (television), 231

Coughlin, Father, 72

Council of Economic Advisors, 194

Council on Foreign Relations, 18

Crowther, Samuel, 21

Cuban missile crisis, 220

Currie, Lauchlin, 96

Daley, Richard, 203, 235, 259

Davis, Rennie, 213, 217

Davis, William H., 125, 129

Dean, James, 216

Deardourff, John, 289–90n.2

DeCaux, Len, 56

Decter, Midge, 230

Deer Hunter (film), 235

deflation, 35, 36

Delano, Frederick, 71

Delinquency and Opportunity (Cloward and Ohlin), 202

demand management, 4

Democratic party: and bankers, 11; and blacks, 192–93, 203, 204, 282; campaign contributions to, 280, 291n.17; and capitalists, xi–xii, 6, 13, 22–23, 24; Chicago convention (1968), 213, 259, 277; and CIO, 127, 137–38, 140, 190; and civil rights movement, xix, 136, 194, 244; domination of, x, 4; and labor, 6, 24, 56, 68, 73, 76, 101, 135, 138, 139, 189, 190, 204, 276, 277; and the Left, 187, 229, 276; liberalism in, xi, xxi–xxii, 278; loss of power of, ix, xviii, xxi, 190, 243; loyalty to, xi, 243,

248, 269; radicalism in, 235; and social reform, 188; struggle for control of, 259, 264, 277–78; support for Republicans in, xxi, 236, 243–44, 248, 249, 262–63; vulnerability of, 245, 269

Demogrants, 262

Deterding, Sir Henri, 16, 23

Dewey, John, 138

Dewey, Thomas, 138

Dickenson, James, 290n.11

Dickstein, Morris, 228

Dies, Martin, 135

DiVall, Linda, 289–90n.2

divorce rates, 154, 155

Doak, David, 289–90n.2

Dohrn, Bernardine, 227

Donnelly, Ignatius, 236

Dos Passos, John, 213

Douglas, William O., 91, 92, 110, 127, 137

Draper, James T., Jr., 284

Drucker, Peter F., 290n.4

Duesenberg automobiles, 40

DuPont, Pierre, 15

DuPont family, 11, 21, 24

Durr, Clifford, 101

Dylan, Bob, 212, 220–21

Eberstadt, Ferdinand, 119n.51

Eccles, Marriner, xiv, 20, 71, 95, 96

Economic Opportunity Act of 1964, 196, 203

Education and Secondary Education Act, 196

Eichmann, Adolf, 219

Eichmann in Jerusalem (Arendt), 219

Eighteenth Brumaire (Marx), 214

eight-hour day, 11

Eisenhower, Dwight D., 137, 187, 194

electoral systems: changes in, x–xi; definition of, x

electronics industry, 48

elite: alliance with labor, xiii; political control of, xxiv, 269, 272, 282–83. *See also* capitalists

Ellickson, Kathryn Pollack, 62

Emmerich, Herbert, 101

Employment Act of 1946, 127

Engel, Ernst, 35

Environmental Protection Agency, 277

Equal Rights Amendment, 234, 251

Equitable Trust, 14
Esping-Andersen, Gossta, 186
European Recovery Program, 139. *See also* Marshall Plan
Evans, Sara, 218
experts, reliance on, 164–65
Ezekiel, Mordecai, 83n.38, 96, 108

Fair Deal, 188, 195, 197, 199
Fair Labor Standards Act (FLSA), 73, 75, 76, 124
Falwell, Rev. Jerry, 252, 279
family, 153–81; commitment to, 167–69, 172; postwar changes in, 153–56, 159, 161–67; rejection of, 175; and security, 153, 157, 161
Farley, James, 20, 70, 235
Federal Reserve, xiii, 13, 17, 71
Federal Reserve Act of 1935, 20
feminism, 228; and feminist scholarship, 178n.9. *See also* women
Ferraro, Geraldine, 235
Filene, A. Lincoln, 23
Filene, Edward A., 19, 20, 23, 26
Folklore or Capitalism (Arnold), 90
Folsom, Marion, 81–82n.24
Fonda, Jane, 234
Foner, Eric, 231
Food and Tobacco Workers Union, 137
food production industry, 36, 41–43, 46, 287
Foodstamps, 196
Ford, Gerald, 204
Ford, Henry, 27n.17
Ford Foundation, 202
Fordism, 57
Ford Motor Company, 49
Forgotson, Edward H., 271
Forrestal, James, 11, 23
Fortune, 142
Fosdick, Raymond B., 19
Foster, William T., 62
Frady, Marshall, 251
Frank, Jerome, 83n.38, 91
Frankfurter, Felix, xiii, 10, 56, 58, 59, 60, 69, 70, 75, 88
Fraser, Leon, 22
Free-Congress PAC, 285
Freeman, Richard B., 290n.4
Free Silver advocates, 7
Free Students for America (FSFA), 222

free trade, xii, 5, 7, 10, 18, 21, 23
Freud, Sigmund, 223
Frey, John, 71
frontier, and economic growth, 98–99
Full Employment Act of 1946, 111, 129, 142, 194
fund-raising, political, 279–80

Gannett media chain, 272
Garin, Geoff, 289–90n.2
Garth, David, 289–90n.2
Garvan, Francis, 21
Gary, Elbert, 10
General Electric, 8, 10, 76, 272
General Foods Corporation, 42
General Motors, xv, 131, 132–33, 140–42
General Theory (Keynes), 192
Genovese, Eugene, 231
Germer, Adolph, 72
Ginsburg, Douglas, 236
glass industry, 44–45
Glass-Steagall Act, 4, 16
Goldberg, Arthur, 134
Gold Democrats, 7
Golden, Clinton, 56, 77
Goldman, Eric, x
gold standard, 4, 13, 16, 17
Goldwater, Barry, 243, 249, 260, 291n.17
Goodman, Bob, 289–90n.2
Good Neighbor League, 23
Gore, Albert, 271
government, role of, 87, 89, 93–94, 97–98, 99–100, 104, 140, 196, 197–98
Government Process (Truman), 191
Graham, Frank, 136
Gramm, Phil, 271
Great Depression: analyses of, 33–34; description of, 3; end of, 95; persistence of, xii, 32–54; and Republican party, 13; and role of the state, 86
Great Society, 185–211; backlash against, 254; characteristics of, 203–4; of the economists, 201, 202; lineage of, 194–95, 200; meaning of, 187–89; optimism of, 48; programs of, 197–98, 202–3; and racial issues, xix, 200; of the social policy experts, 201–2. *See also* War on Poverty
Great Transformation (Polyani), 191

Green, William, 128
Greenstone, J. David, 205–6n.3
Greer, Frank, 289–90n.2
Grenada, 234
Guevara, Che, 213
Guth, James L., 284

Haas, Father Francis, 73
Haber, Al, 212
Hall, Fawn, 233
Hamer, Fannie Lou, 220, 231
Hamilton, Bill, 289–90n.2
Hancock, John Milton, 11, 23
Hansen, Alvin, xiv, 85, 98, 99, 105, 108, 110, 127
Harjes, Morgan, 27n.17
Harriman, Averell, 6, 9, 11, 19, 23
Harris, Seymour E., 127
Harrison, Bennett, 290n.4
Hart, Gary, 236
Hart, Peter, 289–90n.2
Haveman, Robert, 201
Hawkins, Paula, 271
Hawley, Ellis, 5
Hayden, Tom, 212, 213
Hayek, Freidrich, 191
Haywood, Big Bill, 55
Head Start, 196
Hearst, William Randolph, 14, 16
Hecht, Rudolph, 22
Heclo, Hugh, 200
Heflin, Howell, 233
Heller, Walter, 210–11n.39
Helms, Jesse, 271
Henderson, Leon, 88, 91, 96, 110, 116n.31, 132
Heritage Foundation, 272
Hickman, Harrison, 289–90n.2
Hicks, Louise Day, 258
Highlander Folk School, 137
Hillman, Sidney, xiii, 56, 59–60, 62, 70, 71, 74, 75, 76, 77, 78
Hispanics, 287–88
Hiss, Alger, 56, 83n.38
Hoffman, Abbie, 215
Hoffman, Paul, 129
Hofstadter, Richard, 86, 189, 237
Hollander, Paul, 230
home: defined by Nixon, 158; in democracy, 158; rejection of, 175; satisfaction with, 166, 169–71, 173, 174; and security, 153–54, 161; vulnerability of, 159–60, 161
Hoover, Herbert, 13, 15
Hoover Institution, 272
Hopkins, Harry, xiv, 71, 96
House, Col. Edward, 14, 15, 16
House of Morgan, 10, 11, 14, 21, 69. *See also* J. P. Morgan & Co.; Morgan, J. P.
Howe, Frederick, 55
Hull, Cordell, 4, 18, 21, 22
Humphrey, Hubert, 251, 259
Hunt, Guy, 290–91n.12
Hutcheson, William, 61

Ickes, Harold, xiv, 20, 56, 62, 71, 88, 96, 104, 106, 123
income: distribution of, 272–74, 276, 286, 288; stagnation of, 278–79; and voting patterns, 281–83
incomes policy, 124
industrial democracy, 58–59, 62, 64
Industrial Relations Counsellors, 10, 19
Industry Council Plan, 125, 126
Inland Steel Company, 38
Inter-Church World Movement, 10
iron and steel industry, 37–39, 46, 49, 63, 143, 287

Jackson, Andrew, 252
Jackson, Gardner, 74, 83n.38
Jackson, Jesse, 235
Jackson, Robert, 88, 89, 110, 113–14n.8, 116n.31
Jacobstein, Meyer, 59
Jews: and anti-Semitism, 27n.17; as Democrats, xi; and family, 161
Job Corps, 196, 201
Johnson, Haynes, 290n.11
Johnson, Lyndon B., xviii, 186, 187, 195, 200, 243
Johnston, Eric, 128, 129
Jones, W. Alton, 23
J. P. Morgan & Co., 4, 16. *See also* House of Morgan; Morgan, J. P.

Kaiser, Henry J., 129
Kasdan, Lawrence, 215
Katz, Michael, 197, 198, 205
Keefe, Robert J., 271
Kelly, Peter, 271
Kemp, Jack, 271

Kendall, Willmoore, 246
Kennedy, John F., 187, 196, 200, 220
Kennedy, Joseph, 11, 118–19n.48
Kennedy, Robert, 259
Kent State University, 213
Kerouac, Jack, 217
Key, V. O., 24n.2, 193
Keynes, John Maynard, 99, 108, 191–92
Keynesianism: commercial, xiv, xix, 131;
    definition of, xiv; social, xiv, xv
Keyserling, Leon, 69, 127
Kiley, Thomas, 289–90n.2
King, Martin Luther, 232, 261
Kingdon, John, 200
Kolko, Gabriel, 5
Kosters, Marvin H., 290n.4
Kramer, Hilton, 230
Kroll, Jack, 140
Krushchev, Nikita, 158
Kuhn, Loeb, 11, 69
Ku Klux Klan, 72, 137
Kuttner, Robert, 290n.4

labor: alliance with elite, xiii; benefits
    for, 142–44, 151n.60; and civil rights
    movement, 209n.21; as consumers,
    xvi–xvii; curtailment of power of,
    122–23, 187, 191; and Democratic
    party, 6, 24, 56, 68, 73, 76, 101, 135,
    138, 139, 189, 190, 204, 276, 277; as
    economic problem, 55–84; emigrants
    among, 63–64, 67, 73; and national
    planning, xv; and New Deal, xii, 125;
    power of, 57–58; and social democ-
    racy, 122–52; transformation of, xvi,
    xix, 55–56, 62–67, 276–77, 287; two
    welfare systems for, 144–45; and
    unionization, 8, 10, 18, 56–57, 65, 70,
    75, 77, 123–25, 134, 276; women in,
    41, 154, 156, 157, 159. *See also* unem-
    ployment
Labor's Non-Partisan League (LNPL), 70,
    74, 75
LaFollette, Robert, Jr., 56, 62, 71, 75
Lamont, Thomas W., 14
Landis, James, 56, 69, 88, 92–93
Landon, Alfred, 21, 22
Lauck, Jett, 56, 62, 70
Lawrence, Robert, 290n.4
League of Nations, 8, 9, 14
Legal Services, 196

legislation, prolabor, xii
Lehman, Herbert, 11
Lehman Brothers, 11, 14
Leiserson, William, xiii, 56, 59, 60, 62
Lemay, Curtis, 250
Lennon, John, 237
Leon, Rene, 16, 17
Lewis, John L., 56, 61, 62, 70, 74, 76, 77,
    130, 131–32, 133, 142–43
Libby, Joan, 219
liberalism: and capitalism, xv; definition
    of, 87; in Democratic party, xi, xxi–
    xxii, 278; multinational, 3–31; revolt
    against, 258; after World War II, 109–
    10, 112
Liberty League, 21, 22
Lichter, Robert, 230
Lifton, Robert J., 160–61
Lindblom, Charles, 189
Lindley, Ernest K., 108
Lippmann, Walter, 18
"Living Theater," 225
lobbyists, 271–72
Long, Huey, 236
Lorillard tobacco company, 23
Los Angeles Times-Mirror media chain,
    272
Lowenthal, Max, 62
Lubell, Samuel, 245
Lubin, Isador, 69, 91, 96
lumber industry, 37, 46

McAteer, Ed, 279
McCarthy, Eugene, 259
McCarthy, Joseph, xvii, xxi, 246–47, 252
McCarthyism, 156, 157, 243, 247–48
McGovern, George S., 252, 259, 262,
    269, 278
McKinley, William, xii
McNamara, Robert, 201, 210n.37
Madden, Joseph, 71
Made in America Club, 21
Mailer, Norman, 217, 219
Manpower Development and Training
    Act, 196, 201
Marshall, George C., 208
Mao Zedong, 213
Marat/Sade (Brooks), 224–25
marijuana, 223, 224
Marshall Plan, 138, 139
Martin, Homer, 72, 74

Marttila, John, 289–90n.2
Marty (film), 162–63
Marx, Karl, 214
"MASH" (television), 234
Maslin, Paul, 289–90n.2
Max, Steve, 221, 224
Maxwell Company, 40
Mazey, Emil, 138
Meacham, Evan, 232
Mead, George, 19, 20
Mead, Margaret, 165
Means, Gardiner, 108
Medicaid, 196
Medicare, 197, 198
Medoff, James L., 290n.4
Metropolitan Life, 15
Middle America, 244, 262, 266
Miles, Richard, 121n.68
military research, 48, 49
Millis, Harry, 56
Mills, C. Wright, 138, 189, 231
Mine, Mill and Smelter Workers Union, 137
minimum wage, 75–76
Minsky, Hyman, 192
Mississippi Freedom Democratic Party, 220
Model Cities, 196
Moffett, James A., 16, 17, 23
Moley, Raymond, 9
Mondale, Walter, 283
Montgomery, Donald, 128
Moral Majority, 279
Morgan, J. P., 14, 15, 16, 23
Morgan, J. P., Jr., 27n.17
Morgenthau, Henry, 95, 96
Morse, Wayne, 132
Mortimer, Wyndam, 72
Moses, Robert, 217
Mosher, Ira, 130
Moynihan, Daniel Patrick, xviii, 185, 196, 205
multinational liberalism, 9
Murchison, Clint, 23
Murray, Philip, xv, 64, 74, 77, 125, 126, 128, 131, 134, 137, 139

Name for Ourselves (Potter), 227–28
Nathan, Robert, 128
Nation, 88, 105

National Association of Manufacturers (NAM), 74, 134
National Conservative Political Action Committee, 285
National Educational Committee for a New Party, 138
National Industrial Recovery Act, 4; expiration of, 19; 7a clause, 18, 33, 68
nationalism, economic, 8
National Labor Relations Act, xii
National Labor Relations Board (NLRB), xiii, 71, 74, 75, 124, 276
National Maritime Union, 74
National Moratorium Committee, 219
National Organization for Women, 235, 242n.53
National Recovery Administration (NRA): associational vision of, 88; continued by Roosevelt, 17; declared unconstitutional, 18, 29n.38, 68, 124; and price fixing, 5; revival rejected, 4, 23; self-destruction of, 18
"National Resources Development Report," 107, 108
National Resources Planning Board (NRPB), xiii, 71, 106, 189, 194
National Right to Life Association, 272
National Steel, 38
National War Labor Board, 124, 125
Neighborhood Youth Corps, 196
Nelson, Donald, 104
New American Majority, 265
New Deal(s): achievement of, 7, 245; analysis of, 4–7; and bank reform, 14; and capitalists, xi–xii, 88–89; emergence of, xi–xviii; end of, ix–x, xviii–xxiv, 76, 187, 212, 243; and Great Society, 185–86, 197, 199–200, 204; ideological eclecticism of, xiv, 86–87; importance of, 111–12; and liberal concept of the state, 85–86, 112; and role of government, 85–21; two, 25n.8
New Frontier, 48, 188
New Left: and antimilitarism, 234–35; and college students, 215–21, 223; and cultural radicalism, 227–28; failure of, xxi; and individualism, 225–26; and new lifestyle, 224–27; 1980s interest in, 215, 237; and race, 231–32; rise of, 212–15; veterans of, 230–31; and

New Left (*cont.*)
women's issues, 232–34. *See also* Students for a Democratic Society
New Radicalism, 212–42. *See also* New Left; student revolts
New Republic, 56, 58, 88, 96, 105
New Right: and Reagan, 187, 228, 237, 262, 284; and religious groups, 251, 283–85; and Republican party, xxi, 245–46; rise of, 204, 229, 237, 265–66
Newsweek, 9
new unionism, 59–60, 68, 77
New York Federal Reserve Bank, 9, 11, 20
New York Times, 9, 23
Nicaragua, 234
Niebuhr, Reinhold, 132
1919 (Dos Passos), 213–14
Nixon, Richard M., 157–58, 185, 251–52, 260, 261, 262–63, 265, 278
Nofziger, Lyn, 289–90n.2
Norbeck, Peter, 16
Norris, George William, 62
Norris-LaGuardia Act, 11
North, Oliver, 235
Norwood, Janet, 290n.4

Odets, Clifford, 224
Office of Economic Opportunity, 201
Office of Price Administration, xv, 124
Office of War Mobilization and Reconversion, 128
Ogburn, Charlton, 29n.41
Oglesby, Carl, 214
Ohlin, Lloyd, 202
oil: and banking interests, 16; overproduction of, 18; price of, 4, 15, 20–21. *See also* petroleum industry
Oliver, Eli, 62
O'Mahoney, Joseph, 91
On the Road (Kerouac), 217, 218
Open Shop drive, 8
Operation Dixie, xv, 135, 136–37, 248
Oppenheimer, J. Robert, 180–81n.28
Orren, Gary, 263

Packard automobiles, 40
Packinghouse Workers Organizing Committee, 62
Parents Magazine, 161
Parker, Charlie, 217

Partisan Review, 230
Pauley, Edwin, 130
Peabody, George Foster, 23
Peace Corps, 220
peace movement, 223. *See also* New Left
Peale, Norman Vincent, 164
Pecora, Ferdinand, 16
Peek, George, 21
Pennsylvania Retailers Association, 23
Pepper, Claude, 136
Perkins, Frances, 56, 62, 68, 71
Person, Harlow, 56, 59, 60, 62
Personal Politics (Evans), 218
Peter, Paul, and Mary, 221
Peterson, Bill, 290n.11
Petrocik, John R., 283, 284
petroleum industry, 37, 43–44, 46, 48. *See also* oil
Phillips, Kevin, 250, 252
Platoon (film), 234–35
Podhoretz, Norman, 230
political action committees (PACs), 271, 285
political capitalism, 5
political order, definition of, x
political parties: decline of, 270–72, 277; loyalty to, xi
political power, changes in, 269–93
Pollock, William, 143
Polyani, Karl, 191
Popular Front, 137, 139
populism, xi, 7, 236–37, 249, 251, 253, 263, 264
Port Huron Statement, 213, 214, 227, 229
Potter, Paul, 227–28
Preece, Harold, 135
Presley, Elvis, 216, 217
Pressman, Lee, 56, 62, 74, 83n.38, 134
price theory, 33–34
Procaccino, Mario, 258
Progressive Labor Party (PLP), 226
Progressive party, xv, 138, 139
Przeworski, Adam, 186, 187
Pure Food and Drug Act of 1906, 45

Railway Brotherhoods, 133
Railway Labor Act, 11
Rambo: First Blood, Part II (film), 235
RCA, 76
Reagan, Ronald: and conservative intel-

lectuals, 231; Democratic support for, xxi, 236; and end of New Deal, ix, 187, 212, 243; industrial development under, 49; and labor, 276; and moral crisis, xxii; and New Right, 187, 228, 237, 252, 284; regulatory vision of, xiv; and student revolts, 226, 228; and unity of Republican party, 270; voter support for, 283, 284, 285

recession, in 1937, 87, 89

Reciprocal Trade Act, 24

Red Scare, 157, 247

religious groups, and New Right, 283–85

Religious Roundtable, 279

Remington Rand, 16–17

Republican party: and bankers, 7, 11–13; campaign contributions to, 280, 291n.17; conservatism in, 259–60; Democratic support for, xxi, 236, 243–44, 248, 249, 262–63, 264; domination of, x, xxi, xxiii, 7, 243, 269, 278, 285–86; and Great Depression, 13; loss of power of, 11, 22; voter support for, 281

Resettlement Administration, 83n.38

Return of the Secaucus Seven (Sayles), 240n.40

Reuther, Walter, xv, 72, 126, 130, 132, 138, 140, 141, 143

reverse discrimination, xxi, 255

Reynolds Tobacco Company, 135

Rice, Father Charles Owen, 80n.17

Richardson, Sid, 23

Richberg, Donald, 88

Riesman, David, 159

Rizzo, Frank, 258

Road to Serfdom (Hayek), 191

Robertson, Rev. Marion G. (Pat), 279

Robinson, Jackie, 232

Rockefeller, John D., Jr., 10, 14, 15, 19

Roesser, Charlie, 23

Rogers, Adrian, 284

Rogin, Michael Paul, 247, 264

Rollins, Ed, 289–90n.2

Romney, George, 126

Roosevelt, Eleanor, 132

Roosevelt, Franklin Delano, 274; advisors to, 14, 17, 27n.21; and balanced budget, 95–96; bank reform under, 14–16; and CIO, 70, 76; coalition under, 6–7, 14–17, 18–19, 22–23, 26–

27n.16; death of, 56; importance of, to New Deal, 5; and labor, 55, 56, 245; Lewis's exasperation with, 74, 76; 1936 reelection of, xi, 4, 21, 70, 74, 88; 1944 reelection of, 123; social reform under, 3–4, 96–97; voter loyalty to, xi; and World War II, 102, 104

Roosevelt, Theodore, 91

"Roots" (television), 231

Roper, Daniel, 15, 16

Rothman, Stanley, 230

Royal Dutch Shell, 16

Rubin, Jerry, 227

Ruml, Beardsley, 11, 15, 18, 23, 71, 96

Rural Electrification Agency (REA), xiii, 71, 83n.38

Russell Sage Foundation, 62

Sachs, Alexander, 69

Said, Boris, 23

Samuelson, Robert J., 290n.4

SANE, 235

Saposs, David, 62, 71, 81–82n.24

Savimbi, Jonas, 271

Sayles, John, 240n.40

Scammon, Richard, 261

Schecter decision, 68

Schell, Jonathan, 261

Schlafly, Phyllis, 233

Schlesinger, Arthur D., Jr., x, 111, 188

Schneider, William, 265

Schneiders, Greg, 289–90n.2

Schumpeter, Joseph A., 32, 191

Schwellenbach, Lewis, 98

Scripps-Howard papers, 23

Sears Roebuck, 17

Securities Act, 4

Security, Work, and Relief Policies, 107

Seventh Day Adventists, 284

Shero, Jeff, 223

Shriver, Sargent, 210n.37

Shrum, Robert, 289–90n.2

Sierra Club, 235, 272

Silent Majority, rise of, xxi, 243–68

silver, 16, 20

Skocpol, Theda, xiv, 24–25n.3

slavery, x

Slichter, Sumner, 123

Sloan, Alfred P., 20

Smith, Al, 11

Smith, Edwin, 56, 71, 81–82n.24

Smith, Howard, 203
Smoot-Hawley bill, 13
Snyder, Jimmy "the Greek," 232
Snyder, John, 130, 133
Socialist party, 72
Social Security Act, xii, 4, 19, 68, 143, 193, 197, 200
social work, 202
Southern Baptist Convention, 284
Southern Conference for Human Welfare, 137
Spelman Fund, 11, 15, 19
Spencer, Stu, 289–90n.2
Spock, Dr. Benjamin, 164
Squier, Robert, 286–90n.2
stagnation theory, 34
Stakhanovism, 59
Stallone, Sylvester, 235
Standard Oil Company of New Jersey, 8, 10, 16, 17, 21
Stanley, Charles F., 284
Starnes, Joe, 135
steel industry. *See* iron and steel industry
Steelworkers Independent Union, 66
Steel Workers Organizing Committee (SWOC), 62, 71, 74, 77
Steeper, Frederick T., 284
Stephens, John A., 130
Stimson, Henry, 22
Stinchcombe, Arthur, 199
Stock Exchange, reform of, 4
Stockman, David, 211n.40
Stone, I. F., 103, 107, 231
Stone, Oliver, 234
Stone, Roger, 289–90n.2
Stopes, Dr. Marie Carmichael, 174
Strategic Defense Initiative, 49
Strong, Donald, 249
Strother, Ray, 289–90n.2
Student League for Industrial Democracy (SLID), 212
Student Non-Violent Coordinating Committee (SNCC), 218
student revolts, xx–xxi, 213–14, 216–17. *See also* New Left
Students for a Democratic Society (SDS), 212–13, 221–24, 226, 227. *See also* New Left
Studies on the Left, x
Sumners, Hatton, 91
Sundquist, James, 188

Sweden, 4
Swope, Gerard, 19, 20, 23

Taft-Hartley Act, 133–34, 139, 191
Talmadge, Gene, 136
Tarrance, Lance, 289–90n.2
Task Force on Manpower Conservation, 185
taxes, 278, 279
Tax Reform Act of 1986, 285
Taylor, Frederick, 10
Taylor, Paul, 290n.11
Taylorism, 57
Taylor Society, 10, 19, 20, 26–27n.16, 59–61, 69
Teachers Corps, 196
Teagle, Walter, 19, 20, 23
Teamsters, 134
technology, and progress, 160–61
Teeter, Robert, 289–90n.2
Temporary National Economic Committee (TNEC), 89, 91–92
"Ten Days to Shake the Empire" plan, 222
Tennessee Valley Authority, 83n.38, 106
textile industry, 37, 46, 74, 287
Textile Workers Organizing Committee (TWOC), 62, 74–75, 143
Thatcher, Margaret, 285
Thomas, Norman, 138
Thornton, Willie Mae "Big Mama," 217
Thurmond, Strom, 248
Thurow, Lester C., 290n.4
Time, 92
tobacco industry, 46
Tomorrow Without Fear (Bowles), 111
Traylor, Melvin, 11
Tripartite Money Agreement, 22
Truman, David, 191
Truman, Harry S., 128, 129–30, 131, 133, 137, 140, 160, 246, 248, 274
Truth, Sojourner, 231
Tubman, Harriet, 231
Tugwell, Rexford, 10, 83n.38
Turner, Frederick Jackson, 98
Twentieth Century Fund, 20, 62, 81–82n.24, 129, 141

unemployment, 33, 46, 95, 98, 201, 270. *See also* labor

unionization, 8, 10, 18, 56–57, 65, 70, 75, 77, 123–25, 134, 276. *See also* labor
United Auto Workers (UAW), 65, 72, 77, 126, 128, 132, 133, 138, 141–42
United Church of Christ, 284
United Electrical, Radio and Machine Workers of America, The (UE), 65
United Methodist Church, 284
United Mine Workers (UMW), 70, 131, 133, 142–43
United Presbyterians, 284
United Steel Workers (USW), 137
University of Oklahoma, 223
Untermeyer, Samuel, 16
Upward Bound, 196
Urban Institute, 272
U.S. Congress, 270, 271
U.S. Department of Justice, Antitrust Division, 89–90
U.S. Department of Labor, xiii, 71, 189, 194, 276
U.S. Department of the Interior, xiii, 71
U.S. Steel, 10, 20, 76, 131

Vale, Vivian, 142
Veblen, Thorstein, 91
Ventura College, 222
Vietnam War: American view of, 234; and decline of Democratic party, 244; and rise of the New Left, 213, 220, 222–23
voter turnout patterns, 281, 288

wages: and COLA, 141, 142; guaranteed, 126; minimum, 75–76; program for, 128–31; strikes for, 132–33, 141
Wagner, Robert, 20, 56, 62, 69
Wagner-Murray-Dingell bill, 142
Wagner National Labor Relations Act, 4, 19, 21, 57, 68, 69, 74, 76, 128
Waiting for Lefty (Odets), 224, 225
Wallace, George C., xxi, xxii, 236, 249–52, 254, 261, 269, 278
Wallace, Henry, xiv, xv, 56, 88, 96, 129, 138–39
Walsh, Ed, 290n.11
Warburg, James P., 17, 21, 22
War Labor Board, xv
War on Poverty, xix, 187, 195, 196–97, 201, 202

War Production Board (WPB), 102–4
Washington, Harold, 290–91n.12
Washington Post, 290n.11
Watergate scandal, 220, 265, 269, 277
Watson, Thomas, 19
Wattenberg, Benjamin, 261
Weatherman (faction of SDS), 224, 226–27
Webb, Lee, 226
Weber, Orlando, 21
Weinberg, Sidney, 11, 23
Weir, Margaret, 24–25n.3
Whigs, x
White, Walter, 132
White, William Allen, 104
"White Negro" (Mailer), 217, 218, 219
Whyte, William, 159, 162, 163
Wiggin, Albert, 15, 16
Wildflower, Leni, 228
Williams, Aubrey, 96
Williams, J. D., 271
Williamson, Chilton, 252
Wills, Garry, 260
Wilson, Charles E., 130, 140–41
Wilson, M. L., 28n.24
Wilson, William Julius, 287
Wilson, Woodrow, 10, 14, 55, 91
Winfrey, Oprah, 231
Wirthlin, Richard, 289–90n.2
Witt, Nathan, 62, 71
Wolman, Leo, 60
women: in families, 167–68, 170; as workers, 41, 154, 156, 157, 159. *See also* feminism
Works Progress Administration, 45
Works Projects Administration, xiii
World Court, 9
World War I, and economic growth, 100
World War II: and end of depression, 39, 48, 50, 109; impact of, on families, 153–54; impact of, on workers, 123; and role of government, 101–2

Yankelovich, Daniel, 227
Yarmolinsky, Adam, 210n.37
Yorty, Sam, 258
Young, Owen D., 19

Zolberg, Aristide, 263